Internet Philanthropy in China

Yidan Chen

Internet Philanthropy in China

palgrave
macmillan

Yidan Chen
Tencent Research Institute
Beijing, China

ISBN 978-981-16-2565-7 ISBN 978-981-16-2566-4 (eBook)
https://doi.org/10.1007/978-981-16-2566-4

Jointly published with China Renmin University Press.

This Palgrave Macmillan imprint is published by the registered company Springer Nature Singapore Pte Ltd.
The registered company address is: 152 Beach Road, #21-01/04 Gateway East, Singapore 189721, Singapore

Preface

Two years ago, I had the idea of writing a book about the development of Internet philanthropy in China. Now, the idea has matured and it is time to share it.

Since I began working in Internet philanthropy 11 years ago, I have received sincere concern and valuable advice, though this has also been interspersed with a certain amount of turmoil. I've witnessed the establishment of the Tencent Foundation, China's first Internet philanthropic foundation in 2007, and the 99 Charity Day event earlier this year, where more than RMB 1.414 billion was collected in donations from enterprises and foundations, then on top of this, 28 million individuals donated RMB 830 million in three days. Emerging technologies have revealed their explosive potential to the traditional, established philanthropy sector, shocking people from all walks of life. Such integration between philanthropy and the Internet has also been seen in the US, the UK and Japan. In the past few years, Internet philanthropy has undergone such drastic development that it deserves to be recorded and consolidated into one book.

I had three main objectives in writing this book.

Firstly, I want to document the many "firsts" that have occurred as part of this process, such as the first example of an email soliciting international aid, the first small-scale donation made via mobile payment, the first online aid provided to an individual, and the first regulations to be placed on Internet philanthropy. All of these have helped lay the fertile ground upon which Internet philanthropy could expand as it has. But of course, with growth comes growing pains. Far from unconditional support and praise, Internet users hold mixed views towards philanthropy. Some of the most acute criticisms and most influential negative news about philanthropy achieve their viral attention on the Internet. Therefore, it is worth documenting the ups and downs, the twists and turns that Internet philanthropy has gone through, as well as the people and events that have been influential along the way.

Second, the book aims to organize the countless lessons we can draw from over a decade of development in Internet philanthropy. For example, setting up a large-scale environment for Internet philanthropy is always somewhat slower than philanthropic practices on a micro scale. It was not until two years ago that China's *Charity Law* came into being, with provisions for Internet philanthropy. Furthermore, it takes a much shorter amount of time to mobilize masses of internet users than it does to develop regulations for public platforms. Without any motivation from users, regulations cannot make much headway. Moreover, as philanthropic projects gradually increase their level of transparency, sensationalism and blind obedience are giving way to rational thinking. It is high time we looked back at these universal lessons, so that we might find inspiration on how new technologies can be applied to other traditional industries.

Third, the book is designed to inspire us to renew our efforts. Some, though not always steady, progress has been made towards integrating philanthropy with the Internet. We have been on the right track and should not veer off course now. However, mobile phones and the Internet should not be alienating people. Internet philanthropy is something we can all benefit from. We must now look back to move forward, by mastering rather than being mastered by the Internet.

This book has been fully supported by the Tencent Research Institute and the Tencent Foundation.

The research team consisted of three of my friends, Wu Pengyang, Zhou Ziqi and Ma Tianjiao. They visited dozens of influential philanthropic organizations in China and abroad, where many of them witnessed stories that went viral online. Guo Kaitian, Chairman of the Tencent Foundation and the Tencent Research Institute, Si Xiao, Dean of the Tencent Research Institute, Zhai Hongxin, Secretary-General of the Tencent Foundation, Sun Yi, Deputy Secretary-General of the Tencent Foundation, and Li Gang, Director of the Research Center of the Tencent Research Institute, all offered constructive feedback to this manuscript. Researchers Liu Qiong, Sun Yi, and Xu Siyan also participated in the writing of this book. I would like to express my gratitude to all of them.

It took only a few months to write this book due to time restrictions. Any criticism, suggestions or corrections are welcome.

This book is dedicated to all those who have contributed towards the development of Internet Philanthropy in China.

Shenzhen, China
October 11, 2018

Chen Yidan

Prologue: A Painting Connecting You to Charity

Philanthropy begins where society pains.

—Chen Yidan

Core Founder of Tencent, Initiator and Honorary Chairman of Tencent Foundation

"Keynote Speech at the Kick-off Event of the First 99 Charity Day"

September, 2015

In the minds of many Chinese people, the word "philanthropy" is both close to home and yet unfamiliar.

It feels close to home in the good deeds people carry out in their daily lives, no matter how small. It could be giving money to beggars on the street, which is the first image in Chinese people's minds when they think about philanthropy. On the other hand, it is unfamiliar insofar as ordinary people not only don't know what philanthropy itself is, but they don't see how it's relevant to them. In general, only CEOs and the extremely wealthy are seen as being able to make a difference through "philanthropy", and everyone else, the ordinary people, might as well not try. Consequently, most donations in China come from enterprises, leaving the potential of the wider public untapped and undervalued. This is a stark contrast to the U.S. and other countries with highly-developed modern philanthropic systems.

To turn this situation around, what we need is public participation. Given the remarkable ubiquity of the Internet in China, Chinese people are highly connected, allowing philanthropy to find its way into the life of any member of the online community. At a moment when everyone can engage in philanthropy quickly and easily, when everyone's philanthropic contributions can be clearly documented, when everyone can see the progress and effects of philanthropy, it was only natural for China's internet philanthropy to go viral.

WeChat Moments Flooded with Paintings

On August 28, 2017, an H5 campaign entitled Kids Gallery (See Fig. 1) was launched discreetly on WeChat.

It all began when a user named Wang saw an eye-catching update on his WeChat Moments feed. His friend Liu had posted a painting depicting a huge bright sun shining down on a lush cornfield against an indigo blue sky. Wang was transfixed, thinking, "This looks like a work by Vincent van Gogh!" Wang had been fond of van Gogh since high school and had developed an affinity for the Dutch painter's style, which is rich with vigor and vitality. The use of color and brushwork resembled van Gogh's. "When did Liu start to appreciate art?" Wang thought to himself. Noticing a comment written by Liu above the painting saying, "Your painting brings warmth to my heart," Wang became curious, and tapped on the picture for a closer look. Below the painting were a QR code and a caption saying, "Liu has purchased this painting via Tencent Charity to help little kids embark on a journey of art appreciation."

"So, this is a charity campaign?" Wang was surprised. "Liu bought this painting… So, the painting was for sale?" Wang thought. He began to get excited. He had wanted to buy some paintings to decorate his home, but had always been too lazy to go to a gallery. He worried that works by famous artists might be too expensive, or that he could get conned into buying a fake. Paintings by lesser-known artists seemed like a waste of time. "Buy paintings… for charity…" Suddenly, an impulse came over him, urging him to scan the QR code and check out the Kids Gallery H5 page.

Fig. 1 The H5 Page of Kids Gallery

After perusing the site for 30 minutes, Wang decided to donate one yuan in return for a digital painting. This was not only his first time donating money to a charitable organization, but also his first time buying a digital painting. He had never donated to charities because he did not trust charitable organizations, and doubted the donations would be properly used. He was more willing to organize charity events himself or take part in activities organized by his friends. He felt better when he could see the donations reaching those in need with his own eyes. Born as he was in the 1980s, he was used to free online content, and had never bought any digital products when they could be easily copied and shared online. The Kids Gallery changed his mind.

"I was deeply moved when I saw what beautiful drawings the kids had done," Wang explained. "I think seeing how hard they worked really resonated with me and motivated me… In the end, donations became my way of sending encouragement to the kids, showing them my appreciation rather than sympathy." Wang added. "That's right. A donation should not be an act of sympathy. That's not fair to the kids. Donation should be an act of recognition." Speaking on the role of the Internet in this charity campaign, Wang said, "The most important role of the Internet is to connect donors and beneficiaries. It helps me know who I should help next." He paused, then continued, "Additionally, with mobile payment tools, it's getting more cost-effective and convenient to give to charity. Am I right?" Wang asked, gesturing to his phone and smiling.

Later, on his birthday, Wang donated a "substantial" amount of money (20 yuan) through Tencent's charity platform once again. "I want to celebrate my birthday in a more meaningful way," he said.

Kids Gallery: A Popular Online Charity Campaign

What Is The Campaign?

Kids Gallery, which has accumulated an impressive user base of new users like Wang, is an online and offline charity program launched by Tencent Charity and World of Art Brut Culture (WABC). So far, 36 paintings made by children with autism have been selected to be transformed into high-definition digital images. To accompany their paintings, the artists also recorded voice messages thanking the donors. These pictures are featured on a group of H5 pages. If a user likes one of the pictures, he or she can click the "one yuan to purchase" button to buy it. After that, the user can post their donation record, with the child's artwork as the background, to his or her WeChat Moments as an online record of their charitable donation.

What Are Its Results?

Wang's case is just one among millions of others. If someone like him, who had never donated to charity before, is willing to take part so enthusiastically, one can imagine the spectacular effects this campaign could achieve. Indeed, on launch day throngs of users were enticed to take part in the campaign after seeing the images shared by their friends online. Kids Gallery has set a record in the history of charity campaigns—with a mere 36 paintings it has attracted more than 5.8 million donors and reached its fundraising goal of RMB 15 million within its first 24 hours. The project not only eclipsed many traditional philanthropic projects in terms of the efficiency and scale of its fundraising, it also surpassed some middle- and small-sized foundations in the number of participants and donations achieved. As it turns out, there is clearly chemistry between the Internet and philanthropy that has the potential to be explosive.

What Made It So Popular?

According to the organizer, due to unexpected circumstances this event had to be launched early, without any prior promotion. It was participation from the users themselves that made the campaign go viral. If the organizers are to be believed, what on earth triggered such intense user participation? Based on incomplete data, the most frequent words appearing in the forwarded comments were "beautiful" and "touched". It was as if the act of donation had been elevated to a higher level in this campaign. Many users, like Wang, were attracted by the "beautiful" images and were "touched" by the unique artist behind each painting, going on to purchase their paintings and share their messages to their public Moments. In so doing, they were not simply motivated by sympathy, but instead, a higher level of recognition and admiration for "beauty".

When interviewed after the project, the founder shared his thoughts. "There might be two factors contributing to its popularity. On one hand, we didn't present the public with suffering, but rather the vitality and strength of the kids as embodied in their paintings. On the other hand, the public have become more aware. By now, they know that there are many ways of helping others. One way to get involved in charity is to simply pass on the message and let more people understand and get to know this wonderful community."

The Great Potential of Internet Philanthropy

The Power of Perseverance

Did the success of Kids Gallery happen by accident? Many consider it sheer luck, but the program was not developed overnight. The charitable organization that created the program had been in operation for eight years. It takes perseverance to make a non-profit program boom. Its success should be attributed to tenacity rather than dumb luck.

Tencent Foundation: A Key Player

That being said, could this kind of success truly all be down to the perseverance of the project's creators, the World of Art Brut Culture (WABC) organization? According to the Beijing Morning Post, the movement was originally launched on August 17th, 2016, but received a lukewarm response. It was not until the Kids Gallery H5 page went online that things really started to take off and the movement started to go viral. In addition to efforts from the organization itself, a key player in contributing to the craze surrounding the project was Tencent Charity, an online charity platform that has been building its influence over the last ten years.

In June 2017, Tencent funded the launch of the Tencent Foundation, the first national non-public charity initiated by an internet company in China. The affiliated Tencent Charity is one of the most influential internet philanthropic platforms in the country. As a leading IT company, why is it that Tencent engages so actively in the ostensibly "unprofitable" business of philanthropy?

Chen Yidan, core founder of Tencent and the Tencent Foundation, has spoken about the early stages of Tencent's engagement in Philanthropy: "Tencent has a long history of philanthropy. Ever since our initial stages of development, we were so grateful to our users that we began looking for opportunities to reward them and set up meaningful philanthropic projects." When it came to establish a special foundation, he said there were three reasons behind it. "First, we wanted to give back to our users. Second, we had reached a deeper understanding of our responsibility since Tencent went public in 2004. Third, we hoped that we could establish an online philanthropy platform as a channel for more charitable organizations to launch and promote their projects. This platform was to provide groups and individuals from wider society with better access to philanthropic projects, allowing the impact of philanthropy to gradually expand over time."

With the intention of "rewarding users" and a sense of their duty to promote "public interests", Tencent established its charity arm, the Tencent Foundation. The foundation then identified its vision of "being an extensive platform for all to take part in philanthropic projects". They sought to further integrate charity and the Internet through specialized Internet technologies and service capabilities, thus contributing to the rapid development of the philanthropic sector. Following the concept of "Internet Plus" as a model, the Tencent Foundation has gradually helped to develop philanthropic awareness in hundreds of millions of online users. They have succeeded in building a positive environment in which each person can participate in philanthropic activities through innovative platforms, namely, "Tencent Charity Online Donation Platform", "Charity Hiker" and the charity channel of qq.com.

What's more, innovative programs such as WeCountry and Tencent Three-dimensional Relief examine the potential of integrating the Internet and charity in areas such as rural development, education, poverty relief, emergency disaster relief, and employee-driven philanthropy (See Fig. 2). Thanks to their continuous efforts, Tencent Charity enables easily accessible online fund-raising. The platform has raised over RMB 10 million after the Wenchuan earthquake in 2008, over RMB 100 million from the Tencent Monthly Giving program launched in 2013, and over RMB 1 billion with its 99 Charity Day. These charity events have pushed the "Internet Plus Charity" model in China onto the swift path of development from quantitative change to qualitative change.

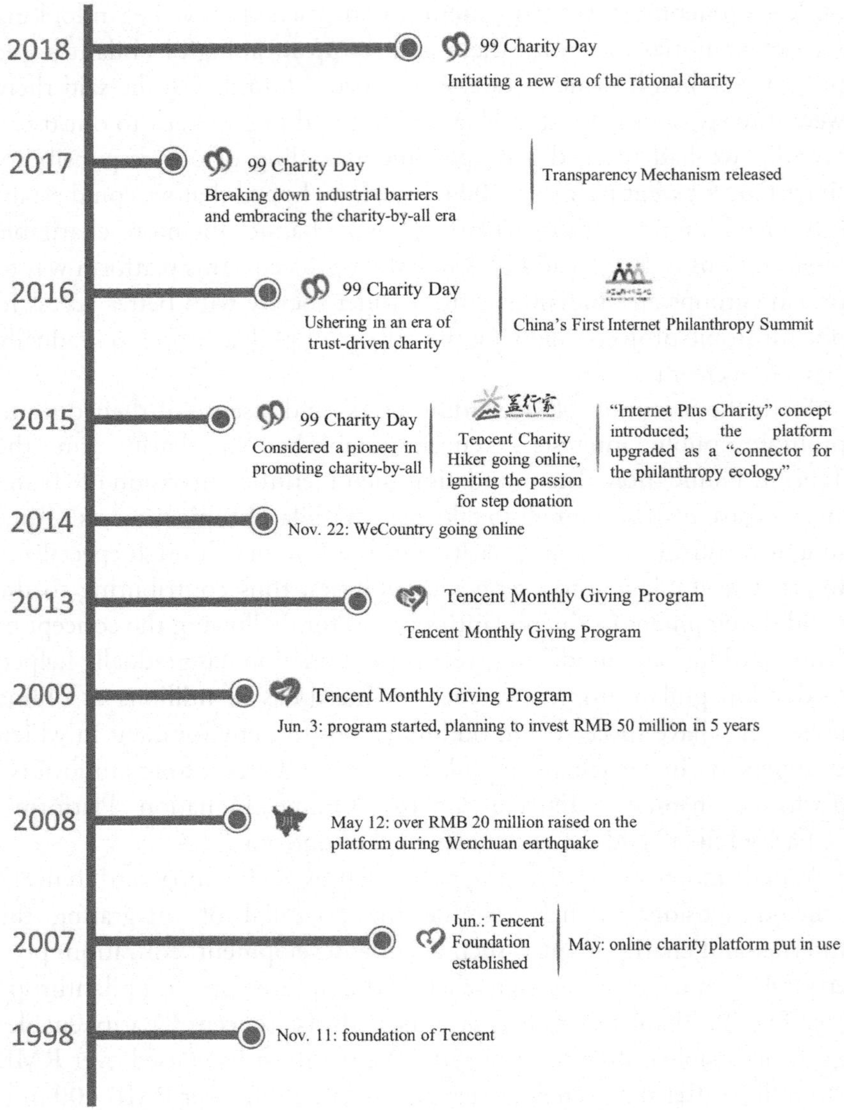

Fig. 2 Milestones of Tencent Charity

A New Era Featuring Philanthropy by All

While the past decade has witnessed Tencent Charity's exploration of Internet philanthropy, it was the 99 Charity Day in 2015 that kick-started truly exponential growth. Prior to that, the major contributors to charitable foundations in China were the government, enterprises, institutions, and the wealthy (a very small part of the population). Due to a lack in systematic fund-raising systems and the traditional individual participation commonly seen in western countries, most Chinese people did not make regular charitable contributions.

The aim of the 99 Charity Day was to make charity more interactive and accessible to all, by taking advantage of modern means such as mobile Internet technology and social media platforms. To that end, Tencent Charity joined forces with hundreds of charitable organizations, well-known enterprises, celebrities, and top creative communication agencies to start a movement wherein Tencent promised to match all donations made by participants. Furthermore, enthusiastic donors were glad to see new ways of getting involved, such as small-sum cash donations, donating one's steps through fitness technology, or even donating one's voice. These stress-free and convenient methods lit a fire in the hearts of hundreds of millions of online users, inspiring them to engage in philanthropy.

The 99 Charity Day has now passed its fourth year since its initial launch in 2015. During that period the number of donors skyrocketed more than thirteen-fold from 2.05 million to 28 million, and the funds raised soared more than five-fold from RMB 228 million to 1.4 billion, according to the data collected by Tencent Charity (See Fig. 3). It is clear that the qualitative change towards "Internet Plus Charity" has already begun.

Progressive Formation of a New Ecology and a New Model of Philanthropy

Tencent Charity Foundation is but one of the bright spots in the vigorous development of Internet philanthropy in China. It is one of the 20 Internet charity fund-raising information platforms designated by the

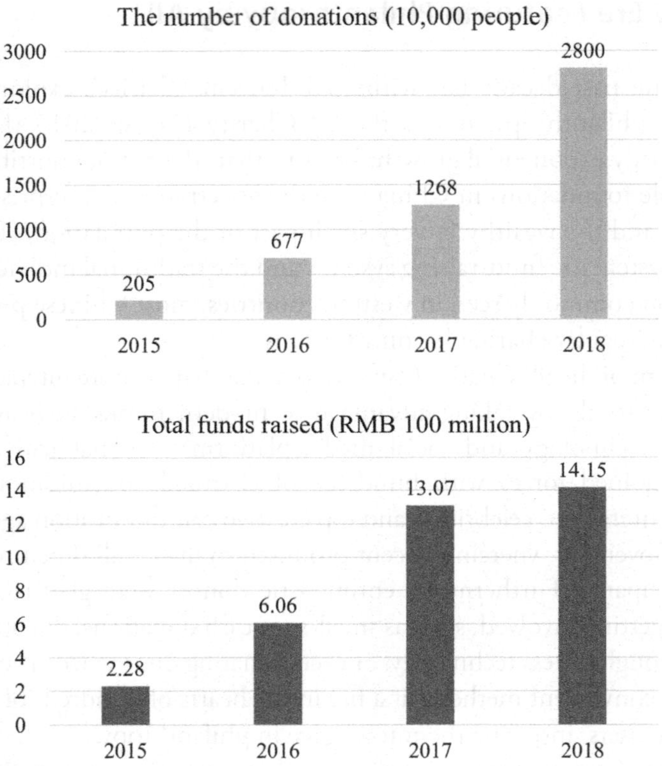

Fig. 3 The number of donors (10,000 people) participating in the 99 Charity Day and total funds (RMB 100 million) raised from 2015 to 2018

Ministry of Civil Affairs (MCA) of the People's Republic of China in accordance with the *Charity Law*.

With the strong support of these platforms, a new ecosystem of Internet philanthropy is rapidly taking shape in China, which effectively helps link and motivate philanthropic powers from all sectors of the society. According to the statistics of the MCA, in 2018, the above-mentioned 20 platforms published 21,000 entries of charity fund-raising information for more than 1400 public offering charitable organizations in China; the number of netizens who clicked the links to information about, paid attention to and got involved in charity fund-raising

Fig. 4 Data on the development of China's Internet charity fund-raising information platforms in 2018

activities exceeded 8.46 billion person-times; and the sum of money raised for charities topped RMB 3.17 billion, up 26.8 percent year on year (see Fig. 4).

With the further integration of philanthropy with the Internet in China, various kinds of philanthropic innovations emerge one after another, initially forming a dynamic "China Model."

First, Internet philanthropy is rooted in community-level institutions. Focusing on the central task and serving the overall situation, the 20 Internet charity fund-raising information platforms prioritized services for poverty-alleviation efforts and community-level institutions in 2018, when the number of services involved in targeted poverty-alleviation projects and the number of services oriented towards community-level charitable organizations respectively exceeded 80 percent of the total number of services.

Second, Internet philanthropy covers a wide range of areas. Comprehensive services were provided for helping the poor and those in difficulty, supporting education and aiding students, giving medical help and treatment, providing disaster relief and rescue to the people, and protecting environment.

Third, Internet philanthropy takes a variety of forms. The relevant platforms design many innovative donation scenarios, among others, presenting donations through walking or reading programs, accumulated points, consumption, enterprise matching gift programs, or virtual reality games. They also make available flexible means of donation such as daily and monthly donation, small change and one-to-one donation.

Fourth, Internet philanthropy is provided through a diversity of channels, including pushing information through official accounts, creating splash screen advertisements, giving out leaflets, making reports on self-owned news apps, and rendering packaged publicity on apps under the banners of different groups.

Fifth, Internet philanthropy involves the participation of people from all walks of life. The innovations in Internet philanthropy are widely popular with people, initiating the trends like "philanthropy for everybody and everybody for philanthropy", "philanthropy at your convenience" and "philanthropy at your fingertips." Most participants in Internet charity fund-raising activities were born in the 1980s and 1990s. Even those born in the 2000s began to be actively engaged in these activities. In sum, the young people constitute an important force in developing Internet philanthropy (See Fig. 5).

In addition, the governments exercise regulation and administration over these platforms, and the platforms also adopt self-disciplinary actions. All these actions provide powerful guarantee for the healthy development of Internet philanthropy in China.

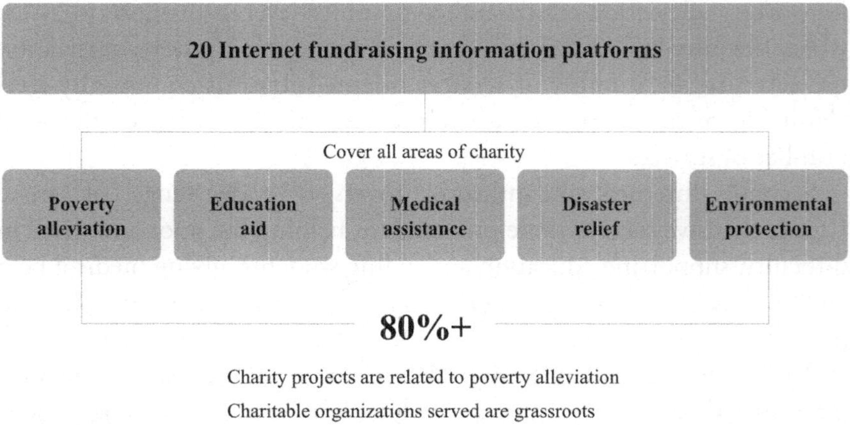

Fig. 5 Main characteristics of the "China Model" of Internet philanthropy

In 2018, the MCA strengthened supervision and control over Internet charity fund-raising information platforms in accordance with two industrial standards—*Basic Administration Standard for Public Fund-raising Information Platform of Charitable Organizations* and *Basic Technical Standard for Public Fund-raising Information Platform of Charitable Organizations*.

These platforms are required to make persistent efforts to monitor public sentiment, conduct daily inspection, accept and handle complaints, and transmit pressure without stop; they are also urged to perform their major responsibilities.

The platforms further strengthen standardized development, intensify disclosure of information, increase the function of lodging online complaints, and make innovative attempts concerning technology and management such as using block chain, the "cool-off" function (which displays Tips on Transparency, encouraging people to think twice before clicking the button of making donation) and financial disclosure package.

These platforms bring into play their characteristics and advantages by providing support for capacity building of small and medium-sized charitable organizations. They help establish the platforms of these charitable organizations, provide consultation, training and coaching sessions, and lend support in terms of technology, capitals and communication. Thanks to these efforts, designated platforms can provide still more specialized services, and Internet charity fund-raising is run in a more standardized and orderly manner.

Three Questions About Internet Philanthropy

The rapid development of Internet philanthropy is shaking up traditional philanthropy, bringing a new lease of life, along with new challenges. In order better understand this new-born phenomenon and make full use of the Internet to stimulate fast and healthy development for philanthropic causes in China, we need to further analyze and explore what lies ahead for charity in its new form. We can start by considering the following three questions:

Exactly How Developed Is Internet Philanthropy?

The Internet develops on a global scale, and so does charity. Due to differences in politics, economy, and religion, countries vary greatly in practice and development with regards to charity. The real question is whether there is also a difference in attitudes towards Internet philanthropy. Is the process of integrating philanthropy with online platforms different in specific countries? Moreover, what advantages does China have at its disposal? The domestic and global overviews in this book will help readers better understand the development of philanthropy both in China and all over the world, as well as what lessons China has to learn from other countries when attempting to enrich itself and clarify its position.

Why Has Internet Philanthropy Developed So Quickly?

While modern philanthropy took 300 years to develop, it has only existed in the People's Republic of China for 30 years, and only made its way onto the Internet 10 years ago. Why has this new form of charity experienced such exponential growth in recent years? What is it that the Internet brings to traditional charity? The "In Retrospection" part of this book will look into the nature of Internet philanthropy from three viewpoints: definition, features, and significance.

Where Is Internet Philanthropy Heading?

With new information technology constantly being developed, Internet philanthropy will continue to integrate itself within this new technology, growing ever more independent and sophisticated. With this in mind, what directions will this development take? How will technology further change philanthropy? What will donation mechanisms be like in the future? How will the philanthropic ecosystems evolve? In "The Future" part of this book, we will discuss the endless possibilities for the future of digital philanthropy.

Terminology Relating to Internet Philanthropy

There are many specific terms and concepts surrounding Internet philanthropy. Some are commonly used by the public, while others have official definitions. For such an emerging field, it is natural that meanings be interpreted in many different ways. For the sake of the reader's understanding and to avoid ambiguity, this section will outline the main terms and concepts in use in this book. Of course, this book is not intended to focus solely on theory, so the concepts and definitions outlined below only represent the views of this book, and is provided as a reference for the philanthropy industry and general public.

"Philanthropy" and "Charity"

The concepts of "philanthropy" and "charity" are closely related but inherently different. There is still contention over the distinction between these two terms in both the industry and academia, but we can still go some lengths to clarify these concepts in a literal sense.

Philanthropy (literally meaning "public interest" in Chinese), representing any pursuit that is made in the interest of society and mankind. What philanthropy emphasizes is working to the benefit of an entire, indiscriminate group and forming a set of structural methods and mechanisms to improve social benefits. Charity, which literally means "love and kindness" in Chinese, implies generous giving to groups of people who are in need. Charity emphasizes working in the interest of specific groups, which often takes the form of donated goods or money.

Of course, in many cases, charity and philanthropy are closely related or even have overlapping meanings. Many charitable acts begin as what we would call charity, and then later become philanthropy, or vice versa. For example, donations made after a major disaster are a kind of immediate charity activity, designed specifically to help the victims. Further along in this process, it becomes a philanthropic undertaking to provide substantial, long-term support and education for the reconstruction of the affected area.

According to Article 3, Chap. 1 of the *Charity Law of the People's Republic of China*, "charitable activities" refers to the following public interest activities, voluntarily carried out by natural persons, legal persons and other organizations through the donation of property, the provision of services or other means: (1) helping the poor and the needy; (2) assisting those who are elderly, orphaned, ill, or disabled, and providing special care; (3) alleviating losses incurred by natural disasters, accidents, public health incidents and other emergencies; (4) promoting the development of education, science, culture, health, sports and other causes; (5) preventing and alleviating pollution and other public hazards, protecting and improving the natural environment; and (6) other philanthropic activities carried out in accordance with this law.

In order to simplify the discussion and maintain consistency with the most common wording within the industry, unless especially stated or explained otherwise, there will be no distinction between how I use the words "charity" and "philanthropy" in this book. For a more detailed analysis of the concepts of "philanthropy" and "charity", please see Chap. 9.

"Civil Society Organization" and "Charitable Organization"

According to the China Social Organizations Public Service Platform, civil society organizations can be divided into three main categories: foundations, social groups ("communities") and private non-enterprise units. According to Article 8 of Chap. 2 of the *Charity Law*, private non-enterprise units are now being converted into "social service institutions". As this transition is still in progress, said organizations are still registered as "private non-enterprise units", and will be referred to as such in this book.

According to Article 8, Chap. 2 of the *Charity Law*, "Charitable Organization" refers to non-profit organizations that have been legally established in accordance with this law, whose purpose is to carry out charitable activities for social benefit. Charitable organizations include foundations, social groups, and social service organizations. At the same time, the *Charity Law* also makes detailed provisions on the registration and recognition of charitable organizations. Before they can be recognized as charitable organizations, civil society organizations are required to meet a series of conditions and register with the Civil Affairs Department of the local people's government (at county level or above).

According to the above definitions, the term "civil society organizations" covers a broader range of institutions than "charitable organizations". Every charitable organization falls under the general category of civil society organizations. However, there are several kinds of civil society organization that are not, in the legal sense, charitable. This book focuses on the role of the Internet in philanthropy, not only focusing on organizations that can be labeled "charitable" on a legal level, but also any civil society organizations that concern themselves with philanthropic activities ("philanthropic civil society organizations"). These two kinds of institution run on very similar concepts and connotations, but also have their own unique differences. In this book, charitable organizations and civil society organizations will be distinguished according to the specific situation under discussion.

"Internet philanthropy"

The phrase "Internet philanthropy" literally refers to "philanthropy with the help of Internet". More specifically, it refers to the ways in which philanthropic activities are carried out using information technology such as the Internet. Internet philanthropy may be carried out by philanthropic or commercial institutions, both of which fall within the scope of this book's research. Commercial institutions usually adopt Internet philanthropy as part of their corporate social responsibility programs, such as organizing their employees to take part in volunteering activities.

References

Min, W., & Yin S. L. (2018, September 30). *小朋友画廊:你可能有的质疑回应都在这里*. ifeng. http://inews.ifeng.com/51802130/news.shtml

Xiang, X. J. (2017, August 29). *"一元购画"刷屏, 发起人苗世明:"罗一笑事件"不会重演*. Southcn. http://kb.southcn.com/content/201708/29/content_176938085.html

Zheng, J. M. (2017, August 31). *半天筹款1500万, 刷屏社交圈的"小朋友画廊"有何秘诀*. YiMagazine. https://www.cbnweek.com/articles/normal/18602

陈一丹:腾讯公益的传统与特色. (2007, July 18). Gongyi. Retrieved October 18, 2018, from https://gongyi.qq.com/zt/2007/txgyj/

互联网慈善的"中国样本"正在形成. (2019, April 05). Gov.cn. Retrieved August 18, 2019, from http://www.gov.cn/xinwen/2019-04/05/content_5379888.htm

中国社会组织动态. (2019, April 05). *2018年, 84.6亿人次参与互联网慈善*. Weixin. Retrieved August 18, 2019, from https://mp.weixin.qq.com/s/NrXV7yZMXMarBNf850Jq7w

Contents

List of Figures

Introduction

Humans are the product of both nature and nurture. The antonym of "philanthropy" is "self-interest".

The fundamental premise of microeconomics is that every individual pursues his/her self-interest. In other words, each rational individual follows the principle of profit maximization, be it in manufacturing, commerce, at work or in their everyday life. In the *Wealth of Nations*, Adam Smith claimed that, although everyone acts in his/her self-interest, through the division of labor and market trade in society, the startling result is not the collapse of order, but the maximized welfare of all.

However, human nature is far more complicated than the premises posited by economic theory. Behavior in economics is strongly constrained by social relations; we do not simply act like atoms in a vacuum. Self-interest is but one of many driving forces, and subject to the framework of established customs. As Adam Smith confessed in The *Theory of Moral Sentiment*, "Of this kind is pity or compassion... The greatest ruffian, the most hardened violator of the laws of society, is not altogether without it" (Smith, 1759). Since compassion is also human nature, neutral observers in social interactions will naturally pity those who suffer injustice, despise the oppressors, and eventually form inner social values, which is the origin of conscience.

Humans are social by nature. If we look at all of history, philanthropy can be seen as the foundation of civilization. And even when you look closely into people's hearts, you'll see that kindness and honesty run deep.

Evolution

The history of human civilization is also the history of philanthropy. Although cultures may differ greatly, in the eyes of history, philanthropy has always followed a similar evolutionary path.

Philanthropy often begins at the subconscious level, an almost intuitive, reflexive behavior. The original form of philanthropy is found in historical records or ancient legends. It can be summed up as the simple emotional reaction of individuals, typically in the form of a helping hand to those in need. According to *the Records of the Grand Historian of China*, "Over 19 years, Tao Zhu Gong's business had thrice earned him large sums of money, but he gave them out to the poor around him. This is what is called the goodwill of the rich." When the king of Kerala in India closed the gate of the palace every day, he asked "*Athaazha Pazhnikaarundo* (Is there anyone who hasn't had dinner)?" And at the other end of Eurasia, Caesar's ally Marcus Agripa said, "Give the people salt and olive oil, cut everyone's hair, and after cleaning the sewers in Rome, take a boat through the main passage into the Tiber River" (Murphy, 2007).

But very soon, people realized that giving based on the whims of people's emotions often occurred as a one-off event and was hardly ever sustainable. The threads of philanthropy gradually weaved behavior into an order based on faith, morality, and the goodness of people. Donations evolved into an indirect model of specialized organizations. In the fourth century AD, a church organization called Diaconiae (meaning "service") was set up in Lower Egypt to distribute food to the poor. In the sixth century, the Diaconiae expanded into Upper Egypt, the Middle East, and Italy, and were able to get the approval of the Roman emperor who ruled Egypt at that time to donate food to the organization every year (Niederer, 1952). In twelfth century Europe, hundreds of clinical places emerged in churches and monasteries, and received all kinds of donations to treat leprosy patients (Davis, 2014).

The modern industrial revolution sparked the era of specialized philanthropic activities. Indirect philanthropy received universal recognition, and was fixed by law and other forms of regulation. Two years before the death of Elizabeth I, the British enacted the English Poor Laws, which became a milestone in the separation from religious ethics to a secular and professional development of charitable work. Among them, the *Statute of Charitable Uses 1601* clearly defined non-profit organizations, their mission, and the principle of preferential policies.[1] The concept of modern philanthropy, accompanied by the momentum of the industrial revolution, spread from England through Europe and across the Atlantic to the United States.

The indirect philanthropy model was an initiative created by a handful of American tycoons during the Gold Rush. The Carnegie, Rockefeller, and Russell Sage Foundations, along with other philanthropic institutes, were established one by one over the course of 100 years. In *The Gospel of Wealth*, Andrew Carnegie believed that it is unwise to use wealth for personal enjoyment, and even more so to not give this surplus to the poor, as the better choice ought to be giving to those who desire to rise in social rank (Carnegie, 1889). He funded the Carnegie Foundation to support education, and donated money to set up universities, libraries, and swimming pools. *The Gospel of Wealth* is also regarded as the "urtext" of modern charitable philosophy. Public interest no longer focused on eliminating hunger and disease, as it shifted its sights to the future and development (Kolbert, 2018). Although this idea has been naively called Tycoon Medievalism, it still has many supporters and a far-reaching influence. To this day, it is still regarded by many foundations as the aim of donations and part of their code of conduct (Davis, 2010).

In modern times, the nature of philanthropy has extended to a large non-profit industry with multiple objectives and flexible organizations. It is also considered as the third major sector (Anheier, 2005), next to government institutions and private enterprises. According to statistics provided by the NCCS, in America alone, there are currently more than one million public charities. Meanwhile, the total number of private

[1] Here, the Statute of Charitable Uses 1601 refers to the Charitable Uses Act of 1601, an Act (43 Eliz I, c.4) of the Parliament of England.

foundations and non-profit civic organizations (like associations and fraternities) are 100,000 and 360,000 respectively (Price, 2018). The size, internal structure, and target markets of these organizations vary widely, ranging from causes like saving a certain wild species to preserving intangible cultures, from protecting ethnic minorities to providing comprehensive medical services, from animal rescue to global warming. Behind this vast range of causes are the countless professionals involved in these non-profit organizations. Kaiser Permanente, the largest public charity in the United States, has 39 central hospitals and 720 clinics, with 21,000 doctors, and 54,000 nurses on the payroll to provide medical services to more than 11.8 million participants. In 2017, its revenue exceeded $72.7 billion, which if this were our only indicator, would put it on the Fortune Global 500 List for 2018.

Three Features

Looking back on the history of philanthropy, we can distinguish three main features of the development of philanthropy over the last millennium.

The first feature is that philanthropic activity developed from an individuals' spontaneous empathetically-driven behaviors into organized and structured public projects. The basic driving force of philanthropy lies in the social nature of humans, who are inclined to show sympathy and compassion for those who suffer. This motivation, though strong and impulsive, is equally unsustainable because it is subject to the whims of people's emotions. Hidden behind this moral dilemma are entrenched social factors that cannot be effectively resolved by depending on emotional impulses. Ceasing philanthropy's reliance on these impulses by instead using organized and structured approaches was the only way that it could persist in the long term. If we compare martyrs like Buddha, who sacrificed himself to feed a dying tiger, to a charity organization that engages a staff of 100,000 in service to society, we can see the first main feature of the evolution of philanthropy over the past thousand years.

The second feature lies in the ever-expanding scope of philanthropy and its increasing market segmentation. As social structures became more complex, the demands upon philanthropy and its corresponding organizations became increasingly diversified. For a long period of history, poverty and disease were the only two problems philanthropy sought to address. In its initial stages, philanthropy was simple and direct: giving relief to the poor. As such, Fan Li (also known as Tao Zhu Gong), an ancient Chinese merchant, only provided financial assistance to his poor friends. Similarly, the Leprosy Revolution was initiated to cure patients during the Middle Ages. As the practice deepened, philanthropy developed more levels. In Jewish scriptures from the twelfth century, even age-old causes such as poverty alleviation were classified by level of merit, the lowest being direct monetary donations, to the highest level of generosity which was classified as offering work opportunities.[2] Nowadays, the objectives of non-profit organizations have been divided into even narrower categories. The International Classification of Non-profit Organizations (ICNPO) divides all non-profit organizations into 12 major activity groups, then further into 27 subgroups,[3] covering almost all social development goals, from education and medical care to culture and environmental protection. Therefore, the second feature worth noting about the evolution of philanthropy is how, as economies developed and societies progressed, public welfare underwent a process of constant expansion and subdivision.

The third feature we can see is the ever stronger connection between philanthropy and the economy, as well as philanthropy's ever growing ability to re-allocate resources. The most fundamental characteristic of nonprofits, however, lies in their social attributes—a nonprofit must pursue fairness for society as a whole, and seek harmony between humans and nature—this is what sets them apart from common private enterprises. In the long period of history preceding the industrial revolution,

---

[2] These obligations were categorized in the twelfth century by the theologian and jurist Maimonides, in the Mishneh Torah, a guide to the edicts of Judaism. Here he set out "eight degrees of charity", where giving reluctantly is the least worthy, while the highest level of generosity could be giving someone a job or helping him or her in some other way to become independent. Maimonides also encouraged anonymous giving.

[3] ICNPO refers to the International Classification of Nonprofit Organizations. The international classification of NPOs was established by the Comparative Nonprofit Sector Project at Johns Hopkins University. The classification was later adopted by the UN in the Handbook on Nonprofit Institutions (2002).

charity organizations, subject to external socio-economic conditions, were usually restricted in their economic functions and struggled to perform any social function within the limited range of their economic capabilities. However, the rapid growth of social wealth during the industrial revolution brought with it an unprecedented boost in the economic function of charitable organizations. Similarly, the principles of economics also started to play a more significant role in philanthropic and charitable causes. Though charities were still non-profit, they experienced the same increase in efficiency due to division and specialization of labor as did the private enterprises. Even though donations and the allocation of philanthropic services are not market-oriented, competition inevitably still exists between different charity projects. It is down to this competition, which is based on efficiency, that philanthropy can fall under the principles of survival of the fittest and evolve.

Looking ahead, these three interconnected features will shape the future of philanthropy into a sophisticated, rational, complex and diverse social ecology. This third sector will be finely structured, specialized and systematic, and undeniably interwoven into the customs of society, as well as in people's personal and work lives.

Rationality for Social Good

Charitable and philanthropic undertakings in the People's Republic of China have gained great momentum since the reform and opening-up policy was introduced. So much so that thousands of years' worth of change has been compressed into just a few decades. The development of the Internet has significantly contributed to this progress.

With the Internet, the flow of information has accelerated. Communication is now instantaneous, social hierarchies have broken down, and more impactful charitable projects have garnered the support of public donations. The barriers of time and space have been torn down, and much kindness and warmth has been gathered and delivered to those in need of help and care. Such pervasive connections have provided small-sized, professional civil society organizations with the platforms to present themselves and have also given them opportunities to amplify their voice, allowing them to be heard by the public. In this sense, Internet philanthropy has offered a platform for participating organizations to compete under the same industry standards and the scrutiny of public donors, promoting healthy competition among different projects and improving the overall professionalism and transparency of the industry.

However, despite the speed of development, the sheer quantity of information and emotional appeals inevitably created a degree of chaos. People's immediate emotional reactions are amplified in the cyberspace. Such emotional impulses have helped put some excellent projects into action, but have also provided a breeding ground for opportunists. Philanthropic organizations naturally bear the weight of living up to a high standard of morality, and it is their duty to do things efficiently and effectively. However, they are not free from fault or error. Even the smallest of flaws are often blown up in exaggerated ways, as they touch on society's most sensitive issues. One single bout of negative press can easily dampen the positive social perceptions of the industry. In one classic case, an unknown woman posted a photo of herself on blogging website Sina Weibo to show off her wealth. This triggered a firestorm of public opinion that nearly destroyed the reputation of the country's most famous public fundraising institution, after decades of painstaking work.

In an age of information overload such as this, it is particularly valuable to maintain a rational attitude towards philanthropy.

A more rational kind of philanthropy is one that emphasizes hard, logical consideration on every issue; the decision to donate money should only be made after careful deliberation, not on an impulse triggered by emotions. Donors who rely on instincts and emotions are often those who do not wish to spend time and energy scrutinizing a project's feasibility before making a one-click payment, nor are they the kind of donor to check the progress or results of a project after donating. However, this extra time and effort may be more important than the money donated. Knowing the facts of a certain program is not only the responsibility of a project manager, but also the mark of a good donor. Donating may be subject to the financial conditions of a donor, but thinking before we decide who deserves our money is the common practice we should try to cultivate. Indeed, philanthropic projects often appeal to emotion and impulse instead of rational thinking; but to make reasonable and lasting charitable donations, it is essential for donors to reexamine the factors leading to their decision before they act upon it.

For rational philanthropy to be possible, civil society organizations and Internet charity fundraising information platforms (Internet platforms) must improve their systems and seek greater efficiency through professionalism and fair competition. In order for a civil society organization to appeal to donors' rational thinking, they must demonstrate internal control, a clear operational process, results assessment and regular feedback on their projects to their donors. Rational donors will also look to whether or not there are rules regarding access restrictions and information disclosure on the Internet and other public information media platforms. Without professional operational mechanisms and sufficient, timely disclosure of information, there can be no rationality in philanthropy. Nor can there be any way of establishing healthy competition between civil society organizations, or creating efficient and long-lasting philanthropic campaigns.

Rational donors abandon the shallow and superficial definition of charity, striking a balance between their financial conditions and high moral standards. Philanthropic causes do require moral support, and upholding public order and good customs have always been the bottom line of these causes. In medieval Europe, there was a distinction between the "deserving poor", who were poor due to circumstances outside of their control, and the "undeserving poor", who were poor due to laziness, reflecting the morals and values of society at that time. However, if morality becomes too pervasive, it can place constraints on philanthropic causes, meaning that any factor that falls short of the public's moral expectations may lead to negative public feedback, precluding any valuable projects or ideals that could have been put into practice. This clearly double-edged sword, on one hand puts pressure on civil society organizations to improve themselves, and on the other, it may cause well-organized, promising projects to be overshadowed by less deserving alternatives. Since civil society organizations are unwilling to raise salaries, they struggle to recruit skilled talent, which often causes influential donors to keep a lower profile. In turn, philanthropic and charitable causes often find it difficult to maintain an attractive public profile.

In the end, we must all hope that everybody comes to understand and respect the inner logic behind philanthropic causes and the way they develop, so that philanthropists are properly understood, and their good intentions can work to everyone's benefit.

The Structure of This Book

This book divides our exploration of Internet philanthropy into four main parts. First, Part I "In China" will review the development of Internet philanthropy in China over the past 20 years. This Part will look at the reasons why Internet philanthropy grew so exponentially in China from various stakeholder perspectives, including the public, the government, public institutions, enterprises, and Internet platforms. I will go on to describe the colossal impact online integration has had on philanthropy. Second, in Part II "Global Vision", we will take a global perspective, introducing the current status of Internet philanthropy in the United States, the United Kingdom, and Japan. Through the analysis of the development of Internet philanthropy in countries with different histories, systems, and cultures, we will explore shared and individual insights on the development of this emerging field. Third, Part III "In Retrospection" takes a close look at the nature of philanthropy and dissects the meaning of Internet philanthropy. Finally, Part IV "In the Future" explores the sustainable development of Internet philanthropy from three core perspectives: science and technology, mechanisms, and culture.

With a view to this book's objectivity, our team visited a number of representative Internet platforms, civil society organizations, corporate social responsibility departments, and government institutions in China and beyond, collecting a large amount of primary data. There are also many organizations and individuals who have greatly contributed to our team over the course of writing this book. We would like to extend our sincere gratitude and appreciation to all the organizations and individuals who have supported the creation of this book.

In writing this book, our team has accumulated a considerable amount of primary and secondary information, and all the material used in the book was carefully curated. Due to length constraints, eventually we had to omit some truly remarkable and moving cases. This is because Internet philanthropy has been created, developed, and promoted by countless industry colleagues and volunteers. Behind every stage of its development are countless real and touching stories. A book is simply too short to encompass the true nature of Internet philanthropy in its entirety. However, we hope that this book not only teaches its readers about the development of Internet philanthropy, but also lets them see a thriving and dynamic China.

In sum, Internet philanthropy is a facet of civilization that deserves to be recognized and documented as a significant part of our ongoing history.

References

Anheier, H. K. (2005). *Nonprofit organizations: Theory, management, policy.* Routledge.

Carnegie, A. (1889). The Gospel of wealth. *North American Review, 148*(391), 653–665.

Davis, A. J. (2014). The social and religious meanings of charity in medieval Europe. *History Compass, 12*(12), 935–950.

Davis, K. (2010). Tycoon medievalism, corporate philanthropy, and American pedagogy. *American Literary History, 22*(4), 781–800.

Kolbert, E. (2018, August 27). Gospels of giving for the new gilded age: Are today's donor classes solving problems or creating new ones? *The New Yorker.*

Murphy, C. (2007). *Are we Rome? The fall of an empire and the fate of America.* Mariner Books.

Niederer, F. J. (1952). Early medieval charity. *Church History, 21*(4), 285–295.

Price, D. (2018, March 23). *Laziness does not exist.* Medium. https://humanparts.medium.com/laziness-does-not-exist-3af27e312d01

Smith, A. (1759). *The theory of moral sentiment.* Gutenberg Publishers.

Part I

In China: The Rise of Internet Philanthropy

Let doing charity work become an attitude, a habit and an everyday lifestyle.
—Huateng Ma
Core Founder, Chairman and CEO of Tencent
(From a letter to all Tencent employees during the third 99 Charity Day)
September, 2017

Internet philanthropy has seen a phenomenal rise in China over the last ten years.

The 2008 Sichuan earthquake was a major milestone in the development of internet philanthropy. Since then, leading internet enterprises such as Tencent and Alibaba have been increasingly engaged in philanthropic activities. The "chemical reaction" between technology and philanthropy has generated an astonishing force in China's philanthropic ecosystem, prompting the appearance of many new internet charity fundraising information platforms with diverse features and functions. These platforms successfully connected philanthropic organizations with enterprises, the public and even the government, and incited the "philanthropy by all" boom in China.

So, what is behind this new and powerful force? How does it affect the various stakeholders of China's philanthropic sector? The answers to these questions will be unearthed as we take a closer look at the historical context from which Internet philanthropy emerged.

1

History of China's Internet Philanthropy

Section 1 The Development of the Internet

For us to better understand the rise of online philanthropy in China, we should start with the Internet, because it is the nature of the Internet that makes online philanthropy different. On September 30, 1995, Yinghaiwei, China's first Internet service provider (ISP), was founded and put into operation in Beijing (Ying, 2018). Its business model was much like that of America Online, which provided users with web services including bulletin board systems (BBS), chat rooms, and online newspapers. This marked the beginning of the popularization and commercialization of the Internet in China.

Over the 20-plus years from 1995 until now, China's Internet industry has been developing at a relentless pace. From rudimentary desktops and laptops to today's mobile phones and wearable devices, from original handful website pages to today's millions of apps with multiple functions, the Internet has permeated practically every aspect of Chinese people' s daily lives. These astonishing changes tell the story of how the Internet and its uses have evolved. As of yet, there is no standardized definition of the different evolutionary stages in this process. Therefore, in order to

Y. Chen, *Internet Philanthropy in China*,
https://doi.org/10.1007/978-981-16-2566-4_1

distinguish between different periods and gain a clearer picture for our discussion, we will rely on the technological divisions between Web 1.0, 2.0, and 3.0, which differ in the way information and services are delivered.

Web 1.0: Institutional Centralization and Portal Network

Web 1.0 began in 1995 when the Internet hit the market. Web portals were a typical feature of the Web 1.0 business model. These web portals extensively used static HTML pages to publish information and provide users with the first browsers to obtain information.

The core foundation of Web 1.0 was in the production and dissemination of information. In terms of production at this stage, information was mainly produced and contributed by a limited number of websites (belonging to institutions). Content and information were posted to websites in a direct and visual way via the World Wide Web. Moreover, these websites offered links directing users to other resources. With regard to the spread of information, this was mainly a unidirectional action from one point (server) to multiple points (users). When content was published on a website, users could log onto the website and browse the content, but they could not modify any information or interact with the providers in real time.

While Web 1.0 catered for the need to collect and browse information, it did not allow for real-time communication or interaction between users. As Graham Cormode and Balachander Krishnamurthy stated in their article "Key Differences Between Web 1.0 and Web 2.0" (Cormode & Krishnamurthy, 2008), "Content creators were few in Web 1.0, with the vast majority of users simply acting as consumers of content." This was the reason why Web 2.0 emerged.

Web 2.0: Platform Centralization and Social Networks

The term "Web 2.0" first appeared in the 1999 article "Fragmented Future" by Darcy DiNucci, who viewed the web as a transmission system which, she predicted, could be incorporated into all kinds of electronic terminals (DiNucci, 1999). This description didn't consider the connection with Web 1.0 and was therefore not widely accepted. It was Tim O'Reilly who accurately defined Web 2.0 and helped it gain recognition. In 2004, his companies O'Reilly Media and MediaLive co-hosted the first Web 2.0 Conference, during which the concept of "Web as Platform" was proposed.

Web 2.0 is the Internet as a large platform where information is spread among multiple parties. In his article "What is Web 2.0" (O'Reilly, 2005) published in 2005, Tim O'Reilly outlined the concept of Web 2.0 and drew a "Web 2.0 MemeMap", in which he described several of Web 2.0's principles and past examples. The biggest difference between Web 1.0 and Web 2.0 is that the latter emphasizes collective wisdom, placing trust in the users as co-developers; i.e., it is the users rather than limited institutions that create online content. From this point of view, each network node has dual identities; it is intended for production as well as consumption. This greatly stimulates the online community's enthusiasm for creation and innovation. Typical applications of Web 2.0 include Blogs, Wikis, RSS, Tags, SNS, IM, and P2P. These applications all reflect the nature of Web 2.0, in that they concern co-development, sharing, and two-way interaction.

Web 2.0 enabled real-time communication and interaction between people, but along with this came new problems. Since content can be produced at any node, the information on the Internet expanded and grew exponentially. The massive amounts of data finally outgrew that which could possibly be processed by an individual, and it became increasingly difficult for users to find and extract useful content from the expanse of information available. To solve this problem, we had to turn to Web 3.0.

Web 3.0: User-centric Smart Internet

As with all new forms of technology, Web 3.0 stirred controversy in the tech world and among the general public. Whereas the uses of Web 1.0 and 2.0 technology were more straightforward, Web 3.0 can be viewed as a data management protocol, an interactive tool, a specific bandwidth, a marketing spectacle, and a host of other applications whose uses have yet to be seen. If this new concept can be introduced to help extract value from the staggering mass of information gained from Web 2.0 technology, Web 3.0 will require "intelligent" networks in order to process information to meet with user demands. To this end, Web 3.0 must be a user-centric smart network, capable of providing information and services that can dynamically customize themselves to the user's ever changing demands.

As to the technologies that will support Web 3.0, there are many ideas being played with among the industry. The three most commonly-held approaches have been classified by artificial intelligence (AI) company, Expert System (Expert.ai Team, 2017). The first proposed technology is the Semantic Web, a concept introduced by Tim Berners-Lee during the World Wide Web Consortium in 1998. According to this theory, metadata processed by computers will be added to documents on the World-Wide Web, such as HTML addresses, so that the entire Internet can serve as a common forum for information exchange, as well as a huge database. The second proposed form of technology is AI, which is mainly used in the processing of human language and image files. Soon, machines are expected to be capable of automatically analyzing a variety of online information, that previously could only be understood by humans, and offer customized results to users as required. The third technology is Software as a Service (SaaS). Since all of the applications and data belonging to users resides in the cloud, which any device can seamlessly connect to, users will have uninterrupted access to their files and programs, even when switching between separate devices.

Web 3.0 promises to be a truly user-centric mode of information services. Every user will have access to a customized information platform and a smart assistant, which will provide dynamic customized information and useful services in real time. However, nothing is certain at this point. Further technological development is needed before Web 3.0 becomes fully realized.

Section 2 The Evolution of Philanthropy

The evolution of the Internet has impacted almost every single sector, including that of philanthropy. In this book, we will divide the history of Internet philanthropy into three distinct phases aligning with those of Web 1.0, 2.0, and 3.0—namely, Internet Philanthropy 1.0, 2.0, and 3.0. Internet Philanthropy 1.0 mainly concerns the distribution of philanthropic information on web portals and forums. During the era of Internet Philanthropy 2.0, various Internet applications such as social networks, e-commerce, and online payment tools enabled philanthropic information to spread via two-way interactions as opposed to the previous one-way mode of distribution. Users were now also able to donate money directly on the Internet, allowing them to become more engaged in philanthropy than ever. As far as Internet Philanthropy 3.0 is concerned, despite the infancy of Web 3.0 technology and applications, Internet philanthropy will most likely keep closely in line with the trends in innovation. We can refer to this as Extensive Philanthropy, where new methods such as "donating your steps" bring philanthropic projects into users' daily lives and routines via Internet technologies. Although available on Web 2.0 platforms, these projects have deployed innovative models that are beginning to demonstrate features of Internet Philanthropy 3.0.

Internet Philanthropy 1.0: Information Distribution

Prior to the Internet, people relied on information about philanthropy from newspapers, broadcasters, and offline events, which limited the scope and efficiency of documentation and coverage. Naturally as a result, the general public did not know much about philanthropy.

As was the case for Web 1.0, web portals became widely used as a low-cost and highly efficient channel of communication for promoting philanthropy, constituting the primary model of Internet Philanthropy 1.0 in China. Major Chinese web portals launched special sections on which to release information about philanthropic projects. These served as the main means of cooperation between charitable organizations and Internet companies.

During the Web 1.0 era, philanthropy was also able to integrate itself to varying degrees with other Internet applications such as email and online forums. These applications played the same critical role: the distribution of information.

The First Case: Saving a Life from Around the World over the Internet

In China, the first philanthropic undertaking to make use of the Internet dates back to 1995, when it was first permitted to use the Internet for commerce.

Shortly after Chinese New Year of 1995, a girl from Shandong Province called Yang Xiaoxia was suffering from a long-term illness, the origins of which her doctors were unable to determine. Noticing these reports, Huang Xiangdong from the intelligence department of the Academy of Military Medical Sciences, the People's Liberation Army of China, and Hu Tiejun of the intelligence department of the Chinese Academy of Medical Sciences decided to take action. They sought help from Chinese scholars based in the US and their international friends, publishing Yang's medical records to several online messaging groups and bulletin boards. In less than two weeks, they received over 500 emails from all over the world. An impressive number of overseas doctors provided their diagnoses and the solutions to previous cases that were similar. Some hospitals offered to treat Yang for free, and many Chinese nationals living overseas expressed their willingness to donate money or medicine. This case demonstrated how efficient the Internet could be as a relay of information, even as a tool to help save lives (Huang, 1996).

In April 1995, a Tsinghua University student named Zhu Ling was struggling to fight off an unknown, life-threatening disease. Her doctors had failed to come up with a solution. In a last ditch effort to save her life, on April 10th students at Peking University started posting her symptoms across nine online medical forums. After three days, they had received more than 100 replies from all over the world, half of which suggested that Zhu had been poisoned by a toxic heavy metal called thallium. Following treatment, the Internet continued to contribute to

Zhu's recovery. She became the first patient in China to be diagnosed via the Internet by the international medical community and successfully treated (Beijing Internet Information Office & Beijing Internet Association, 2015).

Both of these cases concern the benefits of crowd-sourced diagnoses, and are not in the strictest sense examples of philanthropy, which by definition targets society at large rather than the individual. However, these cases do represent attempts to take advantage of the Internet, sharing the same core aims and logic as philanthropy. In this light, it is reasonable to say that the two cases above mark the beginning of Internet philanthropy in China.

Standardizing the Use of Web Portals for Philanthropy

When web portals first came into use, they quickly became the major new channel for distributing information on philanthropic causes.

Thanks to the ease of organizing content and distributing information afforded by web portals, organizations were no longer confined to using print media when communicating their philanthropic message. The public now have seemingly unlimited access to content, from sensational events and individual cases to mid- and macro-level data such as policies, laws, and news regarding the philanthropic sector. Consequently, the general public is more accepting and aware of philanthropic content.

On May 25, 2002, qianlong.com, a local web portal in China, established a charity channel dedicated to all news relating to philanthropic activity. It was the first of its kind in Chinese online media (Li, 2002).

On May 25, 2005, the Internet Society of China launched the first Internet Philanthropy Day (China Internet Association, 2007). It aimed to call on members of society, Internet businesses, and other entities to promote the application of network and information technology in economically underdeveloped areas in western China. Furthermore, the Day sought to provide disadvantaged groups with access to the Internet and opportunities via digital development. The goal was to "create an information-based society that benefits all".

In 2006, Sohu took the lead among China's many commerce websites by inaugurating Sohu's Charity Channel, the first of its kind (Sohu, n.d.). It featured reports on specific themes. Other portals followed suit to meet the public demand for charity news from dedicated channels, presenting relevant information mainly in the form of news stories from a variety of sources.

From then on, dedicated sections on web portals were the main way through which Internet philanthropy released its information during the Web 1.0 era. These dedicated sections would be built by the portal provider and made available for users to browse. This was the initial model for Internet philanthropy and remains in use today. While the model bears a resemblance to the communication methods of traditional media, it also fully utilizes the advantages of the Internet as it achieves low-cost, world-wide coverage, and broadcasts philanthropic information from "1 to N" number of people.

Seeking Help on Online Forums: The Start of Interactive Information Releases

Online forums, also known as bulletin board systems (BBS), form a much more interactive communication model than portals and mark the beginning of Web 2.0. Through these sites, users can post for help and engage in discussions with other users, fostering the two-way communication that marks the transition from Web 1.0. Since BBS was first utilized to spread philanthropic information, the general public has been able to express their own ideas on the subject, which characterizes the beginning of Internet Philanthropy 2.0.

The website tianya.cn was launched in March 1999, and is regarded as one of the most notable BBS systems in China (*Tianya Brief*, n.d.). Tianya has been committed to charitable undertakings since its establishment, whereupon it set up a mutual help section. The website gradually increased its involvement in the charity sector by further developing sections such as Environmental Protection Pioneers, Volunteers, and Together in Philanthropy in 2001, 2005, and 2009 respectively (*Tianya Philanthropy*, n.d.).

It is clear that conducting philanthropy via BBS is highly effective in terms of promotion. Additionally, it sparks active interaction between online users, some of whom even take it upon themselves to monitor and verify the information, helping to detect any false information at little to no cost. For example, on July 15, 2004, Zhang Miao'e, an online user from Kaiping City in Guangdong, registered an account on tianya.cn with her real name and posted a link titled "Friends from All Over the World, Please Click on This Article" (*Report on*, 2004). In the article, she described in detail how she was suffering from an illness, talking about her family and personal information in the hope that other users would lend a helping hand and raise enough funds for a heart surgery. Her article quickly caught the attention of the BBS moderator, who highlighted the title to attract the attention of other users. After extensive online discussion, a number of users decided to visit Zhang's home and verify the information before donating money. Some forward-thinking users discussed setting up a special fund and supervising the way money was spent. Others even invited reporters to cover Zhang's story after they had visited her home. They recorded the progress achieved and reported on each donation Zhang received, using the advantages of the Internet to continuously keep online users updated, gaining the trust and praise of further generous donors.

Clearly, we can see that the "BBS Plus Philanthropy" model has set the precedent for a "self-exposed" way to seek help. Today it is still a primary way for online users to get help when all other methods fail. Zhang's case was the first time that users interacted with each other to share philanthropic information in this way, setting a positive example for future "Social Network Plus Philanthropy" models.

Internet Philanthropy 2.0: Communication Plus Donation

Although Internet Philanthropy 1.0 greatly improved the scope and efficiency at which philanthropic programs could be publicized, it failed to solve the deep-rooted problems faced by traditional philanthropic models. One important factor here is that the spread of information was still essentially one-way. The majority of audiences could only passively receive information, unable to respond to or clarify the content of philanthropic projects. As a result, the projects often lost the public's trust and their willingness to participate. Furthermore, donations mainly came from a small number of large institutions, companies, and celebrities, and were limited to relatively inefficient payment methods such as cash and bank transfers. It was difficult to mobilize the mass of online users to donate to philanthropic causes.

Web 2.0 has successfully addressed the limitations of traditional philanthropy by laying the following two cornerstones of Internet Philanthropy 2.0. The first was the rise of social media, which broke down the barriers restricting the spread of information. Social media also enabled all parties, especially Internet users, to communicate directly and efficiently between each other. The online community was now able to discuss and supervise philanthropic activities at any time, receive faster feedback, and help one another in a philanthropic ecosystem marked by collective trust. The second cornerstone is the rise of online payments, particularly mobile payment. These newly popularized methods make donations incomparably easier. This rings especially true when it comes to minor donations made by the general public, which were never an easy or truly feasible option with traditional donation methods. Mobile payments have lowered the threshold for donations and roused public enthusiasm for donations of any size, made at any time, in any place.

Tencent's Charles Chen Yidan was aware of this trend from early on, and pioneered the concept of online philanthropy 2.0 in China in 2008. He aimed to encourage the advancement of online platforms, and a higher level of interconnectivity between them. In this way, he successfully ushered the charitable sector into an era of "philanthropy by all".

The Effects of Major Disasters on Public Engagement

Both in China and beyond, we have seen the widespread public interest and enthusiasm for social assistance that can be generated by major disasters.

This kind of pervasive public interest could be seen when a catastrophic earthquake struck Wenchuan, Sichuan Province in 2008. This event became a milestone in the history of philanthropy in China, and for the first time the Internet played a key role. One major way in which the Internet was involved was by providing a dynamic online system where people could seek lifesaving assistance. During the disaster relief period, people used online channels such as web portals, forums, blogs, Sina Weibo, and QQ chat rooms to rescue or assist people in a variety of ways. For example, people were able to provide instant coverage of the situation as it developed, organize emergency rescues, collect donations to be put towards disaster relief, share information on missing people, commemorate the victims of the disaster, and send prayers for its survivors. These activities demonstrate the combined effects of online philanthropic platforms at an early stage. The other important role played by the Internet was the effective use of online donations for disaster relief efforts. Various philanthropic foundations quickly launched online donation channels, allowing people from all over China to send their contributions to disaster-stricken areas.

Later, during the 2010 Yushu earthquake and the 2013 Ya'an earthquake, Chinese people were able to actively participate in disaster relief and philanthropic activities thanks to online platforms. By this point, "philanthropy by all" had undergone the necessary refinements and was being practiced in earnest.

Social Platforms: The New Ecosystem for Collective Philanthropy

The most demonstrative change from Internet Philanthropy 2.0 is that the models used for sharing information have expanded from "one-to-many" broadcasts, to "one-to-one", or even "many-to-many" interactions thanks to the newfound prevalence of various social network platforms.

The first change dates back to the 2003 SARS outbreak, when philanthropic activity first appeared on Tencent QQ, an instant messaging platform. Tencent provided tailored QQ accounts for medical staff at Xiaotangshan Hospital to share information in real time and talk with the victims' family members via QQ video chat. This was the earliest use of social media as a tool for philanthropy in China (Tencent Philanthropy, n.d.). Later on, philanthropy became intertwined with more functions such as QQ points and QQ digital medals, meaning users could use their QQ points to make donations, which would in turn award users with a lifelong QQ digital medal for philanthropy. These early attempts at a "Social Media Plus Philanthropy" model were successful in creating enthusiasm for philanthropy among QQ's users.

The next example of social media philanthropy was on Sina Weibo, a microblogging website launched in 2009. Weibo began as a platform connecting strangers, with no preexisting close relationship between them. Then, by introducing celebrity and influential figure accounts, it has formed a social network of VIP influencers which attract massive numbers of fans. Sina Weibo has copied this "Influencer-fan" social media model to create a platform for Micro-Philanthropy. Using this platform, VIP influencers can publish or forward information about philanthropic projects, giving their fans the opportunity to learn about, forward, or even donate to these programs, encouraging people to take an active part in philanthropy on an individual level.

Later on, philanthropy appeared on WeChat, a social media app first released in 2011. Using a more varied and multi-layered social network structure than previous platforms, WeChat centers on close social relationships between friends and personal connections. The more an individual trusts in the core network itself, the more they are willing to use it to interact spontaneously with their online friends. Since WeChat boasts up to 1 billion active users (Pony Ma, 2018), philanthropic projects on WeChat can reach a much wider audience. As a result, the "WeChat Plus Philanthropy" model has a strong and long-term effect on individual participation in philanthropy. This in turn is conducive to a healthier philanthropic ecosystem of donors and beneficiaries.

How Online Payments Help to Normalize Personal Donation

Another obvious function of Internet Philanthropy 2.0 is to encourage a more widespread use of online payments, especially mobile payments.

These payment methods help to ensure that Internet philanthropy can move beyond the information distribution stage and enter into active donation.

For example, both Tencent's Tenpay and Alibaba's Alipay have built their own philanthropic platforms that are easily accessible and convenient to use. Users can donate to and follow the progress of any philanthropic activity at anytime, anywhere. This, therefore, creates a closed loop system where users can go from hearing about a philanthropic cause, to donating, all through the same online platform. Gradually, this helps to form and reinforce donating as a daily habit.

Internet Philanthropy 3.0: Sharing, Donating, and Substantial Action

The growing maturity of Web 2.0 has resulted in a cyberspace that is fed by large amounts of data flooding in from various sources. This data can be integrated and analyzed, which is both a substantial benefit and a daunting challenge for those hoping to use or process these vast reserves of data.

The same can also be said of Internet philanthropy. From one perspective, we can now combine philanthropic data with user data from other areas to create new methods and approaches for engaging people with philanthropy. However, it remains difficult for users to find the appropriate philanthropic causes for them, when there is such a huge volume of different causes and data to sift through. This is why we need an Internet Philanthropy 3.0, which will rely on machine intelligence rather than humans to manage said data.

Internet Philanthropy 3.0 will further develop the system under which Extensive Philanthropy can be achieved. This would mean combining general user data with that relating to philanthropy, allowing ever more philanthropic activities to integrate themselves into users' daily lives. One charity project that is currently very popular is "step donation", which is supported by Web 2.0 in terms of technology, but has already entered the Web 3.0 phase with regard to its everyday format.

More importantly, Internet Philanthropy 3.0 will bring AI technology to the field of philanthropy. Using AI, the user's needs will be the starting point from which philanthropic organizations to release their information, enabling them to design and produce philanthropic activities that are personalized to the users themselves. This is the future of Internet philanthropy, but it is highly dependent on technology and will not be fully realized until Web 3.0 technology has been sufficiently developed.

Section 3 Ten Milestones

As Internet philanthropy evolves, it has encountered numerous milestones, both positive and negative. Some are milestones of technological innovation, some concern natural disasters, and some are related to new systems and policies. According to the timeline of philanthropic activities over the past 10 years (China Lingshan Charity Promotion Association, 2018), there are 10 events that stand out as the most significant.

2006: Sohu Launches China's First Online Charity Platform

Sohu, one of the top three web portals in China, launched its charity channel in 2006. This was the first and largest online charity platform of its day in China, marking a new era for Internet philanthropy. What makes the channel stand out is its affiliation with Sohu news, which allowed for resources and information to be shared between the two platforms, such as posted content, user groups, or Sohu news' relations with other media institutions. As a means of further developing the charity channel, Sohu set up an independent content team and gave them freedom to promote charities as they saw fit. Later on, the channel focused on a series of activities centering on environmental causes, social assistance, humanitarian aid, and celebrity endorsement. The channel's broad coverage and reach have helped to pique the online community's curiosity and raise their awareness of philanthropy.

2007: Tencent Foundation Established, a Key Early Union Between Philanthropy and the Internet

Tencent Charity Foundation was set up in September 2006 by Tencent, and was registered with the Ministry of Civil Affairs (MCA) in June 2007. It is China's first charity foundation launched by an Internet enterprise. Initially, Tencent donated RMB 20 million and pledged to donate a portion of each year's profit from that year forward. Around the time that the Tencent Foundation was established, Tencent also successfully launched its online donation platform. This signified that Internet enterprises had started tapping into philanthropy at a professional level, further encouraging the rest of the Internet industry to start proactively engaging in charity (Tencent Charity Foundation, n.d.).

2008: The Wenchuan Earthquake Attracts Widespread Public Outreach

The largest earthquake since the establishment of the PRC hit Wenchuan County in southwest China's Sichuan Province on May 12, 2008, affecting nearly 48,000 villages across 10 of China's provinces and cities. More than 40 million people were affected by the catastrophe, and over 80,000 were reported dead or missing (Philanthropy Times, 2018). There was widespread alarm across the country, and Chinese citizens began to provide voluntary assistance to help the disaster relief efforts. Only six months after the catastrophe, the ravaged areas had received money and relief supplies totaling RMB 75.197 billion from all around China. Of this figure, RMB 45.8 billion stemmed from individual donations, which, for the first time ever, dwarfed corporate donations (China Lingshan Charity Promotion Association, 2018). Each individual's generous donation had a profound collective impact, resulting in 2008 becoming China's "First Year of Public Donations". Meanwhile, proactive involvement from Internet enterprises such as Tencent and Alibaba also played a significant role in anchoring the concept of Internet philanthropy in the minds of the public. The online payment platforms Alipay, Tenpay, and Yeepay all set up quick donation channels and collected over RMB 60 million (*The Internet*, 2010), gaining 2008 its second title, the "First Year of Internet Philanthropy". A new chapter had been opened, wherein individuals were more informed on philanthropy and had easier access to donation methods than ever before.

2009: Taobao Launches "Philanthropic Products", a Charity Project Accessible to All of Its Shop Owners

Taobao's Goods for Good campaign (Taobao Service Center, n.d.) originated from its Kindness Product. Kindness Products were launched in 2006, when Zhou Lihong, cancer survivor and Taobao shop owner, worked together with the Red Cross Society of China (RCSC) and Taobao to launch a charity project entitled Magic Bean Baby (named after Zhou's own shop, "Magic Bean Baby House"). The project aimed to help disadvantaged mothers to start online businesses. The RCSC also set up a donation account on Taobao and specially designed an automatic donation feature. Any Taobao shop owners engaged in this project could add a Kindness Product label to their products. If a customer buys one Kindness Product, one *fen* (1/6 cent in USD) is automatically donated to the project. Support came in from numerous shop owners and online users, and so Taobao went on to develop the project, changing its name from Kindness Product to Goods for Good in 2009.The new project is accessible to all shop owners and NGOs, and allows shop owners to voluntarily label some of their products Goods for Good, as well as setting a donation ratio to distribute funding between NGOs or charity projects. When a customer buys one Goods for Good product, the previously set ratio is automatically donated to the designated NGO or charity project. This is a standard form of donations involving e-commerce, and has provided an important platform for a vast number of individuals to become directly engaged in philanthropy.

2011: The Guo Meimei Incident Shatters Public Trust in Donation

On June 20, 2011, Guo Meimei caused controversy across China when she posted photos of her luxury villa and Maserati sports car on her Weibo account named "Guo Meimei Baby". As if flaunting her wealth wasn't enough to spark a reaction, she then went on to claim that she was the general manager of a company called Red Cross Commerce. The RCSC then came under public scrutiny for allegedly diverting charity funds to their own staff. The RCSC made repeated announcements saying that Guo's claims were false, there was no such person on their staff and no such subsidiary under that name. Eventually even Guo herself responded on her Weibo account, saying she had no relations with the RCSC and her post about her position in Red Cross Commerce was all fabricated. Ever vigilant, it was the online users who didn't buy Guo's story and, through their mounting doubts and comments, sent it viral. The Internet erupted in a maelstrom of negative reactions, amounting over 700,000 related posts on Weibo in less than 10 days (*The Guo*, 2011). This incident not only damaged the credibility of the RCSC, but also the public's trust in donation. Individual donations to NGOs and charity projects plummeted. According to the Ministry of Civil Affairs of the People's Republic of China, overall donations in July of 2011 were only RMB 500 million, showing a decrease of over 50% compared to June of the same year, while annual donations in 2011 decreased by 18% compared to 2010. Furthermore, total donations in 2012 and 2013 were less than those of 2010 alone. Philanthropic organizations were forced to realize that the Internet is a double-edged sword, offering both truly transformative potential, as well as considerable risk if not utilized properly.

2012: The VIP Influencer Communication Model Launches on Sina Weibo's Micro-Philanthropy Platform

At this time, Sina Weibo (the same platform on which the Guo Meimei incident went viral) was one of the biggest social media sites in China, with more than 100 million registered users in 2011 (*Sina Weibo*, 2011). As more and more philanthropic organizations began to recognize Weibo's potential for interactive communication, there was a boom in philanthropic programs using the platform. Major programs such as Free Lunch and Weibo Crackdown on Child Trafficking have benefitted from the power of widespread attention and support from Weibo's users. The union between social media and philanthropy has proven to work incredibly well. Consequently, Weibo officially launched its Micro-Philanthropy platform in February, 2012 (*Micro public* welfare, 2013) to maximize on the effectiveness of using prominent social media influencers as channels for broadcasting information. Thanks to the unique model of "philanthropic organizations/programs—VIP influencers—Internet users", philanthropic information can now be broadcast with unprecedented efficiency and scale, in newly instantaneous and interactive formats.

2013: The Mobile Payment Boom Brings Philanthropy Right to the Donors' Fingertips

Mobile payments represent one of the most important developments to China's Internet over recent years. They have also been instrumental in the expansion of online philanthropy. In 2013, mobile payments had reached an advanced stage, having exceeded a 25% rate of circulation (*McKinsey released*, 2017). For this reason, around 2013 was when online platforms with third-party payment functions, such as Tencent, Alipay, and WeChat, began adding charity donation features for their mobile clients, effectively integrating mobile payments into philanthropic settings. As a result, users were now able to donate anytime, anywhere over Internet apps on their mobile phones. This made charitable donations vastly easier and marked the entry of Internet philanthropy into the mobile era. Take Tencent's philanthropy platform as an example: in just two years, from 2014 to 2016, donations made through mobile payment rose rapidly from nearly 80% to 98%, according to Tencent Charity's 10th Anniversary Report.

2014: The Viral Ice Bucket Challenge INSPIRES "behavioral philanthropy"

On August 17, 2014, the ALS Ice Bucket Challenge was introduced in China. This activity was originated in the US to promote awareness of the degenerative disease amyotrophic lateral sclerosis (ALS, also known as motor neurone disease). Fueled by support from numerous celebrities and leaders from the world of tech, the challenge garnered more than 4.4 billion clicks and raised over RMB 8 million, making it one of the most successful philanthropic events of the year on social media (*Ice Bucket*, 2015). The success of the Ice Bucket Challenge is largely attributed to the fact that it managed to turn a charitable movement, which would otherwise rely on emotive storytelling, into a fun game which still encouraged people to learn more about a rare disease. This successfully brought people from all walks of life together to take part, generating an enormous viral influence. During this process, a number of innovative Chinese philanthropic organizations also quickly created their own versions of the challenge as part of a widespread effort to promote Internet-based "behavioral philanthropy" in China.

2015: 99 Charity Day Creates a New Charitable System for Widespread Participation

China's first Internet Philanthropy Day was on September 9, 2015. Tencent launched the 99 Charity Day together with a cohort of philanthropic organizations, well-known enterprises, celebrities, and top creative communication agencies. Together, their aim was to use creative and social methods to capture the empathy of hundreds of millions of Internet users in an informal, interactive activity. The 99 Charity Day arguably created a new kind of ecosystem for philanthropy, one that involves society as a whole. This was achieved by combining three key characteristics and advantages of previous online philanthropic practices. The first key aspect of the event is its focus on social connection and interaction. Using their official WeChat platform, individuals, businesses, and public welfare organizations were able to work together more closely.

The second key aspect is mobile donation. Users are able to donate to public welfare programs anytime and anywhere through WeChat Pay. The third aspect of the event is its emphasis on scenario-based participation. Public welfare programs taking part in 99 Charity Day are encouraged to incorporate "behavioral philanthropy" activities such as donating one's steps, so as to better engage users. The 99 Charity Day can be viewed as a role model to other online charities. The event has signaled the beginning of the 3.0 era of Extensive Philanthropy. Popular programs such as Tencent Charity Hiker and Kids Gallery are a testament to this trend.

2016: The Charity Law of the People's Republic of China Standardizes the Development of Philanthropy

The Internet has greatly helped philanthropy to flourish in China, while also increasing the level of risk with regard to online public opinion. Because China's philanthropic institutions were requiring ever more legal support, the *Charity Law of People's Republic of China (Charity Law)* was finally issued in March, 2016 and was officially implemented in September of the same year. This is China's first comprehensive, nationwide charity law, which has opened up an era where philanthropy is fully regulated. The private sector and the government of China are now working together to support the underlying societal benefits of charities. There is now a basic government framework for China's philanthropic institutions, consisting of the *Charity Law*, together with the *Law of the People's Republic of China on the Administration of Activities of Overseas Nongovernmental Organizations in the Mainland of China* adopted in the same year. This new framework is one of the most significant breakthroughs in the history of China's charity legislation. In order to keep up with current changes, the law has also incorporated official identification and regulatory requirements for online fund-raising through information platforms, bringing online charity into a new era of lawfulness and regulatory compliance.

References

Beijing Internet Information Office & Beijing Internet Association (北京市互联网信息办公室，首都互联网协会). (Ed.). (2015). *互联网公益影响力*. 北京日报出版社.

China Internet Association. (2007, April 28). *2005年互联网公益日捐助及表彰情况介绍*. ISC. http://www.isc.org.cn/gyjs/hlwgyr/listinfo1916.html

China Lingshan Charity Promotion Association (中国灵山公益慈善促进会). (2018, June 25). *"2008–2018中国公益慈善十年十大热点" 评选结果出炉*.

Cormode, G., & Krishnamurthy, B. (2008, May 20). *Key differences between Web 1.0 and Web 2.0*. Firstmonday. https://firstmonday.org/ojs/index.php/fm/article/view/2125/1972

DiNucci, D. (1999). Fragmented future. *Print Magazine, 1999*(4), 32, 221–222.

Expert.ai Team. (2017, January 31). *The 5 main features of Web 3.0*. ExpertSystem. https://www.expertsystem.com/web-3-0/

Huang, X. D. (1996). 从杨晓霞，朱令的网络求医到医学信息传递站. *INTERNET世界, 1996*(2).

"Ice Bucket Challenge" where 8.14 million spent on in the first year ("冰桶挑战"一周年814万究竟花哪去了). (2015, August 05). Youth Net. Retrieved October 05, 2018, from http://gy.youth.cn/lyb/201508/t20150805_6964746.htm

Li, J. (2002, May 26). *千龙网正式开通综合性公益频道*. Sina. http://tech.sina.com.cn/i/c/2002-05-26/117259.shtml

McKinsey released a report stating that China's digital economy prospects will far exceed expectations (麦肯锡发布报告称中国数字经济前景将远超预期). (2017, December 12). Cinic. Retrieved October 05, 2018, from http://www.cinic.org.cn/hy/yw/412981.html

Micro Public Welfare (微公益). (2013, September 25). Sina. Retrieved October 05, 2018, from http://gongyi.sina.com.cn/gyzx/2013-09-25/145745632.html

O'Reilly, T. (2005, September 30). *What is Web 2.0*. O'Reilly Media. https://www.oreilly.com/pub/a/web2/archive/what-is-web-20.html

Philanthropy Times. *汶川地震十周年系列:中国公益十年数据观察*. (2018, May 15). ifeng. Retrieved October 05, 2018, from https://gongyi.ifeng.com/a/20180514/44990609_0.shtml

Pony Ma. *马化腾:春节期间微信全球月活跃用户数破10亿*. (2018, March 05). QQ. Retrieved September 30, 2018, from http://tech.qq.com/a/20180305/005666.htm

Report on Zhang Miaoe (《求助帖杂谈惊现》后续报道:关注张妙娥). (2004, July 06). Tianya. Retrieved September 30, 2018, from http://bbs.tianya.cn/m/post-lookout-213-1.shtml

Sina Weibo registered users exceeded 100 million (新浪微博注册用户突破一亿). (2011, March 03). Sina. Retrieved October 05, 2018, from http://finance.sina.com.cn/stock/usstock/c/20110303/03199462932.shtml

Sohu. (n.d.). *关于搜狐, 企业公民*. Sohu. Retrieved September 30, 2019, from https://intro.sohu.com/about

Taobao Service Center. (n.d.). *什么是公益宝贝*. Taobao. Retrieved October 05, 2018, from https://service.taobao.com/support/main/help_quick_new.htm?spm=323.93297.437447.11.37849a9dVQ4CRm&sceneSeq=&q=%25E5%2585%25AC%25E7%259B%258A%25E5%25AE%259D%25E8%25B4%259D

Tencent Charity Foundation. (n.d.). *腾讯公益慈善基金会介绍*. QQ. https://gongyi.qq.com/jjhgy/about/about.htm

Tencent Philanthropy. (n.d.). *2006年及以前腾讯公益大事记*. QQ. Retrieved September 30, from http://gongyi.qq.com/tccf/memo/memo_2006.htm

The Guo Meimei incident ruined the Red Cross for 100 years in 3 days (郭美美事件3天毁掉红会100年). (2011, November 16). Sina. Retrieved October 05, 2018, from http://news.sina.com.cn/o/2011-11-16/150623476066.shtml

The Internet promotes China's "civilian charity" to donate to Yushu through Alipay (互联网推动中国"平民慈善"通过支付宝向玉树捐款). (2010, May 06). People Net. Retrieved October 05, 2018, from http://media.people.com.cn/GB/40606/11532136.html

Tianya Brief (天涯简介). (n.d.). Retrieved September 30, from http://help.tianya.cn/about/history/2011/06/02/166666.shtml

Tianya Philanthropy (天涯公益). (n.d.). Tianya. Retrieved September 30, from http://gongyi.tianya.cn/

Ying H. W. (2018, July 26). In *Wikipedia*. https://zh.wikipedia.org/wiki/瀛海威

2

The Rise of Online Fundraising Information Platforms

Driven by the major earthquake that struck Wenchuan in 2008 and the promulgation of the Charity Law of the People's Republic of China, many major Chinese Internet companies have launched their own Internet fundraising information platforms. Using Sina, Tencent, Alibaba, JD.com, and Didi Chuxing as case studies, this chapter examines the unique Internet philanthropy projects that these Chinese companies have launched.

The Wenchuan earthquake in 2008 was the starting point for the rapid growth of Internet philanthropy in China, marking the beginning of the in-depth integration between Internet companies and the philanthropic sector. Notable charity organizations including Alipay, Tenpay, and Yeepay, all opened online fund-raising channels after the Wenchuan earthquake. With the help of these three major platforms, total funds of over RMB 60 million were eventually raised for victims of the Wenchuan earthquake and Internet philanthropy had begun to play its increasingly important role. (Epay, 2009) Since then, Internet companies such as Taobao, Baidu, Sina, and JD.com have established their own foundations and online fund-raising platforms to promote and sustain the rapid development of China's Internet philanthropy industry.

Y. Chen, *Internet Philanthropy in China*,
https://doi.org/10.1007/978-981-16-2566-4_2

Following the issuance of the *Charity Law* in 2016, platforms began to enter a new stage of official legislation and standardized development. On August 31, 2016 and April 19, 2018, the Ministry of Civil Affairs issued two lists naming all the officially recognized online charity fundraising platforms. With 22 companies altogether, the first list included 13 and the second included 9. Although two companies have since withdrawn from the list, there are still currently 20 platforms in total, which can be roughly divided into four categories based on the attributes of their initiators: Internet companies, banks, institutions (mainly government-backed foundations or charitable organizations), and media companies (See Table 2.1).

The majority of the first batch of 13 platforms are set up and operated by Internet companies, representing a large part of the total cohort. Due to their specific business insights, Internet companies naturally have their own unique ideas when operating philanthropic platforms. In order to explore the differences between these platforms, we must divide them into five categories based on each Internet company's core area of business: social, e-commerce, payment, online-to-offline commerce (O2O), and crowd-funding (see Fig. 2.1).

Section 1 From Social Contact to Philanthropy

At its core, philanthropy can be summed up by a traditional Chinese phrase that translates as "All for one and one for all". That is to say, philanthropy embodies the traditional Chinese virtue of helping one another and viewing the whole world as one community, to be shared equally by all. Philanthropy in China has organically always found itself linked to social activities, as was written over 2,000 years ago in the Western Han Dynasty book called the "Book of Rites". In the "Conveyance of Rites (Liyun)" chapter, it was written that, "When the great way prevails, the world is equally shared by all. Able and talented people are celebrated, and everyone is honest and friendly towards one another. In this kind of world, people do not merely support their own parents and raise their own children, the elderly are well cared for by society as a whole, the middle-aged contribute their talents to society, and children grow up

Table 2.1 Officially Recognized Online Fundraising Information Platforms (as of July 30, 2018)[a]

Category	No.	Platform	Initiator	Launch Date
Internet companies	1	Tencent Charity	Tencent Foundation	May 2007
	2	Micro-Philanthropy	Sina Weibo	Feb. 2012
	3	Baidu Charity	Baidu Foundation	Jan. 2011
	4	Taobao Charity	Taobao	Sep. 2010
	5	JD Charity	JD Foundation	Sep. 2014
	6	Suning Charity	Suning Foundation	Jun. 2018
	7	Ant Financial Charity	Ant Foundation	May 2008
	8	Gongyibao	Beijing Hope Technology Co. , Ltd.	Unclear
	9	Yeepay Charity	Yeepay	May 2008
	10	Meituan Charity	Meituan	Aug. 2o17
	11	Didi Charity	Didi Chuxing	Sep. 2016
	12	Qingsong Charity	Beiing Qingsongchou Network Technology Co., Ltd.	Sep. 2014
	13	Shuidi Philanthropy	Beijing Zongqingxiangqian Technology Co., Ltd.	May 2016
Banks	14	Shanyuan Foundation	Bank of China	Dec. 2017
	15	ICBC E-Mall Charity	Industrial and Commercial Bank of China	Jan. 2014
Institutions	16	China Charity Information Platform[b]	China Charity Alliance, MCA	Apr. 2013
	17	Bangbang Charity	China Siyuan Foundation for Poverty Alleviation, and the United Front Work Department of the CPC Central Committee	Sep.2016
	18	Social Participation in Poverty Alleviation and Development of China	The State Council Leading Group Office of Poverty Alleviation and Development	Jul. 2017
	19	United Foundation Network	Shanghai United Foundation	Dec. 2009
	20	United for Charity	Guangzhou Charity Association	Jun. 2014
	21	China Foundation Center[a]	Beijing Enjiu Research Center for NPO Dvelopment	Jul. 2010

(*continued*)

Table 2.1 (continued)

Category	No.	Platform	Initiator	Launch Date
Media companies	22	Xinhua Charity	Xinhuanet, Xinhua News Agency	Nov. 2016

Source: Official websites of these platforms and publicly available information online

[a]Weibo, which in Chinese means "microblog," exits as a form of microblogging that allows users to edit and post a short text (generally less than 140 words) in a short amount of time. It allows users to control who can read their microblogs. With the development of technology, microblogging services offer alternative ways of publishing information including text messaging, instant messaging, mobile application, E-mail, and webpages. Some Weibo platforms can also publish multimedia content, such as images, videos, and audio files. The "Micro-Philanthropy" mentioned in this section refers to the online philanthropic platform launched by Sina Weibo, and "Weibo" refers to Sina Weibo

[b]China Charity Information Platform and China Foundation Center have dropped out due to strategic adjustments and are no longer included as official online public fundraising information platforms designated by China's Ministry of Civil Affairs.

healthily. Widowers, widows, orphans, those with no children, the handicapped, and people suffering from diseases can all receive support from society. People perform their proper duties. They feel a sense of belonging. They cherish the fruit of labor without appropriating it only for themselves. They make every effort to participate in public affairs without calculating personal gains or losses."

Mobile Internet technologies have significantly lowered the cost of spreading information on philanthropic projects, allowing a considerable number of users to get involved via online social networks and popular applications. In doing so, Internet philanthropy has been able to revive the innate social nature of philanthropy in China, creating widespread impact and appeal throughout Chinese society.

The "Philanthropy Plus Social Networking" ecosystem provides the opportunity for anyone to launch or promote philanthropic activity and ideas. New philanthropic information networks have a "decentralized" structure, meaning that every user of a social platform serves as a potential "node" for the circulation of information on philanthropy. In this sense, philanthropy is no longer confined to a small minority, rather it

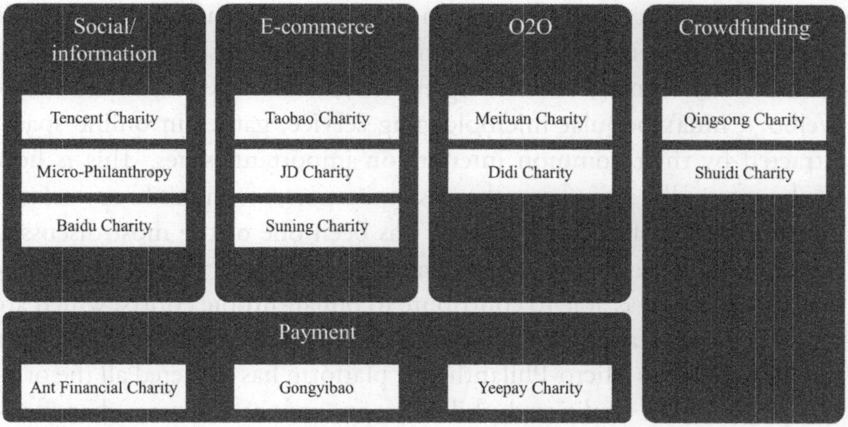

Fig. 2.1 Online Fund-raising Information Platforms Operated by Chinese Internet Companies (as of July 30, 2018)

has turned into a public undertaking in which everyone can take part. Meanwhile, online social networks have given the general public more say on the way information on philanthropy is used and shared, effectively bringing the general public closer to the inner workings of philanthropic causes. This is truly the era of philanthropy by all, for all. Over the course of this transition, fresh changes have seen Sina Weibo's Micro-Philanthropy and Tencent Charity stand out from other online philanthropy-oriented social platforms.

Case Study:Sina Weibo's Micro-Philanthropy Platform

Using 'Weak' Social Relationships to Build a New Kind of Philanthropic Network

The agora was a central public space in ancient Greek city-states where the public would engage in political, social, religious, and commercial activities. There, information and knowledge was shared and spread. In the Internet era, China's Weibo, just like the ancient Greek agora, provides the space for more expansive and in-depth social activity. It allows for complete strangers to come together and discuss public topics, the latest news stories or trending events. Unlike WeChat, users of Sina Weibo, China's popular microblogging service, gather in online space, attracted by their common interests on important issues. This is how Weibo naturally stimulates the dissemination of philanthropy-related information.[2] In fact, philanthropy has been one of the most-discussed topics on Sina Weibo throughout the site's existence. Thanks to microblogging, everyone is able to contribute to philanthropic efforts, which are no longer undertakings involving small groups of people. For the first time Sina Weibo's Micro-Philanthropy platform has gathered all the original players from traditional philanthropy, such as initiators, beneficiaries, and third-party institutions, together in one place.

The Micro-Philanthropy platform's user community is composed of philanthropic organizations, celebrities, media outlets keen on philanthropy, individuals seeking help, and the wider body of kind-hearted Weibo users. In terms of the platform's service community, the philanthropic organizations providing programs include various large-scale charitable foundations, who also launch philanthropic programs in response to the ever-changing demand. The Micro-Philanthropy platform has put in place a series of standards to regulate the programs released, which all users or organizations are required to meet before initiating a help-seeking program.

Currently, the main types of services available on the Micro-Philanthropy platform include the donation of branded products, online auctions, donation via shared news, and individual requests for assistance. The platform can offer systematic brand promotion, fund-raising, and financial supervision for projects that support education, childhood development, medical assistance, animal protection, and environmental conservation, and so on (see Fig. 2.2).

Just as the 140-word limit for each post on a microblog has changed Internet users' posting habits, the Micro-Philanthropy platform is changing the 376 million microblog users' practices and attitudes towards philanthropy. The past six years have witnessed the development of micro-philanthropic causes such as "Free Lunch for Children", "Cracking Down on the Abduction of Women and Children", and "Love Saves

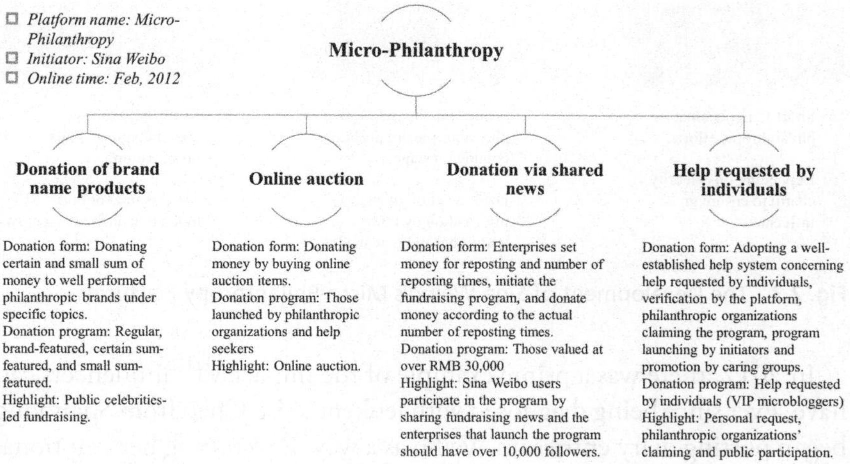

Fig. 2.2 Services Provided on Sina Webo's Micro-Philanthropy Platform

Pneumoconiosis". From the launch of VIP influencers as promoters of philanthropic causes, to the wide-scale participation of general users, the Sina Weibo Micro-Philanthropy platform has now matured as a creative channel for promoting philanthropy (See Fig. 2.3).

The Launch of VIP Influencers

In terms of philanthropy, Weibo serves not only as a platform for voicing initiatives and launching fund-raising programs, but more often as a domain with its own distinct characteristics. Like the ancient Greek agora, Weibo embraces diverse voices, allowing 376 million Chinese online users to exercise the power of their 140 words. As a result, one post can quickly reach all Weibo users at a previously unimaginable scope. Due to the hyper-amplification that can occur when one voices an opinion on Weibo, a celebrity's ripple effect can be enhanced to the extreme, meaning that Weibo's VIP influencers exert a huge influence over general users. Fortuitously, countless VIP influencers staunchly support philanthropy on Weibo, with more and more joining their ranks at a staggering rate—influencers and general users alike.

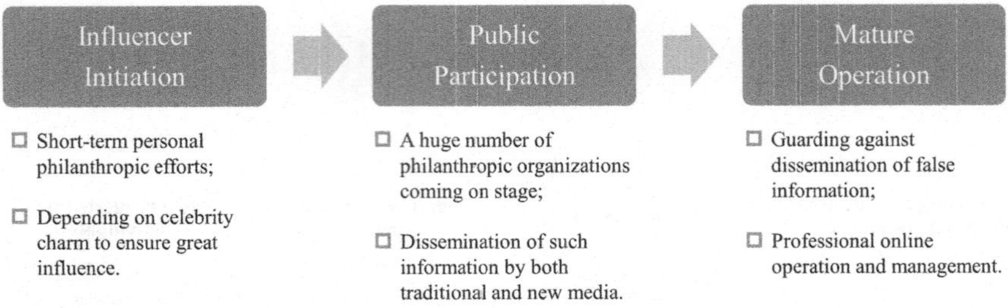

Fig. 2.3 The Development of Sina Weibo's Micro-Philanthropy Platform

In 2012, there was a prime example of the impact VIP influencers can have. Ever since being diagnosed with leukemia, Lu Chao from Shandong began posting diary entries on Weibo as a way of recording her emotional state as she fought for her life. Lu soon attracted the attention of several VIP influencers, who sent her their words of encouragement. Her microblog posts were reposted by emergency room doctor Yu Ying, grassroots web celebrity Sun Jie, film star Huang Bo, and actresses Huang Yi and Yang Zi. She was also contacted by a celebrity couple—singer Christine Fan and television host Blackie Chen Chien-chou—who cheered her on by posting a video they had personally recorded for her. A week later, Chinese-American entrepreneur and angel investor Charles Bi-chuen Xue launched a donation campaign for Lu through his own microblog page, which rapidly drew attention from throngs of Weibo users. Many of them reposted and commented on the microblog, and a large number of celebrities donated online via the Micro-Philanthropy platform. As of June 1, 2012, 8,197 online users had participated in the program, raising a total of RMB 1,049,530 in just four days.

As John Donne wrote: "No man is an island, entire of itself; every man is a piece of the continent, a part of the main. If a clod be washed away by the sea, Europe is the less, as well as if a promontory were."[1] Each person constitutes a basic component of society. One's opinion concerning philanthropy can be plainly seen in his or her reposts on the Sina Weibo Micro-Philanthropy platform. This new level of accountability has caused a subtle but substantial change to public attitudes towards

[1] See John Donn's poem "No Man Is an Island".

philanthropy. The Chinese word "wei" (as in "Weibo") means "micro" in English. Its usage in "Weibo" refers to the tiny power of the individual, the limited content of a microblog, and the small acts of charity we contribute as individuals. As it turns out, when all these tiny elements function in unison and the whole of society begins to do their part, something "micro" can suddenly take on astonishing power.

Widespread Participation from General Users

Through the unmatched effectiveness of celebrity promotion, numerous Weibo users have now brought their attention to philanthropy, but celebrity appeals alone are far from enough. Truly effective philanthropy calls for participation by professional associations and social groups, as well as a more well-established legal and policy system provided by government regulators and law officials.

Following a review of the philanthropic campaigns launched on the Weibo platform, there has been a clear decrease in public fund-raising programs since 2014. In their place, there has been a gradual increase in programs spearheaded by credible and influential philanthropic organizations, mainly mounted through their official Weibo accounts. As a result, Sina Weibo's Micro-Philanthropy platform set up an efficient philanthropic ecosystem by working with government agencies, philanthropic organizations, enterprises, media outlets, celebrities, experts, scholars, and caring online users.

An increasing number of professionals are joining their efforts to the Micro-Philanthropy platform, adding a new level of professional recognition and backing to the benevolent causes therein. For instance, among all of the officially approved philanthropic programs on the platform, the parameters for animal protection and environmental conservation programs are relatively stricter, requiring support from an industry professional. This rings true for the Panda Guardians program launched by the China Green Foundation. As part of the program, participating Weibo users can raise their own virtual baby pandas by feeding them with virtual bamboo, which they can grow within the program. Meanwhile, the staff of the Panda Guardians program uphold their side of the bargain by planting natural bamboo in the Qinling Mountains in Shaanxi Province, which is a wild giant panda habitat. This project works to restore the bamboo forest's ecosystem, hiring local workers to nurse pandas and guard the area. This is just one of the many creative measures used to promote philanthropy, alleviate poverty, and protect the environment.

The Panda Guardians program received immense support from experts and scholars at a number of research institutions. Since going online on November 28, 2017, its posts have received 340 million views from over one million users. It has successfully attracted a growing number of followers on the Sina Weibo platform to participate in the protection of wild giant pandas.

Maturity Period

Given the opinion-driven nature of the Weibo domain, during the early stages of Sina Weibo's Micro-Philanthropy platform, problems began to arise involving the circulation of fraudulent "charitable" information. To improve the transparency, fairness, and the validity of the Micro-Philanthropy platform, as well as the sustainability of philanthropic activities on Weibo, many philanthropic groups have begun using professional online management teams. This has helped these groups to find more flexible and effective ways of maximizing the effects of philanthropy on Weibo. These professional teams have also offered insights on the development of more online products on Weibo, breaking away from the previous one-way communication model.

In 2017, the "Organization, Key-Opinion-Leader, User" (OKU) operation model was first established. Based on the strong user interest in Key Opinion Leaders (KOLs) and trending news, the new model allows Weibo to build connections between philanthropic organizations, KOLs, and users, (SinaCharity, 2018) spreading information across the entire Weibo network, instead of just the philanthropic sector. For example, the widely popular activity, the Ice Bucket Challenge (2014) was launched using the OKU model.

The Ice Bucket Challenge, a campaign launched in the US to raise awareness of ALS disease, was an unexpected viral movement worldwide, hitting China in August of 2014. Beginning on August 17, 2014, an Ice Bucket Challenge (with a focus on rare disorders) was launched by the China-Dolls Center for Rare Disorders[2] on the Weibo Micro-Philanthropy platform. On the same day, Lei Jun, founder of Xiaomi Inc., accepted the challenge after being nominated by Russian investor, Yuri Milner.

The next day, Lei dumped a bucket of ice water over his head in front of his office building and donated RMB 10,000 to the China-Dolls Center. Then a relay of Ice Bucket Challenges swept across every sector, including technology, business, entertainment, and public welfare. As of August 30, 2014, Ice Bucket Challenges had been viewed 4.44 billion times, raising a total of RMB 8.14 million, 81% of which (RMB 6.6 million), came from non-celebrity users. The campaign has provided practical monetary assistance, and drawn unprecedented attention to patients diagnosed with ALS and other rare disorders.

In terms of the OKU operation model, the Ice Bucket Challenge's Organization in China was the China-Dolls Center for Rare Disorders, which launched the campaign on the Micro-Philanthropy platform and successfully drew professional support. The Challenge's KOLs were celebrities such as Lei Jun, Robin Li, Pan Shiyi, Yu Minhong, and Tian Liang who took part in the viral campaign. The Challenge's Users were Weibo's users, without whom the campaign's total 4.4 billion views and RMB 8 million in donations would not have been possible.

Prior to the Ice Bucket Challenge in 2013, the money raised by China-Dolls Center only comprised RMB 6 million. In 2014, the amount totaled RMB 14 million thanks to the Micro-Philanthropy platform. As a result, the first foundation in China to focus on ALS and other rare disorders was established.

The Ice Bucket Challenge, which was designed to help the participants experience how it feels to have ALS, went viral through the nominations of hundreds of celebrities, spreading information related to ALS on an amplified scope within a short time span. Now, an increasing number of organizations are using professional operation models (such as the OKU model) as part of their fundraising efforts.

---

[2] China-Dolls Center for Rare Disorders is a non-profit private organization established in May 2008, dedicated to providing care and support for people with rare disorders.

Due to a strong launch facilitated by VIP influencers and widespread participation by general users, Sina Weibo's Micro-Philanthropy platform was able to reach maturity extremely quickly. The platform has now established itself as one of the leading social channels for promoting philanthropy. Weibo has produced a unique space for social networking and philanthropy to come together, where each charity-related post made by its users receives a professional inspection, a professional operation model for publication, and strong support from charitable organizations.

Case Study: Tencent Charity

Creating a Charity Network That Extends Across Strong Social Relationships

Futurist Alvin Toffler writes in the first chapter of *Future Shock*, "In the three short decades between now and the twenty-first century, millions of ordinary, psychologically normal people will face an abrupt collision with the future. Citizens of the world's richest and most technologically advanced nations, many of them will find it increasingly painful to keep up with the incessant demand for change that characterizes our time. For them, the future will have arrived too soon." This paragraph depicts the 1980s, but also applies to today. "How modern people settle their minds" amid this chaos of progress and change is a question that we will still be trying to answer for many years to come. Whatever the answer may be, it is vital to consider our individual relationships and how they may vary across different social networking platforms.

In the mobile era, if Sina Weibo is the online agora where strangers can come together, what WeChat creates is more like an "online home" for Chinese people; a social networking community composed of friends, family, and acquaintances. Used as a highly efficient networking tool, WeChat's Tencent Charity Platform has triggered a chain reaction in social networking, successfully combining philanthropic practices with its already formidable business edge.

Where It All Began: Using an Existing Business Advantage to Support Philanthropic Causes

In 2007, the number of Internet users in China was only 137 million (CNNIC, 2007), meaning that only 10% of Chinese people used the Internet. In June of the same year, after over a year of preparation and applications for approval, the Tencent Foundation was launched as the first philanthropic foundation established by a Chinese Internet company (See Fig. 2.4).

According to research conducted for this book, when establishing the Tencent Foundation and the Tencent Charity platform, the working team conducted in-depth studies on the philanthropic practices of multinational companies such as IBM, Nokia, Cisco, and HP. As a result, they agreed to design Tencent Charity's philanthropic projects based on Tencent's unique preexisting advantages and core resources. This meant focusing on areas that are easily accessible via Tencent's own products, services, employees and partners to promote public enthusiasm for philanthropic efforts.

That being said, this was still no easy task. At this point in China, there were no established channels for the general public to participate in

Fig. 2.4 Homepage of Tencent Charity

philanthropic causes. Widespread donations were only made in China when large disasters or other major events occurred. Philanthropy and charity were exploits often confined to elite wealthy people, separate from ordinary Chinese citizens.

Coincidentally, as Tencent had already accumulated a large number of QQ users, the company had an established user base ready to be redirected towards a newly built philanthropic platform. 2007 also happened to be the eve of the emergence of mobile Internet, and in 2011, when WeChat was launched, the platform gained even greater velocity.

Since Tencent Charity was established 11 years ago, the platform has moved from the desktops to the mobile phones of users. In 2012, Tencent Charity made its first move to WeChat by setting up a WeChat services account. Then, in January of 2014, the Tencent Charity WeChat Channel was established, providing functions such as inquiry channels, participatory activities, and donation pathways for people interested in philanthropy. By connecting desktop and mobile platforms, Tencent has lowered the participation threshold for charitable donations and other related activities.

Serving as a place for users to post content about their own causes and projects, Tencent Charity provides a range of services including project start-up assistance, donations, interaction and regulation. The platform's core aim is to become a one-stop online service center, where users can seek assistance and charitable organizations can offer help, raise funds, provide project feedback, and maintain public supervision. Individual users can use the platform to donate to philanthropic projects they are interested in, and authorized fund-raising organizations can use it to raise funds for their projects (see Fig. 2.5). As of April 17, 2019, the Tencent Charity platform had helped to raise a total of RMB 5.253 billion, thanks to 227 million donations made by users.[3]

During the time when the Internet was mainly accessed via desktop computers, the Tencent Charity platform launched a number of Internet-based fund-raising programs, including "Monthly Giving", "Self-service

[3] According to the official website of Tencent Charity (https://gongyi.qq.com/), as of April 17, 2019, the total number charitable donations made by users on Tencent Charity reached 227,218,932, pushing the total amount of donations received by the platform to RMB 5,252,686,975.

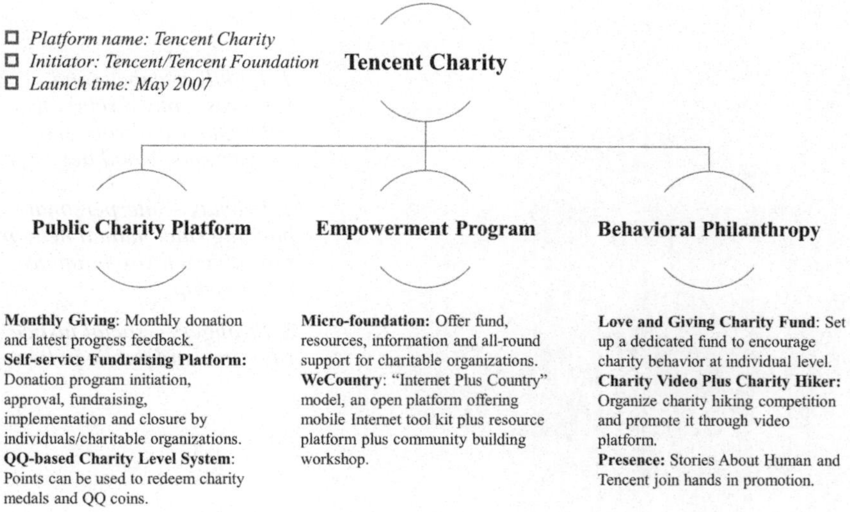

Fig. 2.5 Services Provided by Tencent Charity

Fundraising Platform", and the "QQ-based Charity Level System". Additionally, it has developed Internet-based charity products such as "QQ Public Welfare Icon" and "Charity Fruit". At the onset of the mobile Internet era, new charity products such as "Donate Together" and "WeRun" appeared on WeChat, along with the first "99 Charity Day" in 2015. The arrival of these programs drew attention to mobile social networks as a vehicle for charity projects, bringing philanthropy closer to China's millions of Internet users.

The Logic Behind "Acquaintance Social Networking Plus Charity"

Unlike Weibo users, WeChat users follow their friends and people they already know in real life. In the mobile Internet era, the widespread use of WeChat and WeChat Pay has strengthened ties between Tencent Charity and WeChat.

WeChat users can use WeChat Moments to post their own text and photos, as well as sharing articles and music from other apps. Their

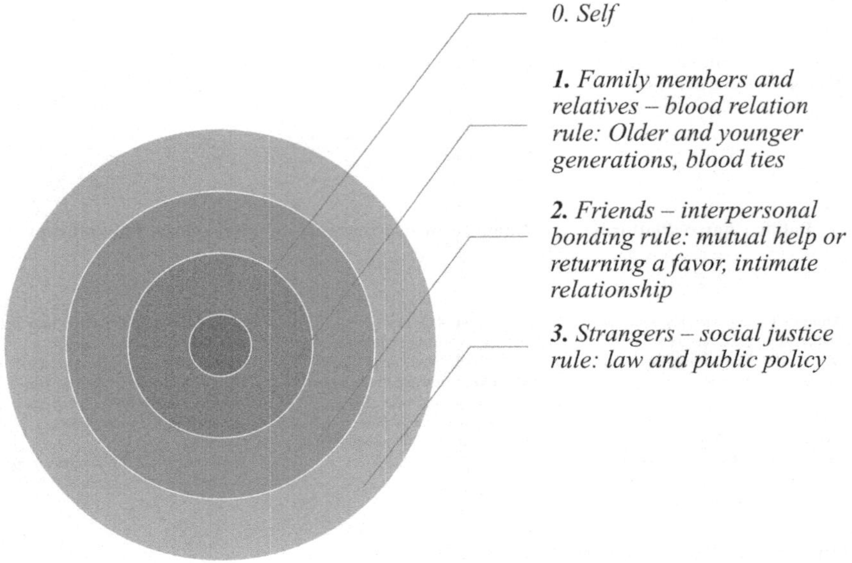

Fig. 2.6 Individual Social Relationships According to the "Differential Mode of Association"

WeChat friends can then add comments and likes on their posts. Consequently, friends can get to know what's happening in each other's lives through recent posts, even without keeping in touch regularly. Therefore, each WeChat user forms their own individual network of connections centering on themselves. This can be likened to Chinese relationships, or the "differential mode of association"[4] proposed by Fei Xiaotong. Within this concept, Mr. Fei compares relationship networks to water rippling from a central point, with the distance from the center indicating the relationships' degree of closeness (Fig. 2.6).

Similarly, a WeChat user's contacts fall into different categories, forming a social network with the user at the center (see Fig. 2.7). Meanwhile, each user may appear in other users' social networks. Compared with

[4]The concept of a "differential mode of association" was proposed by Mr. Fei Xiaotong to describe different degrees of closeness in a relationship network. He uses the metaphor of ripples on a body of water. The distance between the rings on the water's surface is like the different levels of closeness in our relationship networks.

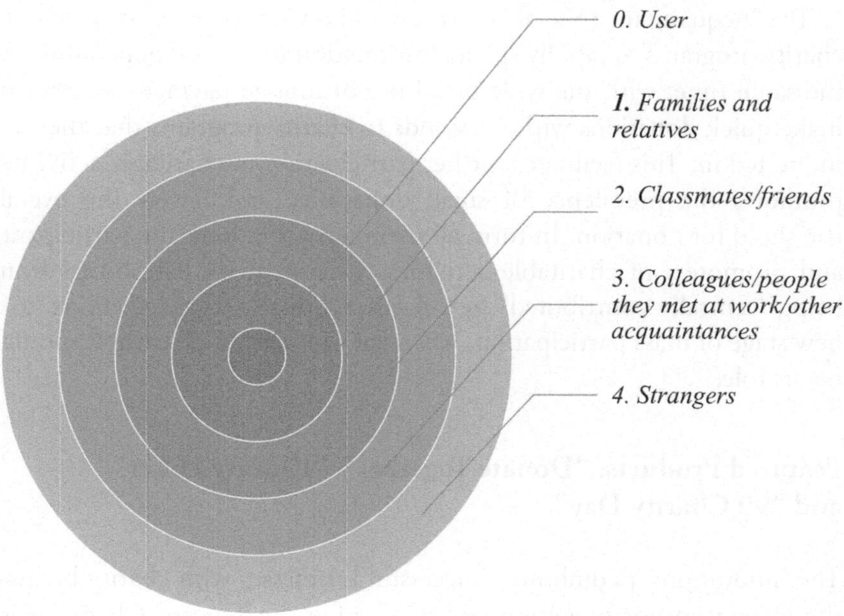

Fig. 2.7 Contact Groups of a WeChat User

Weibo users, WeChat users do not need to make friends and search for the latest news in the agora of cyberspace, or get spammed by the opinions of VIP influence. Their online domain of information is more private. The information users get from WeChat is more related to users themselves because it is either posted by their contacts on WeChat Moments or by the official accounts that they decide to follow based on personal choice.

Under different social network ecosystems, the promotion of WeChat charity programs relies less on VIP influencers and celebrities and more on user-to-user interactions that can help charity programs to go viral. For example, in August 2017, the "Kids Gallery" charity program went viral on WeChat Moments. It attracted participation from about 5 million people and raised a total of RMB 15 million in one day, an unimaginable feat for traditional charity campaigns.

The "Acquaintance Social Networking Plus Charity" ecosystem enables charity programs to rapidly spread information to a broad population. At the same time, with the widespread use of mobile payments, users can make quick donations within seconds to charity programs that they are interested in. This facilitates further participation in charitable activities, promotes the prevalence of small donations, and lowers the overall threshold for donation. In turn, all users can act as both the participants and promoters of charitable activities. Charity work has shifted from being "centrally-contributed" by a few individuals or organizations, to a new stage of mass participation, where all can play an active and spontaneous role.

Featured Products: "Donate Together", "Charity Hiker" and "99 Charity Day"

The innovation of combining successful businesses with charity became the inspiration for operating and developing the Tencent Charity platform. Based on acquaintance social networking on WeChat, Tencent Charity launched "Donate Together", "Step Donation", and "99 Charity Day".

"Donate Together": Charity Driven by Social Networking

In the mobile Internet era, Mr. Pony Ma Huateng, the co-founder, chairman and CEO of Tencent, proposed that Tencent should play the role of connector, enabling the connection of everything on the Internet and realizing "Mobile Internet Plus". In August of 2014, the Tencent Charity launched a new fund-raising product based on mobile social networking, called Donate Together.

Users can launch Donation Together, set target donation amounts for programs posted on Tencent Charity, and then send the Donate Together page to friends or share it on their Moments page. Their friends can then make contributions through the page and forward them on their Moments.

Before Donate Together was launched, the Tencent Charity platform connected large numbers of WeChat and mobile QQ users, but fund-raising activities were still organized by charitable organizations and the platform itself was only responsible for reaching users. Due to this lack of connection, fundraisers for different programs failed to reach sufficient levels of user interaction and communication, and Tencent did not make full use of its social networking advantages with regards to charitable activities. Donate Together turns users into fund-raising agents, and makes full use of each user's social networks to foster charity, driven by the Tencent mobile's social networking advantages.

"Charity Hiker": Workout for Charity

In addition to donating money or goods, people can also donate via workout on the Tencent Charity platform. This is a new method that is being increasingly accepted.

In 2015, Tencent Charity launched the Charity Hiker (i. e. Step Donation) program. Using WeRun on WeChat or Movement on Mobile QQ, users can donate their accumulated steps every day. Their steps then get converted to corresponding amounts of cash which are donated by corporate sponsors and charities towards worthy causes. This innovative combination of individual user fitness and philanthropy gives users new ways to participate in charity campaigns, while also increasing their sense of involvement. Moreover, this program helps build a positive brand image for donating enterprises.

Such functionality has become very popular among users, gaining strong support from corporations ever since the program's launch. As of April 17, 2019, a total of approximately 866 million people had participated in this program on the Tencent Charity platform, raising more than RMB 944 million. The program has not only created new ways for users to participate in charity campaigns, it has also become an important and innovative fund-raising method for the Tencent Charity platform.

"99 Charity Day": Endowing Charity with a Sense of Ceremony

On September 7, 2015, following guidance from the Network Society Bureau of the Office of the Central Cyberspace Affairs Commission and the Administration of Civil Organization of the Ministry of Civil Affairs, Tencent Charity declared that it would join hundreds of charitable organizations, well-known enterprises, celebrities and charitable media in launching China's first Internet fundraising day—"99 Charity Day"(see Fig. 2.8). Charles Chen Yidan delivered a speech at the launch meeting with the topic: "Social issues are the starting point for philanthropy". 99 Charity Day is expected to motivate the general public to participate through festive ceremonies. It aims to efficiently solve the "black box of trust" issue as well as other problems in traditional philanthropy through transparency and social networks, in order to promote philanthropy as a cause in which everyone can participate.

At first, 99 Charity Day functioned through varied channels, including mobile Internet, social networks and many others. Internet users

Fig. 2.8 The 99 Charity Day Launch Event in 2015

were persuaded to participate in charitable activities thanks to their ease, convenience and variety. They could do so through small-size cash donations, regular donations, or voice donations.

Each year during the 99 Charity Day, Tencent Charity also matches the donations made by users towards philanthropic projects as a means of amplifying the benevolence of their actions. That is to say, for each donation made by the user, the Tencent Foundation provides an equal donation to the same project. This enables charitable organizations to receive more donations during the 99 Charity Day, and simultaneously provides a way for enterprises and corporate foundations to creatively contribute funding and resources, further stoking the enthusiasm of charitable organizations during the event.

The 99 Charity Day has empowered charitable organizations, encouraging them to make better use of online charity fund-raising platforms. Additionally, the campaign has substantially bolstered user enthusiasm for philanthropy. Tencent Charity, in collaboration with professional charitable organizations and creative agencies, promotes charitable activities through users' WeChat friend networks, WeChat official accounts, and other online channels, getting more users to participate in fundraising on the Tencent Charity platform.

Section 2 From Shopping to Charity

Since the rapid rise of the mobile Internet in China, its development in the country has taken a different path compared to that in western countries. A variety of mobile platforms with many different functions have emerged to meet people's daily needs, from online shopping to online entertainment, travel booking, take-out orders, and transportation, all aspects of daily life are covered. Mobile Internet platforms can bring convenience to charitable causes by utilizing their combined advantages. For instance, online shopping, a common activity of Chinese consumers, can now be linked to charitable causes, giving online shoppers a new identity as online charity participants.

Case Study: Alibaba Charity

How E-commerce Payments Extended to Charitable Giving[5]

The Alibaba Foundation was established on December 22, 2011 with an initial seed fund of RMB 50 million. Its main goals include awakening public awareness of environmental protection, advocating assistance for vulnerable groups by teaching them practical life skills rather than free giving, and supporting charitable organizations, especially those dedicated to environmental protection.

Alibaba's enthusiasm and practice in philanthropy is closely related to Jack Ma, the founder and chairman of its board of directors. Keen on charity, Jack Ma has been active in the Chinese charity circle for a long time. Under his influence, since the launch of the "Kindness Product" campaign in 2006, Alibaba Group has been committed to philanthropic activities. After that, campaigns such as Taobao's Goods for Good, Alipay's Ant Forest, and Cainiao's Green Logistics all brought the philanthropic model up to date through different Internet businesses. It became an important force for promoting the development of China's Internet philanthropy.

At present, Alibaba mainly carries out charitable practices on two online platforms: Taobao Charity and Ant Financial Charity (See Fig. 2.9), which are fundamentally based on the Taobao platform, funded by the Alibaba Foundation and technically supported by Internet technologies, big data and cloud computing. On these online charity platforms, there are several products with designs similar to the charity choices such as Goods for Good. These products are based on Alibaba's C2C e-commerce model, coming from and eventually returning to commodity trading. During this process, users are not only online shoppers, but also charitable donors.

[5] This section is mostly quoted from the "2016 Annual Report of Alibaba Group Philanthropic Products".

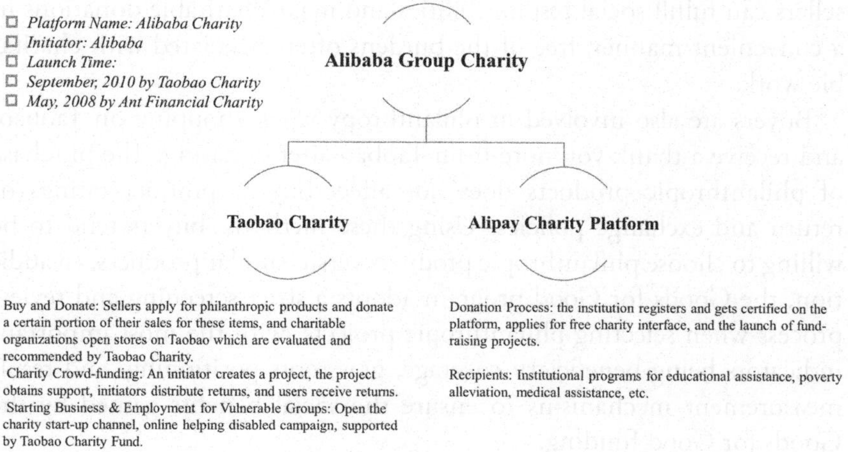

Fig. 2.9 Composition of Alibaba Charity

Goods for Good and Online Stores: Unleashing the Philanthropic Potential of Online Shopping

Originating from the Kindness Product program in 2006, the Goods for Good program empowers participating shopkeepers to label their products as philanthropic products and set a specific donation ratio. Once the product is sold, a certain amount of the payment, based on the donation ratio, is contributed to the designated charity foundation for philanthropic projects. Unlike philanthropic activities with distinct social networking features on Sina Weibo and WeChat, the Goods for Good program adopts a special donation model of transaction.

With its well-designed model, the Goods for Good program can be carried out on a long-term, sustainable basis.

For sellers, the Goods for Good program acts as a tool for engaging in philanthropic activities, providing them with convenience and autonomy. Sellers are free to choose any available philanthropic projects and donation amount, and they can start or terminate projects at any time. The average donation amount of 0.06 yuan per transaction also lowers the threshold for sellers to join the cause. These methods ensure that sellers can fulfill social responsibilities and make charitable donations in a convenient manner, free of the burdens often associated with charitable work.

Buyers are also involved in philanthropy when shopping on Taobao, and receive a thank you note from Taobao after donating. The purchase of philanthropic products does not affect buyers' product ratings or return and exchange policies. Using these methods, buyers tend to be willing to choose philanthropic products versus similar products. In addition, the Goods for Good program adopts a strict screening and review process when selecting philanthropic projects, with the most important indicators being beneficiary coverage, grassroots positioning, and result measurement mechanisms to ensure the social benefits gained by the Goods for Good funding.

The Goods for Good program features a classic charity marketing model, integrating enterprises and charitable organizations to support philanthropic activities while also boosting sales and improving corporate image. On the Taobao platform people who intend to contribute to philanthropic undertakings can select the most appealing projects in a manner similar to purchasing products. Besides, the payment method is more convenient than traditional bank transfers, attracting more public attention. Meanwhile, project web pages come with well-illustrated content, allowing donors to keep up with the latest news about beneficiaries. More importantly, since online donation can be completely anonymous, the original intention behind philanthropic efforts is not as easily marred by the pitfalls associated with utilitarianism (see Fig. 2.10).

Online charity stores can also be opened by philanthropic organizations on e-commerce platforms for fund-raising. The fundraiser is the shopkeeper, who sells items representative of the donor or philanthropic project, and buyers make donations by purchasing these products.

The operation and management of online charity stores requires effort and time from philanthropic organizations, who in turn advance their digitization. Devoted and diligent philanthropic organizations are more likely to stand out.

In short, by utilizing the Taobao platform, the Goods for Good program and online charity stores work to empower donors, fundraisers, and philanthropic organizations to interact with each other via online shopping, greatly unleashing the philanthropic power of online shopping.

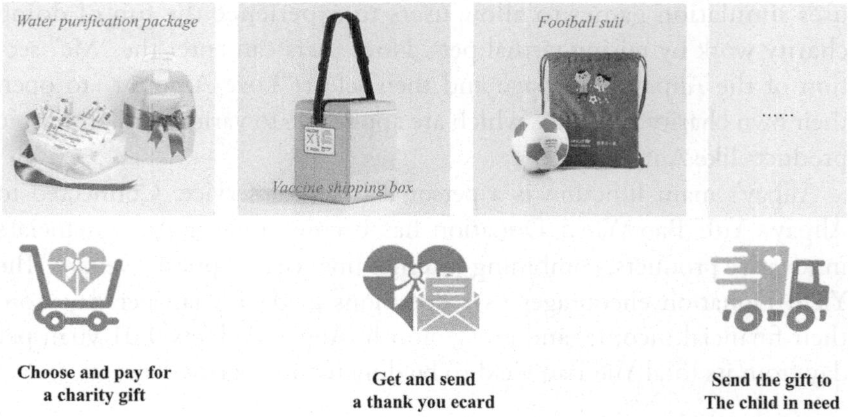

Fig. 2.10 Philanthropic Product Example UNICEF China Gift Shop

Ant Financial Charity Platform: Unearthing Multiple Philanthropic Scenarios

After the Wenchuan earthquake in 2008, Alipay opened an online fundraising channel for One Foundation, and the Ant Financial Charity platform was established. On the morning of August 28, 2017, more than 200 million people made donations using the platform. At the end of the first quarter of 2017, the Ant Financial Charity platform had raised more than RMB 967 million. With competitive edges in big data and Internet traffic, the platform provided public fundraising services for over 50 qualifying charitable organizations, and linked payment channels to more than 1,200 philanthropic organizations.(*The number*, 2017)

Specifically, the Ant Financial Charity platform consists of philanthropic products on Alipay. As one of the major mobile payment tools in China, Alipay brings together large numbers of mobile payment users, utilizing various offline payment scenarios to make more dynamic philanthropic endeavors. For example, Ant Forest integrates offline payment and daily exercise into its credit generation mechanisms to promote low-carbon and environmentally-friendly lifestyles among users. Ant Farm uses simulation games to allow users to experience the fun of doing charity work by raising virtual pets. Now, users can enter the "Me" section of the Alipay homepage and then select "Love Account" to open their own charity accounts, which are applicable to various philanthropic products like Ant Forest.

Alipay's main function is a personal financial service. Connected to Alipay's YuE Bao, Yield Donation has become one of Ant Financial's innovative products, combining Internet finance and public welfare. The Yield Donation encourages user donations of 0.01 yuan per day from their financial income, and every month, Alipay deducts 0.01 yuan per day from its total Yue Bao yield to be donated to charity.

Representative Product: Ant Forest

On August 27, 2016, Ant Financial launched a personal carbon account function on the Alipay platform. The carbon account was firstly introduced in Ant Forest. If users walk, take public transport, pay utility fees online, pay traffic tickets online, make online hospital registrations, book tickets online, or conduct other low-carbon activities they reduce their resultant carbon emissions. These carbon-reducing actions can then be input onto their Ant Forest account and converted into virtual green energy used to grow a virtual tree. Once a user earns 17.9 kilograms of green energy, the virtual tree matures is converted into a real tree, planted by Ant Financial and its charity partner the Alxa SEE Foundation in deserted areas of Alxa in Inner Mongolia.

According to the Ant Financial 2016 Sustainability Report, as of the end of April 2017, Ant Forest users had exceeded 220 million, reducing carbon emissions by 670,000 tons and planting a total of 8.45 million saxaul trees. Data also shows that Alipay users have made 360 million donations altogether via the Ant Financial Charity platform, amounting to a total of more than RMB 1 billion.

Meanwhile, through low-carbon activities such as public transport and online payments, 280 million Ant Forest users have reduced carbon emissions by 2.05 million tons, planting a total of 13.14 million trees on approximately 12,111 *mu* (or 8,074,000 m^2) of protected land. (*300 million*, 2018) In January of 2018, Alipay officially launched its Love Account, which records each user's philanthropic footprint and assets.

Case Study: JD Charity

Using a Background in Logistics to Create the Donation & Love Platform

Another e-commerce platform, JD.com also has its charity practices deeply rooted in the e-commerce business. Its charity products are designed to fully leverage its competitive advantages. It is well known that JD.com has invested significant efforts into building a "Goods Plus Logistics" system, which greatly benefits the organization of charity activities. Currently, JD Foundation focuses on poverty relief, education, environmental protection, disaster relief and social innovation. It has established service platforms, such as Donation & Love, Old Items for New Uses and Donation & Disaster Relief, where charity practices are performed in innovative ways (See Fig. 2.11).

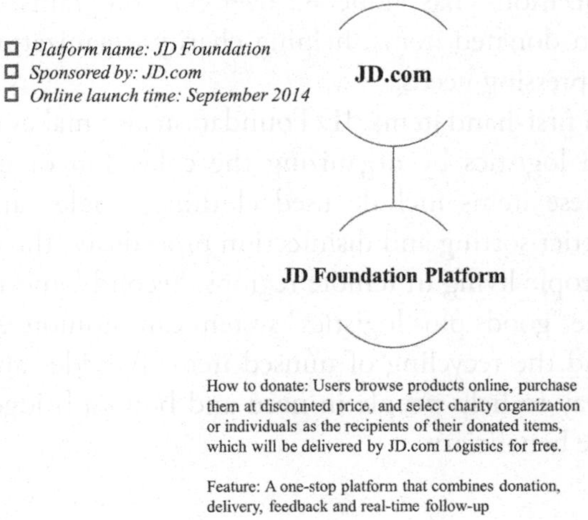

Fig. 2.11 JD Foundation

"Goods Plus Logistics" Capabilities Facilitate Charity

The charity and relief platform Donation & Love, which went live in early 2017, clearly demonstrates the level of integration between the JD Foundation and JD.com's core competitive businesses. Traditionally, in poverty alleviation and disaster relief programs, a long process of fund-raising, bidding, procurement and delivery is required before the donated items are delivered to the beneficiaries. This process may take several months, even for small charity programs. For example, after the 2011 Indian tsunami, there were reports of charity aid intended to help tsunami victims being delivered to the wrong locations, and the overall transport efficiency of disaster relief efforts was low.

JD.com's efficient logistics system allows this process to be simplified substantially. Platform users can directly select the items needed by "charity organizations/beneficiaries", which will then be delivered by JD Logistics. During this process, users can track every logistic detail of the donated items, such as delivery information from large warehouses, through to small warehouses and to the distribution site. Users can also find the contact information for those actually carrying out the deliveries, effectively resolving the two major issues of logistics tracking and gaining user trust. Currently, JD Foundation cooperates with more than 100 charity organizations, has launched over 300 programs, and delivered over 2 million donated items, helping charity organizations meet their beneficiaries' pressing needs.

Along with first-hand items, JD Foundation also makes the most of its advantages in logistics by organizing the collection of used items for donation. These items include used clothing, books, and toys. After undergoing strict sorting and disinfection procedures, the used items are donated to people living in remote regions. Second-hand item donation enabled by the "goods plus logistics" system can promote environmental protection and the recycling of unused items provides an efficient and convenient way to help people in need and build a bridge between the donor and the beneficiary.

Development-oriented Poverty Relief

As the saying goes, "Give a man a fish and you feed him for a day. Teach a man to fish and you feed him for a lifetime". JD Foundation contributes to development-oriented poverty alleviation primarily through driving sales of agricultural products on JD's e-commerce platform.

JD.com drives sales of agricultural products with the aim of helping local farmers find a sustainable way out of poverty. With the support of local governments, the company promotes the development of the agricultural product processing industry. For example, in the "free-range chicken poverty alleviation program", the JD Foundation offers a training allowance for local farmers and establishes a contract responsibility system through which individual farmers are held responsible for their own profits and can pull themselves out of poverty. In addition, the JD Foundation also researches the value of livestock products and analyzes their market potential, which has proven to be effective in improving local farmers' abilities to increase income and boost the development of local industries. In the long run, the sale of agricultural products will not only lift farmers out of poverty, but also help them to build a local industrial brand. Up to now, the JD Foundation has applied the development-oriented poverty alleviation model to over 800 poverty-stricken counties across the nation, creating online sections of agricultural specialty and attracting traffic to those sections by setting up a dedicated "poverty alleviation channel" online.

Aside from providing support for industrial development, the development-oriented poverty alleviation model also includes offering job opportunities and small-sized loans. JD.com's nationwide warehouses and distribution sites have a huge demand for delivery professionals, which offers employment opportunities for underdeveloped regions with a low level of urbanization. In this way, JD.com is joining hands with major civil society organizations and local colleges to hire local people as delivery personnel.

The development-oriented poverty alleviation model also includes offering financial services. The JD Foundation provides low-interest or interest-free small-sized loans for villagers in poverty-stricken regions.

The charity platforms, such as Donation & Love, Old Items for New Uses and Donation & Disaster Relief, benefit from JD.com's strong "Goods Plus Logistics" system, while JD Foundation's poverty alleviation programs rely largely on the overall strength of the JD.com corporation.

Featured Products: "Free-range Chicken" and Children's Book Donation Programs

Children's Book Recycling Program

On the 2018 World Reading Day, the JD Foundation, together with people.cn, China Children and Teenagers' Fund (CCTF), and Stars Youth Development Center organized the "Children's Book Recycling" program in 27 cities. More than 60,000 Internet users donated about 200,000 books, which allowed over 200 schools to make their own "reading corners".

Users can make an appointment on the JD App from the Children's Book Donation Program page under the JD Foundation. Delivery personnel pick up the books from users' location at a scheduled time and deliver them to charity organizations' warehouses. After the sorting and disinfection process, the organizations send these books to remote rural primary schools based on their needs. Meanwhile, users can track the real-time logistics information of the donated books through the JD App.

"Free-range Chicken" Poverty Alleviation Program

Food security has become a subject of major public concern in recent years. Negative news has been reported on the use of growth hormones in chicken farming, one of the most important poultry meat products in Chinese people's daily diets. Consumers have a high demand for grass-fed chicken.

Unlike NetEase's black pig business, JD's "free-range chicken" program focuses more on poverty reduction than the environmentally friendly rearing of livestock. During the "November 11" shopping festival of 2016, JD.com launched its "free-range chicken poverty alleviation program", which made the best use of "unfenced" pastoral farming methods. JD.com promised to buy back all the free-range chicken at a price two times higher than the market value, if the smart devices on the chicken's foot read that they had walked over 1 million steps.

Users with an interest in the poverty alleviation program can easily participate by donating their steps on WeChat Charity Hiking. Each day, every user can donate at least 1,000 steps. For every 100,000 steps that is donated by users, JD.com gives free chicks to farmers and offers small-sized loans to state-level poverty-stricken households. Farmers also receive guidance on how to raise the chicks from JD.com. If the chickens they raise meet the criteria of JD Fresh, they can make money by selling them to JD.com's e-commerce platform and eventually lift themselves out of poverty.

Section 3 From O2O Services to Charity

China's Internet industries have gone through several stages of development12, with the business format changing at each stage, from news and information, online reservation, O2O services to Internet plus industries. By combining these Internet business formats with charity, we have been able to derive new services with varied features.

The O2O service platform typically refers to online-to-offline platforms that give online customers access to a great variety of offline stores. Compared to Tencent Charity, Alibaba Philanthropy, and Sina Micro-Philanthropy, O2O companies such as DiDi[6] and Meituan are latecomers to the charity sector. However, their initial attempts in leveraging online systems and rich offline resources to combine services with charity have offered more possibilities for Internet companies to participate in charity. Currently, DiDi is one of the leading O2O companies in China in terms of their commitment towards charity.

---

[6] Sina and Sohu, two of China's "big four" Internet portals, specialize in information and news; Ctrip and eLong in online booking; Meituan and Didi in O2O services; Haier and Uniqlo in online physical industries.

Case Study: DiDi Foundation

Combining Philanthropy with Mobility Services

DiDi is a major e-hailing/hired car service provider in China and its charity practices are closely linked to its e-hailing platform, DiDi Chuxing. The level of connection between its core business and charity is comparable to that of the Internet companies mentioned earlier. Since DiDi Foundation went live two years ago, it has carried out several transport-related offline charity programs (see Fig. 2.12).

On DiDi Chuxing, drivers and app users play different roles in the e-hailing process, and have both now the gained new roles of charity program organizers and donors under DiDi's charity system.

The idea of donating mileage is closely associated with DiDi's product features. Based on the concept of "resource sharing", DiDi, a company which has thrived from the sharing economy, launched the "Mileage Donation" program encouraging drivers and passengers to donate their mileage in support of charity programs. The "Mileage Donation" program, originally developed in 2016, is similar to WeChat Charity Hiking

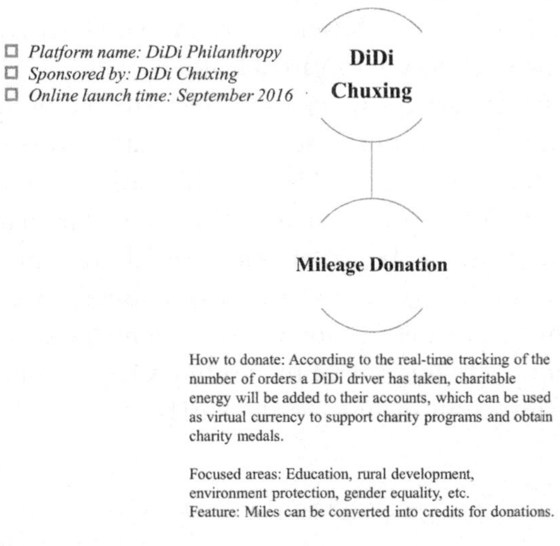

Fig. 2.12 DiDi Foundation

in terms of the means of participation: users and drivers can contribute the mileage of each journey towards charity programs. In 2017, "Mileage Donation" was expanded to DiDi's private car hailing and car hire businesses, which will increase opportunities for charitable donation.

As the most popular philanthropic product on DiDi's platform, Mileage Donation not only combines itself with DiDi Chuxing's business, but also makes use of the mileage which was previously of no real use to DiDi users. Now, each time they use DiDi to contribute to philanthropic causes, they can experience the spirit of charity. Users' membership level in the DiDi Chuxing app will not be affected by mileage donation, so it is a win-win situation for the user. The only thing the user needs to do is touch the donation button to give their support to a specific philanthropic program. With no cost and no threshold for participants, philanthropic programs like this make it easy for people to participate in charity whenever they want. Since the program was released online, it has gained a huge number of participants and has received a strong positive response. For example, the First Aid philanthropic fundraising program initiated by DiDi and One Foundation set their sights on raising funds for Jiuzhaigou Valley National Park which had been hit be an earthquake. DiDi users could donate their recorded travel mileage from their app and DiDi Chuxing contributed the corresponding amount to the philanthropic fund.

Jiuzhaigou Valley National Park in Sichuan Province is a well-known scenic area in China and one of the most popular tourist destinations for domestic travelers. On August 8, 2017, it was hit by a 7.0-magnitude earthquake which devastated the area. Many philanthropic organizations joined the rescue immediately after the earthquake; among them were DiDi and One Foundation who jointly launched the "First Aid" program. For every kilometer traveled and donated, DiDi donated one yuan to the philanthropic fund managed by One Foundation for Jiuzhaigou Valley. By doing so, users could easily team up with the DiDi Chuxing platform to raise much needed funds for Jiuzhaigou Valley. Later, the funds raised by Mileage Donation were donated to One Foundation in the name of DiDi users and DiDi Chuxing which was used directly for emergency aid and post-disaster reconstruction in the area affected by the earthquake.

Being known for transportation, DiDi has also made many charitable attempts at environmental protection. The Green Roof project is one such example of these concerted efforts. In October 2017, DiDi Foundation began working closely with China Green Foundation to launch the Green Roof environmental protection program. This philanthropic program encouraged DiDi Chuxing users to convert their accrued travel mileage into an area covered by green roofs. This program's goal was to turf the roofs of primary and middle school buildings, increasing the amount of local green coverage by utilizing formerly unused rooftops.

As for industry partnerships, DiDi has cooperated with a wide range of philanthropic organizations, including One Foundation, Chinese Red Cross Foundation, China Social Assistance Foundation, Ai You Foundation, China Women's Development Foundation, and World Wide Fund for Nature. By using its everyday service platform to the fullest, DiDi has responded to public demand and garnered amazing charitable results from its users and drivers. Currently, DiDi has approved a series of upcoming new philanthropic programs which include the DiDi Driver Mutual Fund, the DiDi Driver Care Fund, and the Dare to Help special charity project co-initiated with One Foundation.

References

300 million ant forest users plant a million acres of trees annually to green the country (3亿蚂蚁森林用户年种树百万亩系国土绿化行动). (2018, March 12). China. Retrieved October 5, 2018, from http://news.china.com/socialgd/10000169/20180312/32179027.html

CNNIC. (2007, January 23). *The 19th Statistical Report on Internet Development in China*. CNNIC. https://www.cnnic.cn/gywm/xwzx/rdxw/2007nrd/201207/t20120710_31508.htm

Epay. (2009, May 12). *5.12汶川地震一周年 易宝公益圈再掀网民捐赠热潮*. Prnasia. https://www.prnasia.com/story/19673-1.shtml

Sina Charity (新浪公益). (2018, February 26). *互联网公益 让人的善良有处安放*. Sina. http://gongyi.sina.com.cn/gyzx/2018-02-26/doc-ifyrwsqi3139093.shtml

The number of donations on Ant Financial's charity platform exceeds 200 million (蚂蚁金服公益平台捐赠人次超2亿). (2017, September 06). Sohu. Retrieved October 5, 2018, from https://www.sohu.com/a/190029846_102825

3

Philanthropic Civil Society Organizations' "Labor Pains" and "Transformation"

Since modern philanthropy came into being, philanthropic organizations[1] have been the mainstay of philanthropy. Most, if not all, philanthropic activities are organized by philanthropic organizations. Consequently, a country's level of development in philanthropy has, to a large extent, relied upon the capacity of its philanthropic organizations. The now advanced integration between the Internet and philanthropy has reshaped the ecological network through which philanthropy functions. In this sense, the emergence of Internet platforms has brought about significant changes in how each party connects with other members of the ecosystem, and with the philanthropic organizations themselves.

The rise of Internet philanthropy has impacted charities in the following ways:

[1] Civil society organizations in China mainly consist of foundations, social groups, and private non-enterprise units (social service agencies). This chapter mainly focuses on foundations, philanthropic social groups and private non-enterprise units.

Y. Chen, *Internet Philanthropy in China*,
https://doi.org/10.1007/978-981-16-2566-4_3

1. The development of the Internet has lowered the threshold for the general public to take part in philanthropy. This has resulted in a significant increase in the total amount of donations and limited how much control traditional organizations have over philanthropic resources. With increased public participation, traditional fundraising channels have found themselves at a disadvantage. Meanwhile, small organizations have been able to secure funds and users' attention through the Internet, thus making philanthropic resources more evenly distributed. As large organizations lose their edge, small and medium-sized ones have seized this opportunity for growth.
2. As Internet philanthropy becomes more popular, public fundraising has started to play a more important role in the industry. In the age of mobile Internet, online donation and behavior-based philanthropy have gradually become the mainstream models of philanthropy. Traditional thinking, concepts, and models have all been shaken by this new model of Internet philanthropy. For those that cannot keep up with the requirements of these new trends, they will need to renew and evolve.
3. Openness is a core trait of the Internet. The development of the Internet is conducive to transmitting philanthropy-related information. Moreover, public demands for information transparency, especially for charities that raise and use public funds, are higher than ever before. Thus, philanthropic organizations are under more pressure to release information.
4. The development of the Internet has provided a digital way of managing and supervising philanthropic organizations. This has greatly impacted traditional concepts of project design and execution, putting pressure on them to improve the design of their projects and efficiency of their execution through digital means.

Facing these major changes brought on by the Internet, philanthropic organizations have made proactive efforts to transform and innovate.

Firstly, they went from a lack of knowledge and even disregard of the Internet, to actively using online methods to organize philanthropic activities. In the early twenty-first century, when the Internet appeared in China, philanthropic organizations still had limited use of it. Only a few well-funded large organizations could achieve something as simple as promoting themselves online, while the majority of small and medium-sized organizations sank into oblivion due to the lack of technology and funds, as well as the proper channels for going online. Even those that could promote online didn't quite grasp how to use the Internet. Internet philanthropy on the whole was still in its early stage of development.

As the Internet grew, the convenience it afforded quickly became apparent. Especially with the popularization of mobile payments, online donation has become a mainstream practice, impacting the fundraising channels of traditional philanthropic organizations. Shaken by the Internet, they have gradually taken the initiative and embraced this chance as a chance to gain momentum and open up new development opportunities.

Secondly, the Internet has inspired the creativity of philanthropic organizations. Alongside Internet platforms, they are working to actively explore new models of philanthropy such as Ant Forest and Step Donation. For other newly established organizations, their explorations have gone so far as to implement blockchain, big data and AI technology in philanthropy. The full integration of the Internet and philanthropy has thus inspired the industry's creativity, paving the way for organizations to transform and innovate.

Thirdly, a series of transformations have already taken place in philanthropic organizations' project design, models of communication, and operational and organizational structures. These transformations come as part of their attempts to seize the opportunities offered by the Internet and respond to the challenges therein. In other words, many institutional changes have become a reality for philanthropic organizations, all thanks to the appearance of the Internet, with further changes still in the works. A series of reforms have enabled most organizations to adapt to Internet philanthropy's newer features, and to changes such as the increased percentage of funds raised by the public. These reforms lay a solid foundation for sustainable development going forward.

Lastly, huge changes have taken place in how philanthropic organizations regard and practice the disclosure of information. The numerous examples of incidents sparking heated public discussions on the Internet have helped the philanthropic sector realize how important it is for information to be public and transparent. It has become the consensus throughout the industry that efforts should be made to establish and improve organizations' transparency and donor feedback. Philanthropic organizations have begun to offer feedback to donors through various means. The Internet has also become the primary channel for philanthropic organizations to offer input and feedback.

When facing the oncoming wave of Internet philanthropy, no organization can afford not to take part. Different kinds of philanthropic organizations have been proactively adapting to the new changes by using innovative models and concepts to carry out philanthropic activities. Thanks to the continued efforts of philanthropic organizations and philanthropists, the entire sector has seen a distinct increase in digitalization and Internet philanthropy is now the favored model used by an increasing number of people.

Section 1 Public Foundations: A Turning Point in the Transformation of Philanthropy

The *Regulations for the Management of Foundations* (RMF), issued in 2004, made a clear distinction between different kinds of foundations. It defines public fundraising foundations as those that are oriented towards raising funds from the public, and those that are not as non-public fundraising foundations. Raising funds from the public is the key distinction differentiating public foundations from other civil society organizations. As the only kind of civil society organization that can raise funds from the public, public foundations take on the task of connecting donors with other organizations, playing a pivotal role in the philanthropic ecosystem.

A few years after the RMF was issued, given the restrictions on who could raise funds from the public, the foundations to qualify were always few in number, and increased slower than their non-public counterparts. According to statistics, at the end of 2004, the number of public and non-public foundations was 565 and 180, respectively. By the end of 2010, the number of non-public ones had, for the first time, surpassed public ones. As of the end of 2015, their numbers had grown to 1493 and 3324, for public and non-public respectively. (Yang, 2017).

This has shown that public endowments still remain a scarce resource, even in an era when restrictions on distinctions have been loosened greatly. As the public has never been more passionate about participating in charity as now, precisely because public foundations are so few, they will continue to play a very important role in philanthropic activities.

Public foundations can largely be divided into the traditional and the modern, according to their date of establishment and their institutional background. Those that became public not long after the introduction of the RMF in 2004 often had official or semi-official endorsement by the government. Established as they were very early on, they had stable fundraising channels and extensive experience in their own fields. Many of them were fairly traditional in their organizational structure and management concepts. This kind of foundation are commonly referred to as traditional public foundations.

After 2004, a large number of non-public foundations came into being. Then, following the relaxation of public fundraising restrictions in the last few years, some of these non-public foundations became public ones. Often set up by entrepreneurs or social forces without government endorsement, foundations of this kind lack official backing and are more market-oriented in their operation. We would call this kind of foundation a modern public foundation.

Internet philanthropy has been sweeping across the entire philanthropic sector, causing major shocks to both traditional and modern foundations. At the same time, both types of foundation have been able to Internet philanthropy into their practice. However, they have been influenced at varying levels due to their different backgrounds, concepts and operational methods. They share similarities as well as differences in their exploration and practice of Internet philanthropy. Despite their different ways of approaching Internet philanthropy, both have made tremendous contributions to the development of this model. Their persistent exploration has left a valuable legacy for the charity sector in the development of China's Internet philanthropy.

Traditional Public Foundations: Challenges and Opportunities for Internet Philanthropy

The emergence and development of the Internet has presented both setbacks and opportunities for traditional public foundations. The relaxation of policies defining public fundraising has broken the monopoly of traditional foundations, enabling an increasing number of organizations to work alongside them in carrying out public fundraising activities. With the emergence of the Internet, the role of public foundations as the center of the philanthropic ecosystem has been weakened to some extent. On the contrary, the role of public donations in fundraising has been strengthened. Indirectly, the competitive edge enjoyed by traditional public foundations has been made less prominent compared to other, both public and non-public, fund-raising civil society organizations.

In the Internet age, modern foundations are able to compete on the same platform as large public foundations in areas such as fundraising and project execution. The emergence of the Internet has made traditional public foundations more aware of the strong competition, which forces them to keep improving themselves in response to the wave of Internet philanthropy we are experiencing.

When Internet philanthropy was emerging, many large public foundations became aware of changes in the policy environment; they could preempt the oncoming competition, and adapted accordingly. Compared with their non-public counterparts, public foundations have the advantage of excellent fundraising records and wide connectivity. When it comes to a single project, public foundations are not necessarily ahead of non-public civil society organizations in terms of their professionalism and project execution. Therefore, when it comes to coordination and collaboration between civil society organizations, it is reasonable for each party to equally contribute everything they possibly can.

Around the year 2008, some large traditional public foundations proposed converting to grants and funding foundations, focusing on selecting and funding quality projects,[2] while leaving project execution and management to those more competent. (Yan, 2015) In their attempts to transition, quite a few large civil society organizations put in substantial efforts and made several meaningful explorations. However, due to both subjective and objective reasons, a number of large public foundations found that the process was far from easy.

Since then, in a short period of time, the arrival of mobile Internet has given birth to numerous online philanthropic platforms, which offer new pathways to transform. Under the Internet philanthropy model, large public foundations have been able to help small and medium-sized civil society organizations, not by providing them with funding, but instead through joint fundraising[3] with non-public foundations to empower them.

Joint fundraising is by no means a newly discovered philanthropic model. Not long after the RMF was issued, both public and non-public civil society organizations began to unite their respective donors by organizing collaborative philanthropic activities. However, the rise of the

[2] Foundations can be divided into grant-making, operational, and hybrid according to the way they use their funds. Funds raised by grant-making foundations are mainly used to finance other philanthropic organizations in carrying out their own projects. Operational foundations mainly allocate funds for the operation and development of the foundation's own projects. Hybrid foundations do both. Grant-making foundations, most of which are of a non-public nature, account for the greater part of China's philanthropic sector despite their late emergence. In recent years, some large traditional public fundraising foundations have also begun to actively transform into operational or hybrid.

[3] In a narrow sense, joint fundraising refers to fundraising models in which dedicated fundraising organizations effectively allocate social resources on a professional and highly accountable basis, and supervise the use of funds on behalf of the donors. Originating in the UK, this model plays an important role in philanthropy for Western countries. Due to the different national conditions, the practice of joint fundraising in China is different from that of Western countries. The joint fundraising mentioned in this book indicates a joint fundraising model in which the public fundraising institutions cooperate with non-public fundraising institutions via the sharing of public fundraising rights.

Internet, especially that of online philanthropic platforms, has significantly promoted the development and popularization of using the joint fundraising model to unite donors.

Within this model, non-public civil society organizations will propose philanthropic projects and seek to cooperate with public foundations or other charitable organizations that qualify for public funding. When public foundations endorse a project put forward by a non-public organization, they will extend their right to raise public funds, striving to launch the project and raise funds together. After fundraising, non-public civil society organizations will take on the responsibility of follow-up project execution.

During this process, public foundations will also undertake the responsibilities of verifying the accuracy of project information, training non-public civil society organizations in adapting to platform rules, supervising their follow-up project execution, and encouraging follow-up project feedback. By sharing their rights to public funding, as well as providing skills training and credit endorsement, public foundations are able to provide financial aid to non-public civil society organizations. In fact, these public foundations often shoulder greater responsibility in selecting, training and supervising their partners, yet another pivotal role they play within the philanthropic ecosystem.

Through the joint fundraising model, public and non-public foundations have played their respective roles in philanthropic activities. In this way, the efficiency of fundraising and project execution has been significantly improved, compared to when the responsibility fell solely on traditional public foundations. In the Internet era, though there have been certain changes in the ways philanthropic foundations participate in philanthropic activities, they still play an indispensable role in the wider ecosystem of philanthropy.

Many traditional public foundations have utilized Internet tools and technologies to upgrade their digital capabilities and explore what possibilities the Internet has to offer for philanthropy. For example, the China Foundation for Poverty Alleviation (CFPA) has established the "Philanthropy Co-op", its own e-commerce platform dedicated to fighting poverty. It seeks to achieve this by selling products online to assist impoverished regions in increasing their revenue. For the last one or two years and in response to the national targeted poverty alleviation strategy, the CFPA has used big data and other technologies in prioritizing people from low income areas and selecting the right approaches to helping those in need. A number of other organizations, such as the China Youth Development Foundation and China Charity Federation, have also made attempts at connecting the Internet and charity, each pioneering their own direction in the field of Internet philanthropy. They have successfully improved the efficiency of carrying out philanthropic activities and helped even more groups in need, opening a new door to the future development of philanthropy.

Data from Tencent Charity indicates that during the three-day 99 Charity Day event of 2018, China Women's Development Foundation (CWDF), CFPA and several other traditional public charities raised over RMB 10 million, and China Children and Teenagers' Fund (CCTF) raised an amount over RMB 40 million.[4] Making full use of the Internet has helped these traditional foundations gain tremendous benefits, demonstrating the very positive role new philanthropic models have played in the foundations' growth and development.

The rise of Internet philanthropy has on one hand brought about competition while on the other it has inspired the vitality of traditional public fundraising foundations. Spurred by this competition, they now fully utilize Internet technologies and have secured sustainable development, in an era characterized by innovation and challenges. In terms of the future of joint fundraising, traditional public foundations may still face fierce competition and challenges as they work to expand their capabilities.

On one hand, with the loosening of restrictions around what qualifies as a public foundation, we have seen a rapid growth in local public foundations. With their strong grounding in local concerns, these account for a great majority of the newly established public foundations. They are also more strongly connected with local civil society

[4] Source: Tencent Charity platform.

organizations, thereby reducing the cost of coordination and communication between them. When considering cost, many civil society organizations tend to favor local public foundations when choosing their partners, putting traditional public ones at a disadvantage. Two years after the *Charity Law of China* came into force, we can expect a greater number of non-public charitable organizations achieve the right to public fundraising. Said right to public fundraising will thus become less scarce, forcing traditional public foundations to face ever more fierce competition.

On the other hand, increased competition resulting from the joint fundraising model demands higher service capabilities from traditional public foundations. With the rapid increase in the number of philanthropic foundations, non-public civil society organizations are offered more options on which donors to work with, preferring partners that provide better training and services. Adopting more market-oriented operational methods, the modern public foundations enjoy certain advantages in providing their services. Therefore, knowing how to improve their services and collaboration prospects is one of the challenges that traditional public foundations now face.

This wave of Internet philanthropy has presented both challenges and opportunities for large traditional foundations. The rise of the Internet has shaken their role as a nexus of within the wider network, weakening their advantages over other civil society organizations. This is a challenge that can be entirely attributed to the Internet. Yet at the same time, the Internet has also given space for public foundations to play to their advantage by encouraging them to actively partake in industry competition. There are now excellent opportunities for any civil society organization willing to carry out philanthropic activities using the Internet. Traditional foundations need to actively respond to identify, and fully grasp the ever-changing online environment, while actively participating in industry competition and making good use of the Internet tools available to them. If they can successfully do so, traditional foundations will be able to undergo the necessary transformation to flourish in an era dominated by Internet philanthropy.

Case Study: China Foundation for Poverty Alleviation

Promoting Philanthropy for All Through the Use of Internet Platforms (*China Foundation*, 2017)

Profile

The **China Foundation for Poverty Alleviation** (CFPA), established in March 1989, was one of the earliest national and public foundations in China dedicated to poverty alleviation. It was registered under the Ministry of Civil Affairs and supervised by the State Council Leading Group of Poverty Alleviation and Development. From its inception, the CFPA has been one of the largest and most influential charitable organizations dedicated to fighting poverty in China.

In order to carry out high-quality programs, the CFPA launched the New Great Wall Scholarship in 2002, a historically meaningful project that is ongoing to date. The project aims to give students financial aid and assist them in becoming independent and self-reliant. The New Great Wall Scholarship combines poverty reduction with students' development, helping students from struggling households get through their secondary and tertiary education. Thus far, it has supported millions of students with donations of hundreds of millions of yuan.

In the years thereafter, the CFPA undertook a series of impressive charitable programs, including the Care Package Project, Moving Forward, and the Children Companion Plan. As their mission indicates, they aim to "spread goodwill and reduce poverty, help others reach their goals, and instill more goodness in others." With unrelenting efforts, the CFPA has become one of the most influential charitable organizations dedicated to solving social problems caused by poverty in China. The CFPA is dedicated to disbursing donor funds in the most effective way possible to combat rural poverty and stimulate development in remote regions. Current programs of the foundation target rural healthcare, rural education, rural livelihood, disaster relief, and international poverty alleviation issues.

Development History

The CFPA has been known for the boldness it demonstrated when it reinvented itself. When the Internet became more popular, the Foundation was one of the first to use it for charity by integrating it with philanthropy.

Within the first decade of the twenty-first century, the CFPA started to collaborate with SOHU.com to promote its programs helping poverty-stricken students and it earned high praise from around the world. However, limited by the lack of publicity and technological underdevelopment at the time, the Internet still could not play an essential role in the philanthropic sector, as compared to print media, television, and radio broadcasts.

With the advent of Web 2.0, Internet products such as blogs and microblogs appeared by the hundreds. It quickly became apparent to the CFPA that the Internet could make a huge difference within the philanthropic industry, thus the Foundation quickly began to explore how the Internet could be useful to the industry. Two classic examples of this are the 10699999 SMS-Fundraising Platform and Happylife.com.

The 10699999 Platform was an SMS-based fundraising platform developed jointly with China Mobile, China Unicom, and China Telecom. By simply sending text messages to 10699999, donors could donate money to the CFPA on a one-time or monthly basis. The program was an earlier charitable platform that raised funds through SMS in China. Before the dominance of mobile payment, payment through a telecommunication network was the most convenient way. The 10699999 Platform built by the CFPA combined both charitable donations with SMS payments, which lowered the threshold of public participation. During its operation, the platform yielded substantial results.

Technically, the 10699999 Platform was based on a telecommunication network; in essence, it was not really equivalent to the Internet philanthropic platforms that are so popular today. Nonetheless, it was a step forward for the integration of the Internet and philanthropy. Moreover, the monthly donation plan that the 10699999 Platform created could be easily replicated by Internet philanthropic platforms. With the rapid development of mobile payment, long-term monthly donations gradually became the norm of public participation.

Since it was the first of its kind, the 10699999 Platform lacked the features of current Internet products. Happylife.com, on the other hand, could be considered the real pioneer of Internet philanthropy. In 2008, social networks such as Kaixin.com and Renren.com were all the rage because they had hundreds of millions of users. Inspired by Kaixin.com, the CFPA developed Happylife.com, a charitable version of Kaixin.com. Happylife.com hoped to build a large and active online philanthropic community by improving user experience.

Happylife.com failed to meet expectations because of many various limiting conditions and this made it difficult to build an online philanthropic community. After it had been operating for some time, the CFPA decided to shut it down. If we judge by the result, Happylife.com was not a successful venture. Nevertheless, its short existence was of historical significance because it was the first time that a traditional foundation attempted to build its own online platform.

Soon afterwards, the rise of third-party Internet philanthropic platforms in the mobile era that followed, consigned these pioneers of Internet philanthropy to history. Despite this, the CFPA was commended for its daring determination to reform and explore. These failed attempts, in turn, helped the Foundation gain experience and deepen its understanding of the Internet, establishing a solid foundation for its second attempt at platform building.

When the CFPA stepped into the mobile era, it decided to take a double approach to mobile Internet fundraising. It aimed to promote and raise funds on third-party online platforms, while simultaneously building its own platform to record and collect donors' information. Given the fact that WeChat already provided a widely-connected, open, convenient, and efficient system, the Foundation mainly relied on a group of related WeChat official accounts to create its online platform. It was in this way that the Foundation chose a self-owned platform over a self-built one. The most prominent of the first kind are "Let' s Grow Together" and "Philanthropy by All". Apart from opening WeChat official accounts, the CFPA also launched the Philanthropic Co-op, an

Fig. 3.1 Major online philanthropic platforms of the CFPA

e-commerce platform that combines e-commerce and the fight against poverty. It turned out to be a big success in many regions (See Fig. 3.1).

To adapt to the changes brought about by the Internet and to motivate public participation, the CFPA went through several internal structural reforms. Started in 2012, the Public Donation Department was put in charge of online and offline public fundraising. It was then divided into two parts, the Public Interaction Department, in charge of offline public donations and the Mobile Internet Department, which transmitted information and raised funds online. The CFPA is also one of the first organizations to adjust its internal structure to the sudden changes brought on by the Internet era. The constant reforms and innovations show that the CFPA is open to embracing new changes and opportunities. It always keeps pace with the development of the Internet as well as the frontier of exploring how to integrate the Internet with philanthropy.

As a result of its strong involvement in Internet philanthropy, its influence can be seen in every project. The Foundation is propelling the integration of the Internet and philanthropy. In 2017 it raised RMB 580 million in total, 40% of which was donated by individuals; RMB 210 million was donated online, accounting for 90% of individual donations. (China Foundation for Poverty Alleviation, 2019) Currently, the CFPA is not only a pioneer exploring China's Internet philanthropy but is also one of the organizations that has the most thorough understanding of Internet philanthropy, thanks to its effective assimilation of the digital age.

The Main Model of the CFPA's Venture Into Internet Philanthropy

A Self-owned E-commerce Platform to Fight Poverty: The Philanthropic Co-op

The Philanthropic Co-op is the brand of the CFPA's e-commerce social enterprise. The organization's mission is to develop China's Internet Plus Poverty Alleviation initiative for impoverished regions. Based on more than a decade of experience in fighting rural poverty and first-hand research in over 100 countryside communities, the CFPA has creatively developed an e-commerce poverty alleviation model that employs "countryside co-ops as organizational foundations and the Philanthropic Co-op as the umbrella brand". This is how it uses the Internet Plus Poverty Alleviation initiative to give hope to farmers from impoverished regions.

Most traditional poverty alleviation projects merely provide funds to people but the Philanthropic Co-op contributes more than that. It is focused on teaching skills and community building by helping the scattered and small farmer households from impoverished regions to build co-ops in order to increase both the scale and efficiency of their production. At the same time, through consistent guidance and technical training, the Philanthropic Co-op creates rigorous standards of quality control and strictly enforces them, ensuring excellent products. Last, it integrates premium channels such as the Internet, e-commerce, and contemporary retail to support market development and cultivate the public brands of regional agricultural products. Ultimately, with the power of the market, these steps improve farmer households' capacity for self-development from the ground up, resulting in increased market competition.

In 2014, the Philanthropic Co-op used its e-commerce method for poverty alleviation for the first time in areas hit by the Lushan earthquake and received surprisingly good results. The first "trial" was conducted through the red-heart kiwifruits (*Actinidia chinensis*) of the quake-hit area. Within a few days of the marketing campaign, the fruits generated over RMB 300,000 worth of transactions. For the first time, local farmer households "became aware of the immense power of the Internet". Li Shizhong from the Farmers' Professional Co-op for Mingjian Kiwifruit Plantation in Mingshan District in Ya'an said, "The online payments grew continuously. I was dumbfounded". Subsequently, the Philanthropic Co-op invested more time and energy to fine-tune its model and improve its team.

In 2016, the Philanthropic Co-op's "Shimian Yellow Citrus Fruit" made its debut, which it had painstakingly developed. With the support of Tencent Charity, the fruits "made it to the Internet" for the first time after a long trip starting from their home in a small mountain village by the Dadu River. An article entitled "The Flavor of Ya'an Hits the Headlines Again" attracted more people to this campaign and consequently, 50,000 kilograms of yellow citrus fruits were sold in 151 minutes. (China Foundation, 2017) Previously, due to weak quality control and limited channels, local farmer households could only sell these yellow citrus fruits through traditional physical retailers, who usually priced the products at around 3 yuan per kilogram. When the Philanthropic Co-op helped these small farmer households to build co-ops, they then started producing goods under strict quality control procedures and standards. The products that met the requirements were sold at a raised price of 6 yuan per kilogram, leading to a significant increase in profits. As a result, the beneficial cycle of "better quality, better prices" gave these farmer "enough motivation and confidence to diligently improve product quality. But it must be known that such changes would not have been easily implemented in the past".

By the end of 2017, the Philanthropic Co-op had branches in 20 counties in 8 provinces. Over 10,000 rural families and 100,000 urban families from all over the country have benefited from it. In January 2018, the CFPA publicized the Philanthropic Co-op's "Deep Country Fresh" strategy. This will support the establishment of other Philanthropic Co-ops in seriously impoverished counties through methods such as physical operations and model output. These efforts would increase revenue for farmers from severely impoverished regions. (China Foundation, 2017)

Active Use of Third-Party Philanthropic Platforms in Fundraising Activities

By retracing the history of the CFPA, its engagement with Internet philanthropy is apparent. It has always been actively exploring the use of third-party platforms for carrying out philanthropic activities. The CFPA has been among the first public foundations registered under Tencent Charity. According to data provided by Tencent Charity, from when CFPA registered on Tencent Charity in 2009 to the end of October 2018, the CFPA has fundraised for 2037 projects on the platform, engaging nearly 6 million donors who donated more than RMB 243 million. The "Love Package" project operated by the CFPA raised a total of RMB 17.6 million from the public, making it one of the most popular monthly-contribution projects since Tencent Charity went online.[5]

The CFPA has also collaborated extensively with Alibaba Group in a variety of areas. It launched its official philanthropic store on Taobao Charity, which was used to raise funds for its own projects. It was one of the earliest foundations that joined Taobao's Philanthropic Product project. In 2016, the CFPA launched the Alibaba Joint Philanthropy and "Philanthropic Product 2.0 Project" with Alibaba Group as one of the partners. With coordinated participation, it hoped to enhance the Internet capabilities of charitable organizations and build sustainable philanthropic models, using the money raised from Philanthropic Products to support the growth of smaller organizations.

Apart from Tencent and Alibaba, the CFPA has also cooperated with Ant Financial Philanthropy, Sina Weibo's Micro-philanthropic platform, Baidu Charity, and JD Charity.

[5] Source: Tencent Charity. Donation statistics included in this chapter do not take into account deductions over refunds requested by the donors.

Joint Fundraising to Empower Small and Medium-Sized Philanthropic Organizations in All Aspects

The "joint fundraising" model is a mainstream model for fundraising on online philanthropic platforms. Organizations qualified as public unite donors by including their non-public counterparts under the "public" umbrella in exchange for being in charge of project execution. This model is the most popular for collaboration between public and non-public organizations under the framework of China's Charity Law. Such cooperation mechanisms have, on the one hand, promoted the division of responsibility between philanthropic organizations, and on the other, improved the efficiency of every link. Therefore, it has become the mainstream model for Internet philanthropic platforms such as Tencent Charity. The CFPA is one of the earliest adopters of the joint fundraising mode in China; it is also among the first group of foundations to implement joint fundraising on Tencent Charity Platform.

Data shows that third-party NGOs or individuals had been initiators for 92.2%, 93.1%, and 69.8% of the projects whose fundraising was undertaken by the CFPA in 2016, 2017, and 2018, respectively.[6] The continuous increase of the percentage of projects under the joint fundraising model indicated that the CFPA had strengthened efforts in collaborating with small and medium-sized organizations. This model has become an important part of how the CFPA has engaged in Internet philanthropy, as shown by the data.

Building Internet Fundraising Platforms of "Let's Grow Together" and "Philanthropy by All"

Two cases stand out of the CFPA's second round of platform building: "Let's Grow Together" and "Philanthropy by All". Both are based on the "Let's Grow Together" model. They focus on helping the poor one-on-one, using a monthly giving model, and targeting children from impoverished families. As of July 2018, the number of followers of the

[6] Source: CFPA(China Foundation for Poverty Alleviation).

"Let's Grow Together" official account had exceeded 200,000 and the number of users contributing monthly was more than 7000. It has become one of the major third-party platforms of monthly contributions for the CFPA, in addition to Tencent and Alibaba.[7]

"Philanthropy by All", a part of the 10699999 platform, is an Internet donation platform based on WeChat's official account. Because it does not rely on third-party platforms, it has brought together the CFPA's online fundraising projects as well as those launched by organizations under the model that unites donors. Followers can directly raise money for projects by using WeChat's payment system. The "Philanthropy by All" platform collects donors' information while keeping them informed and sends feedback on project progress through its official WeChat account.

CFPA's Model of Internet Philanthropy

As one of the earliest public foundations going through a transformation online, the CFPA has been one of the organizations that have made great use of the Internet. Out of the many aspects of its Internet philanthropy, the following main features can be observed:

Adopting the Double Approach by Simultaneously Building Its Own Platforms While Utilizing Third-Party Platforms

During its ventures in Internet philanthropy, the CFPA adopted a double approach by actively utilizing third-party platforms while building its own platforms. It is the CFPA's view that building its own platforms can help consolidate its resources and develop a deeper and thorough understanding of Internet philanthropy. Therefore, it has persistently promoted building its own platforms during the various stages of its development.

During this process, it made several groundbreaking attempts in the industry, though not without detours and setbacks. The first venture into building its own platforms with 10699999 and Happy Life Website

[7] Source: CFPA.

representing it, sank into oblivion for various reasons. However, the ethos exhibited by the CFPA in its total transformation and innovation became a valuable legacy pushing further development.

Despite failure on its first attempt, the CFPA did not give up and launched the second round in the era of mobile Internet. This time, the CFPA having learned the lessons from past mistakes, avoided over-reliance and simultaneously cooperating with large platforms such as WeChat to reduce cost and improve efficiency.

Until now, the newly established platforms, including the e-commerce platform of "Philanthropic Co-op" as well as the official WeChat accounts of "Let's Grow Together" and "Philanthropy by All", have made great progress during the second wave of platform building and are now an important part of philanthropic models. Through its own platforms, the CFPA has not only secured more resources but also improved donors' experience with charity. Thanks to the CFPA's persistent efforts, the double approach has resulted in enormous success.

Attaching Importance to the Role of Internet Philanthropy in Dissemination and Promotion

Chen Hongtao, Executive Vice Secretary-General of the CFPA, noted that Internet philanthropy does not equate to Internet-based fundraising. The Internet has not only enhanced the organization's fundraising capabilities but has significantly improved multiple links of its charitable activities, the most important of which is the dissemination of philanthropic information and promotion of philanthropic concepts. The Ice Bucket Challenge launched in 2014 is a typical example of how the Internet assists in the dissemination and promotion of philanthropic information. The activity itself has raised a considerable amount of funds but more importantly, aroused the public attention of ALS and facilitated the use of social resources in treating ALS and resolving related social issues.

The CFPA upholds the mission of "spreading goodwill and reducing poverty". The resolution of social issues does not rely on only one organization but the aggregate of society. Therefore, the spreading of goodwill and philanthropy is more important. The influence of philanthropic advocation to a large extent could far exceed the philanthropic fundraising facilitated by the Internet. The CFPA has been living up to this concept during its many years of practicing Internet philanthropy.

The concept is most typically represented by public donation activity of "QQ in Action: Saving Lives by Combating Ebola". The project launched by the CFPA facilitated 105,803 donations for children in Ebola-affected areas through Tencent QQ Wallet guided by the rule of giving away at least one yuan in one single donation with no limit to the number of donations during a 24-hour period starting on December 12, 2014. A total of RMB 1,218,489.3 was donated, all of which was put towards helping people affected by Ebola get through their difficult situation. As confirmed officially by Guinness World Records, this charitable effort set a new fundraising record for the most individual donations on a single online platform in 24 hours. (*Tencent QQ*, 2015) Compared to other large projects, the CFPA considered the donation of RMB 1.2 million to be next to nothing as the value of increased knowledge of the public on Ebola cannot be measured on the same level as money.

Early on came Sohu's Charity Channel, then later on the 10699999 and Happylife.com platforms, leading to the present where they are now the Official WeChat accounts of "Let's Grow Together" and "Philanthropy by All". These platforms have not only provided project fundraising information but also feedback on project execution and information on how beneficiaries' lives have been changed as well as the "charity-by-all" philosophy. The CFPA's commitment to fundraising and spreading of goodwill in practice and transmitting the Internet-based modern philanthropic concept has become one major feature of its Internet philanthropic model.

Attaching Importance to Donor Experience and Offering Feedback to Donors Through the Internet

The CFPA has always insisted that one important reason for building its own platform should be that the donor experience can be better ensured on the platform. It attaches great importance to "experience-based philanthropy" and hopes that donors can get a good experience of participating in philanthropic activities and have a sense of achievement. In the offline Care Package and other philanthropic projects, donors obtain a card from the beneficiary expressing gratitude so that the donors can feel a stronger sense of appreciation for their caring, which exactly embodies the importance the CFPA sets on creating a great donor experience.

Currently, the online philanthropic experience depends mainly on feedback from project execution and results. Therefore, the peer-to-peer, customized donor feedback system is an important means of ensuring donor experience. Though the third-party platforms such as Tencent and Alibaba have a wider range of users and a vast area of transmitting information, it is still difficult for the CFPA to get specific information about donors due to data privacy and other factors, which is why it is hard to provide customized feedback and ensure donor experience.

The CFPA has been sparing no effort to build its own platform for the purpose of improving donor experience in philanthropy. The building of its own Internet platform aims at enabling donors to have a stronger sense of participation and achievement after they engage in philanthropic activities by providing them with customized feedback and follow-up services through the Internet. Thanks to the customized online feedback, the CFPA and donors have built a closer trust relationship, making these donors feel more comfortable to give long-term philanthropic support.

The CFPA has also planned to further cooperate with large-scale Internet-based third-party platforms such as Tencent Charity on the basis of mutual benefit and protection of users' privacy so as to provide donors with more customized and refined feedback, maintain its relationship with donors, and improve user experience of participating in philanthropy. Also, it will actively probe further into the application of new technologies in philanthropy and enhance user experience of participating in philanthropy by upgrading technologies.

Emerging Public Foundations: A New Force in the Era of Internet

After the issuing of the *Regulations on Administration of Foundations* (RAF), a number of emerging foundations sprang up and became a significant force in the philanthropic sector. In recent years, with the loosening of restrictions on public fundraising qualifications based on national laws and policies, a batch of emerging foundations have received assistance in public fundraising. Such foundations often have no government background and are initiated independently by entrepreneurs or civil citizens. Lacking government background, many emerging foundations have no stable fundraising channels or philanthropic-related resources like traditional public foundations have. Nevertheless, because they have a more non-governmental background, the emerging foundations gain unique advantages and characteristics in the development of Internet philanthropy.

Emerging foundations tend to adhere to new concepts about philanthropy and follow the path taken by international organizations in management and project execution. Some of them even have strong commercial management characteristics. Different from traditional public foundations, emerging foundations have formed a relatively modern management structure and governance mechanism since their establishment. They changed the traditional way of de-administrative transformation and adopted a more flexible management system so that it is easier for them to adapt to newly occurring events. Therefore, when it comes to the use of the Internet, emerging foundations are usually more active and even more radical. Most emerging foundations make use of the Internet to practice philanthropy and are firm supporters of the new charitable models.

Emerging foundations attach great significance to using the Internet to raise funds for their own projects, which is also their main mode for participating in Internet philanthropy. Many emerging foundations often enter major Internet philanthropic platforms before they are qualified as public. Then they will work with traditional foundations to unite donors and use the Internet to raise funds for their own projects. After going public, the emerging foundations will no longer rely on the cooperation with traditional foundations to adopt the joint fundraising mode and independently raise funds on the philanthropic platform. As a result, Internet fundraising has become the main mode for emerging foundations to practice Internet philanthropy.

At the same time, the emerging public fundraising foundations are important participants in the effort to unite donors. These foundations started receiving public funding since the year 2010, coinciding with the period where there was a boom in online donations. After obtaining public fundraising certifications, these foundations often unite with grassroots and other emerging institutions to help them grow.

Emerging foundations have also promoted innovation of Internet philanthropic modes. The organizational structure of emerging foundations is more market-oriented, sensitive to new technologies and development, and more daring to adopt new public welfare modes. For example, Ai You Foundation launched a charitable blockchain in August 2018, which fully links all information of its childhood disease projects. The funds can be traced all the way from the beginning of the donation to the hospital to where the treatment is administered. This allows donors to track where their money went and how it was being used. This kind of blockchain mode solves the issues regarding public information disclosure, keeping the information regarding the funds open and transparent. (Ai You Charity Foundation, n.d.)

Although due to budget restrictions and other factors the blockchain mode established by Ai You Foundation may not be replicated in every charitable or philanthropic organization; its attempt is undoubtedly one of the earliest prime examples of the implementation of charitable blockchains in China, exerting a positive influence on the development of charitable blockchains in the country. New foundations represented by Ai You foundation have made bold and advanced attempts in recent years, playing a powerful role in promoting innovations within the philanthropic industry.

The emerging foundations promote the development of Internet philanthropy and undoubtedly benefit from online charity. Thanks to the development of Internet philanthropy, these emerging foundations have achieved rapid growth in recent years. There are two main reasons for this. First, online public fundraising has become an important source of fundraising for emerging foundations. In recent years, the loosening of restrictions on what qualifies to carry out public fundraising has enabled new foundations to go public and start their fundraising. Due to the influence of the Internet, public donations have grown rapidly in recent years, resulting in large amounts of donations.

Many new foundations lack stable fundraising channels that well-established institutions have, thus they mostly rely on the power of public donation. For most of these emerging foundations, small-scale Internet-based public funding already accounts for half, or even more, of the total amount of funds raised. As public donations rise across the industry, the fundraising capacity of emerging foundations has also steadily increased. Public donations from the Internet undoubtedly provide a space that is conducive to the growth of emerging foundations.

Second, the Internet provides the public with more opportunities to become aware of emerging foundations as well as increase their perception and in-depth understanding of them. Unlike traditional foundations, the emerging foundations have only been established for a relatively short time, so they have yet to gain extensive media resources and to generate publicity. Internet-based communication has provided emerging foundations with more opportunities to publicize and present themselves to the public, allowing them to communicate their purpose and intent better. For example, through Alipay's "Ant Forest", many people have learned about SEE and the SEE Foundation; and through 99 Charity Day's "Kids Gallery", they have gotten to know more about Ai You Foundation. In the era of mobile Internet, Internet-based communication is undoubtedly the best way for emerging foundations to gain recognition.

Similar to their traditional counterparts, emerging foundations will also have to face the challenges brought about by the rapid development of the Internet. Due to the improvement of public participation and the convenient access enabled by the Internet, public demands for public information disclosure of public welfare have become increasingly high. Even with emerging foundations, it is also necessary for them to continuously improve transparency regarding their institutions and projects and to meet the increasing public demand for information disclosure.

On the other hand, with the loosening of restrictions on public fundraising qualifications, local foundations and many philanthropic civil society organizations that have previously focused on project implementation will also transform into public fundraising foundations, inevitably leading to fierce competition among emerging foundations and higher requirements for them to connect to and serve small civil society organizations.

Looking back at the history of emerging foundations, the Internet has become an integral part of the public interest mode of such institutions. The mutual achievements and mutual development between Internet philanthropy and emerging foundations have achieved remarkable progress in the past few years. Looking ahead, as the implementation of the *Charity Law* enters its third year, more funds will continue to contribute to the programs of the emerging fundraising foundations. The incoming wave of emerging foundations will further thrive, play a more important role in the public welfare ecology, and bring stronger vitality to the philanthropic environment as a whole.

Case Study: Society of Entrepreneurs and Ecology (SEE) Foundation

Incorporating Environmental Protection into People's Daily Lives

Profile and Historical Background

Since the reform and opening-up policy was launched, China's economy has maintained steady and rapid growth, greatly improving people's livelihood. However, its extensive economic growth has caused differing degrees of damage to the ecological environment in various regions. Ecological problems in numerous areas have become the primary source of social problems threatening the health of local residents. In recent years, with the increasing public awareness of environmental protection, more and more people have realized its importance in their daily lives. However, the conversion of public concern to practical actions is an ongoing challenge for all environmental practitioners.

In 2001, Mr. Song Jun, a Chinese entrepreneur, invested RMB 50 million in Alxa League of Inner Mongolia for the establishment of the Moon Lake Eco-tourism Scenic Spot. Over a span of three years, this scenic ecological desert had attracted approximately 100 Chinese entrepreneurs to visit. First-hand experience in the vast desert has made the entrepreneurs deeply aware of the severity of desertification in northwestern China.

In October 2003, the General Manager of Beijing Capital Group Company Limited., Mr. Liu Xiaoguang, and a dozen entrepreneurs were invited by the China Entrepreneurs Forum to attend a conference at the scenic spot. It has been said that the moment the real estate tycoon arrived he was appalled by the scene. He knelt on the sand, looked up at the sky, and exclaimed, "Human beings are destroying themselves while creating wealth. Can we bring Chinese entrepreneurs together to facilitate desertification control?" His words struck a chord with Song Jun, so the two decided to build an alliance. At their invitation, a number of prominent entrepreneurs joined the cause.

On June 5, 2004, the Society of Entrepreneurs and Ecology (SEE), a social group mainly consisting of entrepreneurs that takes responsibility for society and sets its goal of protecting the ecology, announced its official establishment. Almost 100 entrepreneurs, as SEE's founders, made a commitment that each of them would invest RMB 100,000 every year for the next ten years to make dedicated efforts, starting from mitigating sandstorms in Alxa in protecting China's ecological environment to promoting harmony between humans and nature, humans and society, and human beings themselves.

Through its efforts, SEE initially designed plans to transform deserts into oases. However, an expert in desertification control with strong ties with one member of SEE proposed that its goal should not be turning deserts into oases but desertification control, that is, preventing land from further desertification. The ecological environment is an extremely complicated system. A desert is itself one kind of ecological environment. Changing the ecological environment through artificial means may cause other impacts on the larger environment. Therefore, SEE has set its goal of preventing the expansion of desertification rather than changing the desert environment.

As environmental protection is not the specialty of SEE members, they could only make explorations in various other areas under limited conditions. When SEE was established, it focused on community work by raising cattle and growing vegetables with farmers and herdsmen, in hopes of realizing the goal of environmental protection in this way. However, due to lack of experience in project execution and scientific evidence in project design, SEE encountered many obstacles at this stage, failing to achieve set goals despite much effort. Meanwhile, SEE realized that the overall development of environmental protection could hardly be facilitated by just one organization with limited power and reach. A greater number of environmental protection organizations engaged in this field should work together in building an improved philanthropic environment and promoting environmental protection. In the end, SEE decided to set up a foundation with professional operation, which will be responsible for the execution of environmental-related projects and cultivation of a philanthropic ecosystem focusing on environmental protection.

On December 23, 2008, SEE officially established the SEE Foundation registered as Beijing Entrepreneurs Environmental Foundation, which was dedicated to financing and supporting the development of environmental protection organizations in China. With such a civil society platform, entrepreneurs, environmental protection organizations, and the general public can all participate in and promote ecological conservation and sustainable development.

At the early stage of its development, SEE members had little knowledge in the operation of a foundation, even though they were all successful entrepreneurs with much management experience. Therefore, they decided to visit the US and learn how to manage and operate a foundation. The SEE delegation visited nearly 10 large-scale American foundations and held discussions with the people in charge. In this way, the SEE Foundation has developed a full understanding of the advanced concepts of management and operation of American foundations and set up a mode featuring professional management and delicacy in operation.

With the development of the mobile Internet, the general public has become the mainstay of philanthropic donation. In response to the opportunities and challenges brought by the new trend, the SEE Foundation was upgraded to a public fundraising foundation on November 3, 2014. Apart from the donation from SEE, it also received donations from enterprises, moneyed donors, and the general public. The SEE Foundation has further clarified its core agenda by focusing on three areas of work—desertification control, ecological protection and nature education as well as pollution prevention and treatment, which together with the development of the environmental protection industry constitute its four major areas for funding.

The SEE Foundation distinguishes itself from other foundations mainly in its focus on science. In the complicated ecological environment that we live in, a minor change may cause a significant impact. Engaging in philanthropic activities in environmental protection cannot rely on passion only but also rigorous academic studies and scientific project plans. As the largest philanthropic organization engaged in environmental protection in the industry, the SEE Foundation has attached great importance to science in project design, execution, and evaluation at later stages.

For example, "100 Million Saxaul Trees" (See Fig. 3.2) is a philanthropic project launched by the SEE Foundation to plant saxaul trees in a desert. The SEE Foundation is initially aware of the complicated efforts it requires to curb desertification. Planting trees in a desert is not as simple as it seems. Many factors have to be considered, such as the survival rate of saplings, underground water reserves, and environmental tolerance. To put it more specifically, if the trees are planted at a speed that is too fast for the underground water reserves, this will lower their survival rate and damage the ecosystem even further. However, if they are planted at a speed that is too slow, it might fail to meet the expectations to curb desertification. Therefore, for a project to be successful, it is very important to make a scientific, reasonable planting plan and monitor all the environmental factors in a real-time manner.

At the beginning, the SEE Foundation made a ten-year planting plan for this project and decided to adjust the plan from time to time according to the underground water level, the surrounding eco-environment,

Fig. 3.2 100 million saxaul trees

and the results from continuous testing of the planted trees. In this way, every next-year plan can be further optimized. The SEE Foundation will also keep monitoring the survival rate of the planted trees and make any additional planting plans if necessary. In case the planting plan for each year is successfully achieved, the SEE Foundation will still focus on how to increase the survival rate of the planted trees instead of pushing the project forward without considering the overused underground water and the negative effect on the surrounding eco-environment.

By July, 2018, the "100 Million Saxaul Trees" project has been implemented for five years, achieving its half way success with an increasing survival rate of the planted trees.[8] Thanks to the joint efforts of the SEE

[8] Source: SEE Foundation.

Foundation and other partners, the desertification in Alxa has been mitigated to some extent. In 2006, the SEE Foundation set up a scientific advisory committee led by academicians from both the Chinese Academy of Sciences and the Chinese Academy of Engineering, which aims to fuel the design and implementation of the environmental protection projects with cutting-edge scientific research.

Since environmental protection projects usually require long-term management, and it is impossible to measure their performance in a short period of time, the SEE Foundation specially creates a measurable approach that informs the donors about the effect of the project. Taking "100 Million Saxaul Trees" as an example, when the SEE Foundation raises money for this project, it allocates the cost to each tree so that donors are aware of how much money may be needed to plant a saxaul tree. In this case, donors can have a better understanding of where their donated money goes, thus are more willing to donate to this project.

However, this approach does not apply to all projects, especially for ecological conservation related projects which have a far more complicated process, where it is impossible to measure their performance in the same way. For these projects, it is very important to offer donors feedback about project progress.

The SEE Foundation specially cares about offering feedback on a project's progress. As Internet philanthropy emerges, it continues providing feedback to donors through various platforms and independent websites, meanwhile improving the feedback approaches and details so that donors can receive more personalized and detailed feedback. The SEE Foundation hopes that in this way donors can feel fulfilled in the long-term and slow-moving philanthropic projects and finally become long-standing supporters of these eco-conversation projects.

As one of China's largest environmental protection organizations, as well as a funding foundation, the SEE Foundation facilitates the development of the environmental protection sector and plays as a hub in the philanthropic activities related to eco-conservation. For many years it has helped many environmental protection organizations implement their programs through designated support. It has long realized that for grassroots-level organizations, what they need most is fundamental development rather than the money to implement projects. Therefore, in 2012 the SEE Foundation launched a "Strive Together" project, which aims to help grassroots-level organizations grow by offering them non-designated RMB 0.3 million (without the compulsory rule concerning where the money should be used) as well as mentoring services for three consecutive years. (SEE Foundation, 2015) With the money, they can cultivate talents, develop the organizations, improve their abilities, etc., which will greatly offset their shortcomings.

In 2017, the SEE Foundation received donations worth nearly RMB 200 million, with an increase of over RMB 100 million compared to 2016 (SEE Foundation, 2018), making it one of the largest environmental organizations in China, in terms of its influence and money raising ability.

The Main Mode of SEE Foundation's Internet Philanthropy Endeavor

Leveraging Third-Party Platforms to Raise Funds

As an emerging foundation, the SEE Foundation has been a project-based charitable organization since its inception with a focus on environmental protection. The biggest impact of mobile Internet on philanthropic undertakings is transforming the nature of fundraising, notably fundraising by third-party platforms. For the SEE Foundation, its key Internet philanthropic mode is leveraging third-party platforms to raise funds.

The data shows that up to October of 2018, the SEE Foundation has launched a total of 35 fundraising projects by itself on Tencent Charity since it obtained the right to publicly raise funds in 2014. These projects involved more than 2.94 million donations with a total amount of RMB 100 million.[9] The "100 Million Saxaul Trees", a philanthropic project launched by the SEE Foundation, has marshalled 1.6 million donations with a total amount of over RMB 24 million, during the three years since its launch. It has become one of the most successful environmental/animal protection projects in the history of Tencent Charity.[10]

---

[9] Source: SEE Foundation.

[10] Source: Tencent Charity platform.

The Ant Forest project jointly launched by the SEE Foundation and Ant Financial is widely known to the public. Ant Forest is a philanthropy scheme designed for the Alipay "carbon account": Users can grow virtual trees by recording their low-carbon footprints. When the virtual tree is fully grown, Ant Financial will provide funds to its philanthropy partners for planting a real tree in protected areas.

The SEE Foundation was the major partner of Ant Forest in its early stage, thus the real trees planted were all saxaul trees from the SEE Foundation. Though Ant Forest has gradually formed partnerships with other philanthropic organizations, the SEE Foundation remains the most important partner of Ant Forest. Through the Ant Forest project, the SEE Foundation not only built up a good reputation among Alipay users but also raised a considerable amount of money. By the end of October 2018, the SEE Foundation has cumulatively planted more than 10.35 million saxaul trees through Ant Forest fundraising, covering an area of over 138 million square meters.[11]

The SEE Foundation also opened an official charity store on Taobao Charity to raise funds for projects including "100 Million Saxaul Trees". In addition to fundraising for philanthropic projects, the Foundation also sells goods at its charitable store with all revenue being used to support the Foundation's environmental protection causes.

In the meantime, the SEE Foundation maintains good relationships with large third-party Internet platforms. For example, the Foundation registered an official account on Sino Weibo. In the era of the mobile Internet where third-party platforms form an extensive network of connectivity, the SEE Foundation seizes the opportunity to quicken its growth and achieve wide recognition.

Implementing Joint Fundraising to Help Small and Medium-Sized Environmental Protection Organizations

Given the current institutional and industry environment, the mode of joint fundraising is regarded as a rational system as it makes clear division

[11] Source: SEE Foundation.

of tasks among social groups and enhances the efficiency of philanthropic activities. Traditional large-scale public fundraising organizations such as China Children and Teenagers' Fund (CCTF) and CFPA began to launch the mode of joint fundraising after the rise of third-party platforms. As a representative of emerging foundations, the SEE Foundation quickly adopted the joint fundraising mode after obtaining its public fundraising qualification, sharing public fundraising rights with small and medium-sized environmental protection organizations and endorsing various environmental protection projects. Moreover, the Foundation provides training for its partners in order to support the growth of small and medium-sized environmental protection organizations.

According to the data of Tencent Charity, after obtaining its public fundraising qualification in 2014, the SEE Foundation promptly made joint endeavors for fundraising, pooling efforts of 13 environmental protection organizations and raising nearly RMB 1.88 million on Tencent Charity in 2015.[12]

The following years have witnessed an increased number of projects adopting the joint fundraising mode by the SEE Foundation with more money being collected. In 2017, the SEE Foundation launched 122 fundraising projects on Tencent Charity and raised more than RMB 18.28 million, 9.7 times the amount of 2014.[13] It helped small and medium-sized environmental protection organizations grow and promoted the philanthropic ecosystem for environmental protection.

Facilitating Informatization and Digitalization of the Green Philanthropic Ecosystem by Providing Financial Aid or Training

Since its establishment, the SEE Foundation has been positioned not only as a simple project implementer but also a funding provider dedicated to promoting the development of China's green philanthropic ecosystem. Over the years, the SEE Foundation has funded more than 550 charitable organizations focusing on environmental protection. An

[12] Source: SEE Foundation.

[13] Source: SEE Foundation.

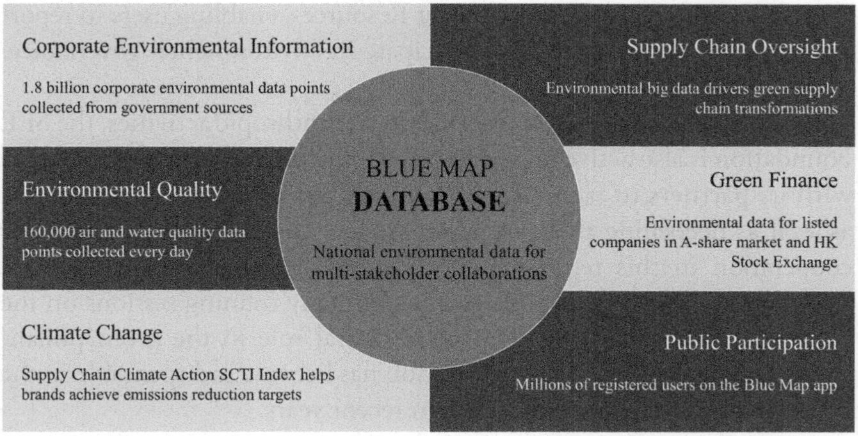

Fig. 3.3 The Institute of Public and Environmental Affairs (IPE) Blue Map

important type of funding target for the SEE Foundation are the organizations that conduct environmental activities on the Internet; a typical representative being the Institute of Public and Environmental Affairs (IPE) that developed the application "Blue Map" (See Fig. 3.3).

IPE is a non-profit environmental organization registered and based in Beijing. Since its establishment in June 2006, IPE has been dedicated to collecting, organizing, and analyzing environmental information published by governments and enterprises to build a database of environmental information. IPE's two platforms, the Pollution Map and the Blue Map, integrate environmental data to serve green procurement, green finance, and government environmental policymaking. Pooling the efforts of enterprises, governments, charitable organizations, research institutions and other stakeholders, IPE drives the green transformation of many enterprises, improves the transparency of environmental information, and optimizes environmental governance mechanisms.

A mobile app developed by IPE, "Blue Map" provides the public with real-time information on air and water quality and soil pollution in surrounding areas informing them of nearby pollution sources. The app is also connected to the reporting platform of the Ministry of Environmental

Protection and the Ministry of Water Resources, enabling users to report pollution sources and directly participate in environmental governance. (*Azure Map*, 2016)

In addition to funding Internet-based philanthropic activities, the SEE Foundation is also active in providing training for and sharing experience with its partners to facilitate their informatization and digitalization as well as deepening their understanding of Internet charity for better cooperation in this regard. Every year on 99 Charity Day, the SEE Foundation will provide its partners with many training sessions on the rules of various platforms. Playing a central role in the green philanthropic ecosystem, the SEE Foundation has become indispensable in the process of promoting green charity in recent years.

Internet Philanthropic Mode

Valuing Cooperation with Third-Party Online Platforms

In the mobile Internet era, cooperation with online platforms serves as, generally one might say, the most important mode of Internet philanthropy for charitable organizations such as foundations, due to the wide connections and tremendous resources of user traffic held by online platforms. Foundations, whether traditional or emerging ones, find it difficult to compete with large-scale online platforms in terms of user resources. Nonetheless, for their intrinsic nature as a platform, the online platforms are usually less professional than foundations with respect to persuading donors, management, and execution. Therefore, such cooperation between the platforms and foundations can not only promote division of labor based on specialties but also enhance the sharing of resources between the two parties, which is undoubtedly a win-win situation for both. The collaboration with foundations enables platforms to accumulate good reputation and gather philanthropic projects and users; and in return, the foundations will be able to connect with more potential donors by virtue of the large user traffic of these platforms and achieve rapid growth of public fundraising.

At the present time, to a large extent, the capability to make good use of third-party tools provided by third-party platforms determines an organization's growth in public fundraising. Looking back on its history, the SEE Foundation's cooperation with large online platforms has played a critical role in its development. The total fundraising of the SEE Foundation increased from RMB 42.99 million in 2014 to RMB 198 million in 2017, indicating an increase of 360%. (SEE Foundation, 2015) From January 2018 to September 2018, the SEE Foundation raised RMB 27.65 million on Tencent Charity for SEE operated projects, which exceeded 64% of the total public fundraising of SEE Foundation in 2014,[14] showing the huge impact brought by large online platforms on the growth of public fundraising for the Foundation.

For philanthropic foundations in this mobile Internet era, taking hold of the resources on leading platforms somewhat means grasping the most extensive user resources. Thus, fundraising via third-party platforms has always been an important part of the SEE Foundation's Internet philanthropic mode. Because the Foundation adheres to open cooperation with online platforms and keeps relying on third-party platforms for online public fundraising, it has succeeded in maintaining rapid growth of public fundraising in recent years.

Encouraging Innovation of the Internet Philanthropic Mode

As one of China's largest charitable institution devoted to environmental protection, the SEE Foundation has always encouraged innovation of the Internet philanthropic mode in the industry. The SEE Foundation works with Ant Financial to create philanthropic products such as Ant Forest, which has attracted a great many users to participate in energy conservation and emission reduction as an initiative to implement new philanthropic modes. Additionally, it also makes venture capital investments to encourage innovation of Internet philanthropic modes in the industry. In the past few years, the SEE Foundation has funded several partners who take Internet-based charitable modes as their main mode, such as the

[14] Source: SEE Foundation.

Institute of Public and Environmental Affairs, and help them to launch innovative environmentally-friendly philanthropic products represented by Blue Map, thus promoting Internet philanthropic innovation in environmental protection.

The development of philanthropy is inseparable from innovation. The SEE Foundation's emphasis on innovation modes has made a positive impact on the philanthropic landscape of environmental protection, while innovation has become an important feature of its philanthropic modes.

Prioritizing Popularization of Scientific Knowledge Related to Environment Protection Through the Internet

As mentioned earlier, environmental protection is an industry which is very reliant on science and in-depth research. It is impossible to accomplish an environmental protection task with only enthusiasm rather than scientific rationales. For any environmental protection project, even if the goal is not that difficult to achieve, it still needs sound scientific theories to serve as guidelines and must be based on rigorous scientific research.

But in real life, awareness for environmental protection of the general public and the professionals presents a certain gap. Despite their passion for the environmental protection charitable causes, many people lack the required scientific knowledge, consequently causing considerable obstacles for the public to participate in environmental protection. Sometimes this kind of gap in understanding will also cause unnecessary misunderstandings. Considering this, for the purpose to motivate more people to participate in environmental charity events, it is necessary to inform the public about scientific environmental protection knowledge in order for them to understand the scientific rationales behind environmental protection actions and enable them to better participate in the environmental protection cause.

Ecological protection and nature education have been one of the three core agendas for the SEE foundation. The SEE Foundation has realized the importance of communicating to the public and advocating the concept of scientific environmental protection for many years and it also has a deep understanding of the Internet's advantages in connecting users and information dissemination. In recent years, with the rise of the mobile Internet, the SEE Foundation has been committed to advocating and popularizing environmental protection among the public through emerging communication channels. The SEE Foundation has opened official accounts on multiple new media platforms such as Sina Weibo, and WeChat and published many influential articles to publicize the knowledge as well as the philosophy of scientific environmental protection.

As Secretary General Zhang Li of the SEE Foundation pointed out, the communication capability of the Internet plays a major role in its combination with the charity industry. As an emerging philanthropic foundation, the SEE Foundation has correctly understood the logic behind Internet communication and has employed the means of Internet communication to disseminate and popularize environmental protection, charity, and science making its Internet philanthropic mode much more meaningful and systematic.

Case Study: Adream Foundation

Promoting Philanthropic Business-Mindedness

Profile and Development

The Adream Foundation is a non-profit organization established and managed by executives with extensive management experience in financial institutions and listed companies. It was registered as a local non-public raising foundation with Shanghai Civil Affairs Bureau on August 14, 2008 and in 2014 it was transformed into a public fundraising foundation.

The Adream Foundation is rooted in the "discoveries" of its founder, Pan Jiangxue.

After graduating from university, Pan Jiangxue went to Hong Kong and became a Board member of China Merchants Securities. Her accumulation of wealth led to more thoughts on the meaning of life so Pan

Jiangxue began her charitable journey in order to give back to society. Since 2000, Pan Jiangxue has actively volunteered in deprived mountain areas, especially in Tibetan areas, and engaged in donation activities with specific beneficiaries, which also sowed the seeds for the establishment of the Adream Foundation.

By chance, Pan Jiangxue set up a field investigation tour in a Tibetan area in northern Sichuan, discovering that the remote areas were totally deprived of reform. In the city of Barkam in the Aba Tibetan Autonomous Prefecture, some students gave up the opportunity to go to school due to the local mindset believing that schooling was useless, which exerted a negligent impact on the lives of children rather than mere poverty.

Despite the huge investment and resources channeled into education by the country and the public every year, many students are still left behind and deprived of the benefits of education, giving them no chance to escape the shackles of poverty. Deeply touched by these children, Pan Jiangxue resolutely forsook her work in financial institutions for philanthropy, establishing the Adream Foundation. With aims to enhance rural children's well-rounded development, she wanted to deploy interesting methods to let children enjoy the fun of learning, improve their capabilities, and cultivate students' key abilities as well as help children grow up with confidence, poise, and dignity.

The Adream Center is where the Adream Foundation begins to promote literacy education for rural children. The Foundation hopes to create a quasi-library environment through the transformation of school classrooms to stimulate students' interest in learning, cultivate their reading habits, and enhance their comprehensive skills. Driven by Pan Jiangxue and other founders, the Adream Center project was launched in the second half of 2007 and the first Adream Center was built in the Barkam area the same year (See Fig. 3.4).

However, libraries are not necessarily the best place for literacy education. The Adream Center equipped with proper materials was not fully utilized by children. Inspired by Professor Cui Yunhuo, Director of the Institute of Curriculum and Instruction at East China Normal University, Pan Jiangxue and the Adream Foundation realized that the classroom was the best place to improve children's literacy levels and abilities and the

Fig. 3.4 The Adream Center

curriculum per se carried educational values. Well-equipped classrooms were important and high-quality curriculum carried more weight in improving the standard of living for children in underprivileged areas.

At the end of 2008, the Adream Foundation and Professor Cui's team cooperated to design and introduce a professional and complete Adream Curriculum consisting of a set of Adream Courses for the Adream Centers nationwide. The Foundation also began to work with local education departments and school administrators by using the Adream Curriculum as a structural supplement to the national basic education curriculum to help students develop sound character and key abilities necessary to adapt to society and make students "truth-pursuing and caring dream-seekers".

With classrooms and curriculum on hand, teachers are then required to impart the content to the children. Teachers responsible for disseminating knowledge are so significant that only their changes may be possible to transform every child they teach. Therefore, with the aim to put into practice and promote the Adream Curriculum, the Foundation launched the Adream Guide program for training teachers at the teaching dais, school administrators, and local education officials, while promoting millions of rural teachers to join the Adream Curriculum system with the overall goal of improving children's comprehensive abilities and literacy levels.

A complete closed loop of knowledge created by the Adream Center, the Adream Curriculum and the Adream Guide has been well received and acknowledged in many deprived areas, bringing continuous and observable changes to millions of children in rural areas. As of August, 2018, the Adream Foundation has built 3135 Adream Centers across the country, designed and implemented more than 40 Adream courses, and organized nearly 1.5 million Adream teachers to participate in the training, benefiting 3.2 million students.[15]

The Application of Transparency, Professionalism, and Business Thinking in Philanthropy

The Adream Foundation is the most transparent among its peers. Over the years, the Adream Foundation has always ranked first in the Foundation Transparency Index (FTI) and has maintained No.1 in the lists of most transparent foundations by Forbes and jiemian.com for many years. Concomitantly, the Adream Foundation is the only non-profit organization in China certificated by SGS (General Standard Technical Service Co., Ltd., 2017) and is hailed as the most transparent foundation in China. (Lan, 2012)

The Adream Foundation's achievement in transparency is rooted in its knowledge of the business world in that it has established a professional management and information disclosure system. In a sense, professionalism is fundamental to ensuring quality transparency for the Adream Foundation.

Finance has always been one of the industries with the highest demand for information transparency. Listed companies have a complete set of information disclosure mechanisms to protect the interests of investors, which is something unseen in philanthropy at this stage. Pan Jiangxue, who has years' experience in the financial industry, has a very deep understanding of information disclosure. She has always been committed to

[15] Source: True Love Dream Foundation. (2018-09-30). http://www.adream.org/.

bringing the thinking and model of the financial sector to the information disclosure of philanthropic organizations.

Pan Jiangxue believes that the information disclosure of philanthropic organizations can be divided into four phases, i.e., Phase 1.0 to Phase 4.0. In Phase 1.0, philanthropic organizations only make general information disclosure on the money, goods, and project effects; after entering Phase 2.0, philanthropic organizations can disclose information in a structural manner, avoiding the concealment of negative information; in Phase 3.0, philanthropic organizations can achieve transparency in both results and processes; and in Phase 4.0, philanthropic organizations should apply blockchain ideology to improve the operation and information feedback mechanism.

This understanding leads to the Adream Foundation's efforts in transparency improvement in both results and processes since its inception. In order to improve result transparency, the Adream Foundation draws on the commercial information disclosure model and has consistently followed the requirements of the disclosure of financial reports of listed companies to make structured disclosures on the Foundation. The Foundation's per capita efficiency, financial data, funding and administrative expenses ratio, executive remuneration, operational capabilities, and related-party transactions are all covered by structural disclosure, which deprives the Foundation of the possibility to hide adverse contents.

The Adream Foundation guarantees its process transparency by adopting a professional management process. Since its inception, the Adream Foundation has designed and implemented a comprehensive budget management system based on the model of corporate management. Each decision is made hierarchically, from the Board of Directors to the Secretariat to the directors' meeting; each project has been subject to a complete set of processes for launch and approval. Such a complete process enables the Foundation to record all the work, achieving both transparent results and processes.

The transparency of results and processes guarantees the overall level of transparency of the Adream Foundation. The high transparency is underpinned by the professional knowledge of transparency, information disclosure guidelines, and management models. To a certain extent, transparency is a by-product of professionalism. While professionally managing with specialized models, the Foundation has generally reached Phase 3.0 of information disclosure and has also borne high-quality fruits in this regard.

Transparency is not the only reflection of professionalism and the skillful application of business thinking of the Adream Foundation. The Foundation also weaves professionalism and business mindset into the fabric of the design and implementation of projects.

Take the Adream Center as an example. At the beginning, the initial Adream Centers were built personally by Pan Jiangxue and other founders of the institute. However, during the process, she also found that due to local differences, the Adream Center could not be easily replicated from place to place because large-scale expansion required the introduction of a business mindset and professionalism. After several practitioners in the retail industry joined the Foundation, the Foundation established the idea of building the Adream Center into a chain of knowledge that can be standardized and applied in scale.

Under the guidance of this idea, the Adream Center can be broken down into 12 standardized steps. Place selection, design, procurement, and tendering are all finished at the headquarters of the Foundation. After the tendering and procurement process, the Foundation then allocates materials based on the area of each Adream Center and the number of students covered and then selects an appropriate logistics provider to ship the materials to the school. Throughout the process, the Foundation has gradually established a relatively complete Adream Center supply chain system.

After materials are shipped to the school, the teachers and staff can independently complete the construction of the Adream Center by referring to the construction manual provided by the Foundation without relying on any construction assistance. In 2016, the Adream Foundation built 448 Adream Centers across the country and the average construction period spanned only 27 days. In fact, there were only four employees responsible for the construction of the Adream Center. (Pan, 2017) Without the support of business thinking and professional models such efficiency would be impossible to achieve.

Professionalism of the Adream Foundation is also embodied in the design of the Adream Curriculum. The Adream Curriculum is the brainchild of the team led by Professor Cui Yunhuo from the Institute of Curriculum and Instruction at East China Normal University. This came after drawing a large number of advanced research results from domestic and international education circles. As one of the curriculum standards development teams for basic education, Professor Cui and his colleagues ensure that the Adream Curriculum system can be perfectly integrated with the national basic education curriculum.

Concurrently, the Adream Foundation also realizes that we are in an era of rapid development. The generalized curriculum system cannot keep pace with the times nor can it help students acquire the knowledge and develop abilities most needed. Therefore, the Foundation's curriculum development team and Professor Cui's team are constantly iterating and upgrading the curriculum. Every year, the Foundation launches new courses based on the latest theories and teaching situations and conducts small-scale pilot teaching and scientific assessments. Only those that pass the assessment can be promoted to a large scale. The launch of Adream courses is not the end, follow-up evaluations are carried out. If the evaluation results are not up to standards, replacement is inevitable. The design, pilot teaching, development, and follow-up evaluation of Adream courses reflect the Foundation's professional requirements and persistence.

Professionalism and skillful use of business thinking make the Adream Foundation stand out. Its commitment to professionalism, in return, also drives the development of the Adream Foundation, helping the Foundation achieve greater value in the field of rural student literacy education.

Major Mode of Internet Philanthropy of the Adream Foundation

As a newly established foundation, the Adream Foundation has been undoubtedly at the forefront of national philanthropic organizations in terms of professionalism and business thinking. In the field of Internet philanthropy, the Adream Foundation is not willing to be outdone and has begun its active practice and exploration early. It has achieved very outstanding results.

Pan Jiangxue and the Adream Foundation have long foreseen the huge impact that the Internet can have on philanthropy. As early as in 2009, the Adream Foundation cooperated with well-known Internet companies such as Tencent to leverage their core strengths and jointly promote projects and services in poverty-stricken areas. Together, the Internet has been part of major projects of the Adream Foundation since the early days: The Foundation uses Internet technologies to provide online interaction and services within the teachers community; all "Adream Centers" have access to the Internet; the monitoring of projects and services, usage of all the centers, and the evaluation of "Adream Curriculum" are mainly Internet-based; and the "Adream Guide" is partially implemented through remote training online. Among them, the most important are the monitoring of the usage of the "Adream Centers" and the evaluation of the "Adream Curriculum".

Without the Internet it is almost impossible to serve every center and be able to monitor their use, much less assess and evaluate the implementation of the "Adream Courses" of each "Adream Center" since they are not only far away from each other but spread around poverty-stricken areas across the country. The solution proposed by the Adream Foundation is Internet-based: In order to monitor the use of "Adream Centers", the development of each "Adream Course", and the offline operation of the "Regional Managers" of the provinces responsible for project operations, the Foundation established the "Adream Box" on the SNS platform serving the teacher community. Teachers can open blogs on the "Adream Box" and publish course plans and teaching and discussion contents. The Foundation can assess the condition of the project operation service and evaluate how "Adream Courses" are being taught via blogs to refine the Foundation's projects and services for the schools involved. In the early implementation stage, Internet technologies played an extremely important role. The proper use of Internet technologies and tools has also enabled the Foundation to overcome the difficulties and obstacles that many traditional means could not have solved in its early development.

In 2014 after the Adream Foundation was approved as a public funding foundation and was able to raise funds from the public directly, the Foundation and its Internet philanthropy were more closely integrated. The same year, the Adream Foundation opened its official account on

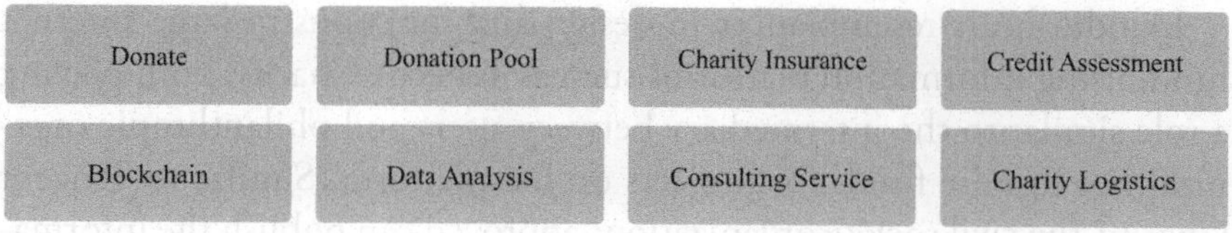

Fig. 3.5 Huodui philanthropic platform

Tencent Charity, the platform for philanthropy established by Tencent, as a public funding foundation to raise funds for projects such as the Adream Center. Since 2015 the Adream Foundation has participated in activities for each session of the 99 Charity Day and evolved rapidly. Data shows that by the 99 Charity Day in 2018 the Adream Foundation has launched a total of 132 projects, whetted the engagement of 410,000 users, and raised a total of RMB 24.38 million. The Adream Quality Education project of the Adream Foundation raised RMB 56.39 million since its inception to the Tencent Charity Platform, becoming a star project in the field of philanthropic education.[16]

With the advance in Internet fundraising, the total amount raised by the Adream Foundation has also risen in the past few years. In 2012, the Adream Foundation raised RMB 45.87 million. By 2017 the amount grew to RMB 141.45 million. (Adream Foundation, 2018) The amounts raised by the Foundation has increased more than twice in five years, showing the explosion of public donations in the past two years and the adept deployment of online, in-depth understanding, and perception of Internet philanthropy by the Adream Foundation.

While actively using third-party platforms for fundraising, the Adream Foundation has not given up its own Internet platform. The most typical one is Huodui (See Fig. 3.5).

Huodui is a platform for providing Internet philanthropy under the Adream Foundation, created and operated by an independent internal team. Huodui is committed to providing public welfare fundraising and management consulting services to small and micro philanthropic organizations. They are also believers that philanthropy is important for making valuable public welfare ideals come true.

[16] Source: Adream Foundation.

Huodui bears resemblances in design and functions to large Internet fundraising information platforms such as Tencent Charity, both playing a role similar to the intermediary between users and philanthropic organizations to raise funds for projects on the platform. Similar to Tencent Charity, the civil society organizations approved can publish the information of philanthropic projects, whose funds will be raised by the Adream Foundation and the civil society organizations. There are, however, many significant differences despite some similarities. The advantage of Internet fundraising information platforms such as Tencent Charity is their wide network, focusing on promoting the connection between donors and public welfare organizations, while the Adream Foundation is superior in its professionalism. Therefore, Huodui provides high-quality and diverse services to small and micro organizations rather than merely acting as an Internet fundraising platform.

In addition to providing small and micro civil society organizations with the opportunity to promote fundraising activities with the Adream Foundation, Huodui also provides a series of additional services for them such as philanthropic insurance, credit evaluation, blockchain technical support, data analysis, online consulting, and offline workshops. More importantly, the management of projects on the platform should follow the same project management model for professional implementation and information disclosure as the Adream Foundation. Through such a mechanism, Huodui ensures the projects on the platform be basically on the par with projects run by the Adream Foundation in terms of management and execution level.

This shows that Huodui has a larger vested scope in comparison to other Internet fundraising platforms. This not only brings in more online funds to small and medium-sized civil society organizations but more importantly, helps them grow rapidly thanks to the development of their own capabilities. This feature also convinced the Adream Foundation to define Huodui as an Internet service platform rather than an Internet fundraising platform.

As of the beginning of September 2018, there have been 641 philanthropic projects on Huodui and the total fundraising amount was about RMB 16 million.[17] Though far from being a peer to larger Internet plat-

[17] Source: Huodui. (2018-09-07). https://www.huodui.org/.

forms such as Tencent Charity in its fundraising ability, Huodui has gathered a large number of like-minded partners through the Internet and through opening capabilities of the Adream Foundation and spread the management model and business thinking to more philanthropic organizations, playing a positive role in promoting the development of philanthropic ecosystem.

In the past few years, both the Internet fundraising and Huodui have become indispensable parts of the philanthropic model championed by the Adream Foundation, implicating its deep understanding of Internet philanthropy. This year, the Adream Foundation set an objective of teaching Adream Courses to over 10 million students in five years, a figure that is difficult to achieve only by traditional means. However, in this mobile era, with the help of the Internet, it is not impossible to achieve. The Adream Foundation has also begun to actively explore new types of curriculum models, hoping to add more technologies. With a deeper integration of technology and philanthropy, the "Internet Plus Philanthropy", the future model of the Adream Foundation, will leave more space for imagination.

Section 2 Non-public Fundraising Organizations: Playing a Bigger Role in Philanthropic Ecosystem

If public fundraising organizations play a pivotal role in the philanthropic ecosystem, then the non-public ones are the most important component. Even with liberalization of public fundraising rights in recent years, the number of organizations without public fundraising rights has greatly exceeded that of organizations with public fundraising rights. The majority of philanthropic projects still count on non-public fundraising foundations and social groups for their development. The emergence of the Internet has also brought about tremendous changes for both types of organizations.

Non-public Fundraising Foundations: The Internet Promotes Innovation of the Philanthropic Model and Supports the Healthy Development of the Industry

The non-public fundraising foundations are those without public fundraising qualifications. Under the current system, non-public foundations have very important functions and are an integral part of the philanthropic ecosystem. With no demand of public fundraising, non-public fundraising foundations are subject to lesser requirements for information disclosure and public information feedback than public ones. Non-public fundraising foundations are also more flexible in their use of resources and are more directly answerable to funders, largely filling the gap between public raising foundations and small civil society organizations and making the public welfare ecology fuller and sounder.

The development of non-public fundraising foundations is closely subject to variations in policies. The *Regulations on Administration of Foundations* (RAF) liberalizes the registration of the foundations and clearly regulates the public fundraising rights, which can be recognized as the starting point for the development of non-public fundraising foundations. In 2004, the year the RAF was published, the ratio of public and non-public fundraising foundations was 565:180 and the number of non-public fundraising foundations was less than one third of that of public foundations. (Yang, 2017) Non-public fundraising foundations at that time were still unfledged and were not the main force in the philanthropic ecosystem.

After the RAF was published, more enterprises and businesses have been engaging in the philanthropy sector. Non-public fundraising foundations also have witnessed strong momentum in development over recent years, exceeding the public ones in growth. According to statistics, non-public foundations started to develop faster than public ones in 2005 and surpassed the latter in number for the first time in 2010. As time goes on such advantage grows even larger. In 2015 a total of 4871 foundations were registered in the Ministries of Civil Affairs of China. Among them, 3324 were non-public ones, accounting for 68% (See Fig. 3.6). So far, non-public foundations have taken up an important role in the philanthropic sector. (Yang, 2017)

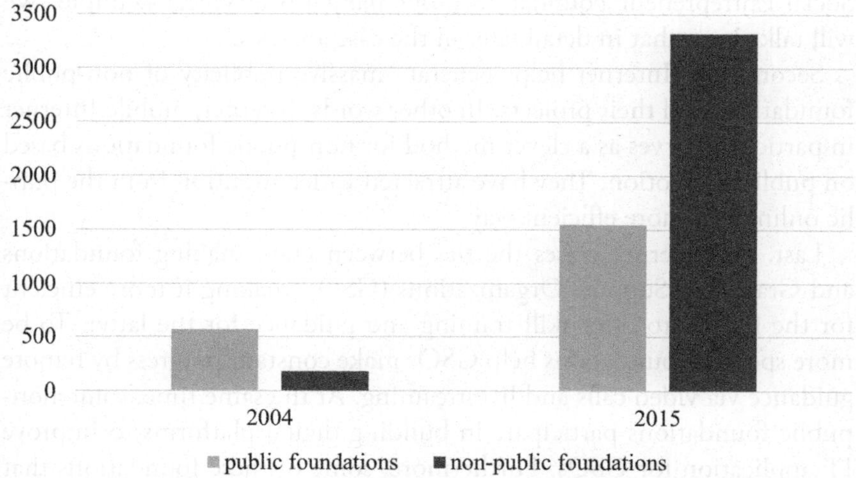

Fig. 3.6 Numbers of public and non-public foundations

In contrast, non-public foundations have not played a major part in Internet philanthropy. Despite the popularity of online philanthropy, non-public foundations are not drawing enough attention from the public in that such foundations are not qualified for public fundraising.

Therefore, such foundations depend on other offline fundraising channels. Online, however, makes the most contribution to fundraising with the greatest public attention among all charitable channels. Being unable to participate in public fundraising via Internet philanthropy (though not equal to Internet fundraising) makes non-public foundations barely known to the public.

Nevertheless, the Internet still yields an influence on non-public foundations which, in turn, proactively embrace the Internet channel. In fact, the Internet has brought non-public foundations critical returns in three major aspects.

First, the Internet brings project-oriented foundations improvement in project management and execution efficiency and inspires brand-new philanthropic projects. These new philanthropic projects, based online, make outstanding breakthroughs in design concept and efficiency, offering innovative solutions to social problems. "Dual-teachers" of China

Social Entrepreneur Foundation (YouChange) is a typical example. We will talk about that in detail later in the case analysis.

Second, the Internet helps generate massive publicity of non-public foundations and their projects. In other words, Internet, mobile Internet in particular, serves as a clever method for non-public foundations based on public promotion. They have attracted wider attention from the public online in a more efficient way.

Last, the Internet closes the ties between grant-making foundations and Grassroots Support Organizations (GSO), making it more efficient for the former to offer skill training and guidance for the latter. To be more specific, foundations help GSOs make constant progress by remote guidance via video calls and livestreaming. At the same time, some non-public foundations participate in building digital platforms to improve IT application for GSOs. Furthermore, some of these foundations that are dedicated to boosting the philanthropic sector, have also invested huge resources in building digital infrastructure in hope of improving the IT application in the philanthropic sector.

The *Charity Law*, since implementation, has freed space for public fundraising. Charitable agencies could apply for transition to public fundraising organizations after two years of commitment. In doing so, the boundary between traditional public fundraising organizations and non-public ones becomes blurred. The market position of the non-public ones is also under threat from other charitable agencies. As a response, non-public foundations must make clear of their development direction and area and take advantage of the Internet. After all, the Internet could help non-public foundations act more efficiently in project execution, public promotion, and grant making.

Of course, non-public foundations do not play a significant role in the first rounds of Internet philanthropy because they are not directly engaged in public fundraising. To them, the Internet is not yet as what it is to public foundations, a structural game changer. Nonetheless, the Internet affects the philanthropic sector in an all-round way. Non-public foundations, as a major part of the sector, surely fall within the range of such influence. As a result, they would produce more structural changes to propel non-public foundations to explore more, apply more state-of-the-art technologies, and improve IT application in the near future. In addition, they will play a more critical part in and have an even closer tie with Internet philanthropy.

Case Study: YouChange Foundation

Creating a New Internet Philanthropic Model

China Social Entrepreneur Foundation (YouChange) is a national non-profit civil society organization approved by the State Council and registered in the Ministry of Civil Affairs of the People's Republic of China. It is the first innovative non-public foundation in China initiated by reputed entrepreneurs from mainland China, Hong Kong, and Taiwan. YouChange strives to promote a just, harmonious society by cultivating talents with leadership in neo-philanthropy and building up online platforms. Additionally, YouChange is committed to forging a neo-philanthropy value chain and upholding social innovation in cross-border cooperation via R&D and experimentation. The goal is to facilitate a more just, efficient, and sustainable social eco-system.

YouChange was founded in 2007 by Wang Ping (Chairman in office) and four entrepreneurs, Huang Zhixiang, Chen Dongsheng, Deng Zhonghan, and Liu Jiren from mainland of China, Hong Kong, and Taiwan. In the past decade, YouChange has been dedicated to poverty alleviation and education. Moreover, YouChange has, via venture philanthropy and social value investment, funded 16 innovative platform projects such as China Alliance of Social Value Investment (Shenzhen), YouChange Volunteer Station, YouChange Eagle Plan, YouChange Evergreen Volunteer Teaching Program, and Lurenjia as well as 171 GSOs in 22 cities and provinces of China.[18]

YouChange also serves as a practitioner and explorer of Internet philanthropy. In 2014, YouChange initiated a people-oriented, multi-dimensional evaluation system on social values—Aim, Approach, and Action—as well as its online version. Together, YouChange initiated and

[18] Source: YouChange. 友成企业家扶贫基金会. (2018-09-30). http://www.youcheng.org/about.php.

reaped fruits from its innovative philanthropic projects featuring IT application and high execution efficiency. A representative among these projects was the Dual-teacher Classroom, a drastically improved one that has received the most attention from broader society.

YouChange devotes itself to education in poverty-stricken areas. Imbalance in educational resources, a problem that still haunts the educational sector, is even more serious between developed and underdeveloped regions. A major reason lies in the rather mediocre faculties in poverty-stricken areas. Therefore, YouChange strives to enhance qualities of professional teachers and promote even distribution of education resources.

Around 2011, Tang Min, Vice Chairman of YouChange, organized retired teachers from cities to go to poverty-stricken areas for voluntary education. These experienced teachers not only imparted knowledge to students but also trained local teachers. As a result, local teachers learned teaching skills even faster than expected.

After some time, however, Tang Min found this project not sustainable as a fundamental solution to educational problems. "Our supporting education would be nothing more than a drop in the ocean, huge needs for rural schools were the ocean. And our teachers couldn't stay there for long", Tang Min said in an interview. How to allocate educational resources more evenly and how to provide children in poverty-stricken areas with education as sound as that in developed areas remain a challenge for Tang Min and YouChange.

Later, an outer space lesson by an astronaut of Shenzhou 10 inspired Tang Min. In June 2013, astronaut Wang Yaping prepared a lesson for children on Shenzhou 10. She presented simple pendulums, spinning tops, and a "ruby" made up of a globe of water. Tang Min, inspired by such a wonderful lesson, came up with an idea for distance teaching. In detail, he wanted to record the best lessons across China and via the Internet send lessons to schools in rural areas where children live in harsh conditions with the scarcest educational resources.

Several times Tang Min reached out to Liu Pengzhi, principal of the High School Affiliated to Renmin University of China as well as a counselor in the State Council. Principal Liu eventually agreed to share the teaching materials of the school. After discussion, they selected Math, whose textbooks are more commonly used and easier to understand, as a pilot subject. In August 2013, YouChange and the High School Affiliated

Fig. 3.7 Dual-teacher classroom system

to Renmin University of China initiated the pilot project of Dual-teacher Classroom. They posted urban educational resources on Massive Open Online Course (MOOC) and display these high-quality teaching videos to students in rural primary and secondary schools. By doing so they attempted to address the lack of high-quality teachers and educational resources in rural areas (See Fig. 3.7).

"Dual-teacher Classroom" means lessons are taught by two teachers; one from the High School Affiliated to Renmin University of China, responsible for online distance courses; the other from the pilot school, carrying out discussions among students and helping them with homework and answering questions after the distance course is over. Dual-teachers is not that complicated: YouChange records lessons delivered by teachers at the High School Affiliated to Renmin University of China every day; teachers at rural schools do some necessary editing on the videos at night and play the videos in class the next day. Teachers at rural schools are not just "playing the videos". When the teacher in the video asks a question, they would pause the clip, ask a student to answer the question, and then make some further explanations and instructions for the students.

According to a third-party assessment by Li Haizheng, professor at Central University of Finance and Economics, Dual-teachers have done a great job in elevating education quality and the rate of graduates enrolled in senior high schools. It also gives these students an opportunity to enjoy higher education and maybe be released from the frame of poverty. (*Dual-teachers*, 2016) Teachers in rural areas, at the same time, also benefit from the Dual-teacher mode because they can watch and learn from the high-quality videos to make progress in their own teaching skills.

Now, the Dual-teacher mode has been spreading to more regions such as Pengshui Miao and Tujia Autonomous County in Chongqing, Weining Yi Hui and Miao Autonomous County in Guizhou, Xianning City in Hubei, and Dongguan City in Guangdong. Via this teaching mode, we record high-quality lessons delivered by excellent local teachers and deliver these videos to the schools nearby where educational resources are needed. During this period, we also find that it is hard to carry out the program of adding IT application in faculty training due to poor access to the Internet in some poverty-stricken counties. For this reason, YouChange and aixuetang.com came up with the Rural Education Innovation Plan. We hope someday to provide teachers at rural schools with better training on IT applications and students with a more immersive Internet education experience.

Case Study: Narada Foundation

A Promoter of the Transformation and Innovation of Non-governmental Philanthropy

Profile

YouChange is both a project executor and an organization sponsor. Meanwhile, Narada Foundation remains a grant-making foundation. For many years it has been focusing on sponsoring the charity sector, yet seldom executing any specific philanthropic projects. But in fact, the Internet and online philanthropy in particular still yield an impact on non-public organizations, i.e., Narada Foundation, that are oriented by "promoting public philanthropy", offering them both opportunities and challenges in the age of the Internet.

Narada Foundation (Narada), was founded on May 11, 2007 as a national non-public foundation approved by China's Ministry of Civil Affairs. Narada was chiefly funded by Shanghai Narada Group Co., Ltd. which invested RMB 100 million as Narada's original fund.

Narada is a typical grant-making foundation. It was founded upon the mission of "promoting public philanthropy" (See Fig. 3.8): the essence of the concept shared by two of its major initiators, Zhou Qingzhi and Xu Yongguang.

The two founders had several in-depth discussions in 2006 and both agreed that China back then was still in a rapid transformation stage, one in which Chinese society would depend on sound cooperation among the primary, secondary, and tertiary sectors. Traditionally, China's primary sector, the government, had been stronger with plenty of resources; the secondary sector, since reform and opening-up was launched, had been growing rapidly; and the tertiary sector was less powerful and influential. However, problems that emerged during social transformation were hard to tackle and we would need a hand from the tertiary sector; more specifically, we need the three sectors to work together. However, the tertiary sector was so less developed than the primary and secondary sectors that it could not tackle social problems. Therefore, promoting the

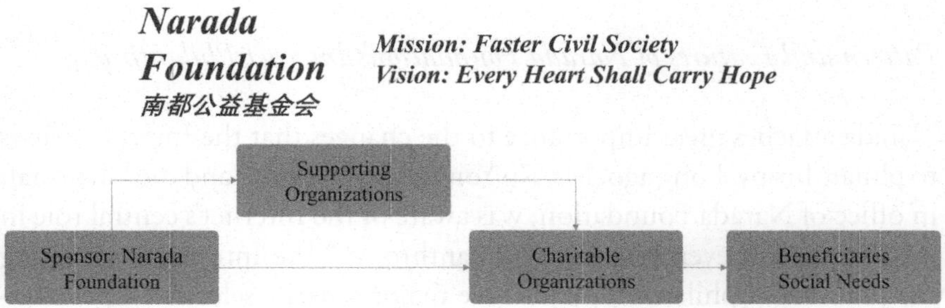

Fig. 3.8 The mission, vision, and operating ideas of Narada Foundation

development of the tertiary sector and philanthropy in civil society organizations became Narada's primary goal.

Narada has worked for public philanthropy since its establishment in 2007. With this mission, Narada carries out infrastructure construction projects to solve fundamental problems, such as lack of talent and growth drive for organizations that impede the progress of the charity sector.

To this end Narada has also conducted a series of projects: New Citizen Program invests in projects; Ginkgo Fellow Program invests in talents; Bright Way Program helps organizations become more influential; and the Effective Philanthropy Multiplier was established by a dozen leading agencies and aimed at producing excellent philanthropic products at scale. What is backing up Narada's rapid development is that they always follow the mission of promoting public philanthropy.

Narada also helps grant-making non-public foundations find who they serve. Many grant-making foundations, besides funding other agencies, have their own philanthropic projects to attend to. This is in contrast to Narada which invests more resources and time in funding other agencies and helping the entire charity sector prosper. Once the *Charity Law* was published, plenty of non-public foundations have transformed into public ones. Narada, on the other hand, held on to its market position and capitalized on its advantage in charity infrastructure construction, philanthropic organization capacity building, and industry promotion to help others. A decade after its establishment, Narada led the grant-making foundations in initiating platform projects that help the charity sector march forward. Now, Narada Foundation has made remarkable achievements in promoting public philanthropy.

Pattern and Features of Narada Foundation's Internet Philanthropy

Narada attaches great importance to the changes that the Internet brings to philanthropy. Long ago, Mr. Xu Yongguang, founder and the Chairman in office of Narada Foundation, was aware of the Internet's central role in promoting and even reforming philanthropy. "The Internet is changing the patterns of philanthropy in three major aspects: selectivity, portability, and transparency," he wrote in an article in 1991. (*The Internet*, 2016)

When mobile Internet sprang up, most of Mr. Xu's prophecies came true, which demonstrates his unquestionable foresight regarding the Internet. In the past few years when mobile Internet prevailed in the philanthropy sector, Mr. Xu advocated for online philanthropy and encouraged agencies to carry out charity events via the Internet to further improve their own management skills. (*Greet the*, 2016) Mr. Xu Yongguang, so to speak, was one of the earliest initiators and pioneers of online philanthropy.

Restrained by the functions of grant-making non-public foundations, Narada could not raise funds directly from the public. It, hence, did not participate in Internet fundraising that received maximum public support and attention. Nevertheless, Narada works to promote public philanthropy and uses Internet patterns and technologies to fund non-governmental projects and build up platforms to facilitate public philanthropy. One representative of the projects is the China Foundation Center.

China Foundation Center (CFC)

Foundations, as organizational entities, play an increasingly important role in social development. As of the beginning of October 2018, the number of foundations nationwide had reached 6877 with an average annual growth rate of over two digits. By the end of 2016, the total assets from foundations in China had amounted to RMB 138.5 billion. The annual revenue from donations and annual expenditure had respectively totaled almost RMB 50 billion, accounting for almost half of the philanthropy industry. (The China Foundation Center, n.d.)

However, contrary to the overall rapid growth of China's philanthropy, the public has raised many questions about the transparency and credibility of the industry. Philanthropy in China suffered a serious crisis of trust in 2011. It has become a top priority for the industry, in such a difficult position, to improve overall transparency and promote honesty and transparency, especially that of the top foundations. This not only helps the sustainable development of China's philanthropy but also has strategic significance for enhancing the harmony and stability of China's society.

Due to this lack of trust, China Foundation Center (CFC) came into being. CFC is a platform for information aggregation and disclosure, co-founded by 35 well-known foundations in China and officially launched on July 8, 2010. The platform looks to advance the transparency of this industry through data pooling, processing, analysis, and disclosure. Narada Foundation is one of the 35 founders. Narada and Xu Yongguang both played a critical role in the process of founding, preparing, and developing CFC.

The planning of CFC originated from a visit to the US by Xu Yongguang. His delegation visited the Foundation Center in America and conducted in-depth communication with the organization's leaders. Xu Yongguang, who has always attached great importance to improving transparency of philanthropic organizations, realized that this excellent model should be introduced to China to promote open and transparent development of China's philanthropy.

Having returned from the US, Xu Yongguang, as well as Narada Foundation, began planning to organize a Chinese Foundation Center with the American one as a reference. To realize this goal, he served as the leader of the preparatory group and visited a number of foundations in support of the preparations for CFC.

With the unremitting effort of Xu Yongguang, Narada Foundation, and their partners, eventually 35 well-known Chinese foundations initiated and co-founded CFC (See Fig. 3.9). Xu Yongguang served as the first chairman of the organization and Narada Foundation became the leading initiator as well as one of the most important sponsors. In the

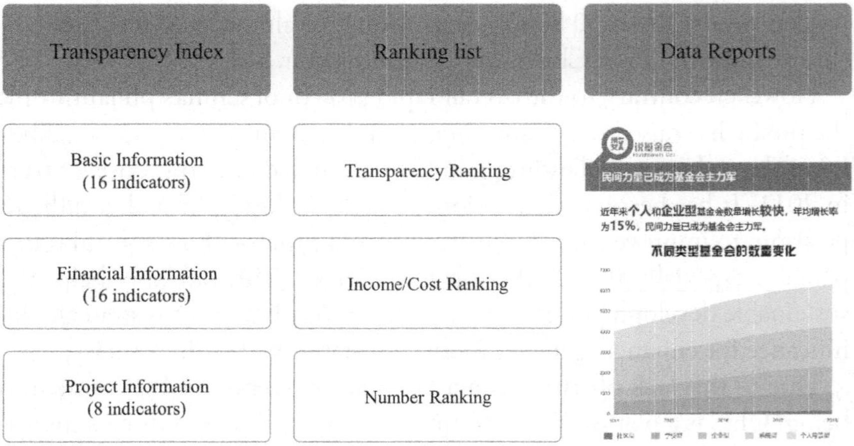

Fig. 3.9 China Foundation Center

following years, Narada Foundation has continued to sponsor CFC with a total amount exceeding RMB 4 million.[19]

Since its establishment, the CFC has made extensive efforts in data collection, processing, and aggregation for the sake of creating an information disclosure platform for the foundation industry, providing required capacity building services for the development of the industry, facilitating the formation of a self-discipline mechanism and the enhancement of credibility, and cultivating a benign, transparent culture of philanthropy. It also discloses the collected and aggregated information online, making it convenient for the public and donors in inquiry and supervision, and simultaneously encouraging further disclosure of information about foundations themselves. Meanwhile, a series of products have been launched, among which the most acclaimed and attention-grabbing by the industry is CFC's China Foundation Transparency Index (FTI).

FTI is a foundation transparency evaluation system that contains parameters such as index, weight, information disclosure channel, and integrity and presents a ranking list as a result. CFC and the Research Center for Anti-Corruption and Governance of Tsinghua University developed the index, which ensures the index design is scientific and precise.

The rankings are updated monthly in accordance with the latest foundation transparency scores. The higher the ranking the more transparent a foundation is. FTI has two major uses: On the one hand, foundations can locate their levels of transparency compared with other foundations across the country via FTI; on the other, the transparency index can also serve as a reference for potential donations so as to promote healthy competition and transparency and credibility in philanthropy.

FTI is the most influential indicator for organization transparency in China, which makes the index undoubtedly a benchmark in the charitable industry. Moreover, CFC's clever use of the Internet has helped the extensive spread of FTI.

The launch of FTI by CFC coincided with the rapid growth of the Internet and the mobile Internet and the Internet has doubtlessly played a significant role in developing and spreading the use of FTI. Before the

[19] Source: Narada Foundation.

Internet, compilations of similar indexes were often collected in libraries. Users were overwhelmed with information and it was also demanding to explore the value of such indexes.

The emergence of the Internet has changed this situation greatly. CFC releases all the relevant information on its website once the index is published, allowing users to make queries about foundations' transparency statuses regardless of time and geographic location. Meanwhile, CFC also makes a detailed display of the index, so that users can not only learn foundations' total scores in terms of the index but also the scores of individual indicators and the raw data required for the calculation, which adds to the depth and breadth of the index's application. Displaying and spreading the index online, FTI has remarkably expanded its reach and reduced the difficulty of its application and has consequently been applied in a wider range.

Since its launch, FTI has won wide recognition by the industry, academia, and the public. It has been used by many government departments, large institutions, and donors as an important reference for cooperation with foundations. The introduction of the index has also encouraged active disclosure of information by some foundations that previously rarely did so. Furthermore, CFC has compiled multiple analysis reports of foundations' categorical data based on FTI and relevant data, analyzing the growing trend of foundations in China in real time. Some of these reports have been translated into English and become an important channel for people overseas to understand the development of Chinese foundations. CFC's data analysis reports are also gradually becoming one of the main sources from which the industry, academia, the public, and the media can learn about a foundation's growth.

The position of Narada Foundation as a grant-making private foundation reduces this organization's association with classical Internet philanthropy. At the moment when online fundraising is in full swing, Narada Foundation still focuses its energy and resources on fostering a non-governmental charitable force featuring offline events, working quietly in a field far away from the hustle and bustle, not boasting about their achievements or their fame. But being away from the hustle and bustle does not mean staying detached from reality. In the era of mobile Internet, all philanthropic models are more or less affected by the Internet. In particular, the advantages of the Internet in dissemination can help organizations better achieve their goals and improve their efficiency.

With further development of digital technology and further integration of the Internet and philanthropy, there is likely to be more innovative "Technology Plus Philanthropy" models on the way to achieve these goals.

Private Non-enterprise Units and Social Groups: The Backbone of Philanthropic Ecosystem Facing the Tide of Internet Philanthropy

Foundations, social groups (SGs) and private non-enterprise units (PNEUs) are the three major types of philanthropy-related civil society organizations. Among them, PNEUs and SGs are the major forces to carry out philanthropic activities. According to the *Blue Book of Philanthropy: Annual Report on China's Philanthropy Development (2018)*, the number of PNEUs and SGs reached nearly 800,000 by the end of 2017.

The introduction of the Internet has brought unprecedented opportunities to PNEUs and SGs. Traditionally, due to the lack of public fundraising rights, PNEUs and SGs relied heavily on cooperation with public foundations. Before the loosening of public fundraising rights, the few public foundations had their respective philanthropic fields to work in and there was no effective competition among these foundations. In this case, unless there was a stable source of donations to specific targets, most other philanthropic organizations and PNEUs relied significantly on large foundations or unstable funding from enterprises.

The popularization and penetration of the Internet has reversed this situation and given a strong impetus to the growth of PNEUs and SGs.

The most direct change to philanthropy by the Internet lies in a remarkable increase in publicly raised funds, which together with relaxed restrictions on public fundraising rights, has directly led to the rise of joint fundraising. Through joint fundraising with public foundations, the financial conditions of many PNEUs and SGs have greatly improved. Although they still cannot compete with public organizations in their fundraising capacity, such a change in models brought by the Internet has lifted a lot of PNEUs and SGs out of the struggle against bankruptcy and brought them more resources and broader space for growth.

According to the *Blue Book of Philanthropy*: *Annual Report on China's Philanthropy Development (2018)*, by the end of 2017 there had been 373,194 registered SGs and 421,567 PNEUs around China. Both had an ever-rising compound annual growth rate of over two digits. The rapid growth of SGs and PNEUs is highly consistent with that of the Internet.

In respect to Internet philanthropy there has been a similar trend in the growth of non-public fundraising civil society organizations. The data from Tencent Charity demonstrate that since 2015, philanthropic civil society organizations without public fundraising qualifications have gradually become the core force in the ecosystem of philanthropy, dominant in the number of projects initiated, the amount of funds raised, and the number of participants. The numbers of projects initiated by public foundations and individuals are also increasing remarkably but their growth rates are obviously less than that of non-public fundraising civil society organizations. Figure 3.10 shows the growth rates of projects by different types of initiators in recent years. From 2014 to 2016 the total number of public foundations that had initiated projects had jumped by

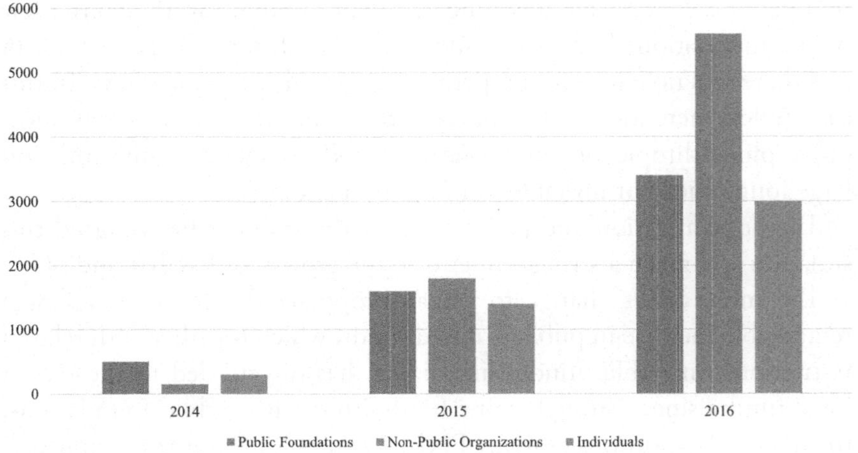

Fig. 3.10 Number of project initiators by type on Tencent Charity

200%, while the figure of civil society organizations participating in joint fundraising had soared by 23 times, from 112 to 2730. (Tencent Foundation., & Tencent Research Institute, 2017) Clearly, in the Internet era, PNEUs and SGs have obtained incredible growth and a rising position in the ecosystem of internet philanthropy, thus playing an important role in fundraising, execution, user communication, etc.

In the Internet era, the PNEUs and SGs not only grow in number, they have also significantly improved their capacity in various aspects and relative position in the ecosystem of philanthropy. Because of such improvement in fundraising capacity and relative position, PNEUs and SGs are playing an increasingly important role in philanthropic activities. In joint fundraising projects, PNEUs and SGs assume more and more responsibility for fundraising, user contact, and notification. Concurrently, as more large public foundations turn to project funding, the difficult task of implementing falls mainly on PNEUs and SGs. In recent years, a series of influential philanthropic projects, such as Kids Gallery and Dandelion Village Library Program, have been organized and carried out by civil society organizations that did not have public fundraising rights. Furthermore, as the information disclosure in philanthropy is gradually focused on project transparency, PNEUs and SGs also participate more in undertaking the information disclosure of philanthropic projects.

With the spread of the Internet PNEUs and SGs have gained significantly more recognition. In the late twentieth century and the early twenty-first century there was generally a low recognition of philanthropic organizations and projects and relatively less knowledge of philanthropy. Those that were widely recognized were often national projects launched by large public foundations with government ties, such as Project Hope and Spring Buds Project. These large-scale philanthropic projects have indeed given play to the kindness of the Chinese people for a long time and have greatly facilitated the development of philanthropy. However, due to the lack of communication channels, the media coverage was mostly confined to these large-scale projects. Thus, it was hard for grassroots organizations and their work to be known by the public.

In the age of the Internet, especially mobile Internet, the rapid increase of communication channels and drastic expansion of media coverage make it possible for PNEUs and SGs to be known and understood. The rise of new media like Sina Weibo, WeChat official accounts, and information flow has enabled PNEUs and SGs, which lack media resources, to have their own ways of dissemination; and the flourishing of We-Media has given them more opportunities to be known by the public. In addition, in recent years the growing public philanthropic awareness and frequent high-profile charitable events have boosted the visibility of philanthropic organizations. Some outstanding PNEUs and SGs, particularly World of Art Brut Culture (WABC) and NGO 2.0, have enhanced their public recognition and accumulated reputation via the Internet, growing into well-known, recognized organizations.

In general, the conditions of PNEUs and SGs, especially their fundraising capacity, have been significantly improved in the Internet era. These organizations have gained higher recognition by the public as well. Nevertheless, weakness still exists in the capacity building of these organizations. On the one hand, the overall information technology application of PNEUs and SGs still cannot meet their demands. For many institutions, the internal IT application is relatively lagging behind leading to the inability of storing information generated in organization management and project execution, low efficiency, and insufficient feedback.

As large organizations further integrate IT with their operation, the gap of IT application capacity between PNEUs and SGs on the one hand and large organizations on the other is likely to be widened. At the same time, while some grassroots organizations do not pay enough attention to project feedback, the ones that attach importance to it are often restricted by IT application capacity or costs. With poor timeliness and lack of details as a result such project feedback fails to meet the public demand for information disclosure.

On the other hand, the implementation capacity of PNEUs and SGs needs further enhancement. In the days when public fundraising was not yet the mainstream approach to raising funds, the biggest obstacle to the growth of PNEUs and SGs was their fundraising capacity. Before the introduction of the Internet, a large number of organizations were oriented toward raising funds but overlooked the capacity of implementing projects.

After the popularization of Internet philanthropy, PNEUs and SGs have seen substantial improvement in their fundraising capacity. For many organizations, limited fundraising capacity is not the only obstacle on their development road; their weakness in execution has been exposed. A PNEU or SO that is not able to carry out its projects smoothly or turn the raised money into philanthropic achievements is destined to lose recognition from donors and eventually fail to survive the competition, even if this organization has a strong fundraising capacity on charity platforms right now. Therefore, since fundraising capacity has been significantly increased, project implementation for PNEUs and SGs is increasingly important. The inadequacy of an organization's implementation capacity has become a major constraint on the growth of many such organizations.

Meanwhile, the stratification of PNEUs and SGs has been more visible. The Internet has encouraged competition among philanthropic civil society organizations. Under the enormous pressure of fierce competition, stratification has become an almost inevitable result of differences in capabilities or resources. Some groups take advantage of online-based tools to maximize the use of valuable resources and philanthropic products provided by online platforms and public foundations. These organizations have attracted much attention and collected most of the donations through high-quality charitable projects. By contrast, PNEUs and SGs with inadequate resources or capabilities in these areas are liable to receive nothing online, only to witness the widening gap between other institutions and themselves. How to help these PNEUs and SGs cultivate their ability to use Internet-based tools and get integrated into the age of Internet philanthropy in the future is also a problem worth exploring and working on in philanthropy industry.

Case Study: Shanghai Association of Volunteers (SAV)

Profile and Development

Founded on July 27, 1997, the Shanghai Association of Volunteers (SAV) is the largest of its type in Shanghai. As a non-profit legal person set up by local volunteers on a free will basis, this social group coordinates volunteer activities throughout Shanghai and works under the management of the Office of the Shanghai Guidance Commission for Guiding Cultural and Ethical Progress.

Shanghai is an old hand at volunteer activities. Many support-oriented SGs have been born here early in the infancy of the reform. They have made great contributions to local public services by getting actively involved in local major events, through which a lot of excellent volunteers stood out.

Despite such remarkable achievements, at that time, Shanghai-based volunteer organizations were on an information island because of ineffective coordination and communication among them. In absence of efficient information exchange, no synergy or coordination was achievable among volunteer activities. Moreover, information disconnection among volunteer organizations and volunteers made it hard to put volunteer activities in order.

SAV was set up by local volunteer organizations on a free will basis as a means to coordinate volunteer activities more effectively. This action opened up a new prospect where city-wide volunteer services could be pooled and units, departments, and industries could take an active part in volunteer activities.

SAV has always been active in major events undertaken or organized by Shanghai. It took the lead in China to provide a volunteer division under the organizing committee of the 8th All China Games in October 1997, making the first appearance of volunteer services for mega events. Subsequent events, such as APEC China 2001, 2011 FINA World Championships, the fight against SARS in 2003, and earthquake relief in 2008 have all witnessed active participation of volunteers organized by SAV. In particular, for the Expo 2010, SAV mobilized 80,000 Expo Park volunteers, 100,000 urban station volunteers, and nearly 2 million urban civility volunteers to receive domestic and overseas visitors, who learned about China through these volunteers. (*Brief of*, n.d.)

SAV remains committed to fostering a social volunteer service system in ways that improve coordination among volunteer organizations and further information disclosure and sharing. With its years of efforts, by 2014 SAV has been home to more than 7000 recurrent projects divided into 20 categories that cover public services, people's demands, and many other topics and its information system has enabled information sharing. (*Brief of*, n.d.) Alongside that, in 2011 SAV began to issue the *Shanghai Volunteer Certificate* that records services in detail across organizations and regions meanwhile serving as an insurance certificate. This action provided volunteers a personal accident insurance with amount insured up to RMB 200,000 as a means to protect their rights and interests. Also, it made volunteer information connected across organizations, facilitating volunteer management and volunteer service management.

With eyes on information connection and sharing, SAV established the website Shanghai Volunteer early in 2005, and has successively launched functions of volunteer recruitment, project presentation, and volunteer project map there. Beyond that, it published volunteer activity information on Sina Weibo. In 2013, the mobile app Shanghai Volunteer was released as part of SAV's exploration in better serving volunteers. Besides, SAV registered the official account Shanghai Volunteer and went through the organization accreditation procedure on WeChat In 2017. This enabled it to serve volunteers in Shanghai via WeChat and made the association an "Internet Plus Volunteer Activity" pioneer in the mobile Internet landscape.

By 2014, SAV has been home to 1,446,593 registered volunteers, more than 7000 recurrent projects, 14,323 volunteer organizations, 76 corps under its direct control, and 83 city-level volunteer service bases. (*Brief of*, n.d.)

Internet Philanthropic Modes and Characteristics

SAV explores the concept of Internet Plus Volunteer Service mainly via its own website (http://www.volunteer.sh.cn/), "Shanghai Volunteer" app and WeChat official account "Shanghai Volunteer". As a volunteer platform that bridges volunteer organizations, volunteers, volunteer projects, enterprises, and the public, SAV has greatly improved the availability of information for volunteer services in the city. This is how the organization has explored the field of Internet Plus Volunteer Service in this era when computers and the Internet prevail (See Fig. 3.11).

Fig. 3.11 Main functions of Shanghai Volunteer website

Soon after it went into operation, the website Shanghai Volunteer launched functions of volunteer organization registration and volunteer registration. The two functions, as a means to submerge the information island, have provided a tool to summarize volunteer organization information and volunteer information and increased the efficiency of volunteer activity management. Beyond that, functions of volunteer project sharing and volunteer activity information publishing were launched to make it possible to transmit volunteer activity information across organizations. Such transmission incurs a lower cost, and allows a volunteer to find volunteer activities satisfactory to him or her in a shorter time. This facilitates upgraded partnering between volunteers and volunteer projects. Later, Shanghai Volunteer website provided a volunteer map, allowing users to find volunteer organizations nearby and learn more about them from their profiles. By doing so this website has made it easier for the people to learn about volunteer organizations and have access to volunteer services.

The wave of mobile Internet has heavily challenged websites that are traditionally presented on computers. As more and more people tend to work via mobile phones, a sharp decrease in traffic has been seen on many PC platforms. Ways to organize and manage volunteer activities also suffer. Impacted by the rise of mobile Internet, many volunteer websites are losing visitors and many functions and information provided there cannot produce expected returns. On the other hand, the rise of mobile Internet is creating exciting opportunities for the Internet Plus Volunteer Service. This is more important because mobile Internet enables a volunteer service platform to be a more efficient bridge between volunteers, volunteer organizations, and the public.

The release of the app, Shanghai Volunteer, represents an action SAV took to quickly seize opportunities created by the mobile Internet for volunteer services. By moving all the functions of the website Shanghai Volunteer to mobile terminals, the app has furthered information-based volunteer activities and improved the efficiency of volunteer activity management via the mobile Internet. As SAV perceived after the app was in operation for some time, the mobile Internet is propelling volunteer project management to be simpler and easier and leading traffic to head to top in the media pile.

In light of changes in external conditions, SAV opened the WeChat official account Shanghai Volunteer and made proper re-adjustment. Now the account is serving Shanghai-based volunteer organizations, volunteers, and the general public. Through links to the website, Shanghai Volunteer, followers of the account can use all the functions provided on that website. Also, the account has completed a range of functional upgrades.

At the activity organizer terminal of the account, management functions like attendance, timekeeping, and volunteer insurance are available to volunteer activity organizers. This means organizers no longer need third-party tools to manage volunteer activities, making volunteer activity management simpler and more efficient. At the volunteer terminal of the account, the function of nearby project query has been added on the basis of the volunteer map to tighten the association between LBS information and volunteer project information. By doing so, the account enables a volunteer to find nearby volunteer projects more easily. Furthermore, detailed user guides respectively developed for organizations, enterprises, and volunteers allow all types of volunteer activity participants to freely use the account and experience how information-based services make things easier.

From the PC-based website to mobile app, then to WeChat official account, SAV remains committed to exploring and practicing Internet Plus Volunteer Activity. It is SAV's unremitting efforts that have digitalized volunteer activities to a large extent: Information sharing is underway among most organizations and volunteers, volunteer project information is communicated effectively, and the efficiency of volunteer activity management continues improving.

Yet, instead of a smooth sailing, SAV's exploration for Internet Plus Volunteer Activity has met a few difficulties and been redirected. Furthermore, attributed to such exploration, volunteer activities organized in Shanghai have made breakthroughs in information connection and improved overall. It is noteworthy that such exploration is not solitary. Many other volunteer organizations have opened official websites and WeChat official accounts alike to digitalize volunteer activity management. As volunteer services increasingly prosper in China, more innovative forms of Internet Plus Volunteer Activity will emerge in the future and technological forces represented by the Internet will help volunteer services scale new heights in the country.

Case Study: China Small Animal Protection Association

Profile and Development

As a national class one professional social group, the China Small Animal Protection Association (CSAPA) was set up with the approval of the Ministry of Agriculture in September 1992 and registered with and awarded independent legal personality by the Ministry of Civil Affairs in December 1992. Advocating life cherishment, cultural and ethnical progress, and humanism the association is committed to protecting animals' rights to life and non-ill-treatment and to improving small animals' livelihood and food quality. Also, CSAPA seeks to fight against behaviors and ideas of ill-treatment or doing harm to animals.

This Beijing-based organization consists of multiple divisions and offices, e.g. organization, publicity, research, liaison, development, relief and detention, health care. Over 20-plus years, it has made great efforts to organize animal protection activities, publicize animal protection information, and rescue sick or injured animals. This is how it has grown into an influential social group in China's animal protection field.

In its infancy, CSAPA focused on policy advocacy and public awareness strengthening. That is, in light of limited objective conditions, it looked to work on animal protection by influencing policy makers and the public at that time. In 1993 CSAPA took part in legislating and practicing dog management in Beijing. During the discussion organized by Beijing in 1995 on draft regulations for dog-keeping limits, the association convened multiple symposiums to offer suggestions on a range of issues like dog keeping levies, prohibited breeds, and allowance time for walking the dog. Subsequently in November 1996, the first anniversary of the entry-into-force of the dog-keeping limit regulations witnessed a symposium convened by CSAPA and attended by personages of all circles, where the participants exchanged views on scientific management and other issues. The symposium attracted the attention of legislators and enforcers. In February 1996 the association held an international academic seminar on rabies to quell people's fear of the disease. At the seminar domestic and overseas experts gave special speeches by invitation, imparting rabies related knowledge to the public.

On October 4, 1996, China Agricultural University saw the first World Animal Day commemoration week successfully organized by CSAPA. In the event that aimed to deepen the public understanding of animals and awaken people's awareness of animal protection, the association realized the limitedness of its publicity and policy advocacy. Unfortunately, CSAPA discovered while policy advocacy and publicity were long-term, they could not immediately alleviate existing problems. Still, many animals lived in hardship or even at death's door. Enlightened by these facts, CSAPA resolved to continue its input to long-term mechanisms while making more direct investment in animal protection.

With this resolve, the association began to take a path of building its own animal protection centers. In 1998 CSAPA brought together different sectors' contributions to set up the first base, Love Education Base, for rescuing and taking in small animals, thus providing a shelter for homeless small animals. With the help of its members, it expanded and reconstructed the base in ways that improved animals' livelihood in 1999.

Alongside the development of the base, CSAPA has built small animal epidemic prevention, health care, and treatment centers in different regions as a means to supply animal health care services to common people. The base and these centers enable the association to grow and thrive.

What animal protectors all over China offered over its years of development has empowered CSAPA to develop and grow stronger. Members of the association include many caring people from Shanghai, Tianjin, Jiangsu, Zhejiang, Guangdong, Guangxi, Sichuan, Anhui, and Heilongjiang in addition to those from Beijing. These members take part in animal protection in different ways as part of their support for the development of the association.

Internet Philanthropic Modes and Characteristics

Respect and care for life are natural characteristics in humans and are an inexorable demand for philanthropy. However, what we respect and care for should not be limited to humankind. Human nature and philanthropy also entail care for small animals. As people's awareness of animal protection grows, recent years have seen improvement in all respects of animal protection. Overall, animal protection is a low-threshold philanthropic activity everyone can take part in and contribute to. The Internet has improved public engagement in the past few years in ways that benefit undertakings more accessible for the public. Accordingly, animal protection has attracted more attention in the wave of online charity.

CSAPA takes the initiative to cooperate with large philanthropic platforms on which it raises funds and feeds project information back online. In this way CSAPA can seize opportunities arising from Internet-improved public engagement. The cooperation with multiple large philanthropic platforms has made the projects from CSAPA known to larger communities and provided them access to more funds from the public, thereby underpinning the long-term development of CSAPA. Among others, synergy with Taobao Charity and Tencent Charity has set a typical model of such cooperation.

CSAPA opened an official philanthropy shop at Taobao many years ago as a means to raise funds for vaccinations, sterilization operations, medical care, and food supply at its animal protection bases. Funds raised from the shop only represent part of what CSAPA has benefited from the cooperation with Taobao Charity. In fact, sales activities and WOM on this platform enable more caring netizens to understand more clearly what CSAPA is and how the association is committed to animal protection, helping the long-term development of CSAPA.

Similarly, the cooperation with Tencent Charity has raised more funds and attracted higher attention from the public for the association. CSAPA has launched three animal protection-themed philanthropic projects: Caring for Life Together, Free Sterilization of Homeless Dogs and Cats, and Small and Medium-sized Pets Care program, as part of its work with the China Social Assistance Foundation to solicit contributions. By October 2018 these three projects have raised RMB 698,000 via Tencent Charity in total with donations from over 21,000 contributors.[20]

Undoubtedly, through the cooperation with Tencent Charity, CSAPA has become more capable of fundraising from the public and receives bonuses from improved public engagement. Moreover, the access control and transparency mechanisms developed for the 99 Charity Day event have motivated the association to strengthen its capabilities and increase the digital coverage and transparency.

CSAPA is a typical social group. Despite obstacles arising in the process of development, its managers and members hold fast to their original intentions and remain committed to contributing to animal protection. Their down-to-earth work has made the association reputable in animal protection circles. As to how it makes use of the Internet, CSAPA raises funds in cooperation with and via online philanthropic platforms and seeks to explore new modes for Internet philanthropy. Thanks to this, both its fundraising and reputation have improved significantly. Without doubt, Internet philanthropic modes have furthered the growth of CSAPA.

However, different from large public foundations, many SGs, including some state-level associations like CSAPA, are in shortage of funds and other resources. They also land in an awkward situation online. Limited by funds and traffic, associations must raise funds and organize other

[20] Source: China Social Assistance Foundation.

charity activities via third-party products and platforms. Though information sharing has been improved after the adoption of Internet technologies, it alone may not be able to fuel persistent development of associations. Increased funds and attention arising from Internet philanthropy are not necessarily satisfactory to projects and long-term development of associations.

In fact, this problem prevails among medium-sized and small civil society organizations. To smaller PNEUs and SGs, to solicit contributions together with public foundations online is a rare opportunity. After all, those that profit from online philanthropic platforms are a minority among the total of 800,000 civil society organizations in China. Even if a small civil society organization gets access to a philanthropic platform, it can only attract about 20% attention, while the remaining 80% is paid to the platform. Such small civil society organization can hardly be noticed or funded by the public.

Online philanthropy has indeed boosted public engagement and awareness and improved resource availability. However, it has intensified competition because funds, traffic, and other resources are limited after all. Consequently, differentiation has worsened among civil society organizations. How can we alleviate the differentiation of resource availability among organizations? How can we allocate resources in alignment with capabilities of organizations? These are what emerging Internet philanthropic modes ask us to discuss in depth.

Case Study: NGO 2.0

Profile and Development

Co-founded by the MIT New Media Action Lab and USTC Knowledge Management Institute in May 2009, NGO 2.0 is a new-type civil society organization committed to offering industrial support and enabling grassroots philanthropic organizations to perform better in regards to publicity. Its major operator is Shenzhen Tu'ou Philanthropic Development Center, a private non-enterprise unit founded in Shenzhen in 2014.

Guided by the "new media, new philanthropy" philosophy, NGO 2.0 remains committed to enabling charitable organizations to perform better in publicity using online tools and social media. As an advocator for Internet Plus Philanthropy, it has conducted a series of investigations on capabilities of Chinese philanthropic organizations to work on and make publicity via the Internet, on the basis of its Philanthropy Map, New Media Workshop, and NGO 2.0 tool box. Also, NGO 2.0 seeks to give instructions on crowd-funding through the Philanthropy Maker Group and serve philanthropic practitioners and civil society organizations by providing online open courses.

The original intention of NGO 2.0 has derived from the founder Professor Wang Jin's critical views on defects of globalization, relating to Creative Commons licenses (CC licenses).

CC licenses were released by Creative Commons in 2011 in the US. Unlike traditional means of copyright protection, CC licenses are intended to protect and allow reuse of user generated content in a more flexible way. Internet elites are empowered to publish CC licenses that contain core enabling clauses selected from six forms so that their works can be freely duplicated or modified under given conditions provided some rights are reserved. This is how CC licenses help protect and use intellectual property in the mobile Internet landscape.

When CC licenses entered China in 2006, the chairman of the CC China Mainland International Advisory Committee, Wang Jin, helped popularize them across the country. Nonetheless, while CC licenses represent an innovative way to tackle defects of traditional copyright protection, many problems have arisen during their promotion worldwide. As Wang considered from the perspective of globalization, CC licenses reflect what developed countries need but have a blind spot and less attention is paid to what developing countries and their disadvantaged groups need and how to close digital gaps. In other words, to developing countries, CC licenses are a pseudo-proposition.

"Web 2.0 must be a communication tool usable for the poor. China's philanthropy 2.0 project aims to reveal the blind spot of CC. We would rather introduce the cornerstone of Web 2.0 culture than introduce CC licenses. To countries like China and India, NGOs are the only entry point for introducing Web 2.0. NGOs and CC licenses share the philosophy of resource and knowledge sharing," Wang said. What NGOs do to help empowerment and development of disadvantaged groups coincides with how Wang critically looks at the Internet, CC licenses, and globalization. She hopes to help NGOs in less developed areas understand what Web 2.0 is all about and get access to more knowledge and resources in the context of globalization, thereby closing digital gaps.

In 2009 while Sina Weibo had not yet risen and the term social media had not come into view, as a starting point for criticizing academic elitism, Wang took the initiative to introduce thoughts and practices of Web 2.0 into Chinese philanthropic circles as part of her move from the American academic elite circle to Chinese grassroots class. Besides forward-looking ideas arising in the new media communication and technology, how digital gaps impact society is also a concern of the founder. The woman who is aware of educators' role in knowledge dissemination set up in person a team of teachers to help Chinese philanthropic circles widely use social media. In addition, offline training that she organized throughout the country has enabled charitable organizations to be more skillful in the use of new media.

July 2009 saw the first session of new media training conducted for charitable organizations by NGO 2.0. Such training has been ongoing since then, representing an unshakable core product of NGO 2.0. Beyond that, NGO 2.0 released the Philanthropy Map in 2010 and the Philanthropy Maker Group in 2013 as it is stepping from new media service into the broader industrial support sector. In 2014 its legal person, Shenzhen Tu'ou Philanthropic Development Center ("Tu'ou" is a transliteration to the English pronunciation of "2.0"), was incorporated in Shenzhen. The incorporation marked that NGO 2.0 formally became a private non-enterprise unit and entered a new phase of operation and development.

By August 2018, NGO 2.0 had organized new media training for more than 1000 charity organizations across the country, enabling them to perform better in communication via new media. (*NGO2.0*, n.d.) Multiple online investigations have been conducted as a means to assess how Chinese charitable organizations work on and publicize via the Internet and improve their capabilities in this regard. By doing so NGO 2.0 has provided reference data for philanthropy and suggestions on communication for those investigated. Furthermore, the organization has developed multiple digital infrastructures that underlie sound development of philanthropy, such as the NGO 2.0 tool box and the Philanthropy Map. By taking these actions NGO 2.0 has achieved the goal of improving the digital communication capability profile of charitable organizations and made meaningful contributions to the growth of Chinese grassroots charitable organizations.

Internet Philanthropic Modes and Characteristics

As an advocator for Internet Plus Philanthropy, NGO 2.0, guided by the "new media, new philanthropy" philosophy, remains committed to helping civil society organizations grow using online tools and social media. All the philanthropic projects under NGO 2.0 aim to meet civil society organizations' demands for communication, resources and technologies, as they are oriented to the goal of making civil society organizations stronger.

NGO 2.0 is a product of innovation itself. The philanthropic projects under NGO 2.0 are all innovative and mostly in close association with the Internet, represented by the New Media Workshop, commitment to higher quality and awareness of online fundraising projects, NGO 2.0 tool box, Philanthropy Map, and Philanthropy Maker Group.

As the flagship project of NGO 2.0, the New Media Workshop works to help Chinese civil society organizations publicize themselves and access resources more easily using online tools. To a certain limited extent its training service has enabled more than 1000 civil society organizations to perform much better in communication, fundraising, and use of tools. Alongside that, NGO 2.0 is planning a trainer fostering project that aims to offer Web 2.0 trainers for philanthropy. This is how NGO 2.0 extended the operation of the New Media Workshop.

Commitment to higher quality and awareness of online fundraising projects, being a focus of NGO 2.0, started early in the organization. NGO 2.0 began to supply crowd-funding services to the Self-service Fundraising Platform very early. At this platform, it offers one-to-one project optimizing and communication positioning services to organizations that need crowd-funding services. In the project optimizing service, NGO 2.0 provides crowd-funding projects a service package comprising goal setting, plan adjustment, budget breakdown, partnering with public foundations, and review before release. In the communication positioning service, it assists charity organizations with audience classification, copyrighting, and packaging (text, image, and video) in alignment with strategies of new media communication. Also, suggestions are given on how to select communication channels, operate communities, and serve donors.

NGO 2.0 has enlisted multiple philanthropic projects for the Self-service Fundraising Platform and provided them a service package comprising copywriting, plan adjustment, budget breakdown, partnering with public foundations, and review before release. Such process service has helped Tencent subsequently release the Partner Program. According to related data in 2015, NGO 2.0 optimized 101 projects of 80 civil society organizations and these projects raised funds of RMB 4,463,735.1 from 111,437 donors via Tencent Charity; in 2017, 179 projects of 142 civil society organizations were optimized and raised funds of as much as RMB 11,391,124.03 from 183,480 donors.[21]

The NGO 2.0 Tool Box and Philanthropy Map are tools developed by NGO 2.0. NGO 2.0 Tool Box summarizes, classifies, and displays digital philanthropic tools and cases prevailing in the market. By doing so, it recommends easy-to-use online tools to civil society organizations, edits philanthropic application scenarios of online tools, and bridges tool suppliers and users. This pool comprising 281 tools and 28 cases has lowered the information cost incurred by civil society organizations in use of new tools and made it easier to select the right tools. (*NGO charity*, n.d.) This is why it is well recognized by civil society organizations (See Fig. 3.12).

The Philanthropy Map, a crowd-sourced civil society organization database, is one of the philanthropic infrastructures NGO 2.0 has worked hard to develop. Now it pools basic information and data of nearly 25,000 civil society organizations in 31 provinces, autonomous region, and municipalities of China (See Fig. 3.13). (*Non-profit*, n.d.) A civil society charitable organization can log in the Philanthropy Map and

[21] Source: NGO 2.0 Written Interview.

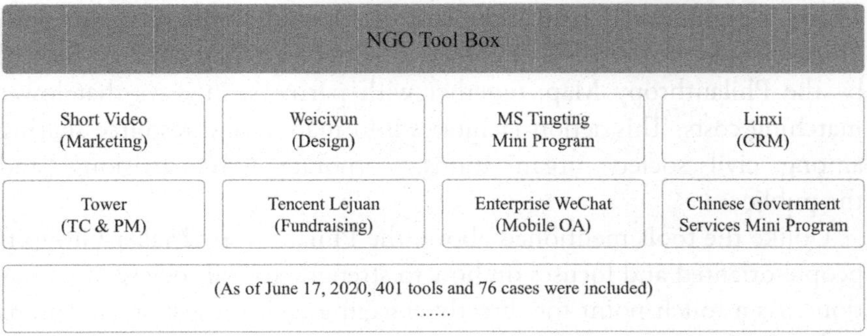

Fig. 3.12 NGO 2.0 tool box

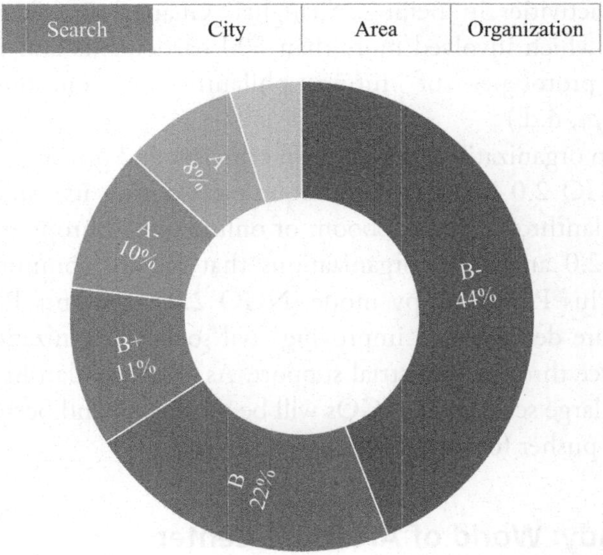

Fig. 3.13 Philanthropy map

enter information about its philanthropic projects. In turn, the database matches civil society organizations and philanthropic projects with LBS location information and displays them on the map. This is how it helps common people, enterprises, and philanthropic practitioners find nearby civil society organizations and philanthropic projects. Alongside such efforts to significantly reduce the cost of matching philanthropists with philanthropic projects, NGO 2.0 has developed a rating database backed by the Philanthropy Map, together with partners, in ways that lower matching costs. This action facilitates information and resource sharing among civil society organizations, corporate CSR divisions, and the public.

Unlike the tools mentioned above, the Philanthropy Maker Group is people-oriented and focuses on how to strengthen civil society organizations. As a touch point for directly engaging civil society organizations and technical teams, it deepens civil society organizations' problem awareness in the forms of a technology salon and hackathon and works to promote ideas and practices of collaborative design. So far, it has organized 17 activities in Beijing, Shanghai, Guangzhou, Shenzhen, and Chengdu, which involved more than 600 participants and ended with multiple prototypes of future philanthropic solutions. (*Maker Philanthropy*, n.d.)

Being an organization derived from criticism and prospering for innovation, NGO 2.0 has blazed a unique path during its exploration for online philanthropy. Today's boom of online philanthropy is attributed to NGO 2.0 and other organizations that remain committed to the Internet Plus Philanthropy mode. NGO 2.0 represents PNEUs and SGs that are dedicated to improving civil society organizations' online performance through industrial support. As online philanthropy propagates on a large scale, such NGOs will be promising and become a more important pusher for progress of philanthropy.

Case Study: World of Art Brute Center

Profile and Development

In the Prologue, we introduced a popular charitable project, Kids Gallery. The project was a milestone event in Chinese philanthropic history as it set several records within one day. While its popularity was partly attributed to accidental factors, its success was a certainty. One of the facilitators for its popularity and its years of commitment to philanthropy and

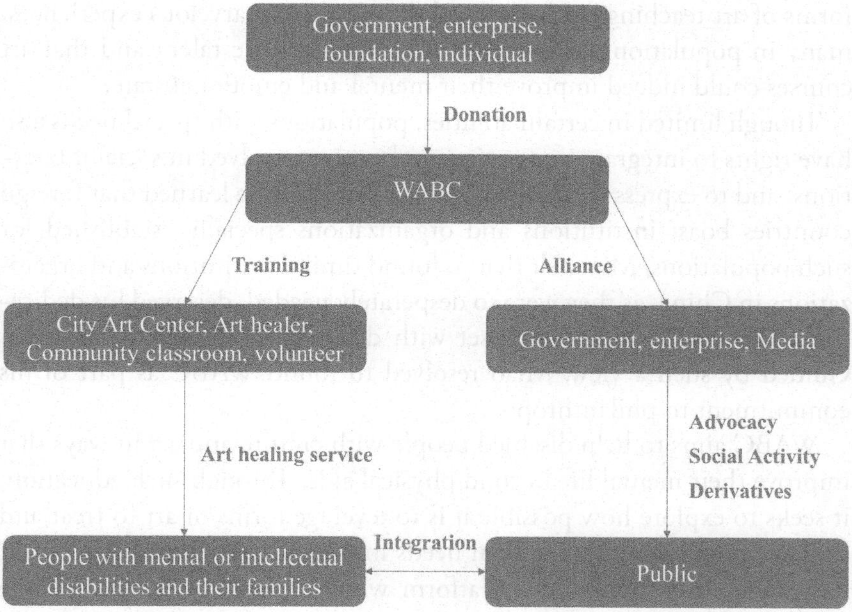

Fig. 3.14 WABC studio

appreciation of creativity and online communication was the initiator and organizer of World of Art Brute Center (WABC).[22] Years of persistence and accumulation and its focus on creativity and Internet communication, are all factors that contribute to the success of Kids Gallery (See Fig. 3.14).

As a private non-enterprise unit registered in Shanghai, WABC is committed to offering art healing courses to the mentally impaired (collectively, "populations with special needs") for free. What WABC looks like today is credited to the sustained hard work of its founder Miao Shiming.

In touch with populations with special needs, Miao was shocked by their living conditions. Inspired by his observations, Miao attempted to make friends with them and go deep into their hearts through various

[22] WABC consists of two parts. One is the Urban Art Center, a private non-enterprise unit engaged in project execution. The other is the WABC Charity Foundation, a non-public fundraising foundation. As the non-enterprise unit part of WABC is more well known by the public, we discuss the case here in this section.

forms of art teaching. As he learned during these marvelous experiences, many in populations with special needs had artistic talent and that art courses could indeed improve their mental and emotional state.

Though limited in certain abilities, populations with special needs also have rights to integrate into society, to become involved in social interactions, and to express themselves artistically. When he learned that foreign countries boast institutions and organizations specially established for such populations, Miao felt that to found similar institutions and organizations in China, as they were so desperately needed, deserved his dedication. The undertaking was beset with difficulties but full of meaning. Guided by such a view, Miao resolved to found WABC as part of his commitment to philanthropy.

WABC aims to help disabled people with culture and art in ways that improve their mental life beyond physical aids. Through such education, it seeks to explore how possible it is to leverage forms of art to treat and heal the population with special needs in present day China. For this, it has made efforts to build a platform where mentally impaired people with artistic talent can present themselves and interact with society. By doing so, WABC expects to reduce prejudice to such populations and enable them to integrate into society over time.

Success of Kids Gallery and WABC's Exploration in Internet Philanthropy

Years of hard work have made Miao Shiming and WABC an influencer in philanthropic circles. Beyond that, the Kids Gallery project, which boomed in WeChat Moments in 2017, has led the organization into public view. Kids Gallery was a major project designed by WABC as a participator of Tencent's 99 Charity Day event. Thanks to "flooding the screen" on H5 pages, August 29 alone saw funds of RMB 15 million raised by the project from more than 5.8 million donors, which made the project a genuine philanthropic fad in the mobile Internet landscape. Such a success has thrust WABC into the spotlight and made it a focus of the public. By way of Kids Gallery many people have become very familiar with the charitable organization and what it is doing for the mentally impaired. However, some of them argue that the success of Kids Gallery was largely a product of luck resulted from synergy of a range of accidental factors.

True, the boom in WeChat Moments and high public attention were partly attributed to accidental factors. Even Miao had never expected Kids Gallery to be such a successful philanthropic fad. In July 2017 Tencent identified Kids Gallery as one of the seven key projects of the 2017 99 Charity Day event. Afterwards, Miao did much to publicize the project. Besides H5 pages which later went viral in WeChat Moments, he designed online pushes via WeChat official accounts, creative videos, offline art exhibitions, and subway advertising. Miao hoped to publicize the project extensively by leveraging synergy of multiple channels so as to achieve the preset fundraising goal. At that time, H5 played a minor part in the channel design and its effects were not highly expected (See Fig. 3.15).

Fig. 3.15 Works exhibited on kids gallery

Yet, it is the minor component that helped to bring about the success of Kids Gallery. Ironically, H5 was released by the supplier in advance without informing Miao or WABC. The fact that the fundraising goal of RMB 15 million was achieved within one day after the release, disqualified the project from following parts of the 99 Charity Day event. As a result, predetermined online and offline publicity and fundraising activities made no sense. In light of this, Miao gave WABC's staff a holiday on September 9.

Contingency entails certainty. During nearly eight years of commitment, WABC has gained much experience in publicity and in the roll-out of charity projects.

Philanthropy, art, and the Internet are the three keywords Miao has defined for WABC. They respectively stand for original intention, form, and as a booster. The organization still puts a priority on creativity. As the best creativity amplifier, the Internet can give full play to a good idea or design.

Miao upholds "perception plus action equals to change" and identifies perception as the basis of action. He has been aware for a long while that the Internet, a super power of communication, has an even more important function: changing public perceptions. To the services for the mentally impaired provided by WABC, public perceptions and understanding sometimes matter more than donations. While donations from the public can extend the service scope and improve project effectiveness, populations with special needs cannot integrate into society without public perceptions and understanding. Guided by these considerations, WABC has been engaged in online advocacy and publicity for years in ways that not only raise more funds for its projects but also raise public perceptions for populations with special needs.

Early in 2013 Miao and WABC set off to explore how to combine online philanthropic publicity with online and offline charitable activities. In the same year, WABC organized an offline activity that featured a Rubber Duck in Shanghai and was chased after both on and off line. The year 2013 also witnessed a WeChat official account opened by WABC, which ranked among the first charitable organizations to appear on the WeChat official account platform. WABC has also maintained an official Weibo account for a long time, so to speak, it is an old hand at new media communication.

As mentioned above, after Kids Gallery was identified as a key charitable project for 99 Charity Day in 2017, WABC made great efforts to publicize the project. The H5 design, the art exhibition, and the trailer and the subway advertising all demonstrated how the WABC team accurately understood online communication and perceptions of the public. Experience and preparatory work reacted with the early release of H5 by the supplier. The reaction enabled Kids Gallery to set the record of raising RMB 15 million in funds within one day. The surprising achievement represented a direct indicator of the huge force of online charity and stood for the direct return on WABC's expertise in online communication, marking that philanthropy is silently changing. In the mobile Internet landscape, a non-public organization can also create a philanthropic fad and grow and thrive as long as it designs quality projects and makes good use of the Internet.

Fundraising is just the first step of a philanthropic project. The most important task is to spend funds efficiently to maximize benefits, especially for campaigns like Kids Gallery which fall under public scrutiny. After raising funds, Miao Shiming and his team shifted focus to implementation of the project. As of 2017, the WABC had implemented several self-operating studios and service centers in 10 cities across China dedicated to providing special services for the needy. As of 2018 its reach has doubled,[23] meaning that beneficiaries, about 3000 children in each city, have doubled. Moreover,[24] the WABC plans to offer art treatment to even more people with special needs in second- and third-tier cities in 2019.

The success of the Kids Gallery stems from a fortuitous combination of circumstances. Indeed, it owes a great deal to years of ongoing contributions made by the WABC and the organization's keen perception of Internet philanthropy, especially in terms of communication. Although luck has undoubtedly played a part in the viral popularity of this H5 campaign, there are other reasons, with opportunity favoring those who prepare.

[23] Source: WABC.

[24] Source: WABC.

Unfortunately, as we have observed, irresponsible remarks on Kids Gallery are spreading in the wake of its success. Though Tencent Charity, Ai You Foundation, and WABC have denied them, these rumors may shatter public confidence. This means that WABC has to set stricter demands on itself while rolling out the project.

The Internet has alleviated the fundraising plight for medium-sized and small organizations and improved public perceptions in many respects. In response, a charity organization needs to upgrade its project roll-out and feedback mechanisms, which otherwise may produce a bucket effect. This is how the Internet makes a difference and enables public fundraising to pressure charitable organizations to be stronger. Only becoming stronger allows a charitable organization to increase its reputation and public awareness and keep moving towards philanthropy of higher good. Stronger charitable organizations make greater contributions to public services.

References

Adream Foundation (上海真爱梦想公益基金会). (2018). *2017真爱梦想年报*. Adream. https://www.adream.org/wp-content/uploads/2018/04/2018-04-25-06380883.pdf

Ai You Charity Foundation (爱佑慈善基金会). (n.d.). *区块链实时图*. Ayfoundation. Retrieved September 30, 2018, from http://blockchain.ayfoundation.org/indexPC.html

Azure Map: The Energy of "Internet + Environmental Protection" (蔚蓝地图:"互联网+环保"的能量). (2016, November 14). Sina. Retrieved September 30, 2018, from http://gongyi.sina.com.cn/gyzx/2016-11-14/doc-ifxxsmif2988443.shtml

Brief of Shanghai Association of Volunteers (上海市志愿者协会概况). (n.d.). Volunteer. Retrieved September 30, 2018, from http://www.volunteer.sh.cn/website/Documents/Sov_Introduce.aspx

China Foundation for Poverty Alleviation (中国扶贫基金会). (2019). *中国扶贫基金会2018年度报告*. CFPA. http://www.cfpa.org.cn/information/institution.aspx?typeid=1

China Foundation for Poverty Alleviation joins hands with Youzan to explore Internet + Poverty Alleviation (中国扶贫基金会携手有赞, 探索"互联网+扶贫"). (2017, March 01). Chinaz. Retrieved September 30, 2018, from https://www.chinaz.com/news/2017/0301/665729.shtml

Dual-teachers teaching project evaluation report conference held in Beijing (双师教学项目评估报告发布会在京召开). (2016, December 12). Gog. Retrieved September 30, 2018, from http://gongyi.gog.cn/system/2016/12/12/015278408.shtml

Greet the new changes that the Internet brings to public welfare (迎接互联网给公益带来的新变化). (2016, May 23). Gmw. Retrieved September 30, 2018, from http://news.gmw.cn/2016-05/23/content_20211197.htm

Lan, F. (2012, December 03). *上海真爱梦想公益基金会被评最透明NGO*. Caixin. http://china.caixin.com/2012-12-03/100467638.html

Maker Philanthropy Group (公益创客团). (n.d.). NGO20. Retrieved September 30, 2018, from http://www.ngo20.org/5

NGO charity toolbox (NGO公益工具箱). (n.d.). NGO20. Retrieved September 30, 2018, from http://tools.ngo20.org/

NGO2.0 New Media Workshop.NGO2.0 (新媒体工作坊). (n.d.). NGO20. Retrieved September 30, 2018, from http://www.ngo20.org/3

Non-profit organization rating map (公益组织评级地图). (n.d.). NGO20. Retrieved September 30, 2018, from http://www.ngo20map.com/

Pan, J. X. (2017, March 07). *把爱当作一场认真的修行*. Sohu. http://www.sohu.com/a/128098450_181327

SEE Foundation (阿拉善SEE基金会). (2015, October 26). *"创绿家"项目*. SEE. Retrieved September 30, 2018, from http://www.see.org.cn/Foundation/Article/Detail/25

SEE Foundation (阿拉善SEE基金会). (2018). *阿拉善SEE基金会2017年度年报*. SEE. http://www.see.org.cn/Foundation/Article/Detail/1566

SGS issued the first domestic NGO benchmark audit certificate to Adream Foundation (SGS为真爱梦想公益基金会颁发国内首张NGO基准审核证书). (2017, December 7). SGS. Retrieved September 30, 2018, https://www.sgsgroup.com.cn/zh-cn/news/2017/12/sgs-issued-the-first-ngobenchmarking-certificate-in-china

Tencent Foundation., & Tencent Research Institute. 腾讯基金会., & 腾讯研究院. (2017, June 12). *腾讯公益十周年报告*. Weixin. https://mp.weixin.qq.com/s/cBd8YgDgFbQ3sp-mN5KAUQ

Tencent QQ, Tencent Charity break the Guinness World Recor (腾讯QQ、腾讯公益打破吉尼斯世界纪录). (2015, January 30). Chinaz. Retrieved September 30, 2018, from https://www.chinaz.com/news/2015/0129/381526.shtml

The China Foundation Center (基金会中心网). (n.d.). *基金会数据总览*. Foundationcenter. Retrieved October 07, 2018, from http://data.foundationcenter.org.cn/data/sjzl.shtml

The difference between social organizations and private non-enterprise units (社会团体与民办非企业单位的区别). (n.d.). Lawtime. Retrieved September 30, 2018, from http://www.lawtime.cn/ask/question_2065158.html

The Internet joins hands with public welfare to start public charity 3.0 (互联网携手公益 开启大众慈善3.0). (2016, April 30). K618. Retrieved September 30, 2018, from http://news.k618.cn/dj/201604/t20160430_7260679.html

Yan, B. (2015, July 22). *做公益没钱?资助型基金会在这里!*. Foundation center. http://news.foundationcenter.org.cn/html/2015-07/92131.html

Yang, T. (Ed.). (2017). *中国慈善发展报告(2017)*. 社会科学文献出版社.

4
The Activated Businesses and Public

Section 1 Philanthropy Integrated Into Business Operation

Businesses play a critical role in the Internet philanthropic ecosystem. In developed Western countries businesses and entrepreneurs have long been contributors to philanthropic undertakings, believing that the success of a business is the result of public support. Specifically, when post-WWII reflections on capitalism prevailed in mainstream western society, businesses were not considered purely profit-driven tools but as entities which could shoulder heavier social responsibilities. In the west, most well-established companies have independent corporate social responsibility (CSR) departments and successful entrepreneurs are often committed to charitable work and are willing to actively contribute to the resolution of social problems.

In the twenty-first century, along with improvements in public living standards, modern charitable and philanthropic ideas are gaining ground in the public sphere. Meanwhile, as more transnational companies enter the Chinese market, which continues to develop and open to the outside world, businesses have brought advanced CSR concepts to China and

Y. Chen, *Internet Philanthropy in China*,
https://doi.org/10.1007/978-981-16-2566-4_4

enhanced CSR awareness of Chinese businesses and entrepreneurs. Nowadays more large and medium-sized Chinese companies are setting up CSR departments with the aim of benefiting society. Some successful entrepreneurs such as Jack Ma, Niu Gensheng, and Charles Chen Yidan established personal or family foundations to support the development of the philanthropic sector.

CSR is a catch-all term. Businesses may foster social responsibility in multiple regards but the most crucial avenue is for businesses to directly engage in philanthropic activities.

Prior to the Internet's birth, businesses were faced with two major weaknesses in direct involvement with philanthropy. First, businesses could only contribute through direct donations and the promotion of philanthropic projects due to lack of experience with philanthropy and were not as adept as philanthropic organizations in campaign implementation, from the design to facilitation, thus did not achieve maximized outcomes relative to their efforts. Consequently, many businesses relied on cooperation with dedicated philanthropic organizations. Unfortunately, this pattern placed businesses at a disadvantage as they tended to lose control over the projects.

The second factor weakening business contribution to philanthropic projects was the fact that they could only obtain limited engagement and recognition from the public. It was quite common for employees to remain unaware of the philanthropic contributions their employers had made, not to mention the general public. If businesses could not increase brand recognition or an employee's sense of identity, they also clearly lacked the momentum to sustain philanthropic engagement.

Since Internet philanthropy has been fostered in the Internet era, these two weaknesses have been mitigated.

For one thing, Internet philanthropy is characterized first and foremost by diversified methods of engagement. Leveraging the Internet, people from philanthropic organizations can unleash creativity and imagination and invent numerous new engagement patterns for businesses to consider. For instance, in the Step Donation campaign launched by Tencent Charity, a business may finance one or more step donation projects. When users donate the digital record of their steps, businesses contribute funds to certain philanthropic projects. In this way the philanthropic engagement of businesses is connected with daily user activities. Without the Internet, such new forms of engagement featuring public data and step-based funding from businesses would be impossible.

Furthermore, Internet-based philanthropic projects are serving as platforms to connect businesses with other donors, volunteers, and even their own employees and significantly helping to improve the recognition of these businesses as philanthropic contributors. As business contributions become increasingly recognized by increasing numbers of Internet users, companies foster a stronger sense of engagement.

Take the Step Donation campaign again as an example. Every time a user donates steps, contributions from corresponding businesses are displayed on the user interface, improving brand recognition. Apart from contributions based on external step donations, a business can also launch internal step donation contests among departments or teams, thus increasing employee morale and awareness of said business's philanthropic endeavors and strengthening its cohesion. As a result, recognition of the business as a philanthropic contributor in both internal and external communities develops.

As Internet philanthropy gains steam and public acceptance, many businesses that have long been devoted to philanthropic undertakings are actively taking advantage of the Internet's resources. Based on strengths and characteristics of businesses, companies continue to create an increasing number of original and customized engagement patterns, greatly expanding the scope of Internet philanthropy. Meanwhile, the Internet has magnified the reach of philanthropic endeavors, making them more well-known among employees and the public. They also benefit from a heightened sense of employee identity for those taking part in such endeavors and receive societal recognition. Businesses taking the lead in online philanthropy include SF Express and Yum China.

Case Study: SF Express

Promotes Its Corporate Social Philosophy of "Philanthropy by All" Through the Internet

SF's Engagement in Philanthropy

Committed to giving back to society, SF Express has been an active participant in philanthropic activities since its establishment. In an effort to provide fair education opportunities for more children in rural areas, SF Express has supported child development efforts and saved the lives of many children suffering from congenital heart diseases.

SF Express started engaging in the philanthropic undertakings in the 1990s. Lacking an online model, it contributed to philanthropy and education aid projects such as Project HOPE and Fengxia Middle School Project to directly help children in rural areas suffering from congenital diseases. In 2008 when a catastrophic earthquake hit Wenchuan, Sichuan Province, SF Express launched a voluntary donation project on the Internet, raising a total of RMB 10 million. (*Charity*, n.d.)

In 2009, SF Express set up the Guangdong SF Foundation, which is operated by a specialized agency with dedicated funding via the Guangdong Bureau of Civil Affairs. In 2012 the Shenzhen Mingde Holdings Development Co., Ltd. (the parent company of SF Express) and its six subsidiaries established the SF Foundation through the Ministry of Civil Affairs (MCA) to ramp up philanthropic undertakings, marking a new stage of SF Express's innovation in philanthropic activities. As of September 2018, the Foundation had funded 14,263 senior high school students with low economic means, 989 college students, and 420 teachers in extreme poverty. It donated 10 SF Lotus Primary Schools, 19,376 sets of desks and chairs, and helped 6637 sick children. In recent years, SF has participated in the earthquake relief of Ya'an, Qixian, and Ludian and has contributed RMB 27 million worth of disaster relief supplies. It also supported earthquake relief in Yushu and the Nepal earthquake by sending special planes.

In addition to participating in philanthropic activities itself, SF Express endeavors to raise public awareness of philanthropy and to promote the engagement of more people. By designing activities which are accessible to volunteers, SF Express seeks to make each project sustainable, drawing more people to philanthropic undertakings.

According to internal records, the number of volunteers in SF Express who have participated in philanthropic projects totals 20,812, discounting those not recorded. In 2017, 17 volunteer organizations affiliated with SF Express launched a total of 104 philanthropic activities, participated in by nearly 80,000 people.[1] The philosophy of philanthropy has been rooted in the company's corporate culture and has become a vital part of its everyday operation.

The relentless efforts of the executives of SF Express and the SF Foundation have allowed the company to continuously support philanthropic undertakings. Using its advantages, the company has made remarkable achievements in philanthropy by launching a series of projects such as the SF Lotus Education Aid and SF Children Medical Assistance. Most importantly, SF made a significant breakthrough by proposing the philosophy of "Philanthropy by All", promoting the engagement of businesses in this monumental undertaking.

An Introduction of SF Foundation

The SF Foundation is a charitable organization initiated by Shenzhen Mingde Holding Development Co., Ltd., the former SF Express (Group) Co., Ltd., and was established in 2012 with the approval of China's Ministry of Civil Affairs. The Foundation is mainly committed to financing the development of education in remote and impoverished areas and providing medical assistance to children amongst others. Concurrently, relying on the advantages of SF Logistics, it actively engages in disaster relief and tries to explore other philanthropic fields such as poverty alleviation and ecological protection.

[1] Source: SF Foundation.

The SF Foundation advocates "Philanthropy by All" and looks to introduce volunteers to the implementation of philanthropic projects by lowering the threshold; and encouraging and guiding volunteers to participate in and make philanthropy known to others, that is, promoting philanthropy as a way of life. Based on this, internet philanthropy quickly became the preferred means.

The Main Model of SF Foundation's Internet Philanthropic Endeavor

Before the mobile Internet began to thrive, SF Express realized that the Internet could breed better philanthropic products and engage more people in philanthropic activities. Consequently, the SF Foundation began to actively explore the possibilities of Internet philanthropy.

The SF Foundation carries out its internet philanthropy in cooperation with third-party platforms to give full play to the advantages and characteristics of corporations. The application of internet philanthropy can reduce the threshold for participation, spread easily among people, transmit the slogan of the Foundation, and enable more employees to engage. In this way, philanthropy as a habit is promoted.

Internet Based Charity Hiking Program

Tencent Charity Hiker is a natural fit for SF Express. SF Express is a labor-intensive enterprise, employing a large number of employees who travel around delivering letters and parcels every day. During work employees accumulate a lot of steps, which are then converted into donations to philanthropic projects. By donating steps, deliverymen develop a stronger sense of value, which can enhance their self-confidence and self-esteem. Furthermore, group donation activities launched by Tencent Charity Hiker engage more employees in step donations as teams, stimulating a sense of camaraderie among team members. Step donation is not merely a philanthropic campaign but also helps to shape corporate culture and deepen employee understanding of company ethos.

Synergy between SF Express's main business and Tencent Charity Hiker model allowed SF Foundation to become one of Tencent Charity Hiker's earliest partners. The SF Foundation launches "step" donations according to their own projects within the Hike for Charity. Philanthropic competitions in SF have been promoted to encourage employees to actively participate in "step" donation and make the concept of "Philanthropy by All" known.

After exploring its options in 2015 and 2016, the SF Foundation and Tencent Charity jointly launched the SF Sunshine Hiker in 2017, a variant of Tencent Charity Hiker for employees. SF Express formed five major leagues with more than 80 teams participating in various online and offline activities over the period of half a year. Half of SF's employees, or about 200,000 people, were expected to participate in the project. However, the project's popularity exceeded expectations, as many employees also invited friends, relatives, and customers to join.

The SF Sunshine Hiker campaign involved more participants than the total number of company employees. According to statistics, a total of 2.81 million people participated in the SF Sunshine Hiker campaign within just six months.[2] In 2018 SF Express continued to actively promote the Action for Good campaign launched by Tencent Charity, starting a craze for "walking to give" within the company. As of April 17, 2019, the SF Foundation has teamed up with 170 million philanthropy hikers to donate nearly RMB 180 million, ranking the first among all companies and corporate foundations.[3]

Distributing SF Giving Mails to Promote the Idea of "Philanthropy for All"

SF Love Mails are another important form of internet philanthropic activity that the SF Foundation can use to promote the concept of "Philanthropy by All". On the 99 Charity Day in September 2016, SF Express worked with Tencent Charity to send 9.99 million pieces of SF

[2] Source: SF Foundation.

[3] Source: Tencent Charity.

Giving Mails, passing on kind regards via the postal service. (*Together with*, n.d.) On the 99 Charity Day in 2017, since September 1, SF Express distributed 20 million "giving opportunities" in Beijing, Tianjin, Shanghai, Shenzhen, Hangzhou, Changzhou, and many other cities in the form of 4.5 million pieces of SF mail and 15.5 million SF bags containing "giving secrets". (*Public welfare*, 2017)

On the cover of the giving mail there is an image with the slogan "Philanthropy at Your Fingertips, Love Will Be Everywhere". Those who received them were granted the opportunity to scan a QR code at the top right of the image and follow a process to make donations. In just ten seconds, donations would be sent to underprivileged girls with excellent character and academic performance who were living in remote, mountainous areas. The business model and philanthropic efforts of the giving mail campaign encouraged more people to participate in philanthropic activities and enhanced public awareness of philanthropy.

Meanwhile, on 99 Charity Day, SF Express also actively matched users' donations for philanthropic projects such as One Desk for Each, Education Support in Rural Areas to Build a Beautiful China, and Sports Gift Packs for Village Schools. According to statistics, on 99 Charity Day in 2017, SF Express successfully supported seven philanthropic projects, involving nearly 3 million people and raising a total of RMB 25 million.[4]

Compared with other platforms and charitable organizations, SF Express has simple Internet philanthropic models but adheres to an approach combining core resources and corporate strategies, maximizing company roles in the undertaking of philanthropic activities, and using the Internet to fully mobilize its employees to join in. Although Internet-related philanthropic projects only account for a small percentage of the SF Foundation's annual philanthropic expenditure, the exposure and reach these projects provide is invaluable. As a representative of labor-based enterprises, SF Express has blazed a trail to unite people through Internet philanthropy.

[4] Source: Tencent Charity.

Case Study: Yum China

One Yuan Donation Program Connects Online and Offline Philanthropy to Make Donation Much Easier

Yum China, the parent company of KFC and Pizza Hut, is a long-established catering corporation with a globally recognized reputation. It has been actively engaged in philanthropy after entering the Chinese market and also in making contributions to society through social responsibility programs.

Early in 2008, Yum China co-sponsored a nationwide fund-raising campaign with the slogan "Donate One Yuan, Give Benevolence, Offer Nutrition" with the China Foundation for Poverty Alleviation. The program encouraged everyone to donate one yuan for a one-year nutrition program going to students in poor mountainous regions. It provided an extra meal for students every day, including a bottle of milk (200ml), a vacuum-sealed marinated egg, and donated kitchen equipment including stoves, rice steaming carts, sterilizers, freezers, kitchen work tables, and ventilators. The program also included tutorials on nutrition.

When the program was launched, Yum China spent almost six months upgrading the company's financial and cashier systems and setting up a special button for the One Yuan Donation program. When customers made a donation at a restaurant, a cashier just needed to press the One Yuan Donation button and the system automatically added one yuan to the overall amount to ensure that donated money was separated from the company's turnover. By doing so, cash registers could record each donation made in each restaurant during the One Yuan Donation event, then use the powerful financial system to quickly and accurately count the money and then transfer it to the China Foundation for Poverty Alleviation.

Ten years after the One Yuan Donation program was launched, a total of RMB 170 million has been raised and more than 110 million people have participated in the program. At the close of 2017, the program has provided more than 37.4 million nutritious meals to 547,000 primary school students in 60 counties of 34 cities in 10 provinces including Sichuan, Yunnan, Guizhou, Hubei, Guangxi, Hunan, Fujian, Hebei, Heilongjiang, and Xinjiang. It has also provided 860 schools in impoverished mountainous regions with kitchen equipment including electric stoves, rice steaming carts, sterilizers, kitchen work tables, and ventilators.[5]

The program has mobilized substantial offline efforts and successfully promoted the concept of "Philanthropy by All" prior to the ubiquity of the mobile Internet. With the popularization of mobile devices and the rise of online philanthropic platforms, the program now enjoys renewed momentum. During the 99 Charity Day in 2015, Tencent worked with KFC and the China Foundation for Poverty Alleviation to launch the One Yuan Donation program on its philanthropic platform, inviting KFC customers to donate one yuan to the program. When customers walked into KFC stores, they found display boards both inside and outside restaurant locations. They could then make donations by scanning a QR code and entering the donation page on the Tencent Charity platform.

The launch of the One Yuan Donation program online marked the dawn of a connection between online and offline philanthropic activities. Previously, customers made offline donations in physical stores. Since 2015, such donations can be made online. As a result, customers understand more about charity programs before donating and can follow programs more closely via WeChat push notifications from Tencent Charity's official account. Prior to this innovation, donations were untraceable once made. Now money raised online goes directly to the bank account of the China Foundation for Poverty Alleviation rather than being collected in Yum China affiliated stores and transferred through its account, in turn speeding up capital turnover and reducing costs for stores.

The combination of offline fund-raising and online donation not only helps to reduce costs for stores and philanthropic organizations but also helps people to better understand philanthropic programs, therefore encouraging more people to participate. After several years of trial and error, the overall amount of funds raised through the One Yuan Donation program both online and offline has seen record highs.

---

[5] Source: China Foundation for Poverty Alleviation.

Both SF Express and Yum China are companies utilizing manpower in traditional industries. Although these two companies are famous innovators in their respective fields and committed pioneers of philanthropy, the models they have adopted are still largely based on offline activities and their specific advantages. The Internet has brought high-quality projects, effective communication tools, and explosive creativity to traditional corporate philanthropic models, helping to solve problems and achieve real results. Unfortunately, the Internet, which mainly acts as a catalyst and booster, only has a relatively moderate impact on the traditional model.

In modern times, emerging Internet companies have mushroomed in the market. These companies are founded on inclusive and philanthropic ideals and have quickly embraced the infinite potential of Internet Plus Philanthropy thinking. They carry out philanthropic activities via Internet-based innovation and are redefining the concept of corporate philanthropy. Because of their Internet backgrounds, these companies have embarked on a radically different path of corporate philanthropy from traditional counterparts, while also constantly broadening their scope and pushing the boundaries of philanthropy. Among these emerging Internet companies is Kuaishou, a video-centric communications application. Its philanthropic department is also adopting new methods as well as adding a brand-new connotation to corporate philanthropy in the era of the mobile Internet.

Case Study: Kuaishou

Kuaishou's Emphasis on Inclusive Philanthropy and Its Attempt with Short Videos

Kuaishou Initiative: A Brief Introduction of Kuaishou's Corporate Social Responsibility (CSR) Department

The initial idea to engage in philanthropy came from Kuaishouюs idealistic founder and management team. Su Hua, CEO and co-founder of Kuaishou, graduated from Tsinghua University, one of the most prestigious universities in China. Despite achieving such heights, he comes from a humble background, being raised in the countryside and possessing firsthand knowledge about the lives of impoverished people in rural regions. When creating and developing his company, he and other co-founders looked forward to making contributions to society through the Kuaishou app and so assisting people living in poor regions.

As Su Hua said, “One of the most important values in Kuaishou is inclusiveness. There is no superior or inferior way of life and everyone is worthy of being recorded and remembered. I care more about long-term value instead of instant gains and losses”. (Li, 2018) This business philosophy distinguishes Kuaishou from its competitors in terms of corporate logic. Kuaishou always insists on inclusiveness in product design and traffic distribution and provides no preferential treatments to the top streamers. Kuaishou hopes to connect more individuals unreachable in the past through short videos, help them to see the world through the app and make their voices heard by others.

As the company grew in strength with its short video products increasing in popularity, Su Hua and other senior managers decided to set up a CSR department to pool the company’s resources and invest more intensively in charity efforts.

After deciding to set up an independent department for philanthropy, the company conducted a survey online to investigate current philanthropic products and their connection with the industry. After nearly 10 months of surveys, the company’s CSR department, Kuaishou Initiative, was formally established on June 17, 2017. The new department is responsible for organizing and coordinating most of the company’s philanthropic efforts, marking the beginning of a more professional stage of the company’s philanthropic undertakings.

Since its establishment, Kuaishou Initiative has participated in a number of philanthropic activities such as disaster relief and reconstruction after a devastating mudslide hit Maoxian County, Sichuan Province. It also worked with organizations including the China Foundation for Poverty Alleviation, China Youth Development Foundation, and One Foundation to launch promotional campaigns. As of August 2018, Kuaishou Initiative has nine full-time employees,[6] the number of which

[6] Data source: Kuaishou Corporate Social Responsibility Department.

tops among other such companies and far exceeds the industry average. This shows Kuaishou's determination and dedication to philanthropy.

The Main Models and Characteristics of Kuaishou's Online Philanthropy

Kuaishou's philanthropic activities consist of three main strategies: Happy Growth, Happy Village, and Happy Partners, which are all related to Kuaishou's core business model and are based on its core resources and advantages of live broadcasts and short video products. These strategies are all Internet-based and innovative in nature.

The Happy Growth strategy focuses on the healthy development and protection of juveniles. As we know, many young Internet users lack self-control and are more likely to be addicted to the Internet or affected by inaccurate information than adults. While it is impossible for Kuaishou to completely control either the content on its live broadcast and short video platform or the behavior of its teenage users, it can guide young people to use the Internet rationally and let the Internet play a positive role in their growth, which is therefore an important task facing Kuaishou.

Kuaishou has made several attempts in this field. First, it strives to educate young people. Kuaishou has worked with the China Youth Development Foundation and several leading content creators to launch a series of educational activities concerning Internet use by young people, encouraging them to follow advice and develop awareness of how using the Internet incorrectly can negatively impact their lives. Second, Kuaishou establishes a strict system to protect the young and introduces a parental control model. In this mode, when minors use the Kuaishou App, they can only stream suitable content. They can neither start a live broadcast nor charge, recharge, or withdraw cash. At the same time, in order to prevent minors with lack of self-control from becoming addicted to live broadcast video, Kuaishou also adds an "antiaddiction" notification. When minors "continuously" use Kuaishou for 60 minutes straight, a prompt box will pop up to prevent overuse. Kuaishou also internally launches an automatic identification mechanism for minors and it will repeatedly confirm and verify when minors carry out live broadcasts and give rewards. Thirdly, Kuaishou works with the Academy of Social Sciences and other relevant institutions to establish a grading system for videos. This helps to solve the root cause of Internet overindulgence by young people.

The Happy Village strategy focused on rural vitalization rural areas and targeted poverty alleviation. The aim was to take advantage of short videos and traffic distribution to help users in poverty-stricken areas find long-term ways to shatter the shackles of poverty and live better off. This strategy also helps to promote sound governance in the countryside.

As the saying goes, "give a man a fish and you feed him for a day; teach a man to fish and you feed him for a lifetime". For poor people, the root cause of poverty lies in a lack of sustainable ways to enrich themselves. What Kuaishou hopes to do is to use its advantages to find new sources of income for poor people and eradicate poverty.

Happy Village strategy is comprised of three main methods. First, it sets role models. Kuaishou uses live broadcasts and short videos to find individuals experienced in local business operations or those who have successfully escaped poverty in the past. They receive training before shouldering the responsibility of acting as role models and sharing their successful experiences through the Kuaishou app with audiences from neighboring impoverished regions. With support from Kuaishou, those role models could gain more exposures and play a more important role in poverty alleviation in the neighboring areas.

The second is "high-quality products from the countryside". Many "high-quality rural products" from villages, large and small, scattered across the vast land of China, are often unknown to the outside because of the lack of communication. For example, many high-quality ingredients and hand-crafted products are difficult to sell and represent a source of income for farmers. High-quality products from the countryside are agricultural products that themselves can alleviate poverty or directly boost employment and income for the poor farmers who produce them. Users sell their products through live broadcasts and short videos. With their influence over internet fans and understanding and enthusiasm for their hometown products, they introduce reliable home-made agricultural products, attracting more attention. Kuaishou also uses its own influence and brand advantages to provide a variety of displays and introductions to featured agricultural products. On Kuaishou, these products become more known by more people, have access to larger markets, and help the people in poor areas to increase their incomes and wealth.

In addition to promoting high-quality local products, Kuaishou also cooperates with traditional philanthropic organizations and uses its corporate strengths to help implement poverty alleviation programs. Kuaishou has established a long-term partnership with the China Foundation for Poverty Alleviation. In early 2018, it became one of the strategic partners of Good and Fresh, an e-commerce poverty eradication program launched by the China Foundation for Poverty Alleviation. Kuaishou is responsible for implementing the Good and Fresh program in poor regions and many Kuaishou users there have already used the platform to become rich.

The last component of the Happy Village is the protection of intangible cultural heritages and cultural tourism. Live broadcasts, short videos, and cultural tourism are naturally related. Live broadcasts and short videos outdo text and pictures when it comes to giving tourists an idea of what it feels like to actually visit a place. There are many beautiful sceneries and a vast and precious intangible cultural heritage in rural areas. There are also many users who are constantly publishing content related to folk customs, festivals, traditional crafts, etc. and have made their hometowns famous through short videos and live broadcasts, bringing more attention to the cultures and intangible cultural heritage of their hometowns. Some cities even have new city name signs. Kuaishou, seeing the integration of rural cultural tourism with its own business and core competencies, hopes to promote the development of the cultural tourism industry with the help of the platform's ecosystem.

Happy Partners focuses on leveraging the strong community and core resources of Kuaishou, uniting professional philanthropic organizations and conducting public advocacy activities based on its unique community. During important philanthropic festivals, Kuaishou also explores the use of innovative short videos to transmit the concept of philanthropy to charitable organizations and prioritize high-quality philanthropic topics so that philanthropy can have wider access to people. For example, on the World Sleep Day celebrated on March 21, 2018, Kuaishou, together with Wakey-Wakey China Next, launched the "Sleep with Me" activity. Its aim was to invite Kuaishou users to release videos showing a variety of sleeping positions, call on awareness to the narcolepsy, and debunk myths surrounding it. On May 12, 2018 the National Disaster Prevention and Mitigation Day and the 10th Anniversary of the Wenchuan Earthquake, Kuaishou and the One Foundation launched a short video competition under the theme of #Learn About Self-help Devices# to inspire people to make shift self-help devices with ordinary objects in life, both online and offline, and remind the public to pay attention to safety, develop awareness of disaster prevention and mitigation, master skills of self-help, and calling for help.

Another key component of the Happy Partners strategy is promotion based on magical memes. It is a new app function combining image recognition, image synthesis, and AR technology allowing users to choose different memes to change the way videos are presented. It is quite popular with users and also provides an important addition to other forms of philanthropy.

During the 99 Charity Day in 2018, Kuaishou launched a magical meme aiming to draw attention to people with visual impairments. After users selected a meme, a filter was added on videos and photos, displaying a visually impaired effect on the screen. This gave users an opportunity to experience the world of visually impaired people and understand more about what life without sight was like. This was a rare philanthropic experience for Kuaishou users.

In April 2018, Kuaishou joined the Action for Good program launched by Tencent Charity and designed a magical meme as part of the program. During the Action for Good campaign, if users selected the magical meme and held up their hand to show a "6" in front of the camera, little penguins appeared on and ran across the screen. Kuaishou promoted the Action for Good in this way and let more people know that they could contribute to charity by walking. This encouraged users to donate their steps in exchange for money that was given to various philanthropic projects.

In addition to these three main strategies, a happy laboratory has been established in Kuaishou for innovation. It sets up philanthropic accounts which link user behavior with points going towards a number of charities, which can be exchanged for philanthropic contributions. Furthermore, Kuaishou also aims to apply emerging image and video recognition technology to animal and plant protection, hoping to take the advantage of live broadcast, short video, and image recognition to propel breakthroughs and innovation.

Kuaishou is an Internet company of the new generation and its values are the same as those of the "indigenous peoples on the Internet". The Internet itself is inclusive and even philanthropic in nature. It brings people closer to each other and gives them opportunities to watch, listen, and express themselves. The concept of inclusiveness is earnestly practiced at Kuaishou and is what underpins Kuaishou's continuous investment in philanthropy.

As an Internet company, Kuaishou's philanthropic model is closely tied with the attributes of the Internet. Its philanthropic products are all based on its business model of live broadcasts and short videos. The philanthropic model of emerging Internet companies, represented by Kuaishou Charity, is distinct from models adopted by traditional companies. For traditional companies, the Internet is a tool and the Internet-based philanthropic model is an effective supplement to traditional philanthropy. However, for emerging Internet companies, business and philanthropic models are driven by the same philosophy and this is what fundamentally differentiates philanthropic activities carried out by Internet companies from those of traditional ones.

Besides Kuaishou, many emerging Internet companies have already followed their predecessors and embarked on the path of online philanthropy. As more and more Internet companies are getting involved in philanthropy, will the boundary between online philanthropy and e-commerce disappear? Is it fair to say that the Internet is equal to philanthropy? Will we see a cyberspace with stronger philanthropic and inclusive attributes in the future? Only time will tell.

Section 2 Philanthropy Integrated into People's Daily Lives

In China, traditional Internet and mobile Internet have been important components of people's daily lives. The mobile Internet plays a major role in shaping Chinese lifestyle and having a mobile phone at hand is very common among Chinese people. Additionally, the Internet and its mobile counterpart are of great significance to philanthropy in China. Benefiting from the "decentralization-featured" Internet that can address information asymmetry, China's charity and philanthropy continue to attract numerous donors, realize diverse philanthropic efforts, and demonstrate vibrancy as all kinds of philanthropic activities thrive together and all forces of society join in.

Welcome to the Era of "Philanthropy by All"

Internet philanthropy has connected the general public of China and popularized philanthropy on a massive scale. In the past, the main players of China's philanthropic arena were the government, enterprises, and a small group of wealthy people. However, thanks to Internet philanthropy, members of the general public at different ages and income levels can easily contribute to philanthropic efforts today and play dominant roles as philanthropists.

Such a distinct change can be clearly seen when comparing data from the China Charity Alliance and the 99 Charity Day. According to the China Charity Alliance, of the donations collected by Chinese charities in 2017 only 21% came from individuals, while 65% were contributed by enterprises. (China Charity Alliance, 2018) In contrast, data from the 99 Charity Day showed that individuals played a leading role in donations in 2017, accounting for 63.5% of the total and making public donations a core component of Internet philanthropy.

Backed by the Internet, China's philanthropy is mainly joined by grassroots efforts, the young, and long-term participants.

Grassroots: Scale Effect of Small-Sum Donation

The success of China's public philanthropy is dependent on the fact that it has mobilized a large number of grassroots forces to get involved in small-sum donations with the help of the Internet. Data from Tencent Charity shows that small-sum donation has become a dominant component and indicates that a great many netizens have become engaged in philanthropic activities. On one hand, donations of less than 20 yuan are the most popular, with the number of donors accounting for over 70% of the total. On the other hand, the number of donors with donations ranging from 20 to 100 yuan is on the rise while that of donors giving less than 20 yuan is declining. It can be safely concluded that many small-sum donation contributors have become more generous than before (See Fig. 4.1). (Tencent Foundation & Tencent Research Institute, 2017) Indeed, Tencent Charity platform users can participate in fund-raising according to their own financial capabilities. Regardless of economic background, all users are able to contribute to philanthropic efforts on the platform, reflecting its feature of "Philanthropy by All".

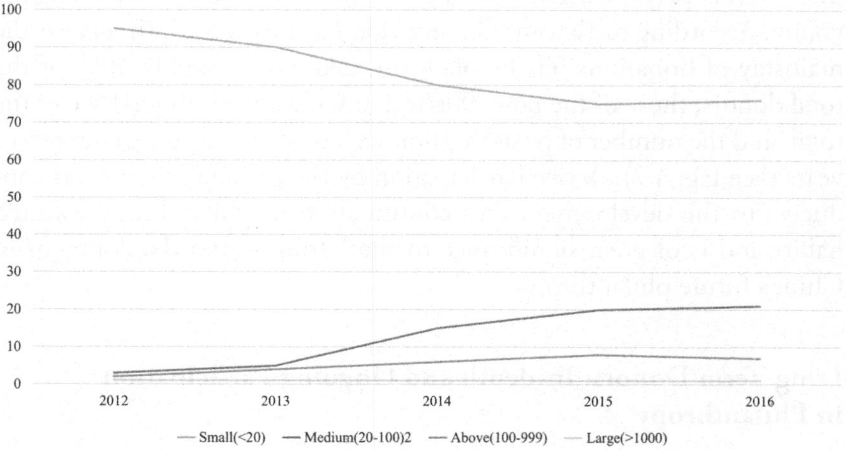

Fig. 4.1 The proportion of Tencent Charity's Donors by Sum of Donations (2012–2016)

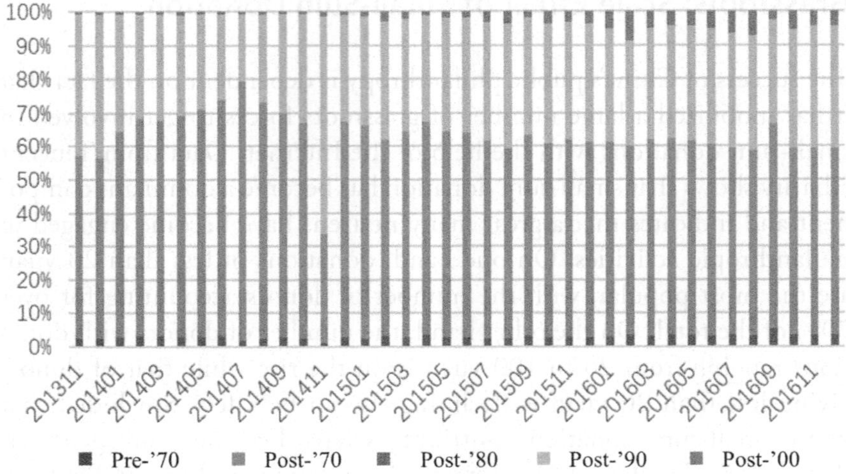

Fig. 4.2 The proportion of Tencent Charity's Donors at different ages (2013–2016)

The Young Main Force: Post-'80s, '90s, and '00s

The Internet plays an active role in public philanthropy by mobilizing the young. According to Tencent Charity, donors of the post-'80s serve as the mainstay of donations on the platform, taking-up roughly 40% of the total donors; those of the post-'90s and '00s constitute about 40% of the total, and the number of post-'00s donors has been increasing over recent years (See Fig. 4.2). Active participation by the young generation is conducive to the development and continuation of philanthropy-featured habits and is of great significance to the lasting sound development of China's future philanthropy.

Long-Term Donors: In-depth and Ongoing Participation in Philanthropy

The Internet's connection to philanthropy makes it possible for donors, project executors and sometimes even beneficiaries to connect and interact with each other. Previously, donors would leave at once after donating money. They were rarely involved in philanthropic projects in a direct manner and disappeared completely at most times after the donation. Today, by using the Internet people can easily take part in philanthropic projects, making donations, sharing news, supervising work, and even implementing projects. When discovering an online philanthropic project, netizens can donate money quickly through mobile payment and share news about the project on social media platforms, thus encouraging others to become donors. After that, donors who have any questions about a project can track it on the platform and view the real-time progress of the project and the whereabouts of donations. Hence, donors become social supervisors for the project. Those who want to know about how the project is implemented may contact relevant philanthropic organizations through the platform and even engage in the implementation process themselves. As a result, donors get deeply involved in philanthropic projects, increase their trust in the projects and organizations, thus become long-term participants. According to Tencent Charity, the rate of second donations by its users exceeded 20% in 2016, constituting a growing group of long-term donors.

Everything Can Be Philanthropically Made

Why can the Internet mobilize the general public to participate in philanthropic activities? Most importantly, the Internet has enriched the form and content of philanthropy. As a result, philanthropy is not only about donations in the traditional sense any more but is also closely related to people's daily lives. Benefiting from the Internet and digital technologies, users can donate their steps, voice, time, amount of consumption, and other entities on platforms. Theoretically, any daily performance that can be digitized can serve as a donation. Consequently, by effectively combining philanthropy and users' daily lives, philanthropic activities have become more interesting and diversified, thus attracting more and more participants.

Sentiments such as "Everything can be philanthropically made" show the nature of the Internet for the public, "the hide comes from the pig's back", that is, an Internet platform provides its users with free products or

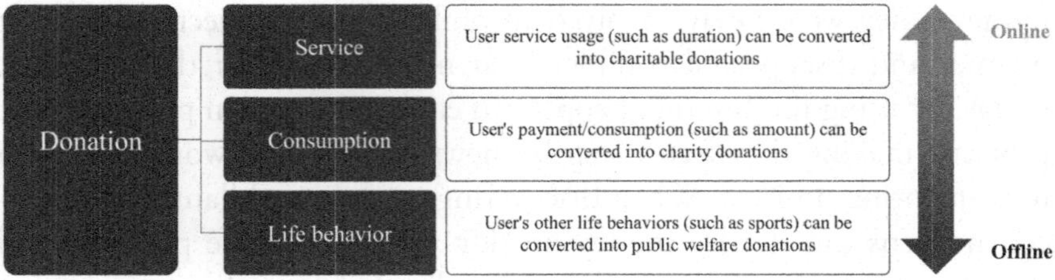

Fig. 4.3 Three new ways to participate in philanthropy

services which will be paid by other market players. Indeed, the public donates no money and their participation incurs no cost, which is known as the "free" model that can greatly motivate people, especially those who hardly ever get involved in philanthropic activities to become donors. The real fund donors are enterprises that provide project services for users. They are willing to do so due to the fact that it can on one hand increase online traffic and encourage users to obtain services, while on the other can also fulfill their social responsibilities through philanthropic activities.

Currently, there are a variety of ways to contribute to philanthropic efforts, which may be mainly classified into services, consumption, and daily life by the degree of its online and offline focuses (See Fig. 4.3).

Internet Service Usage for Philanthropy

Users can convert their online service usage into rights and interests for donation in accordance with rules set by service providers. For enterprises, this strongly correlates to services and links up with corporate and social responsibilities. Their input produces better results. Consequently, many enterprises, particularly newcomers to the Internet philanthropic industry, want to make an attempt at the integration of services and philanthropy. For users who decide to use the service first, they can make philanthropic donations and obtain philanthropic interests immediately, so why not go for it? Certainly, as users do not need to input costs directly, they may be uninformed about and lack enthusiasm for philanthropy. So how does one find interesting ways to attract more users, an especially important role in philanthropy of this kind?

At present, the core method of ensuring philanthropic donations and interests is to convert service usage amounts. Sometimes, users can convert the usage amount of overall services. In this case, the conversion is aimed at attracting more views from some core functions, for example tool-related services. Additionally, users can convert the usage amount of derivative services, which is applicable to platforms. It can encourage users to utilize derivative services more frequently and enhance connections between all the services on the platform.

Case Study

Reading News for Philanthropy

In September 2017, China's top news aggregation service, Jinri Toutiao, launched a philanthropic project called One Minute of Your Love. By accumulating daily reading time, users are able to convert said time into philanthropic funds that can be used on various projects. This event launched eight projects, including Action for Making Mothers Smile which helps children with cleft lip-palates.

The time donation allows users to get involved in philanthropic activities with ease. For instance, a long-time user of Jinri Toutiao, a network engineer who usually paid attention to philanthropy, found it difficult to participate due to his busy work schedule. Thanks to this project, he could donate the reading time he accumulated on Jinri Toutiao app, more than half an hour every day, and convert it into one surgical coat and one bandage for children with cleft lips and cleft lip palates within just a few days.

In reality, this is a process of converting online virtual information consumption into tangible donations. News service platforms have established relations among users, philanthropic organizations, enterprises, and assistance recipients. The philanthropic funds donated by users are directly converted into donations that enterprises participating in the project will claim and fund, and then the philanthropic organizations will deliver the donations to assistance recipients. All these efforts form a virtuous circle.

The virtuous circle plays a key role in accelerating the production of results and expanding the effect of philanthropy. The reading time donated by users reached approximately 55 million minutes and the number of participants reached 939,000 within three days after the projects went live. The I Want to See the World project for children with eye diseases in poverty-stricken areas raised RMB 12 million in total and contributed over 100,000 donations of time. (Ren, 2017)

Case Study

Cleaning Up for Philanthropy

Tencent's PC Manager and Tencent's Mobile Manager joined hands with Tencent Charity in December of 2015 to launch the "Clean Up Plus" campaign (Zhu, 2015), taking the lead in the security software sector to combine the cleanup function of products with philanthropy (See Fig. 4.4). Every time a netizen cleaned up his or her computer or

Fig. 4.4 Tencent mobile manager "clean up plus" campaign

mobile phone, the junk files that were cleared were converted into a sum of cash which was donated to philanthropic organizations and eventually used for trash cleanup covering an area of 50,000 square kilometers in the Sanjiangyuan area, literally "Source of Three Rivers", of Qinghai Province.

To provide easier access to the public, this philanthropic campaign adopted a new model instead of the traditional way of offline fund-raising or participation. Therefore, netizens could accomplish good by simply clicking or tapping love brooms online. The users could also learn more about the "Clean Up Plus" campaign in the Event Details section after donating, such as the total number of love brooms one had donated, the national donation landscape, and other relevant information. In an effort to encourage user participation, the campaign also set up a philanthropic medal system wherein the more donations one made, the more highly ranked one's medal was. Users could also invite friends to take part in the campaign and help influence others.

In accordance with the plan, if there were 10 million people participating in the phone cleanup project and donating the love brooms they had obtained from the cleanup, the Tencent Foundation would provide financial support for trash cleaning efforts in the Sanjiangyuan area. Exceeding expectations, the project turned out to be a highly sensational event that attracted more than 20 million netizens to participate. (Chu, 2017) Half a year later, in May 2016, Tencent Mobile Manager took the next step to promote the Trash Cleaning Action in eight major cities across the country where users were encouraged to serve as environmental guardians and get involved in philanthropic activities, while reflecting the initiator's endeavors to cultivate philanthropic habits of the public by gradually switching online philanthropic behaviors offline.

Case Study

Playing Games for Philanthropy

Ant Farm is an online philanthropic game that Alipay launched on August 6, 2017 which can be accessed through the Alipay app. In this game, users collect chicken feed awarded by making Alipay payments to feed digital chickens and get eggs. For every five eggs collected, the user can make one donation.

Due to a game's feature and the fact that users only need to use short bursts of time to play, Ant Farm has done a great job in influencing Alipay users to participate in philanthropic projects. Active behavior of the user can be transformed into philanthropic donations and interests via the game, bringing more fun to users. In addition, the user and the user's chicken can also steal food from other users and there is a ranking to show who has donated more eggs among the user's friends. This socially interactive function also increases user adherence to philanthropy and benefits the establishment of Alipay's social attributes.

For many Internet businesses that are less entertaining, it may be a good idea to design new games whose points can be converted into philanthropic donations and interests in ways to give users incentive to use their business, while also driving public participation in philanthropic activities at the same time.

Consumer Behavior for Philanthropy

Consumer behavior for philanthropy means that users can convert a sum of cash consumed into philanthropic donations and interests according to the conversion mode on the platform. It is not a new idea. Many companies already adopted this method when they were primarily selling goods offline. It is a common philanthropic marketing method, i.e., every time a consumer buys a commodity, the company will extract a part of the profit as a philanthropic donation. For example, Nongfu Spring's previous "Drink a bottle of water to donate a penny" philanthropic campaign was highly effective in terms of marketing and communication.

In the era of Internet philanthropy, this approach has now moved online and become quite diversified. It becomes widely applied by different businesses from large to small and medium-sized as well as businesses in poor rural areas on platforms such as Taobao's Charity Products, JD.com's E-commerce for Poverty Alleviation section, and Vipshop's Only Love Workshop with consumer donation modes upgraded from the old passive methods of donating via purchases to the new ways of voluntarily donating after buying, such as what we have seen in Tencent's Charity Coins and Alipay's Ant Forest. As a result, this approach enables further utilization of consumer behaviors, or a kind of behavior that is financial, for philanthropy on a wider range and in a more proactive way, thus stimulating the enthusiasm of all parties involved in philanthropy.

Case Study

Purchasing for Philanthropy

In recent years, in response to the national poverty alleviation strategy, various e-commerce platforms have delved into philanthropy and launched various campaigns of e-commerce philanthropy and e-commerce poverty alleviation with the aim of encouraging consumers to make philanthropic contribution while purchasing goods. Among them is an interesting platform entitled the Only Love Workshop, launched by Vipshop on May 27, 2017.

Unlike most e-commerce philanthropic platforms which put focus on the sale of local agricultural products and byproducts, the Only Love Workshop is solely for local handicraft products. The products' folk culture origins add to their market value and further expand the influence of the place of origin and the target of poverty alleviation. Vipshop provides funding in early stages to help people in poverty-stricken areas to organize production as well as support in design, packaging, operation, logistics, and other areas for free. The products are sold for zero profit during the Only Love Workshop event and the sales income from these special activities is used to help vulnerable groups.

As of the writing of this book, Vipshop has already organized three Only Love special activities to sell products for poverty alleviation. All these products, including tie-dye works from the Bai and Dai ethnic groups, design works of unique embroidery from Tu ethnic group, and paintings done by autistic children have been sold out within 24 hours following launch. For consumers who participate in these special activities, they are doing it out of concern for vulnerable groups and also out of love for handicrafts that possess unique artistic and cultural values, enabling consumers to acquire special value in return by participating in these activities.

Case Study

Paying for Philanthropy

In addition to contributing to philanthropy with purchases, Alipay, WeChat Pay, and some other payment tools also have designs that convert users' payments into philanthropic donations and interests to promote business use, such as Alipay's Ant Forest and WeChat Pay's Charity Coins.

Take Charity Coins as an example. It was a philanthropic innovation campaign organized by WeChat Pay and Tencent Charity around the 99 Charity Day campaign from August 9 to September 9, 2017 during which users who paid with WeChat Pay at stores participating in this campaign in China were awarded Charity Coins for each payment. These coins could be donated to support certain philanthropic projects (See Fig. 4.5) which would later receive actual funding from the Tencent Foundation to achieve their philanthropic goals based on user coin donations.

The Charity Coins campaign effectively utilized online payment habits users had already formed and seamlessly connected them with donations to philanthropic projects, representing a beneficial attempt to cultivate voluntary online donation habits of users at zero cost.

Daily Behavior for Philanthropy

By engaging in philanthropic causes through daily behaviors, we mean users' daily activities are digitized via the Internet and turned into rights and interests donated in the form of public service after conversion. When compared with the former two categories, this model is closer to user lives and better helps to cultivate habits of continuously participating in philanthropic events and activities in different scenarios.

Fig. 4.5 WeChat pay's charity coins

Of course, it is impossible to convert every daily behavior into philanthropic donations. There are several dimensions to be considered when designing such projects. First, no upper threshold should be set against the behaviors, meaning that it is something easy for most people to do, for example, talking. Second, the behavior should benefit the donors and bring positive value to most people, such as running. Third, the behavior should relate to public service as much as possible and it is better to do philanthropic work while performing the behavior, such as traveling. Judging from current industrial development, representative methods including donating voices, steps, and energy have successfully aroused the public enthusiasm for doing philanthropy.

So why do we need to achieve the pattern of life plus philanthropy via the Internet? Han Jing, founder and CEO of Lurenjia, explained in an interview, "Why are we always talking about bringing philanthropy into life? It is because such behaviors as buying a pot of tea, drinking a cup of coffee, and singing karaoke help people to form a habit of doing philanthropy. When a donor has led a life like this for three years, he will continue to be involved with philanthropy even if he no longer receives discount coupons for doing this, as it has become his habit". (Wang, 2017)

Case Study

Step Donation for Philanthropy

Actually, donating steps has a long history in philanthropy, as there have been various philanthropic oriented races, both at home and abroad since long ago. But in the recent past, as the time and number of participants of the offline public events were limited, their sphere of influence was usually not large.

The popularization of intelligent terminals and the Internet has truly brought donating steps into the daily life of the public. For example, the Tencent Foundation initiated the Charity Hiker project in 2014. With this project, users can donate their steps after they reach a certain number of steps by walking every day. Essentially, the cooperating enterprises convert the steps donated by users into actual funds and donate the money to relative philanthropic projects (See Fig. 4.6).

Fig. 4.6 Tencent charity hiker

Starting with fund-raising sports competitions at universities, this activity has attracted participants from all over the undivided platform and has gained the support of a large number of users. It has become a public activity in which citizens are willing to participate on a long-term basis.

Case Study

Voice Donation for Philanthropy

While tens of millions of blind people in China can only rely on their ears and hands to perceive the world, more than 73% of the 1.3 billion population can speak Mandarin. (Ministry of Education & National Language Commission, 2017) If speaking is one of the most common social behaviors in daily life, then why not motivate these 900 million people to help the blind by speaking?

The WeChat team came up with this idea in 2014 and initiated a creative philanthropic campaign named Reading for the Blind.[7] In 2015 they launched the Team Lead Reading campaign. By simply connecting to the Voice Donor WeChat, account users could read the texts sent by the system or read their favorite paragraphs in a book. The system would record the voice, produce audio files, and provide them to the blind (See Fig. 4.7).

Indeed, the program did encounter some controversy. For example, the performance of non-professional readers was the most criticized aspect since it could influence the quality of audio books. The WeChat team developed a close loop which could automatically select, integrate, and optimize voices by utilizing their own voice recognition technology and an AI-driven big data operating system. In other words, they sent different paragraphs to different users and then collected voice files. After comparing them with the AI voice recognition technology-based standard human voice model, only the best voice files could be integrated into the voice bank and optimized to be part of an audio book. Despite

[7] WeChat account: voicedonate.

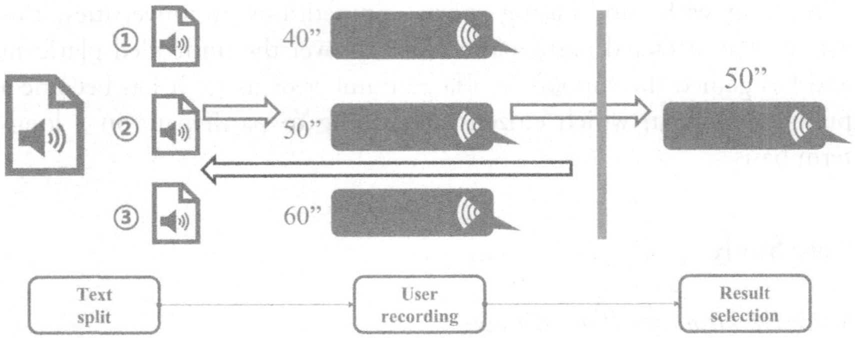

Fig. 4.7 WeChat's voice donor

some flaws, the process of crowd sourcing and late optimization enabled it to demonstrate close-to-professional performance.

Extensive social attention was aroused by this campaign. Celebrities such as Yi Zhongtian, Xu Jinglei, and Wang Han also participated in these activities. By May 2015, the "Voice Donor" WeChat account attracted over 1.3 million people and collected over 1.3 million voice files (*Reading for*, 2015) which finally generated more than 100 audio books, 3 million visually impaired people listened to them, and 10,000 visually disabled children from 100 schools for the blind received Pleasant Reading Boxes donated by the program. (Yang, 2015)

Case Study

Carrying Needed Materials for Philanthropy

As early as ten years ago, the desktop Internet era had already witnessed success in initiating Action for Philanthropy online and called for voluntary participation. In 2004, Yu Zhihai (username "Angel") traveled to a remote village in Yunnan Province and learned that only two girls out of over one hundred families could go to middle school. He decided to start the One More Kilogram program which aimed at encouraging tourists to carry books and stationery when they traveled between villages and give them to local schools. Volunteers were also encouraged to disseminate knowledge and broaden local children's horizons by face-to-face communication and the online sharing of information about local schools after the tour.

After several such activities, the number of participants began to grow and the Internet-based model proved quite effective. Angel decided to develop it into a long-term project. The website 1KG.org was then set up to collect and provide information on rural schools so that tourists could prepare before traveling. Within one year tourists from Guangzhou, Shanghai, and Beijing organized over 20 activities with more than 200 participants. Volunteers went to places such as Hunan, Guangxi, Guizhou, and Yunnan and donated over 10,000 pieces of stationery and over 3000 books to local schools. (Yang, 2006)

As for how to use the Internet to promote philanthropic campaigns, they summarized it in three core steps in their blog. First, spread information online and call on tourists to carry one more kilogram and give these needy materials to rural schools. Second, communicate through playing games with children and joining their events in schools to provide knowledge, share happiness, and record content. Third, share information online after the tour so that more people could be informed and get involved (See Fig. 4.8). In its later development, the One More Kilogram campaign reached out to mainstream online communities and social

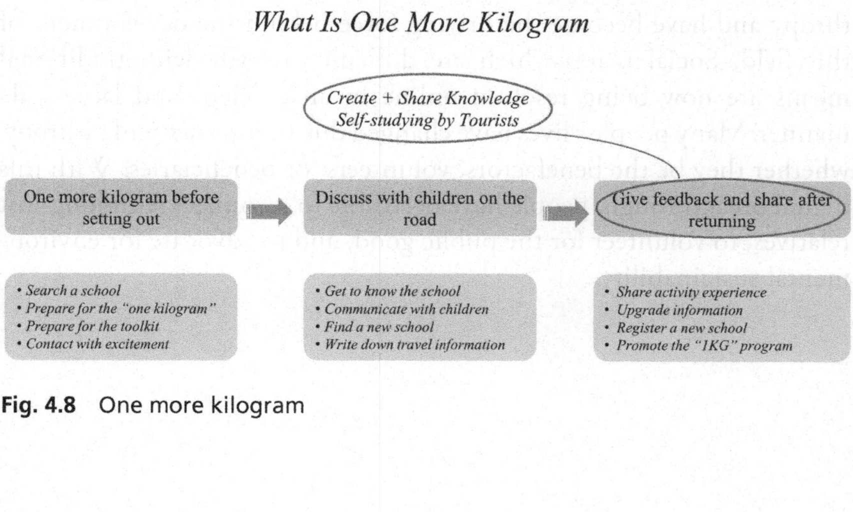

Fig. 4.8 One more kilogram

networks such as Douban, Renren, and Kaixin to conduct activities and manage volunteers, pioneering a model of combining social networks and philanthropy.

The key factor of Internet integration has enabled One More Kilogram to operate successfully for nearly 10 years and receive many philanthropic awards both at home and abroad such as the Golden Nica of Digital Communities of Prix Ars Electronica in 2008, which was rarely given to grassroots philanthropic organizations. Angel considered the biggest difference between One More Kilogram and traditional charitable organizations was that "rather than taking the place of volunteer users, One More Kilogram leads and builds platforms and processing and information structures. Therefore, we should constantly understand the needs of schools, classify them, and improve the presentation of school information and the management of public service process in the community". The grassroots organizations did so more than a decade ago, using the Internet as a platform for empowerment in order to build a public service ecosystem and create a scale effect. More than ten years later, this has become the rule of success on online philanthropic platforms.

Those That Are Connected by Internet Philanthropy

Indeed, the Internet has changed philanthropy in China. With its help, a large number of people have shifted their focus to pursuing philanthropy and have become the driving force behind the development of this field. Social issues which are difficult to settle with traditional means are now being resolved online in an efficient and large-scale manner. Many people's lives have changed due to Internet philanthropy, whether they be the benefactors, volunteers, or beneficiaries. With this digital breakthrough, people have been able to reconnect with long-lost relatives, to volunteer for the public good, and to advocate for environmental sustainability.

Restoring Blood Ties: The VIP Micro-blogger Policeman Online Person Finder Service

In recent years, a saying became popular in Xi'an: "One who seeks to find a missing person can turn to Officer Cao." Officer Cao's full name is Cao Jinsheng. He was a communication officer who worked in the Political Work Section of the Public Security Bureau of the Lianhu District in Xi'an. At the start, he was not in charge of looking for missing people. He helped a young girl with amnesia get back to her family in Henan Province by means of the Internet six years ago when she had been missing for five years. Because of this, Officer Cao decided to help look for more missing people using his influence as a VIP micro blogger.

On the afternoon of January 12, 2013, a young girl came into the Lianhu branch of the Public Security Bureau (PSB) of Xi'an City for help. She reported that she did not know her name or where she lived. She just wanted to go home. Cao and his colleagues could not find any substantial clues in the handbag she was carrying, leaving them no choice but to send the girl to a rescue management station. However, the girl slipped out of the rescue station, spent a day and a night at a nearby McDonald's, and returned to the Lianhu branch of the Xi'an PSB, again asking for help. Cao and the other officers had to put the girl in the police dormitory temporarily. After that, they tried to find her family through the citizen registry on the public security network but they could not find a match with the girl's information. The search had led to a dead-end.

In frustration, Cao suddenly thought of the Internet. He posted two notices separately on Sina Weibo and Tencent Weibo regarding the lost girl on his own social media accounts. Unexpectedly, his post went viral. Within a week it was reposted more than 50,000 times and had over 80 million views. (Xu, 2017) Before long, a certain Mr. Zhao of Shangqiu City, Henan Province, who saw the photo of the amnesia girl confirmed that she was his daughter who had gone to work in Qingdao and lost touch with her family for five years. Soon after, Zhao and his family took an overnight train to Xi'an and finally reunited with their missing daughter.

Since then, Cao understood the enormous power of the Internet. He began to learn how to use Sina Weibo and WeChat in his spare time and tried to incorporate his experience into his daily work. Every time he received a report of a missing person, he would post the information on the Internet. Understanding the immense potential of the Internet, Cao was able to achieve three things. First, using the popularity of the WeChat social platform, he created a group with several hundred people called "Officer Cao's Person Finder Group" that was joined by Cao's media friends, good-hearted citizens, and those who had received Cao's help while enlisting support for the core force of his public quests. Second, he succeeded in coordinating with new media platforms to partner with his cause. Third, he was also able to attract the attention of other VIP micro bloggers in various fields such as culture, entertainment, etc. as well as use these well-known figures' influence to aid his cause.

With this efficient and effective use of the Internet, Cao has served the public for more than six years. During this period he has responded to the queries of more than 15,000 people online, posted more than 6000 articles regarding safety and security information, and found more than 600 missing senior citizens and children, averaging about one every three days. (Song, 2017) A journalist once asked him, "Why do you still keep doing this after so many years? After all, looking for missing persons is neither your job nor a lucrative business." Mr. Cao replied, "As a public security officer, I'm well positioned to quickly and accurately verify information with the resources I have. Also, I've already gained people's trust. I feel obliged to keep doing it. By helping the others, I've found fulfillment in life." According to Cao, mobile phones are the most preferred method for people to obtain information nowadays. The traditional method of putting up posters is no longer effective. Platforms such as WeChat and Sina Weibo need to be fully utilized. Mr. Cao also said, "It's quick and convenient. You don't have to do anything but move your fingers. It's also easier for people to spread the information, increasing the chances of finding people."

Strengthening Social Ties: Protecting and Revitalizing China's Countryside via the Internet

China is a large agricultural country and its countryside is an important social component. However, with the rapid progress of economic development and urbanization, a large number of villages, especially the ancient ones, continue to wither and disappear from the country's map. According to statistics from 2000 to 2010, the number of China's villages dropped from 3.63 million to 2.71 million, with a shocking decrease of over 900,000 in just over ten years. On average, 80 to 100 villages cease to exist every day. (Feng & Song, 2016) With the disappearance of these villages, a large amount of cultural information and patterns are getting lost, causing irreparable social losses.

Zhou Yin, mayor of Heshang Town, Xiaoshan District, Hangzhou in 2013 had such sentiments during a visit to a village named Fengwu in his town. The village had once been the headquarters of the Xiaoshan County government during the war of resistance against Japanese aggression. Many sites and relics remained but most of the architectural structures were in ruins. The county government site, an old building with over 100 years of history, was in danger of collapsing. Next to it was a dilapidated old house that had once housed the Flying Tigers, a group of US pilots who supported China during WWII. Amazed by the historical significance of these two old buildings, Zhou had intended to turn them into museums but failed due to lack of funds. Later on, he came up with the idea of crowd-funding and established a public crowd-funding platform with the help of the Zhejiang Provincial Love Charitable Foundation. Finally, after a series of online and offline marketing events, he was able to receive help from teachers, students, war veterans, social celebrities, and even local villagers. From 2015 to 2017 a total sum of RMB 1 million was raised to establish two museums, namely the Xiaoshan Memorial Hall for the Anti-Japanese War and the Memorial Hall for Sino-US Cooperation in the Anti-Japanese War (See Fig. 4.9).

In a notable anecdote, when the first museum was built, not a single local villager donated a penny. However, after the first museum opened, many people started visiting after learning about it through the media.

Fig. 4.9 The memorial hall for Sino-US cooperation in the Anti-Japanese War Crowd-Funded by Heshang Town

All the names of the donors were written on the wall, which sparked interest among the villagers. They wanted their names on the wall, too. And so when the construction of the second museum started, many of the villagers made donations. Of the RMB 300,000 raised, about 20% was from the villagers. (*Practical experience*, 2018) What everyone learned from this was that under the guidance of a responsible, capable village leader, a village without a sense of unity and poor public ethos can be brought together. This case highlights a feasible way of rural reconstruction projects in the country.

Connecting with Nature: Internet Plus Environment Protection to Foster a Public-Government-Corporate Relationship

Due to rapid economic development, China has been facing detrimental environmental problems in recent years. Smog, water pollution, and soil pollution, among others, are frequent issues that occur on a daily basis, posing an increasing threat to public health. Even though environmental issues and their harmful effects have already become public knowledge, few people have access to sufficient data and opportunities to participate in environmental governance and protection. Due to the lack of information and means, responding to the appeals of experts and the media is the only way for most of the citizens to get involved. As a result, the general public has limited awareness of how to combat these problems in China, which in turn leads to slow progress with regards to environmental sustainability.

A veteran in the field of water resources and protection, Ma Jun came to realize how dire the situation was becoming and that something needed to change. In June 2006 he established the Institute of Public and Environmental Affairs (IPE). The institute aims to disclose environmental information and promote environmental governance. In order to increase public awareness and encourage participation in environmental protection efforts, IPE launched the first China Water Pollution Map, a non-profit water pollution database. Open to the public, the website collects and compiles information about water quality, sewage emissions, and delinquent companies that violate environmental regulations. With the development of the Internet, IPE took the opportunity to develop a mobile app that would provide convenient access to real-time environmental information. The mobile app, officially launched in 2014, has been renamed Blue Map since its upgrade in 2015. (*Chronology of*, n.d.) With three million downloads in 2014, Blue Map became successful, despite being an app of such nature. In 2015 the app was able to track the sewage emissions of more than 9000 companies across the country. Over 70,000 incidents of pollution were put into the database in 2016, contributing to a total number of 300,000 by the end of the year. (Public

Environmental Research Center, 2017) Due to this, Ma Jun won the Skoll Award for Social Entrepreneurship in 2015 and the Prince Claus Award in 2017. Both are globally renowned awards for social services. The success of Blue Map can be attributed to the combination of the Internet and environmental protection. Blue Map connects the public, the government, and the private sector by fostering a beneficial interaction amongst them, thus effectively solving environmental problems. Its impact has been achieved through the following three factors:

First, Blue Map relies on credible data. Since 2006 the IPE has collected and displayed environmental data released by the government. It also collates sewage emissions data from companies to provide supplementary resources to the public. These are done to establish the credibility of the data and to avoid conflicts and disputes caused by unreliable information as well as to ensure that enough attention is given to the problem. During environmental monitoring, the IPE thoroughly analyzes and researches the data to check whether the data gathered actually reflects the reality of the situation. When the data is proven to be invalid, the IPE removes it and sends feedback to the authorities, thereby ensuring the authenticity and accuracy of the data.

Second, it encourages the public to contribute via the Internet. Blue Map provides a platform where users can participate in current pollution regulations. Consequently, with the influence of public opinions, the efficiency and effectiveness of the pollution control efforts can be massively improved. Industrial pollution often happens in the production of energy and raw materials but at the upstream of the supply chain, it is difficult to pinpoint when it occurs exactly. For example, a steel plant in Shandong Province once exceeded the emission standard by 10 times the legal limit. When the IPE negotiated with the plant, it removed itself from the equation by claiming that the company was not restricted by the environmental protection regulations. However, when the real-time data was reflected on Blue Map, local residents repeatedly shared the records on social networks and tagged the local authorities in their posts. In the end, the authorities responded to their online reporting and mandated the company to rectify the situation. This is an example of how important the role of public opinion is in environmental protection.

Third, it urges companies to take corrective measures. To make sure that corrective measures are being implemented, the IPE uses the influence of the market as leverage. The institution collaborates with each part of the supply chain to emphasize joint social responsibility of upstream and downstream companies. In 2007 the IPE started to promote the idea of green choice. When the pollution source or the raw material suppliers refused to take measures, the IPE turned to their clients. It sent the data to large enterprises and brands, who valued environmental compliance for the sake of corporate social responsibility and public image. To promote environmental sustainability, these large companies became cautious when choosing their suppliers. The supplier selection process has now evolved into a search for green suppliers, confirming green practices, and disclosing green operations. Moreover, the Corporate Information Transparency Index has also been established. Over 40 famous international and domestic brands, such as Apple, Adidas, Dell, and Huawei regularly check on their suppliers with Blue Map's database. For the past 10 years, the Green Supply Chain has encouraged about 2000 suppliers to take actions and about 1000 of them to disclose emission data. (*Ruan Qingyuan*, 2017)

References

Charity (公益慈善). (n.d.). *Sf-express*. Retrieved September 30, 2018, from http://www.sf-express.com/kr/sc/about_us/about_sf/Philathropy/

China Charity Alliance (中国慈善联合会). (2018). *2017年度中国慈善捐助报告*. *Charityalliance*. http://www.charityalliance.org.cn/u/cms/www/201809/20232201v09l.pdf

Chronology of Institute of Public and Environmental Affairs (IPE历程). (n.d.). *IPE*. Retrieved October 05, 2018, from http://www.ipe.org.cn/about/about.aspx

Chu, X. (2017, May 05). *"清理+"引发全民公益热潮超2000万网友参与*. *Cctime*. http://www.cctime.com/html/2017-5-5/1285498.htm

Feng, J. C., & Song, Y. (2016, May 15). *有故土, 才记得住乡愁*. *Infzm*. http://www.infzm.com/content/117062?b0h

Li, X. (2018, January 01). *时间的朋友:速度、价值观和选择*. *Baijiahao*. https://baijiahao.baidu.com/s?id=1588376244475322510&wfr=spider&for=pc

Ministry of Education, & National Language Commission (教育部., & 国家语委). (2017, July 18). *中国语言文字事业发展报告(2017)*. *Baidu*. https://baike.baidu.com/item/中国语言文字事业发展报告%282017%29/22032052?fr=aladdin

Practical experience: How to use Internet crowdfunding in rural revitalization (实战经验:互联网众筹如何运用于乡村振兴工作中). (2018, January 19). *Sohu*. Retrieved October 05, 2018, from http://www.sohu.com/a/217737482_737595

Public Environmental Research Center (公众环境研究中心). (2017, January 19). *寻找蔚蓝——公众环境研究中心2016年度报告*. *IPE*. http://www.ipe.org.cn/reports/report_19060.html#

"Public welfare + express delivery" 20 million copies of love are on the road on 99 Charity Days (99公益日试水"公益+快递"2000万份爱心已上路). (2017, September 02). *QQ*. Retrieved September 30, 2018, from https://news.qq.com/a/20170902/115087.htm

Reading for the blind, turning good motivations into effective actions (为盲胞读书, 将良好动机转化为有效行动). (2015, May 18). *QQ*. Retrieved September 30, 2018, from http://gongyi.qq.com/a/20150518/027250.htm

Ren, X. N. (2017, September 27). *今日头条上线公益项目*. *Chinaxwcb*. http://www.chinaxwcb.com/2017-09/27/content_361797.htm

Ruan Qingyuan: From knowing to acting-the Internet realizes "cloud environmental protection" (阮清鸳:从知情到行动——互联网实现"云环保"). (2017, June 19). *QQ*. Retrieved October 05, 2018, from https://news.qq.com/a/20170619/038771.htm

Song, J. J. (2017, April 24). *网络寻人找"西安莲湖曹警官"*. *Sanqin*. http://www.sanqin.com/2017/0424/293561.shtml

Tencent Foundation., & Tencent Research Institute (腾讯基金会., & 腾讯研究院). (2017, June 12). *腾讯公益十周年报告*. *Weixin*. https://mp.weixin.qq.com/s/cBd8YgDgFbQ3sp-mN5KAUQ

Together with SF Express to focus on rural education in China (和顺丰一起, 关注中国乡村教育). (n.d.). *QQ*. Retrieved September 30, 2018, from http://gongyi.qq.com/m/html5/home_list.htm?id=117

Wang, Y. M. (2017, October 13). *社企的时代现象:公益+商业+互联网*. *Shanda960*. http://www.shanda960.com/shandaguan/article/5039

Xu, K. (2017, April 24). *有一种感动叫曹警官寻人*. *Sanqin*. http://www.sanqin.com/2017/0424/293561.shtml
Yang, B. (2006, June 09). *《市民》杂志:安猪:人人多背一公斤*. *Tianya*. http://bbs.tianya.cn/post-books-80025-1.shtml
Yang, X. D. (2015, May 18). *花一分钟为盲人读书, 微信平台上公益可以这样做*. *Tmtpost*. http://www.tmtpost.com/1007828.html
Zhu, H. W. (2015, December 27). *手机管家公益版发布:清理手机垃圾就能做公益*. *Leiphone*. https://www.leiphone.com/news/201512/FAX6guqF2p5GXHxV.html

5 Governmental Support and Regulations

As China continues to make progress in social development, the Chinese government is attaching greater importance to charity and philanthropy. On March 16, 2016 the *Charity Law of the People's Republic of China* was adopted at the Fourth Session of the 12th National People's Congress of the People's Republic of China, with 2636 in favor, 131 against, and 83 abstentions. The law was finally adopted on September 1, 2016 (Wen, 2016) marking the triumph of charity legislation, which had been under dispute for more than a decade. Legally speaking, this paved the way for a new chapter of conducting charitable and philanthropic activities in China.

As the first charity law in China, the *Charity Law* provides a widely encompassing definition of charitable activities, which are now officially defined as those that promote the development of education, culture, and environmental protection in accordance with international consensus. This new definition no longer limits charitable activity only to helping the poor and the needy. The broader meaning of charity guides and guarantees the diversified development of philanthropic cause. The *Charity Law* also specifically stipulates the forms and operations of charitable organizations, the sources and uses of charitable property, charitable

Y. Chen, *Internet Philanthropy in China*,
https://doi.org/10.1007/978-981-16-2566-4_5

services, and the development of charitable cause. Considering the boom of unregulated charitable organizations in China, the *Charity Law* will forcefully promote the healthy growth of the industry.

Moreover, the *Charity Law* is up-to-date with the current cyber landscape, considering the flourishing of online philanthropic activities. Consequently, this law specifies the qualifications of online fundraisers and charitable information platforms. Considering the differences and distinct features of online charities as opposed to traditional ones, such as their expansive reach, the law had undergone several revisions to accommodate philanthropic platforms. In the end, it was stipulated that the charitable information platforms shall be designated and regulated by the civil affairs department of the State Council. The institution not only effectively supervises the platforms but also addresses the demand for centralized and simplified management. Ultimately, it serves to achieve a balance between enforcing the law and encouraging development at the same time.

Section 1 The Progress of Charitable Legislation

2005 to 2015: A Long Period of Time Before Its Birth

In Chinese culture, decades carry particular cultural significance. As the famous Confucian saying goes, "At thirty, I stood firm. At forty, I had no doubts". Ten years is a tipping point for many. Within a decade, one's knowledge can turn into wisdom and social development has changed from quantitative to qualitative.

The legislation of China's *Charity Law* has gone through exactly a decade of development. Its legislative research started in 2005 and the legislative deliberation followed in 2015. In 2005 the Social Policy Center of the Chinese Academy of Social Sciences and other institutions began legislative research in the field of charity and in the same year, in September, the MCA formally proposed to the National People's Congress (NPC) and the State Council to draft the law supporting charity, marking the beginning of charitable legislation. However, it was not until three years later in 2008 that the Charity Law was finally approved by the MCA and included in the first category of legislative planning of the Standing Committee of the 11th NPC. Then, in 2009, the MCA submitted the draft to the Legal Affairs Office of the State Council, enabling the Charity Law to undergo the legislative process. In 2010, the head of the Legal Affairs Office of the State Council announced that the draft of the Charity Law had taken shape and would likely be published not long afterwards. Unfortunately, the delay lasted for four lingering years. In 2014 the first plenary session of the leading group for the charitable legislation was held by the NPC's Internal Affairs Committee. Only in this year were the timetable and framework of the legislation for the Charity Law studied, thus paving the way for its final approval. Finally, in October 2015 the draft of the Charity Law was finally completed and submitted to the NPC Standing Committee for review.

Why was the progress so slow? For one thing, it had something to do with the institution in charge of it. The legislation of the Charity Law was initially led by the MCA, which is a relatively weaker body compared to the other ministries. If a law is to be passed by the State Council, it must consider the different opinions of all the ministries and commissions. It was difficult for the MCA to balance the different demands of the ministries and commissions, which consequently slowed the process of legislation. In November 2013 the Charity Law was included in the legislative plan of the Standing Committee of the 12th NPC, and it was finally put into the hands of the NPC's Internal Affairs and Judicial Committee. Since the new leading institution was more powerful than the old one, the disputes between ministries were more easily settled, causing the legislative process to enter a "fast track". Additionally, the legislation itself needed substantial investigation, research, and discussion to fully accommodate all the stakeholders' opinions. Traditional philanthropic activities have always been about social relief in China, thus modern charity is a fairly new concept. Therefore, people found it difficult to understand.

These disagreements and misunderstandings were almost impossible to resolve in such a short period of time. In 2009 Wang Zhenyao, Director of the Department of Social Welfare and Charity Promotion, revealed that the draft of the *Charity Law* had been submitted to the State Council for review. However, due to countless challenges, it was not successfully submitted to the NPC Standing Committee immediately (Zhou, 2015).

It usually takes special events for the unification of different viewpoints to happen. Two kinds of events played a pivotal role in shaping the law. The first kind is social. The Wenchuan earthquake in 2008 is a perfect example; it traumatized the aggregate philanthropic industry in China. At the time, donations from all over the country flooded in, increasing the total amount of donations received by the MCA and civil society organizations by 5 to 6 times that of the previous year.[1] While concerned citizens actively participated in charity, various problems surrounding charity management and mishandled funds were exposed. As reported by Financial Network, only about RMB 15.1 billion worth of expenses, or 23.16% of the RMB 65.2 billion donated in the Wenchuan earthquake, was disclosed to the public. The remaining RMB 50.1 billion has not been clearly shown in public data and even the source of it cannot be verified (Zhao, 2018). The rapid outpouring of donations and the chaos caused by it attracted the attention of the government and all sectors of society. This pushed the *Charity Law* to be listed as first type of legislative planning of the NPC in that year and then into the legislative process the following year.

The second kind is technological. Around 2015 online philanthropic innovations represented by the 99 Charity Day emerged. Rapidly spreading, cross-regional, and gamified the innovations encouraged netizens to donate. The amount of third-party online donations surged three times as fast as that of the previous year (Charity Fundraiser Alliance, 2017). However, the amplification effect of the Internet also brought new problems, such as pressure from the public caused by the Guo Meimei incident, which had a tremendously negative impact on the Red Cross Society. The development of philanthropy, especially in the form of Internet philanthropy, has become an urgent problem for regulators to solve. Therefore, a draft of the *Charity Law* was completed in 2015, which included relevant articles on Internet philanthropy and entered the final stage of deliberation by the NPC.

[1] Calculated based on annual social donation data published by the Ministry of Civil Affairs.

A Hundred and Thirty-Nine Days

Compared to the twists and turns of the previous decade, it took less than half a year, or 139 days to be exact, for the Charity Law to be reviewed after it entered the legislative cycle of the NPC in 2015. It was quite rare for bills submitted to the NPC to be processed so quickly. The media even called it super speed, which only highlighted the importance of the *Charity Law* and the urgent need for it.

Han Ke, head of the Commission of Legislative Affairs, detailed the 139 days of work in his book, *The Affairs of the National People's Congress*, under the chapter "Charity Law Journal". From the beginning of the legislation, the method used for creating the law was unusual. Public opinion was solicited and many seminars and symposiums were held continuously within academic circles, various charity organizations, relevant ministries, trust institutions, people in charge of philanthropic enterprises, and other parties. With avid research regarding representative institutions and internal revisions of the active committee, the final revision was completed during a long night's work before being submitted on the day before the deadline. Four days later, the *Charity Law* was adopted by the NPC on March 16, 2016 with a 92.2% approval rate and was officially declared effective on September 1, 2016 (Ma, 2016).

Extensive and adequate communication was the key to the smooth and rapid introduction of the Charity Law. During the 4th session of the 12th NPC, a total of 1231 deputies commented on the draft of the *Charity Law*, proposing nearly 4000 suggestions for amendments, with 110 amendments actually made (Ma, 2016).

With its legislation charitable activities, organizations, and behaviors were standardized under the supervision and management of the Chinese government. It also marked the end of the chaotic situation in the field of philanthropy, which had been poorly regulated and difficult to manage. Furthermore, it managed and promoted sound and orderly development of charitable and public welfare undertakings in China.

Section 2 The Five Stages of the Most Important Article Legislating Internet Philanthropy

The article of the Chinese *Charity Law* that has the most impact on online philanthropy is Article 23, which regulates charitable information platforms. It dictates who can launch online fund-raising campaigns and through which platform. Due to the article's considerable importance, all those involved in its legislation offered different judgments on the strictness of its enforcement. Because of this, it ended up going through repeated modifications over five stages: An initial inclusion in the law, its removal in the second draft, followed by a re-inclusion of a revised version more like the original, then a slight modification, and last, a revised final draft, where the task of assigning platforms was handed over to the Ministry of Civil Affairs under the State Council. A vote settled the matter and the final draft was passed. Though the process was cumbersome, it reflects the democratic character of the legal system regulating charity, as it was able to make room for a plurality of views, thus gaining the approval of those involved in its making.

The Inclusion of the Article in the First Draft: Management at Different Levels

Online philanthropy was right in the middle of a development boom a year before the first draft of the law was produced. According to the findings of the *2014 Research Report on Chinese Online Donation Third-party Platforms*, funds raised on third-party platforms that year reached RMB 436 million, with the number of individual donations amounting to 1.118 billion.

While the aggregate industry was progressing at full speed, it was also plagued by donation scams. One instance of this was in August of 2015, when a Gen Z girl was arrested on the charge of duping netizens into making donations on Weibo, a popular social platform in China. The girl, under the pseudonym "My heart always belongs to Bayern Munich" (literally) begged for cash donations under the pretense that her father had died in the notorious explosions at the port of Tianjin. Though some sharp-eyed netizens saw through the hoax in a timely manner, according to incomplete statistics, more than 3700 Internet users contributed over RMB 90,000 to the girl (*Father died*, 2015).

Against this backdrop, those who drafted the first version took on a cautious attitude to online fund-raising. First, the article calls for management at different levels, providing that "charitable organizations registered at the civil affairs departments at the provincial or higher level may raise money either on their own websites or other websites. Those registered at the district or county civil affairs departments may do so only on online charity platforms established or designated by such departments". Second, the article put geographic restrictions on public fund-raising, setting forth that "public fund-raising campaigns by charitable organizations should be conducted within the area administered by the civil affairs department they registered with". During first drafting of the article, Wang Shengming, Vice-chairman of the NPC Supervisory and Judicial Affairs Committee, expressed that: "This legislation is based on the need and possibilities of conducting online fund-raising. At the same time and to a large extent, it avoids duplicate donations and donation scams. According to preliminary estimates, the number of charitable organizations registered at civil affairs departments at the provincial or higher level has soared upwards to several thousand, enough to require online fund-raising here in China; there is also a huge number of those registered at lower levels, most of which specialize in charity services. There is a need to regulate charitable information platforms through which organizations established or designated by civil affairs departments raise funds in a beneficial manner" (Ma & Sheng, 2015).

The Deletion of the Article in the Second Draft: More Open and Inclusive

The strict management at different levels of the first draft provoked widespread controversy. During the one-month period soliciting public opinion before review, 1803 comments were received (Ma & Sheng, 2015).

The major concerns lay in the four following aspects: Whether individual fund-raising should be limited, including whether it was legal through social platforms like Weibo and WeChat; whether it was necessary to set a two-year inspection period since the NGOs were already granted the permission to raise funds publicly; whether management at different levels and geographic restrictions were reasonable; and last, what preferential policies for taxation were in place and if there was a way to update them.

The second draft took these opinions into full consideration, in particular by deleting differentiated management and geographic restrictions on online fund-raising. This move marked a more open and inclusive attitude benefiting online philanthropy. Insiders in the industry believed that as online philanthropic development was still in its early stages, management at different levels and strict regulation could hinder its development. More leeway should be left for it to grow. Wang Zhongfang, Secretary-general of Guangzhou Charity Association, said in an interview, "Limiting charitable organizations' online charitable campaigns by consigning them to management at different levels, reeks of 'control and censorship'. Many organizations at the municipal and district levels have already put up their own fund-raising functions on their websites. If differentiated management is adopted, most of them will be severely affected" (Wang, 2015).

Therefore, the second draft abandoned "differentiated management" and lifted the restriction on what platforms charitable organizations could use. The new article provided that "charitable organizations should specify the authority with which they are registered if they are to raise funds through the Internet", and that "Internet service providers should verify the registration credentials and the public fund-raising certificates submitted by the charitable organizations that use online platforms".

As for geographic restrictions, some NGOs and experts at the NPC Standing Committee had already expressed their disagreement during the first draft. They held that many charitable organizations release their public fund-raising information through multiple channels such as broadcasting, television, newspaper, and the Internet. Hence, it is unnecessary and almost impossible to place restrictions, much less geographical ones, given that these media channels typically span different districts by nature.

The second draft basically adopted the aforementioned advice, lifting geographic restrictions on public fund-raising campaigns publicized through broadcasting, television, newspaper, and the Internet. However, public fund-raising activities such as putting a collection box in public places or organizing a benefit performance, bazaar, charitable competition, charitable auction or charitable party, would all be subject to geographic restrictions and ought to be carried out within their respective administrative region of the civil affairs departments under which they were registered.

The Re-Introduction of the Restrictive Article: A Return to Conservatism

During the review of the second draft, some authorities were convinced that online charity should be standardized and as the idea prevailed, the Legislative Affairs Commission of the NPC Standing Committee formulated an article similar to that in the first draft. It stipulated, "Charitable organizations raising funds on the Internet shall release relevant information on unified charitable platforms designated by civil affairs departments and those registered at civil affairs departments at the provincial or higher level, may release their fund-raising information on other websites".

The return to conservatism for online charity was obvious for two reasons. First, the power of verifying and managing charitable information platforms was granted to the civil affairs departments. Second, geographical restrictions for online fund-raising were again imposed on small and medium-sized organizations registered at lower levels, limiting them to officially certified platforms, while those registered at the provincial or higher level would be able to use their own online platforms.

This conservative tendency reflected the previous cautious attitude to online charity. The major risk legislators were trying to avoid was the potential chaos for the industry due to the lack of management.

Slight Modifications to the Second Draft: Removing Differentiated Management

After the second draft was revised, the Legislative Affairs Commission of the NPC Standing Committee held a symposium to hear the opinions on online fund-raising provisions in the draft, inviting relevant companies to participate, including China Minsheng Bank, HNA Group, Alibaba, and Tencent.

The major concerns of these companies were the restrictions on charitable information platforms. For non-governmental platforms, the expression "unified charitable platforms designated by civil affairs departments" did not imply anything specific, making the provision hard to enforce. For well-established small platforms, "officially certified platforms only" could mean bankruptcy. For those organizations registered at lower levels, already deficient in resources and capability, the fact that their fund-raising information could only be published on official platforms would further deny them the access to more resources. That could result in institutional inequity.

The modified draft partly accepted the feedback and removed differentiated management but still maintained the request for government supervision. "Charitable organizations that raise funds through the Internet shall publish the fund-raising information on the unified charitable platforms designated by the civil affairs departments; they may also publish such information on their own websites".

Final Adjustments to the Modified Draft: Unified Management

The modified draft retaining the article about government supervision reflected outdated thinking typical of traditional philanthropy conducted offline. For such charity, the supervisory power was delegated to local governments for decentralized implementation. This might work for traditional offline fund-raising activities but it would be almost impossible for charitable information platforms to apply for government authentication at all levels, given that they spanned many administrative areas by being on the Internet.

A special meeting of deputies was held during the 4th session of the 12th NPC to discuss the issue. On the question of whether the authentication of online fund-raising platforms should be handed over to the civil affairs department above provincial level, Pony Ma Huateng, the core founder, Chairman and CEO of Tencent, and an industry representative held an opinion in opposition to Chen Shu, an expert on legislation. They had an in-depth conversation to share their opinions on the matter.

Pony Ma Huateng insisted on changing the department in charge of authentication to the "the Ministry of Civil Affairs of the State Council or perhaps a civil affairs department above the provincial level". He might have good reason to worry. According to the article, these platforms would have to be authenticated at over 3000 civil affairs departments at different levels before they could operate legally. He argued, "They would waste almost all of their time on each process, greatly undermining their capability to organize charitable events".

Chen Shu objected that it was not in the interest of charitable organizations to set a "provincial level threshold" as it would not ensure equality. "I am afraid I don't agree with Mr. Ma. By eliminating this threshold, all charitable organizations would be on an equal footing".

The clash divided the debate into two camps: What is more important for the development of technology-driven philanthropy, efficiency or equality? In later discussions, Chen expressed that she did understand Mr. Ma's point, saying, "The crux of the issue is to distinguish 'form' from 'content'. Platforms such as Sina Weibo, Sina Weibo's Micro-Philanthropy, and WeChat are just different platforms for fund-raising. But it is the charitable organizations dealing with public fund-raising that need to be regulated. The law must make that point quite clear. The form is just the outside appearance, it's the 'content', i.e., the organizations that need to be regulated" (Zhou, 2016). She indicated that in the end they were different, thus the regulation of platforms could be different from that of the organizations that used them.

The final draft took into consideration the opinions from many parties. According to Article 23(3) of the *Charity Law*, "Charitable organizations using the Internet to carry out fund-raising shall publish relevant information on the unified charitable information platforms designated by the Ministry of Civil Affairs under the State Council. They may also release such information on other websites". This time, this law confirmed regulation on charitable information platforms was necessary, and the power to oversee them was given to the national-level civil department so that the cost to obtain authentication was drastically reduced. This draft was finally passed and online charity entered a new era where information platforms were to be overseen by a unified authority.

Section 3 Three Questions about Internet Philanthropy

When first inducted into China, the *Charity Law* inevitably faced disputes in its formulation and promulgation. Especially for newborn Internet philanthropy, there was not much world experience related to building a well-established system. Therefore, different questions and doubts are easily recognized before all sectors of society when it comes to making specific legal provisions on philanthropy. In general, there are mainly three questions: Can individuals raise money "publicly" through the Internet?

According to Article 26 of the *Charity Law*, organizations or individuals not eligible for public fund-raising may, for charitable purposes, run public fund-raising campaigns in partnership with charitable organizations eligible for public fund-raising; and charitable organizations with public fund-raising qualifications are responsible for running the campaign and managing the funds raised.

Does it mean that individuals cannot publicly seek help or raise donations through the Internet? Actually, this is not the case. The *Charity Law* does not prohibit individuals from seeking help or collecting donations online. According to different types of individual behaviors related to releasing philanthropic information, three cases can be summarized and discussed.

Case 1: Personal help-seeking behavior is not prohibited. It refers to the fact that individuals who want to solve their own or their family's problems can publish help-seeking information online. Such behavior is not explicitly prohibited by the *Charity Law*. According to Kan Ke, Deputy-head of the Bill Division at the Secretariat of the 4th Session of the 12th NPC, "Charity is altruistic, which means to benefit unspecific and most people. Self-interest has nothing to do with charity, for it is all about personal help-seeking, which is not included in and regulated by the *Charity Law*". The Regulations on the Management of Public Fund-raising Platform Services also clearly stipulate that personal help-seeking does not belong to the public fund-raising scope specified by the *Charity Law*. However, it should be noted that individuals who contribute fake donations or commit donation fraud will be held accountable to the law.

Case 2: The public online fund-raising behavior of individuals for the sake of another person is not prohibited. Such a behavior benefiting only a particular individual does not fall within the scope of Charity Law. As Kan Ke said clearly, "Charity means to benefit unspecific and most people". Article 26 of the *Charity Law* also specifies that only in pursuit of charitable purposes can individuals cooperate with organizations eligible for public fund-raising to run public fund-raising campaigns. A charitable purpose means that the fund-raising aims at benefiting a group of people rather than a specific individual. That is, the beneficiaries should be unspecific individuals and groups.

Case 3: The public online fund-raising behavior of individuals for the sake of unspecific individuals or groups is prohibited. Such a behavior pertains to the public charitable fund-raising regulated by the *Charity Law* which clarifies that individuals must cooperate with charitable organizations eligible for public fund-raising to initiate such campaigns. If an individual does so, it will be considered illegal according to the *Charity Law* and he or she shall assume corresponding legal responsibilities.

What charitable organizations are the legal agents for running a fund-raising campaign through the Internet?

According to the *Charity Law* and the *Regulations on the Management of Public Fund-raising Platform Services*, charitable organizations that have obtained qualifications for public fund-raising according to law can run public fund-raising campaigns, while organizations and individuals who are not eligible for public fund-raising shall not run a public fund-raising campaign.

As shown in Fig. 5.1, only those public fund-raising charitable organizations legally eligible for fund-raising and having obtained certificates of

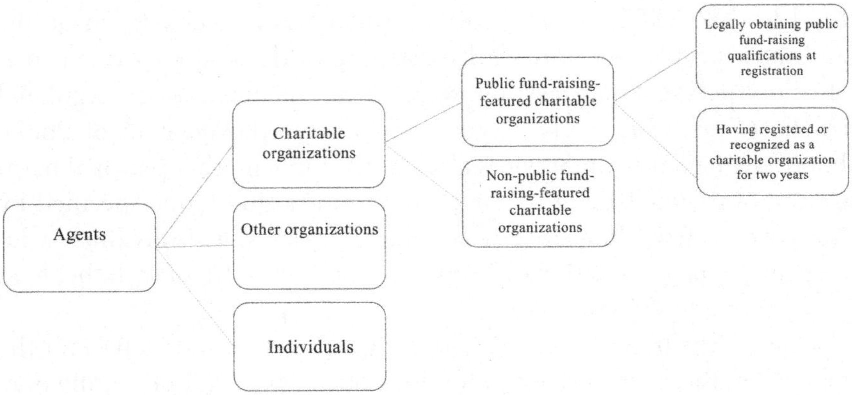

Fig. 5.1 Agents of charity and philanthropy

registration and the qualification certificate of public fund-raising can carry out public fund-raising activities online, while those indicated by dotted lines have no right to conduct such activities.

What Are the Obligations of Charitable Information Platforms?

Since a charitable information platform can obtain the statutory right to release charitable-oriented information, it naturally needs to bear corresponding responsibilities and obligations. The *Charity Law* and the *Regulations on the Management of Public Fund-raising Platform Services* clearly stipulate that the charitable information platforms shall mainly undertake obligations from seven standpoints:

1. Verification. When providing public fund-raising services, the platform shall check, on behalf of donors, that the registration certificate and the qualification certificate of public fund-raising of the charitable organization to release charitable-oriented information is legitimate.
2. Signing of agreements: When the platform provides charitable organizations with public fund-raising services, an agreement shall be signed to clarify the rights and obligations of both parties in terms of information released and the authenticity of fund-raising matters.

3. Reporting: If the platform finds any charitable organizations in violation of any laws or regulations during public fund-raising activities, it shall report to the corresponding civil affairs department in a timely manner.
4. Recording and preservation: The platform shall record and retain a copy of relevant certificates of charitable organizations and related information released on it.
5. Support: If the civil affairs department finds any charitable organizations in violation of laws or regulations on the platform and asks for assistance in the investigation, the platform should give full support to this effort.
6. Informing: If the platform stops publishing public fund-raising information for charitable organizations, it shall inform the public.
7. Reminding: Regarding the help-seeking information released by individuals, the platform shall remind the public to guard against risks with a reminder in a prominent place, saying the information is not public fund-raising and that the responsibility for its authenticity is assumed by the individual who released it.

In a word, the official enforcement of the *Charity Law* has had great impact on China's Internet philanthropy. The charitable information platforms have been included in supervision, marking the fact that China's Internet philanthropy has ushered in an era of regulated development. How to encourage innovation allowed by laws and regulations will become a big question for the government and the philanthropic industry.

Section 4 Internet Plus Civil Affairs Services

In fact, the Chinese government noticed the significant role of the Internet years ago. In 2015 Premier Li Keqiang gave a report on government work where the "Internet Plus" had turned into a national strategy. Since then China's Internet philanthropy has greatly expanded and the government has seen the Internet play a huge part in social work. The MCA of the People's Republic of China, as a competent department for national charity and philanthropy, promulgated the *Action Plan for the Internet Plus Civil Affairs Services* ("The Plan") on May 28, 2018 (Ministry of Civil Affairs, 2018), which indicated its vision and commitment to promoting further integration of the Internet and civil affairs services, upgrading the entire civil service system, improving the quality of public services, and enhancing management.

The Plan includes 10 typical "Internet Plus" featured services, four of which are closely related to the great cause of philanthropy. They are Internet Plus Social Organization, Internet Plus Social Assistance, Internet Plus Volunteer Service, and Internet Plus Lost Relatives-Seeking Service. Thus, it is easy to see the importance of charity and philanthropy to "Internet Plus Civil Affairs Services".

Internet Plus Civil Society Organizations

Since the reform and opening-up policy was launched, China's civil society organizations have achieved significant development with their scale expanded and their types enriched day by day. Furthermore, they have become useful supporters and assistants of the government in social governance. However, due to the immaturity of infrastructure, management mechanisms, and supporting tools healthy and ailing civil society organizations have been mixed up in society, which may bring about further risks.

It is difficult to efficiently handle the complex problems related to civil society organizations via traditional offline methods. For example, false online information sent by some organizations can easily affect the majority of users and it is nearly impossible to give warnings to the public through offline methods, thus we must resort to the Internet to energize and manage civil society organizations.

Therefore, the MCA made clear the "Internet Plus Civil Society Organizations" via four points in the Plan, including the legal person stipulation, the WeChat matrix, charitable donation information platforms, and credit system. The implementation of this part of the Plan is led by the China Social Organization Administration under the MCA and joined by the MCA Information Center in addition to the MCA Service Center for Civil Society Organizations.

First, all civil affairs departments work together to build a national legal person database for civil society organizations while establishing a comprehensive regulatory system for civil society organizations connected to the civil affairs system. When managing the registration of civil society organizations, relevant departments should streamline administration, delegating more power to lower-level government entities and society, improving regulation, and optimizing services. More efforts should be made to solve problems of work difficulties, low efficiency, and cumbersome procedures when it comes to registration. Until now, the legal person database has completed public bidding and entered the construction stage. The base is to be built according to the instructions from both ministerial and provincial levels, which aim at developing an information system that is able to improve services concerning the business registration and credit disclosure of main market players as well as the reporting, registration, and annual inspection of civil society organizations, ensuring that the main market players' information is over 99% accurate and complete, and 80% of the supervision information about those players has electronic records.

Second, all civil affairs departments work together to build a quality WeChat matrix and a web platform that features quick data inquiry about civil society organizations, advanced warning, online complaints and tip-offs, and the subscription account of new developments of China's civil society organizations (Fig. 5.2). Such an effort is aimed at facilitating benign interaction between civil society organizations and the public and creating an environment where the development of civil society organizations is supported and supervised by society. At present, the web version of China's civil society organizations' public service platform and the WeChat subscription account have gone live, which have collected statistics from nearly 800,000 civil society organizations (Public Service Platform for Chinese Social Organizations, n.d.) and 4880 charitable organizations (Charity China, n.d.). By virtue of these two tools, it is more convenient for users to search for relevant information or to voice complaints through personal computers or mobile devices.

Third, all civil affairs departments must work together to strengthen the selection and daily supervision of online charitable fund-raising information platforms, providing guidance on how to create easy,

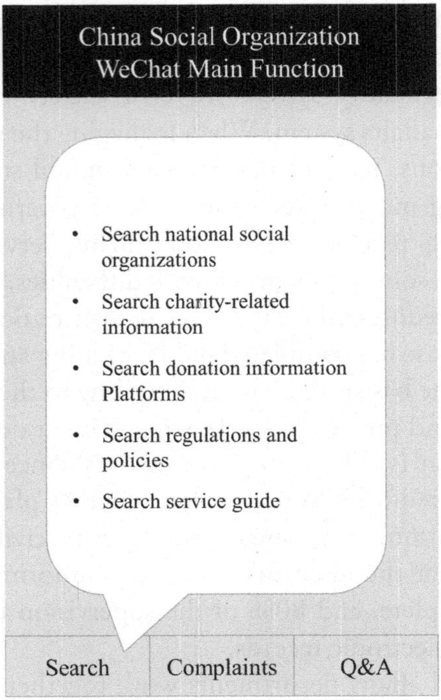

Fig. 5.2 China's civil society organizations' public service platform

normative, and smooth access to fund-raising as well as give impetus to the efforts towards the sharing of information on charitable donations and the establishment of a reward and punishment system so as to create cleaner cyberspace featuring "All for philanthropy and philanthropy for all". Furthermore, more efforts should be invested in giving full play to the collaborative advantages of Internet platforms, ensuring that civil society organizations' service projects meet social needs and exploring more approaches to information sharing and social participation in a bid to provide more chances for the public to participate in charity and philanthropy. As mentioned above, the MCA has authorized 20 online fund-raising information platforms after two rounds of selection, almost covering all major existing types such as social networks, e-commerce, O2O, and crowd-funding.

Fourth, all civil affairs departments work together to strengthen cooperation with members contributing to the building of the national credit system and domestic large-scale Internet platforms; ensure the sharing of credit information of civil society organizations in an attempt to build and share credit information of civil society organizations; and intercept online information about illegal civil society organizations in an attempt to safeguard and protect the rights and interests of the public. To this end, the MCA promulgated the *Measures for Managing Credit Information of Civil society organizations* in January of 2018. It stipulates that all of China's administrative authorities for the registration of credit information of civil society organizations should record those who fail to fulfill their obligations according to law or violate laws and regulations. Presently, the "list of entities with abnormal operations" and the "list of illegal and dishonest entities" exclusive to the MCA have both been released on the China's civil society organizations' public service platform. Nevertheless, the MCA is still exploring ways to cooperate with other information systems. It may be a while before the birth of an all-around credit system.

Internet Plus Social Assistance

As a major part of social work, social assistance relies heavily on the Internet in enlarging influence and simplifying its complicated work system. It is an important point of the government's work plan to integrate information through the Internet, accurately identifying the assistance objectives and shorten the assistance-delivering time frame.

First, the aim is to build a comprehensive service information platform for social assistance, extend service area, and strengthen cooperation in providing services so as to ensure resource sharing. At the same time, more efforts should be made to get the utmost out of websites, WeChat, apps, service hotlines, self-service terminals, and other means of providing the public with policy interpretation, trouble-shooting and inquiries, supervision, and reporting services. Social assistance-related information should be accessible to the public and subject to social supervision.

Second, the aim is to give full play to "Internet Plus", big data, and other technologies in promoting the establishment of a checking mechanism on the economic status of families who receive social assistance and contributions to accurately identify social assistance objectives. The relevant departments should give advice to local sectors on how to deal with assistance application, carry out household surveys, and recheck and supervise social assistance-related work while developing mobile apps to improve work efficiency and information sharing.

The social assistance section of the action plan is led by the MCA Department of Social Assistance and joined by the MCA Center for Monitoring and Verification of Low-income Families, and the MCA Information Center. Presently, due to the obvious regional characteristics of social assistance and civil affairs departments' fresh start in applying information and digital technologies to social assistance, this section of the action plan explains the present condition, i.e., that the central departments assign tasks and give advice and support while local sectors execute the tasks independently. Local sectors, such as Hainan and Qinghai at the provincial level, Baotou and Changsha at the municipal level, and Chongqing's Jiangjin and Yan'an's Ansai at the district level have all opened official WeChat accounts for social assistance to provide online services (See Fig. 5.3).

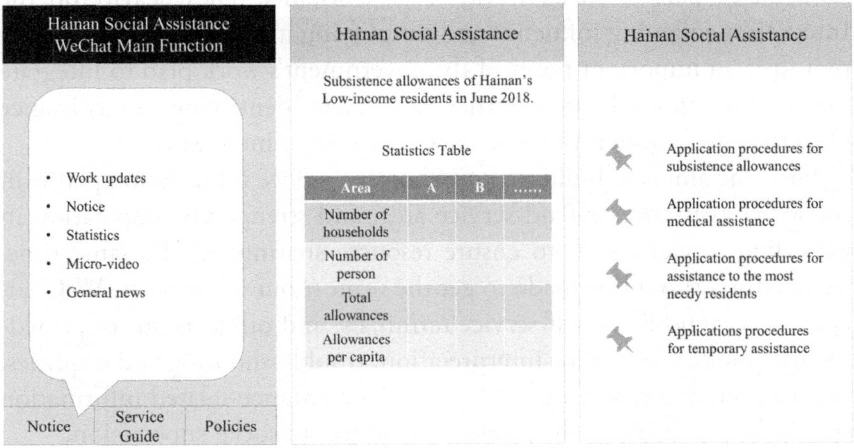

Fig. 5.3 WeChat account of Hainan social assistance and its services (as an example)

Internet Plus Volunteer Service

Volunteers serve as the core force in implementing social work. According to the *China Volunteer Service Development Report (2016)* issued by China Volunteer Service Federation, the total number of officially registered volunteers and unregistered volunteers in China reached 134.8 million in 2016, accounting for 9.75% of China's population. This means almost every one out of ten people is a volunteer in China, which demonstrates the important role of volunteers in China's social work force, especially with regards to charity and philanthropy.

However, with a short history, Chinese volunteer services have run into several problems. For one thing, the volunteer service in China takes on obvious regional imbalances. According to the aforementioned report, the number of rural volunteer service organizations only accounts for 5.53% of the total and the number of volunteers in eastern developed areas is 11 times that of volunteers in central China. For another, the industry lacks norms. Incidents concerning illegal employment of volunteers and substandard volunteer services happen occasionally. All these problems have restrained the sound development of China's volunteer services.

Given the popularity of the Internet, it is inevitable to connect, support, and manage volunteer services by the Internet. As a result, problems such as information asymmetry, procedure redundancy, non-transparency, and lack of incentives can be readily solved.

First, information asymmetry: We can promote the connection and communication between different information systems and gather big data resources for integrating volunteer services by upgrading and rebuilding the national volunteer service information system and authorizing eligible systems.

Second, procedure redundancy and non-transparency: We will give full play to the role of Internet platforms in providing volunteer services, better the digitization of volunteer service information, and provide easy-to-reach services for volunteers and voluntary-service organizations involving real-name registration, activity search and sign-up, personnel recruitment, service time recording, certificate issuing, query and printing, etc., forming a good environment for the public to participate in volunteer activities.

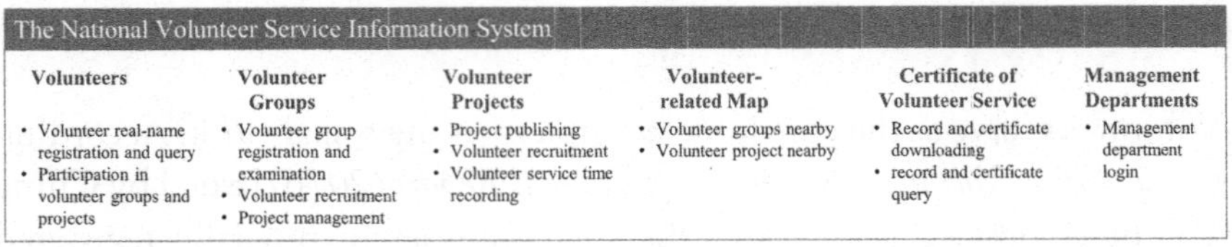

Fig. 5.4 Main functions of the national volunteer service information system

Third, lack of incentives: Relying on the development of the volunteer service information system and data sharing, we will strengthen the efforts to offer praise and favored treatment to volunteers, complete citizens' credit information, enhance online communication of volunteer activities and volunteerism, and mobilize all parties to participate in volunteer services.

The volunteer service section of the action plan is led by the China Social Organization Administration under the MCA and joined by the MCA Information Center. Actually, the national volunteer service information system was first tested in November, 2016 and officially launched online in June 2017. Until now, nearly 480,000 volunteer groups and more than 90 million volunteers have registered, the number of published volunteer projects has exceeded 1.4 million, and the total volunteer service time has reached 1 billion hours (China Volunteer Service Network, n.d.). We can safely conclude that volunteer service has covered a wide range (See Fig. 5.4). In the future, we will further focus on refining the functions of applications of the system to attract more volunteer groups, projects, and volunteers to frequently use the system and let the efficiency-featured Internet come into play.

Internet Plus Lost Relatives-Seeking

Helping people seek lost relatives is a variety of social assistance that shows both caprice and possibility in daily work. The speed and scope as well as the veracity of information dissemination both play decisive roles in the result of lost relative-seeking efforts. It is widely recognized that the 24 hours after one's disappearance is the "golden time" for seekers. Traditional offline methods get nowhere if we want to quickly disseminate a notice for missing persons on a large scale, while the Internet can effectively and quickly reach netizens and mobilize them to provide useful information. In addition, machine intelligence technologies such as face recognition have been developed, which greatly increase the possibility of finding missing persons.

The lost relatives-seeking section of the action plan is led by the MCA Department of Social Affairs and joined by the MCA Information Center and aims at facilitating the upgrade of the Internet Plus Lost Relatives-Seeking platform and the development of its technologies and applications.

On one hand, we should innovate means and broaden channels of the lost relatives-seeking services by making full use of the Internet's strengths so that it can easily reach people and share information; upgrade and improve the national platform of missing children's information; enhance the functions of the national information system for assistance management; and focus on the development of assistance management-featured mobile app, the WeChat account for the national lost relatives-seeking service, and the VIP Weibo account. We will try to achieve the sharing of population information within the public security sector, enlarge the coverage of family seeking and assistance, and make more progress in helping vagrants and beggars find their families and giving assistance to children who lose touch with their families. We will also continue to make efforts to raise social awareness and credibility of the website of the national lost relatives-seeking service.

On the other hand, we need to actively embrace new technologies and make full use of machine intelligence, deepen cooperation with Internet-enabled platforms, and actively explore the application of emerging technologies such as face recognition and fingerprint identification so as to improve the efficiency of lost relatives-seeking efforts and help those who have lost touch with their families.

In September 2015, the MCA worked with the Ministry of Public Security and launched a national platform of missing children's information. Presently, it only has a web version that features limited functions and is mainly used for disclosing and searching for information on rescued children. In the future, it is possible to work with companies who specialize in cutting-edge technologies such as face recognition and blockchain for the purpose of upgrading the platform's functions.

References

Charity China (慈善中国). (n.d.). *慈善组织查询*. Chinanpo. Retrieved October 05, 2018, from http://cishan.chinanpo.gov.cn/biz/ma/csmh/a/csmhaindex.html/

Charity Fundraiser Alliance (公益筹款人联盟). (2017, December 20). *2015–2016第三方线上平台公众公益参与方式研究报告*. Read01. https://read01.com/zh-sg/Q3a7o0D.html#.YBkQ0ugzY2x

China Volunteer Service Network (中国志愿服务网). (n.d.). *全国志愿服务数据统计*. Chinanpo. Retrieved August 07, 2018, from http://www.chinavolunteer.cn/

"Father died in an accident asking for money on Weibo" is a fraud ("父亲在事故中身亡微博求打赏"系诈骗). (2015, August 16). People. Retrieved October 05, 2018, from http://society.people.com.cn/n/2015/0816/c1008-27467900.html

Ma, D. H. (2016, March 21). *人民日报:中国慈善事业进入法治化时代*. People. http://opinion.people.com.cn/n1/2016/0321/c1003-28212539.html

Ma, W., & Sheng, H. (2015, December 09). *慈善法草案公开征求意见结束诸多争议如何解决?*. People. http://politics.people.com.cn/n/2015/1209/c100127903842.html

Ministry of Civil Affairs (民政部). (2018, July 08). *民政部印发《"互联网+民政服务"行动计划》*. MCA. http://xxzx.mca.gov.cn/article/zcwj/201807/20180700010370.shtml

Public Service Platform for Chinese Social Organizations (中国社会组织公共服务平台). (n.d.). *全国社会组织查询V3.0*. Chinanpo. Retrieved October 05, 2018, from http://www.chinanpo.gov.cn/search/orgindex.html

Wang, Z. (2015, December 23). *慈善法草案二审:网络募捐分级制拟取消不限平台*. Chinanpo. http://www.chinanpo.gov.cn/1940/92320/index.html

Wen, J. (2016, March 17). *有故土, 才记得住乡愁*. Infzm. http://www.infzm.com/content/117062?b0h

Zhao, Y. S. (2018, May 12). *汶川地震十年系列—捐赠者的质疑:怎么捐?捐给谁?*. BBC. https://www.bbc.com/zhongwen/simp/chinese-news-43945981
Zhou, C. X. (2015, October 31). *首部慈善法提交审议政府摊派捐赠构成犯罪可追刑责*. Xinhuanet. http://www.xinhuanet.com//politics/2015-10/31/c_128378150.htm
Zhou, W. (2016, March 12). *广东团热议慈善法草案 马化腾与陈舒坐下来"私聊"*. Gzmz. http://www.gzmz.gov.cn/gzsmzj/mtgz/201603/fb58b799239b4b1c998d12f28d1aedd6.shtml

Part II

Global Vision: Internet Philanthropy in Charitable Countries

The challenge here is to design a system where market incentives, including profits and recognition, drive those principles to do more for the poor. I like to call this idea creative capitalism.

—Bill Gates

Founder of Microsoft Corporation and Bill & Melinda Gates Foundation

A New Approach to Capitalism in the 21st Century

—World Economic Forum 2008

January, 2008

Internet philanthropy enjoys a significant presence not only in China, but also around the world.

The past 20 years of the Internet' s growth and widespread popularity have jumpstarted online philanthropy on a path towards far-reaching growth. Fast-growing modes for Internet philanthropy and mechanisms in the US, EU and Japan have increasingly extended the scope of charity and philanthropy, offering innovative solutions to social problems. The development path for Internet philanthropy, however, is different for each country. The influence of multiple factors such as economics, culture, institutions, and the level of Internet development, has led to strikingly different, and diverse results.

China, for its part, has made great strides in online philanthropy up to now. Be that as it may, there is still a pressing need to take on an international perspective to promote its development, while learning from other countries' success stories. By doing so, we can pave a path for further growth of online philanthropy, one that is both in line with its own internal rules of development but also imbued with Chinese characteristics.

6
The United States: Voluntary Spirit and Technological Innovation

The American charitable spirit has a long, rich history in the United States, which is greatly influenced by the country's historical background and political system. Since entering the 21st century and the era of innovation, Internet enterprises have assumed more social responsibility towards philanthropy, and formed a distinctly American Internet philanthropy model. This includes a number of large tech enterprises such as Facebook, Twitter, Paypal, and Google.

The US is a country that leads the whole world, not only in terms of economy, but also in the development of its philanthropic sector. The US has the highest level of public involvement in philanthropy in the world, as well as the most professional charitable organizations[1] and the most influential philanthropic services. On top of this, America enjoys a long history of a public charity culture and a sound system of charity regulation. These two constitute the fountains for constant innovation in

[1] The English equivalent to Chinese word "慈善组织" is "charitable organization", referring to organizations that are aimed to improve public welfare. It includes non-profit charitable, religious, educational and other philanthropic organizations. The "charitable organization" defined in China's *Charity Law* has a narrower range than the original "charitable organization" in English. The two are different in concept to some extent.

Y. Chen, *Internet Philanthropy in China*,
https://doi.org/10.1007/978-981-16-2566-4_6

American philanthropy and have had a significant impact on its development.

As the top player in Internet applications and technological innovation, the US, without doubt, leads developed countries and the entire world in its Internet philanthropy. This includes the strength of American fundraising, initiatives, and innovative modes that integrate online and offline methods. Rooted in a profound cultural base and a sound system of laws and policies, Internet philanthropy in the US has been propelled towards constant success and innovation over the past 20 years. Therefore, it is indispensable for us to study carefully and learn from America's achievements and experience.

Section 1 The Philanthropic Culture in the US

The Christian tradition of giving to charity and the public's activist involvement in public affairs are the two main sources of America's culture of philanthropy.

The US has deep religious roots. The first immigrants that came on the Mayflower colonial period were pious Protestants. They were persecuted in Britain because of their religion and finally ended up fleeing in search of a new home until they settled in the New World. In this sense, religious faith ran deep throughout the whole North American colony. Even the first universities and charitable organizations had close ties with religion.

Henry Allen Moe, the American philosopher, once said that "Religion is the mother of charity in both ideology and originating process." Even though Christianity stresses that the afterlife is about salvation and eternity, the religion has also been a proponent of "doing good" ever since it first began. Christianity rests on the premise that humans are born with original sin, and hence, their souls can only be saved if they believe in God. To this end, it stresses loving God (i.e., committing acts of charity). Nevertheless, charity, as a virtue, is not only about loving God. Christians believe they ought to follow the edicts "Love the Lord your God with all your heart and with all your soul and with all your strength and with all your mind"; "Love your neighbor as yourself" (Pope John Paul II, 2019);

and even "Love your enemies, do good to those who hate you"[2]. Such love for God and others constitutes the foundation of the loving Christian spirit, which underpins all Christian teachings.

Due to these teachings, it has become a moral obligation for the rich to help the poor. It is universal love that Christianity teaches; to help others even at the cost of material wealth is a good deed that guarantees one wealth in the afterlife. The Bible says, "If thou wilt be perfect, go and sell that thou hast, and give to the poor, and thou shalt have treasure in Heaven"[3] Aside from this, Christianity advocates that the poor are God's chosen people, so that helping the poor is helping God. The rich, therefore, are encouraged to help the poverty-stricken to earn God's praise.

Since the collapse of the Roman Empire, Christian churches have gradually taken over the responsibilities of social security and emergency relief. During war or disaster, famine or plague, Christians always play a major part in offering relief and security. Over thousands of years, this love for God evolved into the distinctively Christian spirit of the Good Samaritan.

After the Protestant Reformation, many of the emerging religious branches reflected on how the Church controlled our world, and came up with Christian ethics. Good deeds still played a major part of these ethics across all branches. In addition, the Protestant Reformation enabled many branches to pay more attention to life here on Earth, encouraging more believers to donate, do good deeds and put God's words of "love your neighbor as you love yourself" into earthly practice. Under such guidance, many churches carried out philanthropic events with a certain religious character in their communities during the early days of the American colonies.

Later, philanthropy in modern America shifted towards more secular values, leaving religion on the sidelines. Nonetheless, the Christian virtue of "loving others" still comprises an integral part of modern philanthropy. Given that the US is still a deeply religious country, the influence of this Good Samaritan spirit is felt widely, forming the long-lasting core of philanthropic culture in America.

---

[2] The Gospel of Luke 6:35.

[3] The Gospel of Matthew 19:21.

The philanthropic tradition in America also comes from people's voluntary spirit, driving them to participate in public affairs. Out of the major Western countries, autonomy and governance by the people have the deepest roots in Britain. There, governmental power is relatively weak and hardly centralized. The *Magna Carta* has been capping the power of governments since the 13th century. In North American colonies, governments could wield even less power.

After the War of Independence, America's founding fathers were wary of an excessively powerful government, and they endowed the Constitution with multiple checks and balances to cap governmental power. These laid the foundation for the American social structure "That government is best which governs least". However, such a government could hardly handle all public affairs, and it required the voluntary participation of more citizens.

Hence, "volunteer groups" with American characteristics emerged across the Americas, covering all facets of public life. Via "volunteer groups", American people have participated in a great number of public affairs for many years, during which they have also nurtured their "volunteer spirit". For Americans, participating in affairs related to public interests is not just the obligation of governments, but also the responsibility of common citizens. Therefore, in the spirit of volunteering, numerous American citizens are dedicated wholeheartedly to public affairs and services, which constitutes another major source of the philanthropy tradition in the country.

Section 2 The Institutional Base of Philanthropy in the US

American philanthropy, though resting on a profound cultural and historic tradition, also owes a great part of its progress to national institutions and policies. Over the past century, its rapid growth was aided by a series of preferential policies, key among which was tax relief.

The *Wilson-Gorman Tariff Act of 1894* proposed tax exemptions for certain philanthropic organizations in the US for the first time. As the philanthropic sector boomed and large private foundations emerged in the late 19th and early 20th centuries, the American government amended its tax policies to offer further relief. More specifically, the *Revenue Act of 1913* explicitly stipulated the first tax exemptions for non-profit organizations; the *War Revenue Act of 1917*, on the other hand, provided tax deductions for individual charitable donations for the first time. (Arnsberger, et al., 2008)

In the following years, the US Congress made dozens of amendments to tax policies for non-profit organizations, including more specific tax acts benefiting charity organizations. Some laws implemented in the second half of the 20th century further reduced the tax burden of charity organizations and encouraged donations through tax incentives. Take the *Revenue Act of 1978* for example, the tax on philanthropic organizations' income through investment, such as private foundations, was reduced from 4% to 2%. The *Tax Reform Act of 1969*, meanwhile, strengthened administration on charitable organizations via new provisions dictating their minimum annual expenditure.[6] Therefore, through adjustments to taxation, America had solved non-profit organizations' problem of registration once and for all, and initiated a distinctively American tax deduction system for the philanthropic sector.

Today, if a non-profit organization in the US wants to enjoy favorable tax deductions stipulated by article 501 (c) (3) of the tax code, it needs to submit Form 990 to the tax department and meet a series of requirements for registration, meanwhile strictly adhering to the tax department's information disclosure regulations. Once approved by the tax department, such an organization can finally enjoy tax deductions. At the same time, American citizens who donate to non-profit organizations can also enjoy reasonable tax deductions, which in turn encourages people to make more donations. Besides, many rich Americans, to circumvent high estate tax, choose to donate most and even all of their wealth when they reach a certain age, and set up foundations or donate to non-profit organizations.

Of course, once philanthropic organizations receive tax deductions, they are obligated to be regulated by the government. In the US, each state's government shoulders such responsibility. State governments can, based on local conditions, set up a local code of supervision on philanthropic organizations in order to avoid the discrepancies and shortcomings of national laws. According to statistics, 45 of 50 states in America have passed related laws and regulations, and some include more specific demands on registration for fundraising events. (United States, 2018)

Federal tax regulation, and industry regulation at the local governmental level are the two pillars of American regulation of the philanthropic sector. Such a system not only keeps citizens and enterprises active in charity events via tax deductions, but also reduces fraud and forgery by working together with local governments. While economic strength and the culture of philanthropy serve as the source of progress for the philanthropic sector in the US, this system of regulation is the best guarantee for such progress. After hundreds of years of experience, America has forged a comprehensive, efficient system to regulate philanthropy. The lessons of its experience have also spread to other countries and regions across the globe.

Section 3 The Philanthropic History in the US

Although the United States of America was founded for no more than 250 years, philanthropy on this land has gone through a history of 400 years. Religious philanthropic events were initiated nearly as early as the founding of the American colonies, which was the seed of modern philanthropy in America. Over the following 400 years, American philanthropy went through five stages: the colonial period, from the War of Independence to the Civil War, from the Gilded Age to the Progressive Era, middle and later periods of the 20th century, and the early 21st century.

The Colonial Period: The Beginning of Modern Philanthropy in the US

The colonial era is widely seen as the beginning of American philanthropy, and shares close ties with voluntary religious organizations. In the colonies of New England, the Congregational Church and Anglican

Church were supported via tax collected by the colonial government. Meanwhile, other more voluntary branches, such as the Methodists and Baptists, more depended on the voluntary support of their followers.

Branches that received little governmental support, though a considerable amount of voluntary support from their congregations, prospered rapidly. (Philanthropy in the United States, 2018) Later, they founded their own charity departments and facilities such as schools, clinics and hospitals, offering more services designed to serve public interest. Such voluntary religious activity also became the origin of modern philanthropy in America.

In this stage, *Bonifacius: An Essay to Do Good*, written by Puritan priest Cotton Mather, was the book that best represented the religious spirit of philanthropy in America. Mather believed that the traditional idealism of his times was being undermined, and the best countermeasure was to see good deeds in daily life as a medium to communicate with God. He also thought that any conflict of interest could be reconciled by belief, volunteer work and private charity. He concluded that everyone, regardless of gender or age, should strive to have a long-lasting, meaningful effect on the world, thus is the core purpose of faith. (Philanthropy in the United States, 2018)

As a missionary, Mather composed works filled with religious fervor, and volunteer work back then was at the service of religious faith. Nonetheless, his works exhibited clear American characteristics, and even encompassed modern concepts of public philanthropy that went beyond traditional Christian ones. His ideas left a legacy for later generations, including Benjamin Franklin, a pioneer of American philanthropic activity.

Benjamin Franklin, born in the 18th century, was a great American scientist, inventor and author. He was also a statesman, diplomat, and one of the founding fathers of the United States of America, as well as one of the signatories on the *Declaration of Independence*. Whenever his name comes up, people tend to talk about his outstanding achievements in natural science or politics, and yet his contributions to the development of philanthropy should not be overlooked.

Based on Mather, Franklin further enriched the concept of philanthropy in the US, shifting the emphasis from religion towards secularization. He paid more attention to the actual practice of giving and encouraging more people to participate in philanthropic activities. In

1792, Franklin founded the *Philadelphia Weekly* to advocate philanthropy and to drive innovation in social services. (Benjamin Franklin, 2018)

Since the beginning of the 18th century, Franklin had directly and indirectly helped Philadelphia carry out a series of voluntary charity projects, including setting up the first public library, the Academy and College of Philadelphia, the first volunteer fire department in North America, a local police force, a post office and hospital, and so on. (Benjamin Franklin, 2018) He is widely praised as a major pioneer of philanthropic events in America because of the wide influence of his ideas and practices.

From the War of Independence to the Civil War: Early Rapid Development

The United States of America was founded after the War of Independence, and this was when philanthropy in America entered a new stage. Many philanthropic events and even public enterprises during this period were started by "volunteer groups", which are essential to understanding the American social system.

In 1835, Tocqueville, a French political thinker and historian, composed his masterpiece *Democracy in America* after his tour of the US. In the book, he said: "I met with several kinds of associations in America, of which I confess I had no previous notion. (These associations are) serious, futile, extensive, or restricted, enormous or diminutive. The Americans make associations to give entertainments, to found establishments for education, to build inns, to construct churches, to diffuse books, to send missionaries to the antipodes." (Tocqueville, 1989)

The "volunteer groups" Tocqueville saw were something unique to the US, a phenomenon markedly different from that of Europe.

The US Constitution places a considerable amount of restrictions on government authority. Therefore, since the first sector (public sector) is relatively weak in authority, the third sector (voluntary sector) takes on the responsibility of a great number of public services. As Tocqueville said in his book, American volunteer groups are more powerful than ordinary civil associations since the powerful third sector is not only a popular part of American society, but also serves as the central pillar maintaining

America's democracy and national institutions. Thus, a constitutionally powerful third sector and a well-liked volunteer spirit further contribute to the foundations of philanthropic causes in America.

During the 100 years between the War of Independence and the Civil War, the economy was still booming, and ever more people were amassing large fortunes. Logically speaking, the American wealthy classes in the 19th century had to find out what to do with their enormous wealth. Against the background of a popular volunteer spirit and an influential third sector, many emerging rich Americans turned to charity.

1820 was when these newly rich Americans started to participate in charity. They founded schools, hospitals and libraries; they helped orphans and the elderly; and they even invested in public facilities built by the federal government. James Smithson, founder of the Smithsonian Institution, and George Peabody, regarded as the father of modern philanthropy, were typical of these rich American citizens. In this stage, however, philanthropists and the public carried out charity events chiefly in local communities. A philanthropist with national or global influence was yet to appear.

In this stage, non-religious charity organizations such as the Magdalen Society, were progressing in more specialized directions. This was also when new forms of charitable organizations such as foundations started to appear. In less than 100 years spanning the War of Independence and the Civil War, American philanthropy went beyond religion to take in more secular values, increased in scale and offered more professional services.

From the Gilded Age to the Progressive Era: The Rise of Scientific Charity Movements and National Foundations

The end of the American Civil War united the once-separated North and South, abolished slavery, reshaped the United States, a costly affair for many regions. People and refugees across the country were destitute and homeless. The war caused casualties and deteriorated sanitation, and many people became refugees. However, governments lacked the funds to improve sanitary conditions on their own. Thus, philanthropic organizations shared the burdens of sanitation and health care.

In 1861, Henry Bellows, Frederick Olmsted and George Strong established the United States Sanitary Commission (USSC) with other fellows to work with volunteer organizations scattered across America and help the federal government improve sanitary conditions for the military. The USSC then raised a substantial amount of funds, setting up mobile hospitals to offer medical treatment for the wounded, thereby greatly improving sanitary conditions during the Civil War.

The American Red Cross was also founded at that time. During the Civil War, many non-governmental organizations helped treat the wounded and take in refugees. In 1881, Clara Barton, a philanthropist known for her outstanding charitable contributions, founded the American Red Cross and served as its first president. Since then, the Red Cross has played a critical part in American humanitarian activities. America, with the help of Barton, became a member of the Geneva Convention in the following year.

As America entered the Gold Rush, society and economy went through sharp changes, driving philanthropy to embark upon a new path. As the economy picked up, the wealth of the upper class skyrocketed, and the number of millionaires soared compared with that of the early 19th century. However, the accumulation of wealth was accompanied by dramatic polarization, a wider economic gap, chaos in the public order, class struggle, and even social conflicts. All these problems posed a huge threat to traditional charity.

The Long Depression between 1873 and 1878 further exacerbated the situation. Some philanthropists found that many traditional philanthropic activities were having no imperceptible effect. The reason was that traditional charity organizations were essentially "giving a man a fish to feed him for a day" rather than "teaching a man to fish to feed him for a lifetime". Therefore, philanthropists like Josephine Lowell and Humphreys Gurteen, together with non-profit organizations, initiated the Scientific Charity Movement.[4]

[4] For more information concerning the Scientific Charity Movement, please refer to "Scientific Philanthropy 1873-1893" by R. H. Bremner.

The Scientific Charity Movement was dedicated to helping low-income groups shake off poverty by applying the then most advanced knowledge of health and sociology. More specifically, initiators of this Movement tried to use their expertise to help the poor get employed and make a living on their own in order to get out of poverty. In addition, the Scientific Charity Movement promoted the abolishment of poorhouses.[5]

Nevertheless, there are always two sides to every coin. Limited by the people's misconceptions and narrow-mindedness at the time, the Scientific Charity Movement also aimed to eliminate the whole class of people with physical and psychological disabilities by isolating them in asylums and subjecting them to "scientific experiments". In retrospect, it was far from humane or scientific. As science advanced and people's conceptions changed accordingly, the Scientific Charity Movement gradually faded into the background. However, the philanthropic concept of "teaching a man to fish to feed him for a lifetime", i.e., aiming to solve social problems and improve social structures, started to be widely accepted.

The Progressive Era marked the point where philanthropy in America became even more specialized. The increasing number of billionaires also set the stage for foundations of an even larger scale. The most notable examples of this were the Carnegie Corporation founded by Andrew Carnegie, and the Rockefeller Foundation founded by petroleum tycoon John Rockefeller Sr., among others.

Andrew Carnegie, founder of Carnegie Steel Company, by triggering the booming American railway and steel sectors of the end of the 19th century, swiftly became the wealthiest American of the time. On top of that, he was the first philanthropist in the American history to hold such great influence over the entire country and even the world.

Carnegie had been contributing to charity ever since the early days of building his wealth. In the 1880s, he funded a number of local libraries

---

[5] In the mid to late 19th century, the government accommodated people who couldn't make a living in poorhouses funded by tax revenue. The poorhouse was a supplement to the welfare system, but it also placed these people in a vicious circle. Once a person was placed in the poorhouse, it was difficult for them to leave since they were unable to make a living in the first place. Traditional charity lacked a solution to this. Though charity helped poor people for some time, they would eventually end up back in the poorhouse.

and other public infrastructure projects. In 1889, Carnegie wrote his widely influential book *The Gospel of Wealth* and encouraged the rich to use their wealth and jump on the philanthropic bandwagon for the sake of social progress and reform. After selling his own steel company in 1901, Carnegie began to carry out philanthropic activities on a broader scope, actively engaging in various fields such as peace advocacy, education and public facilities construction. He also established a series of philanthropic organizations such as the Carnegie Endowment for International Peace, Carnegie Institution for Science, and the Carnegie Hero Fund Trust.

However, by 1911, there were still more than USD 150 million-worth of assets under his name, which deeply troubled him. At the suggestion of his friend Elihu Root, Carnegie decided to donate the majority of his wealth and pool together all the money to set up a foundation to coordinate all his ongoing philanthropic activities. At first, Carnegie contributed USD 25 million to the foundation, and in the following years, additional funding reached a total amount of USD 135 million, which accounted for 90% of Carnegie's total remaining assets. (Zi, 2015)

Under Carnegie's influence, the Carnegie Corporation, since its inception, has channeled most resources into education. A series of adult education programs for marginalized groups of society were launched in the 1920s to help these people better integrate into society, with impressive results. Later, the Carnegie Corporation made efforts to improve the quality of and access to education, and carry out a comprehensive overhaul of the entire education system. He was able to accomplish a great deal in both aspects. At the same time, the Carnegie Corporation was also concerned about the issue of race and actively carried out various philanthropic programs to help African-Americans improve their living conditions and gain social acceptance.

Two years after the establishment of the Carnegie Corporation, John Rockefeller Sr., the "richest man in American history", founded the Rockefeller Foundation in New York. John Rockefeller Sr. possessed even more wealth than Carnegie. According to common consensus, John Rockefeller Sr. is regarded as the richest person in American history, even after accounting for inflation. When it came to business, John Rockefeller

Sr. was a cunning, calculative and frugal business tycoon, while in philanthropy, his achievements were by no means any less impressive.

Before the Rockefeller Foundation, the University of Chicago had been the most important recipient of John Rockefeller Sr.'s contributions. Between 1892 and 1910, more than USD 35 million was donated to the University of Chicago, setting the record donation amount made by an individual to a single university. (John D. Rockefeller, 2018) In 1901, John Rockefeller Sr. considered setting up a large, specialized foundation to carry out his philanthropic undertakings.

In 1906, John Rockefeller Sr.'s personal adviser and close friend, Frederick T. Gates, told him that his wealth had grown so fast that it had doubled. Gates was deeply concerned that Rockefeller' s heirs would "exhaust their inheritance or would be corrupted by such amount of money unless a permanent philanthropic foundation was established". Considering Gates' advice, John Rockefeller Sr. made up his mind to donate most of his wealth in 1906 to create a dedicated foundation. However, due to the ongoing antitrust case against Standard Oil, the Rockefeller Foundation was not established in New York until 1913. (Rockefeller Foundation, 2018)

In comparison to the Carnegie Corporation, the Rockefeller Foundation focuses more on health care, which absorbed almost all of the Foundation's funds in the early days. The Rockefeller Foundation actively promoted the prevention and treatment of infectious diseases such as hookworm infections, malaria, and typhoid fever, positively contributing to the improvement of medicine and health in many areas of the US. At the same time, the Rockefeller Foundation was also committed to promoting the study of medicine. The Rockefeller Foundation sponsored a number of medical research projects and popularized higher medical education in various countries and regions around the world to improve local healthcare standards. The Peking Union Medical College (PUMC) and its affiliated hospitals were among the key overseas projects of the Rockefeller Foundation during that period. (Zi, 2015) In addition to the healthcare sector, the Rockefeller Foundation also actively sponsored highly successful philanthropic projects in various areas such as reducing hunger, ethnic civil rights and in the humanities and social sciences.

The establishment of the Carnegie Corporation and the Rockefeller Foundation are hallmarks in the history of American philanthropy. Carnegie and Rockefeller, as the richest people in American history, donated most of their wealth when they were still alive and set up professional foundations to coordinate the development of philanthropy, exerting profound influence on the wealthy class at that time. Moreover, these two foundations undoubtedly shaped the US philanthropic mode, given that more and more rich people have applied this private foundation mode to carry out specialized philanthropic activities. Inspired and led by the two foundations, private foundations in the United States have seen rapid growth, ushering in the era of foundations in US philanthropy.

The 20th Century: The Era of Mass Philanthropy

The development of philanthropy in the middle and late 19th century was dominated by the upper class, especially the billionaires. Then, with the emergence of innovative new forms of donations and organizations in the 20th century, public donations rose, public participation became ever more popular, and mass philanthropy gradually became mainstream.

At the beginning of the 20th century, scarce methods for donations prevented the public from giving donations, despite Americans' strong enthusiasm for charitable giving. Innovative fund-raising methods were what successfully resolved this standstill. In 1907, the United States introduced a new fund-raising method by selling Christmas seals. In 1908, the amount raised through stamps reached USD 135,000. By the 1960s, a total of USD 26 million had been raised (Xu, & Zhu, 2017), a remarkable achievement in a period without electronic payment methods. Therefore, "fundraising stamps" are often regarded as the starting point for "mass philanthropy" in the United States. Enlightened by the "fundraising stamp", a series of everyday donation activities became popular in the United States, greatly triggering the enthusiasm for public donation.

Meanwhile, the rise of community foundations, a type of philanthropic foundation with a clear target community coverage, allowed the public to participate directly through an increased number of channels.

The first community foundation in American history was the Cleveland Foundation, set up in 1914 by Frederick Goff. In the years that followed, community foundations flourished.

Unlike large private foundations, community foundations have a clear community coverage, meaning that they tend to build more detailed and complete local philanthropic networks that are well-rooted in the community's actual requirements. Community foundations serving local areas can often encourage more ordinary people to participate actively in public services and philanthropic activities, being an important driving force for public participation.

By 1930, more than 20 cities had seen the emergence of community foundations. As of 2010, the number had exceeded 700, raising more than USD 4.2 billion annually. (Foundation Center, 2012) Community foundations do not outnumber other types of foundations in the US, but they play a very important role in solving local social problems. Every year, tens of millions of Americans participate in philanthropic activities through community foundations.

Of course, traditional foundations did not fall behind in the period of mass philanthropy. While traditional foundations such as the Carnegie Corporation and the Rockefeller Foundation continued expanding and playing an important role, other large and influential philanthropic foundations such as the Ford Foundation and the Bill & Melinda Gates Foundation appeared on the scene. They pushed US philanthropy towards more specialized and scientific development with a more detailed division of labor.

The development of philanthropy in the United States could not have succeeded without the support of taxation and policies implemented during this period. Since the end of the 19th century, the United States introduced tax relief measures for charity organizations, effectively promoting the prosperity of foundations. The *War Revenue Act of 1917* defined tax deductions for individual donations for the first time, establishing a tax incentive system for individuals to carry out philanthropic activities. In the ensuing decades, Congress amended charity tax deductions several times through various bills, further expanding the tax deduction coverage for individual donations. Finally, the modern tax system for charitable organizations was officially established with the passing of the *Internal Revenue Act of 1954*. (Arnsberger, et al., 2008)

Tax deductions for donations provided the public with long-term and stable incentives to engage in charity. Alongside these incentives and a tradition of volunteerism, American people's enthusiasm for philanthropy burgeoned. Donations gradually became part of the American way of life for both the upper and middle classes. Similarly, the rise in public donations prompted the emergence of more specialized fundraising organizations in the United States, dedicated to full-time fundraising activities and fundraising-related training. The professionalism and transparency of the sector was consequently improved, transforming the entire American philanthropic industry.

Statistics show that in 1954, the total amount of donations in the United States was about USD 54 billion. By 2017, the total amount of donations in the United States had reached USD 410.02 billion, an increase of nearly eight times in the span of 60 years. The share of public donations in total reached 66.91% in 2017, far exceeding the total amount of donations from foundations and companies. (Giving USA, 2018) About 6.2 million US citizens participated in various forms of volunteer activity in 2015, making up 24.9% of the US adult population, based on data from the United States statistics bureau. (US Bureau of Statistics, 2016) It can be said that the 20th century paved the way for the rise of "mass philanthropy" in the US. The emergence of new modes, methods, and tax reforms were an unprecedented injection of enthusiasm for the American people, making the US the leading country in the development of, and public participation in, philanthropy.

The 21st Century: The Age of Philanthropic Innovation

Philanthropy in the United States has maintained steady and rapid development since the beginning of the 21st century, characterized by three new trends.

First, American charitable organizations, especially large ones, are more actively involved in global governance and providing aid and support to developing countries. Established, well-known foundations such as the

Rockefeller Foundation have always looked outside national borders, seeking to contribute to the resolution of public health and social issues at the global level. However, plagued by the two world wars and then the Cold War, US foundations' global influence has not yet been expanded to its full extent.

Following the collapse of the Cold War barriers, globalization underwent 30 years of development at breakneck speed. US charitable organizations, be they long-standing foundations such as the Carnegie Corporation and the Rockefeller Foundation, or newcomers like the Gates Foundation and the Clinton Foundation, became more actively involved in tackling global problems. As such, they played a more important role in fighting global warming, AIDS prevention, poverty eradication and even public governance. In some developing countries, these foundations have even become the proxy of government agencies, playing a vital role in the social governance of these regions.

Second, more and more innovative philanthropic concepts and modes continue to emerge. New types of philanthropic modes deeply influenced by business thinking have been proposed, such as venture philanthropy, social enterprises, and impact investments, and ever more widespread experiments are being launched in the US. These innovative ideas have further blurred the boundaries between the second and third sectors, forcing the philanthropic community to further think and explore the core issues of philanthropy. "How should we define philanthropy?" "What is the substance of philanthropy?" The impact of these emerging concepts of philanthropy has been to push our consideration of these fundamental issues to a whole new level.

At the same time, emerging modes and concepts such as venture philanthropy and impact investment have been introduced outside the US by many countries and regions in Europe and Asia, where they have had considerable impact. Born in the US, these emerging modes are then replicated in other countries and areas, becoming the mainstream practice in global philanthropic development.

Third, since the Internet-based philanthropic mode emerged, it has attracted more people to participate in philanthropic activities. With the development of the Internet, large Internet companies, such as Google, Facebook, Amazon, Twitter, and PayPal, have all entered the field one after the other and actively used the Internet to raise money. Some also provide traditional philanthropic organizations with digitalized technologies and tools to help them make better use of the technology available. The popularity of Giving Tuesday means that in the United States, where philanthropy is deeply woven into people's daily life and offline networks are very strong, Internet philanthropy has been able to successfully show its presence and maintain its current growth rate, far outrunning its traditional counterparts.

After 400 years of development, US philanthropy is now well established: the concept has been deeply rooted in the hearts of the people, the habits have been ingrained, the system has improved, and innovation has been endless. In the field of philanthropy, compared to other developed countries, the US has undoubtedly been at the global forefront, becoming one of the most developed countries in this sector.

Section 4 Major Modes of Internet Philanthropy in the US

Over the past two decades, America's Internet philanthropy has developed fast. Innovative ways of carrying out philanthropy have appeared in various fields leaving a lasting impact and breathing new life into the US philanthropic sector. Similar to China, Internet giants have played a great role in the development of online philanthropy in the US. In this process, non-profit organizations in the US have also played a part, doing groundbreaking work in changing the way philanthropy is done.

According to the *2016 Charitable Giving Report* released by Blackbaud, a research agency serving non-profit organizations, in 2016 overall charitable giving in the United States showed a year-over-year increase of 1.0%, with online giving increasing by 7.9% compared to 2015. That same year, the percentage of funds that were raised online reached a record high. About 7.2% of overall fundraising revenue, excluding grants, was raised online.

Non-profit organizations of all sizes increased their online fundraising in 2016, as compared to 2015. Large-scale non-profits, which raise funds of more than USD 10 million annually, grew their online fundraising by

6.3% in 2016. Medium-sized non-profits, raising an annual amount between USD 1 million and 10 million, saw a yearly increase of 11.4% in their online fund-raising. For large organizations, 7.7% of their fund-raising revenue came from online donations in 2016. This was followed by medium-sized organizations at 5.1% (see Fig. 6.1). (Blackbaud, 2017)

The analysis also showed that 89% of large online donations in 2016 were between USD 1,000 and 4,999. Another 8% of large online donations were between USD 5,000 and 9,999. Finally, 3% of large online donations were USD 10,000 or higher. The largest online donation in this group was USD 100,000 (see Fig. 6.2). (Blackbaud, 2017)

The prosperity of Internet philanthropy can be seen in the data of Giving Tuesday. In 2016, online donations increased by 20% during Giving Tuesday, and 22% of online donations were made through mobile devices. (Blackbaud, 2017)

Generally speaking, as new online business models develop, the formats used for Internet philanthropy in the US become more diversified. Traditional charitable organizations promote new ways of donation through campaigns on online platforms. Social media, e-commerce websites and payment platforms are also exploring the charity sector. In addition, new tools have emerged such as independent information disclosure platforms, crowd-funding websites and blockchain-based philanthropic

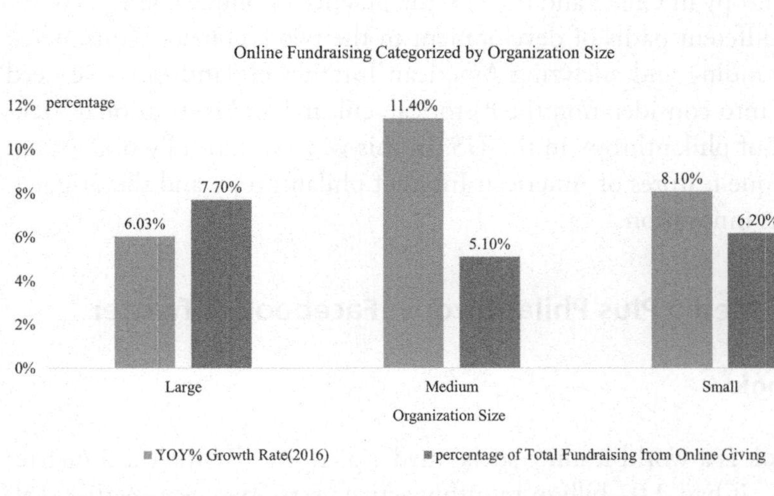

Fig. 6.1 Online Fundraising Categorized by Organization Size

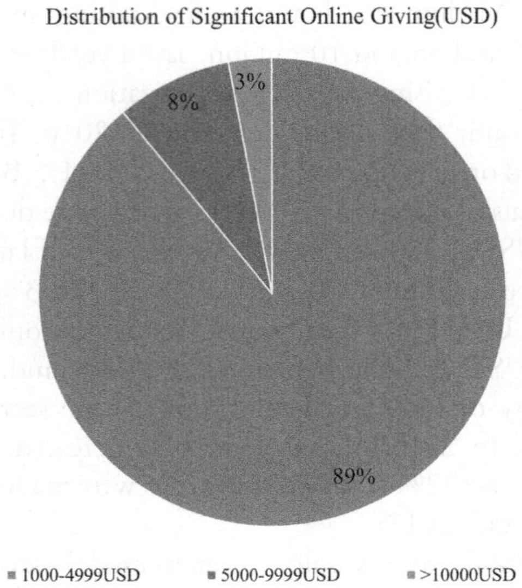

Fig. 6.2 Distribution of Large Online Donations (USD)

platforms. Charitable organizations are now more specialized and professional, and charity campaigns have become more entertaining and diverse.

It is worth noting that, due to numerous differences between Internet philanthropy in China and the US, the practice of online charity has followed different paths of development in the two countries. Thus, when understanding and analyzing American Internet philanthropy, we need to take into consideration the historical, cultural and institutional background of philanthropy in the US. In this way, we can fully understand the unique features of American Internet philanthropy and the originality of its innovation.

Social Media Plus Philanthropy: Facebook & Twitter

Facebook

Facebook is a world-leading social media platform. By the third quarter of 2017, it had 2.07 billion monthly active users. Two years earlier, 150 million people (Gleit, 2015) were already connected to a charitable cause or philanthropic activity through Facebook. By giving its users an opportunity to interact at a large scale, Facebook gathers together volunteers, donors and activists from across the world to donate to all kinds of causes. Given its current development, Facebook is not only a platform for promoting charity campaigns and charitable organizations, but also an ever-expanding platform for donating online.

Philanthropic organizations promote their campaigns on Facebook by establishing a Facebook account, creating group chats and organizing unique activities.

Facebook developed the “Donate Now” feature in 2014, enabling charitable organizations to organize fund-raising events in a variety of ways. Personal fundraisers are also available for users of 18 years or older.

For example, a charitable organization can add the “Donate” button to its page and posts, making it easier for supporters to contribute in just a few taps.

A charitable organization can build a page for their fundraising campaigns on Facebook. Donors can then repost this page or share it on their profiles so that more people can learn about the campaign and make a contribution to it.

As social media networks incorporated ever more multimedia features, Facebook has added the “Live Fundraiser” feature to attract more donations (see Figure 6-12). A “Donate” button can be added to a live video on Facebook. In this way, charitable organizations can showcase their work and how they run through live streaming, giving people an inside look.

In 2017, Facebook also introduced “Birthday Fundraisers”, another new, fun way of combining charitable causes with the Internet.

Every day, more than 45 million (Nowak, 2017) people receive birthday wishes on Facebook. Nowadays in the US, two weeks before your birthday, you will see a message from Facebook in your News Feed giving you the option to create a fundraiser for any of the 750,000 (Nowak, 2017) US non-profits currently available for donations on Facebook. You can choose a charitable organization, and set a fixed donation amount and a deadline for your campaign. You can also choose the title and cover picture of the fund-raising page.

Previously, users were encouraged to send a virtual flower or gift to congratulate a friend on his or her birthday. Now, Facebook will send a birthday notification to your friends, inviting them to take part in your fundraising event, making your birthday even more memorable and meaningful.

According to its official website, in 2017, the "Donate Now" function was available in 38 countries including Australia, Canada, Denmark, France, Japan, South Africa, the UK and the US. Furthermore, philanthropic organizations in 17 countries including Austria, Finland, Germany, Italy, the US and the UK could raise money on Facebook. Personal fundraisers were available to users in 17 countries including Australia, Canada, Denmark, Spain, the UK and the US. By May of the same year, personal fundraisers had to fall within at least one of the eight following categories: community service, sports, education, health-care, pet, personal emergency, crisis relief, and funeral. For personal fundraisers in the US and Canada, Facebook charged a transaction fee of 6.9% and 8.8% respectively, in addition to a flat fee of USD 30.

Mark Zuckerberg, founder of Facebook, has been very passionate about philanthropy. As a social enterprise, Facebook has exhibited strong concern for charity work during the growth of Internet philanthropy. It combines its core strength as a social networking platform with creative philanthropic methods, making it easier and more convenient for individuals to give to charity and empowering them to do so. Looking at the features yet to come, Facebook will continue to promote philanthropy, and is expected to come up with more innovative activities, formats and themes for users and organizations to take part in philanthropic campaigns.

Twitter

Twitter is a world-renowned social network, providing microblog services for users. It had 330 million monthly active users in the third quarter of 2017. Twitter has become a charitable platform for organizations and individuals alike. According to the *2017 Global NGO Online Technology Report* published by Public Interest Registry and Non-profit Tech for

Good, 72% of charitable organizations had Twitter pages. On average, small organizations had 3,755 Twitter followers, medium-sized organizations, 12,815, and large organizations, 80,371. (Nonprofit Tech for Good, 2018)

Like Facebook, Twitter is a useful social platform for both promoting philanthropy and organizing fundraising events.

First, philanthropic organizations or philanthropic campaign organizers can open a twitter account and use it to post articles, pictures, videos and podcasts. Second, they can also establish a corresponding hashtag topic for users to re-post or comment.

For example, the American Red Cross created its twitter account in June 2007. By January 18, 2018, it had posted 5,594 tweets, followed 39,600 Twitter accounts, and had 5.35 million followers. Another example is Giving Tuesday, one of the days on which the most money is donated in the US. The event's Twitter account was created in January 2012. By October 10, 2018, it had posted 15,300 tweets, and had been followed by 63,400 users[6]. This event is also a hashtag on Twitter; different versions of Giving Tuesday have been created in several countries.

In 2015, Twitter launched its fundraising function called "#Donate". It is a new system that allows Twitter users to donate to a charity by retweeting or tweeting a hashtag that is registered with the service. First, Charities or individual users must get their Twitter accounts verified and link their accounts with PayPal. After they are verified, they need to register a hashtag containing the name and amount to donate, then tweet it. Charities could set specific hashtags so that, upon seeing the tweet, Twitter users can retweet it or use the hashtag to make a donation. Those who donate receive a confirmation from the fundraiser's Twitter account.

In terms of Internet philanthropy, Twitter's main role is to provide a platform for circulating and sharing information. Through endorsement from celebrities and influential charities with large numbers of supporters, charity campaigns and programs can be sure to get promoted, and transparency of charity events is also improved. Twitter's fundraising feature is relatively standardized, but it is fairly complex to use. In terms of user experience, there is still room for further improvement.

[6] Source: Giving Tuesday Twitter official account.

Payment Plus Philanthropy: PayPal

Founded in the US in 1998, PayPal now has 218 million active users. As one of the world's largest third-party payment platforms, it has offered itself as the donation method for a great number of online charity platforms. In 2017, more than USD 8.5 billion was donated through PayPal. In 2016, over 8 million PayPal users in 181 countries and regions donated over USD 971 million to 282,000 charitable organizations. (*PayPal Exceeds*, 2017)

In terms of its involvement in philanthropy, PayPal has built a fundraising and donation platform and set up a charitable foundation to encourage its users to take part in charity. The PayPal Giving Fund is a registered non-profit organization, supported by PayPal payment technology. It has partnerships with PayPal, eBay, and Humble Bundle. Linking fundraisers with donors, the PayPal Giving Fund aims to make it easier for people to make donations. In the US and the UK, the PayPal Giving Fund raises more than USD 35 million every year. (PayPal Giving Fund, 2019)

PayPal users can donate directly on the PayPal Giving Fund homepage. They can choose to donate to one of the philanthropic organizations like St. Jude Children's Research Hospital, the American Red Cross, Feeding America and UNICEF. They can also choose one of the eight charity categories: Arts and Culture, School and Education, International, Human Services, Environment and Animals, Religion and Spirituality, Society and Communities, and Sports and Recreation.

After choosing a category or organization, users can donate using PayPal. Charities enrolled with the PayPal Giving Fund will typically receive funds in their PayPal accounts within 15 to 45 days after a donation goes through the PayPal Giving Fund. Charities not enrolled with the PayPal Giving Fund will be additionally vetted and if eligible, will receive funds via other means, such as a check, which typically arrives within 90 days. Additionally, users will also receive a tax receipt confirming their donation.

Users can also make a donation via the PayPal mobile app, where they can choose the organization or category to which they would like to donate.

Generally speaking, PayPal features a simple way of donating. It connects charity organizations with donors, so that donations can be sent using its simple payment technology. As a non-profit charitable organization, the PayPal Giving Fund uses PayPal's extensive payment platform as the means to cooperate with other e-commerce platforms and charity websites. It has played a uniting role in facilitating the payment processes of Internet philanthropy.

E-commerce Plus Philanthropy: eBay & Amazon

eBay

Founded in the United States in 1995, eBay has become recognized globally for shopping and online auctions. In the third quarter of 2017, eBay boasted 168 million active buyers and a registered revenue totaling USD 2.4 billion. (eBay, 2017) As an e-commerce platform, eBay has made philanthropy one of its top priorities. For example, it has made PayPal Giving Fund a main hub for buyers and sellers among charity organizations, and encourages its users to contribute to philanthropy through buying and selling. Through eBay, the PayPal Giving Fund raises GBP 19 million every year for British charity organizations.

This e-commerce platform has embedded operations for donations and fundraising into the regular transaction processes.

A charity organization can directly sell philanthropic products at the official eBay website (www.ebay.com) by linking the page of its shop to the "charity shop" section under the official eBay Charity site (charity.ebay.com). There, a buyer can directly access a charity shop via www.ebay.com or the "charity shop" section under charity.ebay.com There, they can buy philanthropic products, for example such as those sold to fund the vaccination of children in poverty-stricken areas.

A buyer can donate by shopping at www.ebay.com, or directly donating at charity.ebay.com. They can then choose to follow any number of charity organizations in order to receive their latest updates.

For example, when buying a product at www.ebay.com, a buyer will see a donation option during the completion of the transaction. After checking the option, the user can select an amount (USD 1-25) to be donated to a charity organization recommended by www.ebay.com or to another charity organization which the buyer chooses.

Alternatively, a user can directly donate to a charity organization via charity.ebay.com by simply selecting the organization from the recommendations or via search page of charity.ebay.com, then clicking the amount to be donated.

At charity.ebay.com, a seller can add a donation option to their products on sale. In doing so, when a product is sold, eBay will automatically transfer the donation amount into the account of the selected charity organization via the PayPal Giving Fund. When creating a product page, a seller can click the "Charity" button, and then select the percent of the transaction price to be donated, as well as the recipient charity organization. When a transaction is finished, PayPal Giving Fund will automatically withdraw the amount to be donated from the seller's PayPal account and transfer it to the selected charity organization.

eBay practices online philanthropy through two channels (www.ebay.com and charity.ebay.com) where buyers, sellers and eBay itself are all involved in philanthropy during the e-commerce process. This demonstrates how all parties can make joint contributions to philanthropy. Thanks to the fact that donations and fundraising are a straightforward part of the eBay transaction platform (equally so for the buyer, seller and charitable organizations), eBay has successfully raised the effectiveness and level of engagement charitable activities.

Amazon

Amazon is a major Internet-based e-commerce and cloud computing enterprise. It practices philanthropy through its affiliates, the Amazon Smile website and the Amazon Smile Foundation, which are currently only available for American users. Its charity practices through Amazon Smile began in 2014.

Amazon Smile, which is independent from the official Amazon website, is a website specially operated by Amazon for charitable donations. As a private foundation established by Amazon for managing Amazon Smile projects, Amazon Smile Foundation is dedicated to managing the charitable donations and transaction costs received through Amazon Smile. When a user buys a product at the official website (www.amazonsmile.com), Amazon Smile will donate 0.5% of the transaction price to a charity organization selected by the user. The platform collects no service charges from charity organizations or donors.

A user can log in Amazon Smile using his or her Amazon ID, and must select a charity organization either from the popular charity organizations recommended by Amazon Smile, or by searching for themselves. Following the selection, users can begin shopping. After the user successfully buys a product, Amazon Smile Foundation will transfer the amount donated to the selected charity organization a specified amount of time. The selected charity organization will remain a fixed recipient, unless the user manually changes his or her choice. Each successful donation can be shared by the user via social media, such as with Facebook, Twitter and email.

Amazon Smile has expressed high requirements for charity organizations to qualify for its services. Only registered formal charity organizations can apply for enrollment into Amazon Smile, while private foundations are not considered. An eligible charity organization needs to enter its organizational information, bank account information, and contact information at www.amazonsmile.com; organizations are not recognized by Amazon Smile until they have signed a thorough agreement. Beyond that, organizations can apply to become a "Spotlight Charity" to increase their exposure by featuring more prominently in users' recommended charities. Additionally, subsidies from Amazon Smile are also available to unregistered charity organizations. Through its cooperation with Guide Star, Amazon Smile shares information about American charity organizations that meet regulations on its official website. As a result, an unregistered charity organization can also be searched out by a user and become a fixed recipient. When each quarter ends, donations received in that quarter will be processed by Amazon Smile Foundation, and delivered by direct electronic transfer to the accounts of specific charity organizations in line with donors' choices.

Amazon's online philanthropic practices, which feature donations via the independent Amazon Smile and Amazon Smile Foundation, are simple and direct. While these easy donations can further stimulate public engagement, Amazon does need to consider how best to lead users to Amazon Smile. Another question Amazon Smile must answer is how to expand its global presence and engage more users worldwide, since Amazon Smile is currently only open to American users.

Technical Empowerment Plus Philanthropy: Google

Search engine giant Google has also made its own appearance in the field of online philanthropy. Unlike Facebook and Amazon which focus on the users themselves in their online philanthropy practices, Google has mainly involved utilizing online platforms and technologies as its means of supporting charity organizations and philanthropy.

Google organizes most of its philanthropic activities by means of its non-profit organization Google.org. Founded in October 2005, Google.org plans philanthropic activities and events on behalf of Google. Every year, the organization spends USD 100 million aiding the charity projects of its partners. (*Our Work*, n.d.) Through this affiliate, Google has launched a range of projects revolving around issues such as racial equality, education and digital skills, support for the disabled, and emergency crisis responses.

As a non-profit organization under an Internet giant, Google.org has developed a close association between its charity projects and the Internet, and has made many pioneering explorations by leveraging Google's strong expertise in Internet technologies.

Pratham Books, a major project partner of Google.org, seeks to help children in remote areas of India by promoting reading and literacy. Participants of this project translate English and Hindi books into Indian dialects for the remote target children to read. Specifically, Google.org has launched StoryWeaver, an online reading platform, to connect readers, authors and translators. However, a lack of translators has restricted the quantity of translated works.

As part of its partnership with Pratham Books, Google supplies funds while keeping its technological capabilities open to its partner. Google has made its machine learning-based translation API and transliteration tools available, and assigned its volunteer engineering team to give technical instructions to Pratham Books. These efforts from Google have greatly increased the efficiency of the translation project, allowing more books to be successfully translated into Indian dialects for the targeted beneficiaries. By 2018, there have been more than 20,000 translated books and over 500,000 active users on StoryWeaver. (*Helping Pratham*, n.d.)

Backed by its cumulative technical strengths, Google.org has helped many similar projects, including the Equal Justice Initiative and the Code for America. The Equal Justice Initiative aims to use data to discover and change the narratives of racial inequality, and the Code for America seeks to improve the American labor market using digital tools. While these projects are not led by Google, they have alleviated many chronic social problems in a new "technology plus philanthropy" mode by using Google's core technical strengths. This is how Google supports innovative non-profit organizations through technical support and digital tools.

Yet among the numerous charity organizations that exist all over the world, only a few enjoy funding and cooperation from Google. In light of this, Google has launched a philanthropy support program as a means to make high-quality services and information tools available to more charity organizations. This program works to help these organizations raise funds more easily, get involved in more efficient collaborations, and share their ideas and visions with more target groups. This highly recognized program has reached many non-profit organizations and plays a major part in Google's Internet philanthropy mode.

Google has offered charity organizations a complete series of products based on its core technological and commercial strengths. An organization involved in the program can get access to the charity version of the G Suite email service, and also raise awareness and deepen interactions with donors via Google AdWords' free advertising service. Among the numerous Google subsidiaries, the YouTube charity program enables participants to view amazing videos and interactive content, while Google One Today empowers connections with more potential donors and helps to streamline fundraising, and Google Earth Outreach tells the success stories of charity organizations more vividly and efficiently using customized maps and global location data.

Now, the program has reached more than 50 countries and regions around the world. (*Google For*, n.d.) Millions of charity organizations are receiving help to improve their information-based systems, improving their publicity and connecting with more potential donors. By doing so, the program has become an important player in strengthening the capability of charity organizations by expanding IT applications across the board.

Instead of simply attaching an online philanthropy model onto Google's search services, the search engine giant has developed an open and innovative strategy in which its core technological capabilities and core products are open to charity organizations. By doing so, Google has enhanced the digital capabilities of many charity organizations and improved the use of information technology throughout the American non-profit sector. Moreover, in the process of funding innovative non-profit organizations, Google has taken the initiative to roll out many entirely new charity projects which combine sophisticated technologies with philanthropy. Thanks to the company's efforts, the "Internet plus philanthropy" mode has gone beyond just fundraising and publicity, and revealed even more possibilities promised by "technology plus philanthropy".

Crowd-funding Plus Philanthropy: Mightycause

As the US government has no strict controls over the right to public funding, Internet-based philanthropic crowd-funding platforms have emerged in the country in the wake of the rapid growth of the Internet. Many of them, such as Mightycause, have become very familiar with the public.

Mightycause is a US-based philanthropic crowd-funding platform. By connecting potential donors, charity organizations and individuals in need, it enables under-funded non-profit organizations and individuals in need to raise sufficient funds online.

Mightycause classifies crowd-funding projects into organization and individual projects. The initiator of an organization project is required to provide the name and Employer Identification Number (EIN, assigned by the tax authority) of the organization, and to register the organization's official name. Such requirements do not apply to individuals, who can initiate a crowd-funding project simply by providing a personal profile and bank account information. After an organization or individual has registered, they can initiate a crowd-funding project, then all that is left is for Mightycause users to make their donations.

Unlike what usually prevails on Chinese crowd-funding platforms, crowd-funding on Mightycause is not directly linked to specific projects. On this platform, a user can access a non-profit organization to learn about its organizational structure and how it operates and executes its projects, then they can donate directly to the organization. This model caters better to American donation habits and attitudes about philanthropy.

This platform has developed new and interesting modes for individual crowd-funding projects. On Mightycause, the creator of an individual project can set up a project fundraising team. However, donations from users are counted per team member, not to the team as a whole. This encourages competition between the team members, and motivates the project creator's enthusiasm for fundraising. Furthermore, Mightycause encourages online interaction between crowd-funding initiators and donors through Facebook and Twitter's social networking interfaces, thereby deepening the connection between them.

Mightycause also provides a gift matching option. For some specific projects, donors and organizations can set up a matched donation fund. With one of these funds, whenever other users make donations, the fund will make a matched donation based on predetermined guidelines. This system compounds the influence of each subsequent donation and appeals to users' sense of charity, effectively attracting more people to take part.

When a crowd-funding project is complete, or partly completed, the initiator (whether an organization or individual) can regularly disclose the project's progress to donors via the information disclosure module offered by Mightycause. Updates and feedback give users a clear picture of how funds are used and how the project progresses, which helps bring about long-term mutual trust between the project's creator and its donors.

Compared to many other crowd-funding platforms, Mightycause has a very low threshold for initiating crowd-funding projects. There is neither an upper nor lower limit of fundraising, nor any charges collected from charity organizations or donors. Mightycause has also raised its visibility by optimizing web content to be displayed on mobile terminals, and has therefore attracted more mobile users to take part in donation activities via this platform (see Fig. 6.3).

Mightycause also supplies a range of other services, including data analysis, donor profiles, and social interaction, which helps project creators locate more potential donors and actively accelerate fundraising. Additionally, well-oriented custom-built services are made available to organizations and individuals with certain specific demands.

Thanks to the platform's usability and refined services, Mightycause has won universal praise from charity organizations and donors, as well as raising more than USD 600 million for thousands of organizations and individuals over the past 12 years. The platform now enjoys 12 million active users. (*About us*, n.d.-a) It has grown into one of the largest and most recognized crowd-funding platforms in the US.

American peers of Mightycause include WebCharity, JustGiving, and many more. The crowd-funding community, which most American Internet giants have not been actively involved in, are enjoying a

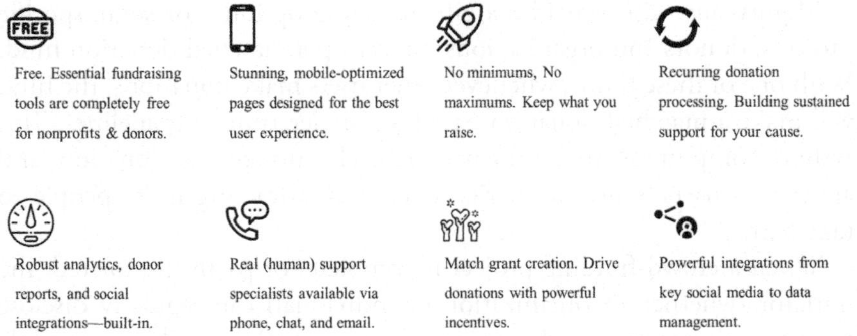

Fig. 6.3 Features of Mightycause. Source: Official Website of Mightycause

promising period of growth in their somewhat less developed sub-section of philanthropy. Crowd-funding plays a smaller and less important part in philanthropic donations in the US than in China, and is more characterized by decentralization.

Transparency Plus Philanthropy: Charity Navigator

The Internet responds well to transparency when it comes to philanthropy. Sharing information between different sections of the Internet is low-cost, far-reaching, and efficient. Via the Internet, a charity organization can disclose information about donations and share its progress to the public, and users can learn about charity organizations and charity projects more clearly. As such, the Internet has become a common tool used in various countries to disclose information more effectively across philanthropic circles, especially the US.

In the US, there are many institutions dedicated to disclosing philanthropic information and rating charity organizations over the Internet. These include Charity Navigator, CharityWatch and BBB Wise Giving Alliance. Among them, Charity Navigator is particularly well-known.

Founded in 2001, Charity Navigator is one of the world's first third-party websites that aims to be a valid source of information as well as a performance assessor for charity organizations. This website is committed to summarizing and disclosing information and giving objective, impartial and inclusive comments on charity organizations in order to help the public make well-informed, correct choices. After about a decade of exploration, the website has developed a relatively impartial and objective data-based assessment system which covers more than 8,000 well-known charity organizations. On that basis, Charity Navigator leads public donations to flow into the most efficient charity organizations all over the US. According to its official website, in 2018 Charity Navigator conducted complete transparency and financial status assessments for more than 9,000 charities across the United States and provided the public with basic information on more than 1.8 million other charities. (*About us*, n.d.-b) The Charity Navigator assessment system focuses on two key indicators: one is the charity organization's financial health, and the other is its accountability and transparency.

As to accountability and transparency, Charity Navigator seeks to answer two essential questions through data disclosure. First, is the philanthropic organization equipped with a good governance structure and is it compliant with ethical standards? Second, has the philanthropic organization provided donors with easy access to key information concerning its accountability and transparency? Accountability and transparency assessments by Charity Navigator are based on data from two sources: the attached information within IRS Form 990, and charity organizations' official websites. Charity Navigator extracts 12 data indicators from IRS Form 990 and five from official organization websites. All 17 data indicators are available at its website, and constitute an accountability and transparency assessment system of philanthropic organizations. (*How Do,* n.d.) In the system, each philanthropic organization is awarded stars, and its position compared to its peers is shown as reference for users when selecting philanthropic organizations. The system also allows users to find the merits and shortcomings of philanthropic organizations through comparison.

It is of note that Charity Navigator pursues an "apples to apples" principle of comparison in its comprehensive assessments. With a view to the comparability of assessment results, Charity Navigator divides philanthropic organizations into 11 classes and 35 sub-classes, and bringing similar philanthropic organizations together in the same assessment and comparison pool, rather than comparing various philanthropic organizations without discrimination. Although incurring high costs with regards to information disclosure and assessment, such divisions minimize direct comparisons of entirely different philanthropic organizations, and ensure fairness of assessment for each of the various types of philanthropic organizations.

As mentioned above, there are many agencies similar to Charity Navigator who are also dedicated to disclosing philanthropic information and rating philanthropic organizations online. They collect and summarize tax returns and information disclosed from websites of philanthropic organizations as a basis for their comprehensive transparency assessment systems. This is how they leverage philanthropic information as a way of reducing the search costs incurred for the public. In this country where philanthropic organizations are traditionally meant to have a high level of transparency, Internet-based information disclosure makes the philanthropic sector even more transparent, and has been a major help for regulators.

International Philanthropy Festival: Giving Tuesday

Giving Tuesday has been a major philanthropic and charity movement in the US in recent years. It falls on the first Tuesday after the Thanksgiving holiday, and aims to encourage individuals, families, philanthropic organizations, and companies to contribute their time, money and skills to help those in need through independent and creative approaches. Since its inception in 2012, Giving Tuesday has been gradually expanded to various countries and regions. This movement is supported by the Bill & Melinda Gates Foundation as well as PayPal.

Through both online and offline activities, Giving Tuesday encourages organizations and individuals to join through various channels.

As officially registered philanthropic organizations, and non-profit enterprises, schools and religious or community groups may also register to join the Giving Tuesday platform. If a registered organization or agency needs to plan and promote a philanthropic activity, it may refer to the "tool package" provided by Giving Tuesday. This "tool package" includes examples of successful activities from the past, templates of press releases, ready-to-use media platforms, and recommended schedules. These registered philanthropic organizations often use such social media platforms as Facebook and Twitter to promote their activities, as they can use the donation pages on these platforms and also redirect donors to donate on their own official websites.

There are various ways for individuals to support Giving Tuesday, such as donation, volunteering, and the sharing of philanthropic and charity stories. Giving Tuesday encourages individuals to take part in community volunteering, and provides a link on its website for individuals to search for nearby philanthropic organizations and join specific volunteering services. Individuals may also donate through social media platforms or through the websites of philanthropic organizations. When an individual joins a philanthropic activity, he or she can share their experience online. Sharing content can be enhanced by, for example, using the hashtags #UNSelfie and #MyGivingStory.

In 2017, Giving Tuesday entered China and cooperated with Tencent Charity to encourage people to raise money through donations. From November 23 to 28, 2017, Chinese users could participate in donations

Fig. 6.4 Screenshot of the Result of Tencent Charity Step Donations

through WeChat or Mobile QQ after walking at least 1,000 steps every day. The donated steps were changed to money to help children suffering from leukemia. According to the official report of Giving Tuesday, up to the night of November 27, 2017, over 5 million users of Tencent Charity had participated in this step donation campaign, and donated 66.8 billion steps, which were converted to RMB 4.44 million (about USD 683,000) for charity (see Fig. 6.4)[7].

Giving Tuesday has achieved significant philanthropic results and a high global participation rate. In 2016, 18% (CM Public Welfare

[7] Source: Giving Tuesday Twitter official account.

Communication, 2017) of the US public knew about the Giving Tuesday charity day. This is already a large proportion, successfully manifesting the trend of "philanthropy by all". On the exact day of Giving Tuesday, the hashtag "#GivingTuesday" ranked the highest among trending topics on major social media platforms. In 2017, Giving Tuesday raised USD 274 million online, and received 2.4 million gifts, the average value of which was USD 110.98. It was mentioned over 1 million times in social events, and received 21.7 million "likes" on Twitter and other social media platforms. During the movement in 2017, the hottest five topics were: Public and Social Benefits, People-oriented Services, Education, Health, and Animal Protection. People from over 150 countries and over 100 US community coalitions participated in this movement. A total of 42 countries participated through official channels, among others who promoted the movement independently.

Giving Tuesday has made a huge impact on online philanthropy in the US. According to Blackbaud's analysis in its *2016 Charitable Giving Report*, as of December of 2016 (Blackbaud, 2017), the total amount of online donations in the US had increased for two years in a row and accounted for 21.8% of the total donations made online. Specifically, American online donations in November made up 9.7% of the total donations made online. This may be the result of the continued increase as part of #GivingTuesday.

Section 5 Special Features of Internet Philanthropy in the US

Given that the US enjoys a strong tradition of philanthropy and a leading position in the Internet sector, online philanthropy in the US is taking the lead worldwide. Moreover, thanks to the unique history, culture, and traditions there, online philanthropy tends to have the following distinctive features in the US:

1. Internet philanthropy in the US has rapidly developed over the past two decades, already reaching a considerable scale. However, in the philanthropy sector, online philanthropy is still playing a supporting role. In

2017, the funds raised by the philanthropy sector in the US amounted to USD 410.02 billion. In terms of the absolute scale, this amount ranked the first in the world, but only 7.6% of this was raised online and the proportion raised by the public was only 11.36%.[41] The reason may be that the traditional charity network is very advanced in the US, so the public more often rely on offline channels to take part in philanthropy. As a result, online fundraising still represents only a small share in the wider philanthropy sector despite its rapid growth.

2. Online philanthropy in the US is distinctly decentralized. As decentralization is an important feature of the Internet, online philanthropy is also an innately decentralized philanthropic model. The US Internet philanthropy network also works around a central section. Internet giants in the US, such as Google, Facebook and Amazon, all take an active role in online philanthropy. Unlike their Chinese counterparts, such as Tencent Charity and Taobao Charity, these giants have not extensively connected potential donors, charity organizations, enterprises, and recipients to the extent comparable to their counterparts in China. Meanwhile, traditional US charity organizations and small and medium-sized enterprises have also been conducting large amounts of research during the development of online philanthropy in the US. Some platforms operated by smaller Internet companies, such as Mightycause, have also been able to connect a large number of potential donors, effectively weakening the giants' central position in this field, and making the US's feature of decentralization more distinctive.

3. Online philanthropy is more diverse in the US, where there are more attempts to apply cutting-edge technologies. In China and some other countries and regions, the main mode of online philanthropy is online fundraising or Internet-based initiatives. Some platforms and organizations are attempting to use emerging technologies to improve the implementation efficiency of projects. In the US, as traditional fundraising channels are well developed, many organizations do not rely on online fundraising, so their explorations online tend to be more extensive. Meanwhile, as those organizations responsible for the implementation of projects are more professional, American enterprises have accumulated more expertise in the field of science and technology. As a

result, more organizations and enterprises in America apply state of the art technologies, such as the blockchain-based smart contract, AI-based image recognition and big data, to carry out charity projects. These innovative methods have achieved fruitful results. With the development and application of new technologies in the field of philanthropy, online philanthropy is more diverse in the US.

4. In the US Internet philanthropy model, desktop computers take up a large part. The development of mobile Internet applications has taken a very different path in China. A number of technologies such as mobile payments, among others, are not as popular in the US as they are in China. Therefore, the use of mobile terminals in Internet philanthropy remains of no great value in American people's everyday lives, and home computers take up a higher proportion of Internet philanthropy activities. Such platforms as Amazon Smile, eBay, and Mightycause rely more on desktop computers to carry out charity activities, and desktop computers secure the larger part of online donations. This is clearly different from China, where the mobile terminals play a dominant role.

5. Transparency in philanthropy is an integral part of the US online philanthropy model. The US has a long tradition of philanthropy and a sound system for governing charitable organizations. There have long been professional organizations concerned with promoting the transparency of this sector, such as the early examples of foundations. In recent years, with the expansion of the Internet, a lot of professional organizations have emerged in the US that devote themselves to pursuing information disclosure and ratings for charity organizations. By virtue of the Internet, these organizations collect information on charity organizations, and disclose this information online. It is without a doubt that the emergence and rise of the Internet has improved information disclosure, and helped professional organizations to significantly raise the transparency of charity organizations and the industry. Although the Internet has greatly improved the transparency of organizations and the industry, there are still only few countries with numerous websites and professional organizations promoting transparency. However, the importance attached to transparency in charity is certainly one of the distinctive features of Internet philanthropy in the US.

References

About us. (n.d.-a). Mightycuase. Retrieved September 30, 2018, from https://www.mightycause.com/about

About us. (n.d.-b). Charitynavigator. Retrieved September 30, 2018, from https://www.charitynavigator.org/index.cfm?bay=content.view&cpid=1653; https://www.charitynavigator.org/index.cfm?bay=content.view&cpid=1093.

Arnsberger, P., Ludlum, M., Riley, M., & Stanton, M. (2008). A History of the Tax-exempt Sector: An SOI Perspective. *Statistics of Income Bulletin, 27*(3), 105–135.

Blackbaud. (2017). *Fifth-Annual Charitable Giving Report: How Nonprofit Fundraising Performed in 2016*. Blackbaud. https://institute.blackbaud.com/asset/2016-charitable-giving-report/

Benjamin Franklin. (2018, September 30). In *Wikipedia*. https://en.wikipedia.org/wiki/Benjamin_Franklin

CM Public Welfare Communication. (CM公益传播). (2017, September 18). *国外也有"99公益日"?英国人把募捐玩成一种时尚, 美国人悄悄弄了个公益大IP*. Sohu. http://www.sohu.com/a/192689686_712346

eBay. (2017, October 18). *eBay Inc. Reports Third Quarter 2017 Results*. ebayinc. https://www.ebayinc.com/stories/news/ebay-inc-reports-third-quarter-2017-results/

Foundation Center. (2012). *Key Facts on Community Foundations*. Foundationcenter. http://foundationcenter.issuelab.org/resources/14079/14079.pdf

Giving USA. (2018, June 13). *Giving USA 2018*. Givingusa. https://givingusa.org/giving-usa-2018-americans-gave-410-02-billion-to-charity-in-2017-crossing-the-400-billion-mark-for-the-first-time/

Gleit, N. (2015, November 18). *Introducing New Tools for Nonprofits*. Facebook. https://about.fb.com/news/2015/11/introducing-new-tools-for-nonprofits/

Google For Non Profits. (n.d.). Google. Retrieved September 30, 2018, from https://www.google.com/nonprofits/

Helping Pratham Books increase children's access to reading material in their own language. (n.d.). Google. Retrieved September 30, 2018, from https://www.google.org/our-work/

How Do We Rate Charities' Accountability and Transparency?. (n.d.). Charitynavigator. Retrieved September 30, 2018, from https://www.charitynavigator.org/index.cfm?bay=content.view&cpid=1093

John D. Rockefeller. (2018, September 30). In *Wikipedia*. https://en.wikipedia.org/wiki/John_D._Rockefeller

Nonprofit Tech for Good. (2018). *2017 Global NGO Online Technology Repor*. Nptechforgood. https://www.nptechforgood.com/wp-content/uploads/2020/10/2017-Tech-Report-English-FINAL.pdf

Nowak, M. (2017, August 16). Celebrating a Birthday? Now You Can Make It Even More Meaningful. Facebook. https://about.fb.com/news/2017/08/celebrating-a-birthday-now-you-can-make-it-even-more-meaningful/

Our Work. (n.d.). Google. Retrieved September 30, 2018, from https://www.google.org/our-work/

PayPal Exceeds $7 Billion in Charitable Giving in 2016 as Mobile Giving Continues to Surge. (2017, January 10). Businesswire. Retrieved September 30, 2018, https://www.businesswire.com/news/home/20170110005744/en/PayPal-Exceeds-7-Billion-Charitable-Giving-201

PayPal Giving Fund. (2019). *Annul Report 2018*. Paypalobjects. https://www.paypalobjects.com/marketing/web/PPGF/US/PPGF_US_Annual_Report_2018_final_clean_for_proofing_BBB_edit.pdf

Philanthropy in the United States. (2018, September 30). In *Wikipedia*. https://en.wikipedia.org/wiki/Philanthropy_in_the_United_States

Pope John Paul II (Ed.). (2019). *Catechism of the Catholic Church*. USCCB.

Rockefeller Foundation. (2018, September 30). In *Wikipedia*. https://en.wikipedia.org/wiki/Rockefeller_Foundation

Tocqueville, A. D. (1989). *论美国的民主*(G. L. Dong, Trans.). 商务印书馆.

United States Non Profits Laws. (2018, September 30). In *Wikipedia*. https://en.wikipedia.org/wiki/Non-profit_organization_laws_in_the_U.S.

US Bureau of Statistics. (2016). *Volunteering in the United States in 2015*. BLS. https://www.bls.gov/news.release/pdf/volun.pdf

Xu, Y. S., & Zhu, Z. N. (2017). *美国公益图谱:从传统到现代*. 社会科学文献出版社.

Zi, Z. Y. (2015). *财富的责任与资本主义演变:美国百年公益发展的启示*. 上海三联书店.

7

The UK: The Tradition of Philanthropy and Government Support

The charitable causes and the culture of philanthropy have a long tradition in the United Kingdom. The British public's enthusiasm in various philanthropic activities is greater than most other countries. Charity organizations emerged very early on in British society; according to some relevant studies, mutual assistance organizations in the UK date back to 55 AD. (Wang et al., 2009) As early as the twelfth to thirteenth century, there were about 500 civil volunteering charity organizations in the UK.[1]

Section 1 The Foundation of Philanthropy in the UK

At the very beginning, philanthropic causes in the UK were mainly civil or non-governmental movements pursued out of Christian benevolence, but the success of philanthropy must be attributed in great part to

[1] According to British experts, charity organizations are "non-profit and non-government organizations which are established for extensive public interests and dedicated to various charity activities". In China, the definition of charity organizations is relatively narrower. The two are different to some extent.

Y. Chen, *Internet Philanthropy in China*,
https://doi.org/10.1007/978-981-16-2566-4_7

support from government. The UK has already developed a diversified charity system which features private charities and government aid.

Benevolence of Christianity

In the previous section of this chapter, we referred to the influence of Christianity on the charity culture of the US. The charity of the UK, which is also mainly a Protestant country, is also deeply influenced by the traditions of Christianity.

In the sixth Century, Pope Saint Gregory I sent a mission headed by Augustine of Canterbury to preach in Great Britain and reintroduce Christianity to the country. During the seventh century, Wilfred and Theodore of Tarsus had successfully converted the region to Christianity, and established the organizational structure of the British church. Since then, Britain has always been a predominantly Christian country. The core doctrines of Christianity, such as "original sin", "redemption", and "sola fide" have spread across the country and become an integral part of the British culture.

With the development of Christianity, the Christianity culture of "Rich as Sin" gradually became popular in British society. If the rich did not contribute to society, it was regarded as sin. During Roman rule, early Christian theologian and philosopher Saint Augustine pointed out "Wealth furthers the voracity of people and makes them give up the pursuit of God. This is more sinful than theft. Arrogance and voracity are the sins of the rich, and only modesty and giving can lead to redemption." (Gao, 2012) Such a philosophy became the motivation for charity in these early times. In order to show their faith in God and achieve redemption, groups of the merchant class took an active part in charity under the guidance of the doctrines of Christianity. Specifically, they funded the construction of various charity facilities, such as poorhouses, workhouses, correctional facilities, hospitals, primary schools, and universities. In the mid-sixteenth century, there was a boom in charity organizations. In London, "46% of charity donors were businessmen, who contributed 56% of the total donations." (Jordan, 1960)

Therefore, during this period, Christian churches and businessmen were the mainstay of social charity in the UK, and they met the demands of vulnerable groups in the society. However, this kind of volunteering and occasional donation seemed unorganized due to the lack of any systematic guarantees. In addition, churches became weaker and weaker with the passage of time, meaning philanthropy by early churches and business were unable to effectively organize complicated donations.

The Development of Charities

Since the Industrial Revolution, charities in the UK have started to take on more important functions, replacing the role of wealthy individuals and churches in philanthropy. This came about as part of an intensification of the Christian spirit of charitable giving and an increase in public awareness of social responsibility. The Industrial Revolution boosted not only the economy, but also education. Education and economic development facilitated social mobility and lay the foundations for the rise of the middle class.

The British middle class, now accounting for the larger part of society, rose to significance because of the Industrial Revolution and increased commercial activity. Compared to the upper class, they were more familiar with the lives of ordinary people and showed more concern about social issues. Compared to the lower class, their higher economic and social status enabled them to be actively involved in public philanthropy. This was how early modern civil society started to gradually take shape in Britain.

Charles Margrave Taylor, a Western political philosopher, defined civil society as "a web of autonomous associations, independent of the state, which binds citizens together in matters of common concern, and by their mere existence or action could have an effect on public policy." (Wang, 1998) These citizens actively devoted themselves to philanthropy and voluntarily set up numerous charities and non-governmental mutual-aid groups, both to protect their own interests and alleviate social issues.

Meanwhile, after the Renaissance, the spirit of liberty, equality and humanitarianism was increasing in popularity. The majority of the middle class acted in accordance with these notions and believed that each individual, whether poor or rich, should love and help each other. Without a doubt, such altruistic and humanitarian values helped spread a sense of philanthropic consciousness throughout society. The public were now encouraged to participate in philanthropic causes through various means, as a way of expressing their love for God and other people. During this period, British citizens started to value their self-worth and more members of the middle class contributed to public philanthropy.

In terms of specialized development, the UK saw all kinds of charitable organizations appear in this period. Statistics show that "In 1861, there were 640 charities in London alone, 103 of which were founded before the eighteenth century, 114 between the eighteenth and nineteenth century, 279 during the first half of the nineteenth century, and 144 in the 12 years between 1850 and 1861. By 1863, London was already home to 770 charitable organizations, and the number rose to 989 in 1869." (Harris, 2004) Among these, the more well-known nationwide charities were the National Children's Home and Orphanage, the Royal National Lifeboat Institute, and the Royal Society for the Prevention of Cruelty to Animals. Such organizations were involved in sectors of public life such as emergency social relief, healthcare, education, scientific research and environmental protection.

Charitable organizations could not have seen such development without fostering volunteer involvement. A volunteer spirit encourages people to selflessly contribute towards improving their communities, promoting social progress and advancing human development, without demanding any reward. (Salamon, 2002) Volunteerism in the UK dates back to 55 AD, when the Friendly Order first came into existence, perhaps the earliest voluntary organization in the world. More formal voluntary activities appeared around the twelfth and thirteenth centuries. During the two world wars, the participation of the British public in voluntary services reached its peak due to mobilization as part of the war effort. With time, volunteering one's services for your country became an individual drive for the British public. (Xu, 2013)

With the development of voluntary activity, the public came to realize that on such occasions, they could not only help others, but attain self-worth and spiritual satisfaction. This encouraged people to became more active volunteers. A survey showed that 27% of British people took part in voluntary activities for all types of organizations at least once a month in 2002, and 39% at least once a year. In 2005, 29% of people volunteered at least once a month and 42% at least once a year. Paid employees in charitable organizations take up only a minority of the work force, while the majority are volunteers of varying types. On average in the UK, every adult over 16 offers some kind of voluntary service every month. (Wang, 2012)

By March 31, 2018, there were 167,972 charitable organizations registered in the UK, with an annual total income of GBP 76.015 billion. (The Charity Commission for England and Wales, 2018) Many of these organizations, such as the Lloyd's Register Foundation, Save the Children and Oxfam, play an important role in domestic affairs, and also offer aid to developing countries and regions to help those affected by poverty, disasters or war. According to the 2017 statistics from the Charities Aid Foundation (CAF), donations used for overseas aid and disaster relief accounted for 12% of total donations in the UK. (CAF, 2018)

Support and Regulation from the Government

As mentioned above, after the Reformation, the secular power of Christian churches was taken over by the government. Its authority under serious threat from the growing class divide, the government organized a law-based system for poverty relief.

At that time, the church and government found themselves at odds when it came to philanthropy. The government regarded emergency relief as a sacrifice of the beneficiary's integrity and honor, and thus set forth strict regulations for those receiving relief. For example, in 1530, British law mandated that, except for the elderly and disabled, any vagabond or beggar was to be arrested and whipped. The *Act for the Relief of the Poor of 1597* still divided the poor into those that were fit to receive relief, and those that were not. Those fit included the elderly, sick, pregnant, and mentally or physically disabled. These people were then placed in poorhouses to be overseen by the government. Meanwhile, the able-bodied poor were not entitled to any relief, they were also made to work in exchange for a place in the poorhouse, facing imprisonment if they refused to do so. (CPRI & CCOH, 2013) In 1601, the *Act for the Relief of the Poor 1601* (also known as the *Old Poor Law*) was enacted, along with the *Charitable Uses Act of 1601*, the first law on charity in the world. Since then, the UK established an official system for helping the poor, with the government taking over control of philanthropy and institutionalizing all practices. Though the system was still morally restricted by religion, it no longer offered unconditional or unregulated charity, as the government believed that not all citizens were entitled to relief.

Charitable culture in the UK has never been unconditional. The Industrial Revolution provided a chance for everyone to make a living—a historic opportunity for workers. During the Renaissance, however, British culture came to value the recognition of people's desires and abilities as the preferred means of promoting self-reliance.

Despite charitable relief, it was believed that poverty and unemployment are due to personal laziness, not the structural shortcomings of society. In 1834, the British government enacted the *Poor Law Amendment Act 1834*, also called the New Poor Law, in which the "less eligibility" and "workhouse test" policies were developed. The former meant that the living conditions of those receiving relief in the workhouses had to be worse than any independent laborer outside. The latter stated that relief was only to be available within a workhouse, where the poor were to be under strict supervision. This aimed to improve the morals of the poor, and make the idle poor more hardworking. (Chen, 1996) Encouraging the rich to do kind deeds while deterring them from saving the incurable poor formed a charitable tradition that was religiously and historically unique.

In the modern era, the government adopted a more scientific and sophisticated approach to regulating the philanthropic sector. The government's daily functions began to include poverty relief as part of regular social welfare, and a series of security policies and legislation was put forward such as the *Unemployed Workmen Act 1905*, the *Old-age Pensions Act 1908*, and the *National Insurance Act 1911*. Since the twenty-first century, laws on philanthropy and charity have been updated and cover a wider scope to meet new needs.

Meanwhile, the UK government attaches great importance to cooperation among charitable organizations. It offers tax deductions and subsidies by signing the instructive Compact, an agreement between the UK government and voluntary and community organizations, to promote cooperation between authorities and civil society organizations.

Moreover, the Charity Commission was founded to supervise these organizations on behalf of the government. The Commission provides five types of service: (1) registration services for organizations which are established only for charitable purposes; (2) taking enforcement action on charity projects involving malpractice or misconduct; (3) ensuring charities meet their legal requirements, including providing annual disclosure of information; (4) ensuring the widespread availability of information about each registered organization; and (5) online services and instruction.

Section 2 The Realities of Internet Philanthropy in the UK

The UK is a traditional, developed European country, with a population of 65 million people and a land area of 94,268 square miles. Its GDP in 2016 totaled USD 2.63 trillion, accounting for 3.85% of global GDP and ranking 5th in the world. The per capita GDP was USD 40,096 in 2016, and ranked 9th in the world.

It is a country rich in culture, where 60% of its inhabitants are Protestants. Since the Middle Ages, the aristocrats and nobility have made up the British upper classes, and slowly the essence of aristocracy developed into the modern-day culture of the gentleman. This gentleman culture and elitism are infused with two further characteristics outlined above: Christianity's universal love and the humanitarian notions of the Renaissance.

The country's unique culture never impeded technological progress. When the world entered the Digital Age, the UK, as one of the major developed countries, saw a high rate of Internet access and a high level of activity in e-commerce, online social networking and entertainment compared to the rest of Europe. This relatively exhaustive Internet infrastructure, together with the country's cultural richness, constitute the ideal preconditions for Internet philanthropy to development in the UK.

According to the *European Ecommerce Report 2017* published by the Ecommerce Foundation, European e-commerce sales exceeded EUR 530 billion in 2016, with an annual growth rate of 15%. This figure is projected to reach EUR 602 billion in 2017. The UK accounts for the largest share of these figures, with the largest e-commerce market in Europe. E-commerce sales in the UK have reached EUR 197 billion, 37% of the European total (see Fig. 7.1).

Moreover, statistics from studies by Newzoo, an American provider of technology market analytics, showed that there is a high rate of smartphone usage in the UK. According to this study, 69% of the population are smartphone users, which is 45 out of 65 million.

In terms of e-payments, card payment is the most popular payment type in the UK, taking up 57% of the market share (divided into: 40% debit card, 17% credit card). The second most popular type is e-wallet payments, with 22% of the market share (see Fig. 7.2). This also shows that mobile payments, a real hit in Asia, has not yet received widespread interest from the majority of British people.

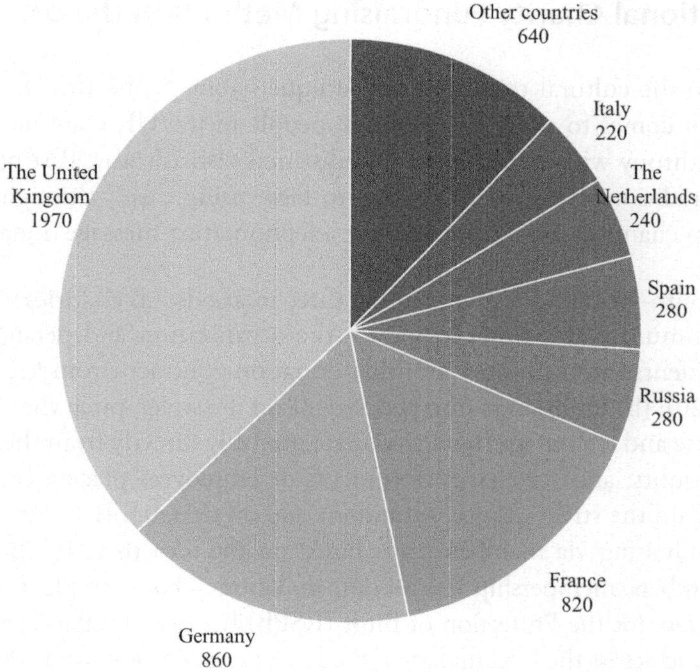

Fig. 7.1 Sales of Ecommerce in Europe (Unit EUR 100 million). (Source: European Ecommerce Report 2017 by Ecommerce Foundation)

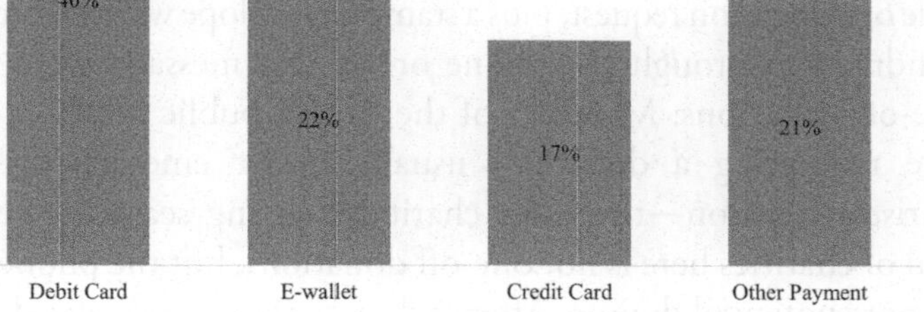

Fig. 7.2 E-payments in the UK. (Source: WorldPay)

Traditional Charity Fundraising Methods in the UK

Due to the cultural traditions and unique habits of the British people, when it comes to using the Internet, people in the UK combine public philanthropy with the Internet in a distinctly British way. Past practices have traditionally raised funds face-to-face (using cash), through membership channels, mail donations, or telephone/text message donations.

1. Face-to-face fundraising includes three methods: (a) charities visit one community at a time, introduce the organization and persuade the residents into signing a monthly donation contract (from GBP 3 up to 20); (b) fundraisers stop pedestrians on the street, pitch the charity's cause and encourage them to donate monthly directly from their bank accounts; and (c) charity volunteers or employees place a collection box on the street to receive random one-off donations.
2. Fundraising via membership is based on the idea that "by increasing members, membership fees become donations". For example, the Royal Society for the Protection of Birds (RSPB) has over a million members spread across the UK, making it the largest organization for wildlife protection in Europe. There are three types of memberships: children, adults and families. The membership fee starts from GBP 3 per month (GBP 1.5 for children). As supporters of the charity, members can receive magazines on wildlife protection from the RSPB and free tickets to over 200 natural reserves all over the country. Members also have access to events organized by the RSPB, such as outdoor activities and talks. (Qiu, 2014)
3. Fundraising via postal mail helps build strong relationships between the charity and donors to keep them in the long term. Usually charities enclose a monthly donation form with a letter of the charity's work, gratitude or a donation request, plus a stamped envelope with a return address.
4. Fundraising through the phone or via text message often results in one-off donations. Members of the British public receive a text message requesting a donation, usually under emergency or during Christmas season—the UK's charitable giving season. The ultimate goal of charities here is not one-off donations, but the phone numbers of more potential donors. After each donation, a specialized team calls back to thank the donor, introducing the role of the organization and encouraging them to sign a monthly donation contract.

The Development of Online Fundraising Methods

With the development of the Internet, a new way of fundraising has emerged: online fundraising, a more convenient method compared to traditional ones. More people are now willing to donate online. An increasing number of British charities have also realized that the Internet is an effective way to communicate with the public. They have started to build their own online donation platforms and strengthened cooperation with charity websites already in existence. The government has responded with policies to regulate these thriving platforms. Internet donation has built up a promising momentum with the help of the public, charitable organizations and the government.

Active Public Participation in Internet Donation

According to statistic from relevant British organizations, besides government funding, 7.6% of charitable donations in the UK came from the Internet in 2017, 21% of which were donated on mobile devices, up 12.1% compared with that of 2016. Among charitable organizations, the share of donations made over the Internet increased by 18.5%. The largest increase occurred in religious charities (18.1%), organizations for environmental or animal welfare (17.6%) and organizations for art and culture (17.2%). (NPT UK, n.d.)

Among all the Internet donations made in 2016, 10% of one-off donations were no less than GBP 800 and 40% of charities received a donation through the Internet worth as much as GBP 800 at least once. From January 2010 to December 2014, the average online donation in the UK increased by 20% to GBP 63.69, from GBP 52.87. (NPT UK, n.d.)

Charity Organizations' Move to the Internet

Charitable organizations have directed more focus towards the Internet, with the intention of increasing publicity through charity websites. Now, there are 10 famous websites for charitable donations including

JustGiving, Everyclick, BT MyDonate, and GlobalGiving UK. These websites operate not only on a desktop version, but also on corresponding mobile applications for the convenience of both the public and the charities themselves.

There are 8000 charities registered and collaborating on the JustGiving website. In 2015, BM Charity received a considerable click-through rate and over 100,000 views. Over 430 local charities registered with BM Charity could also promote themselves through the website, or even have access to international donations. (*How does*, 2016) Online platforms open up new sources of funds for charities, adding to their donations. In effect, 55% of surveyed charities claimed that the Internet donations they received in 2017 had further increased. (Blackbaud, 2014)

Regulation and Support from the Government

Britain's thriving industry would not be the same without the support of the government, which has played a substantial role in developing Internet donation. The Fundraising Standards Board (FRSB), the Institute of Fundraising, and the Public Fundraising Regulatory Association were founded to professionally and comprehensively regulate the sector.

The FRSB is responsible for monitoring and analyzing public complaints, as well as working with the charitable sector to raise standards for donations. The Institute of Fundraising is composed of professional fundraisers who compile and publish the Code of Fundraising Practice and assess the analyses made by the FRSB. Lastly, the Public Fundraising Regulatory Association regulates public donations.

UK charity law and the Charity Commission have also contributed towards the regulation of Internet donations. These regulations concern the use of private donation accounts, the ways in which online platforms guarantee the designated spending of donations, refunded donations, complaints from donors and fundraisers, and charge policies of donation websites. The regulation from the government and relevant organizations on Internet philanthropy enables a well-organized, functioning system. Such regulation also guarantees the rights of the donors, fundraisers and websites and sets boundaries to differentiate responsibilities.

Overview of the UK's Large-Scale Online Fundraising Websites and National Philanthropy Days

After more than a decade of development, the use of philanthropy websites in the UK is ever more sophisticated. While traditional charity days and charity organizations have strengthened their influence through the Internet, Internet philanthropy has been playing an increasingly important role in British public life. In the following sections, we present the three most well-known charitable fundraising websites and the UK's biggest charity day, Red Nose Day.

JustGiving

Founded in 2000, JustGiving is currently the largest UK charitable fundraising website, covering a vast range of areas for possible donations. Anyone can become a fundraiser; all they have to do to start fundraising is create a page, without having to pay any fee whatsoever. Users can start a page if they are receiving donations for charity projects or personal causes—but only if those projects and causes serve a social purpose. For example, a disabled person used JustGiving to raise funds to install more disabled facilities in their house. Another example was in 2010, when a 7-year-old British boy named Charlie Simpson raised money for the Haiti earthquake through JustGiving, eventually raising a total of GBP 210,000, with as much as GBP 145,000 received in the first 48 hours. This was a landmark in the history of online fundraising in the UK. (BBC News, 2010)

In 2013, JustGiving also launched Yimby.com, a crowd-funding platform, which marked the company's official entry into crowd-funding. During the open beta test, 250 campaigns opened on Yimby, pledging funds of over GBP 250,000. More than 100 of them successfully met their goals by the deadlines. The success rate was reported to be 64%. (Lomas, 2013)

As of now, JustGiving has more than 22 million registered users in over 160 countries and has raised a total of USD 4.5 billion, helping 25,788 charities worldwide. (JustGiving, n.d.)Donors can donate directly through the website. At the end of the fundraising campaign, the company deducts 5% of the money raised for operating costs, and the rest goes directly to the fundraiser. At the same time, JustGiving also charges its registered users GBP 15 a month, and for each donation of GBP 1000 and above there is a service fee of GBP 79.

Everyclick

Created in 2005, Everyclick is an Internet company providing online fundraising services for British charities. It promises to donate half of its revenue to charities. In 2010, Everyclick launched a new product called "Give as You Live", a website where you can search for online retailers that offer cashback to charitable organizations. In other words, the retailers donate a percentage of revenues to charity when users purchase their products. Through this website, it is easier and more convenient for users to find philanthropic retailers and participate in causes for social good. To date, this website has raised 9,872,000 GBP for British charities. (Give as you Live, n.d.)

BT MyDonate

BT MyDonate is a non-profit online fundraising service provided by the British telecommunications company BT Group for British charities as part of BT's community investment. BT MyDonate was officially launched in 2011. The site transfers all the donations it receives (excluding credit/debit card fees) to charity organizations without charging any subscription fees or commission. By December 31 of 2015, BT MyDonate had made donations to 8750 charities (My Donate, 2016) and thus became one of the most popular donation platforms in the UK.

Red Nose Day

Red Nose Day is a long-established charitable campaign in the UK with a distinctive British character. It was first organized in the UK in 1988 by

Comic Relief, and has since been held every two years, which means this year it turns 30. Red Nose Day advocates using joy to deliver positive social energy. Its most prominent feature is that it allows people to raise funds in a fun way; people typically wear a red nose, weird red costumes, or dye their hair red. The campaign looks to draw attention to the disadvantaged through a series of fun activities. At the end of the event, 40% of the proceeds are used to help disadvantaged groups in the UK and 60% to assist the impoverished in Africa.

When established, Red Nose Day was a national festival in the UK, but has now gradually spread to other countries, turning into a global charity event. It has been held in the US, Germany, Ireland, and Iceland among others. In June 2017, it was also introduced in China.[2]

Offline events in the UK mainly include a live, televised fundraising show, baking, short films, and Red Nose Day merchandise. In addition, people can also participate in online charity events.

As for Internet philanthropy, fundraising projects on the Red Nose Day website fall into categories such as vaccination, mental health, education, domestic violence, and malaria. The public can make donations on the website at any time. Six buttons for donations of GBP 30, 50, 100, 250, 500 and 1000 are displayed on the "Donation" page, though users can also choose a customized amount to donate. Payments can be made by credit card (American Express, Mastercard, Visa, etc.) or through Paypal. Meanwhile, the website also livestreams the fundraising events featuring celebrities on its "News Media and Events" page, where users can not only watch the live events, but also make donations on the donation page by following the links on the livestream.

The campaign encourages fundraising projects created by schools, so as to motivate the younger generation to take part and to enhance their philanthropic awareness, raising money through a unique "offline activities plus online promotion plus online/offline fundraising" model. Red Nose Day classifies young people into four age groups—kindergarten, primary school, middle school, and young adults—and provides differentiated, targeted fundraising methods for young people of different ages.

---

[2] Rage Comics has been authorized along with a number of charity organizations to hold the Red Nose Day campaign on June 1.

Red Nose Day charity events have provided support to more than 2000 projects, covering problems such as homelessness, dementia, and the mental health of young people. For instance, in Africa, these donations are destined to help 11.7 million people to address issues such as immunization, malaria, education, maternal health, etc.

Red Nose Day has received extensive participation and support from the British public. In 2017, the amount raised online reached USD 38.17 million (about RMB 250 million). From the launch of the campaign to 2017, Red Nose Day donations in the UK had exceeded USD 1.8 billion. (CM Public Welfare Communication, 2017; Huang, 2017)

Section 3 The Impact of Internet Philanthropy in the UK

Benefits

The increasing popularity of online donations in the UK helps the British philanthropic sector make use of new technologies to stimulate its own growth and allows charitable activities to be more convenient and transparent. Similarly, since online donations make other people's donations clearly visible, from the psychological perspective, this also stimulates the public to make donations.

Convenience

British users only have to open a charity organization's webpage or app online to make donations. At the same time, they can also start fundraising on various crowd-funding platforms, participating in philanthropic activities without ever having to leave their home. In a survey on philanthropy in the UK by the CAF, 26% of the people surveyed had participated in philanthropic activities via online donations in the past 12 months, ranking 5th out of all fundraising methods (see Fig. 7.3). Among these, online donations were most popular among users in the 25–44 age group, which may be attributed to the

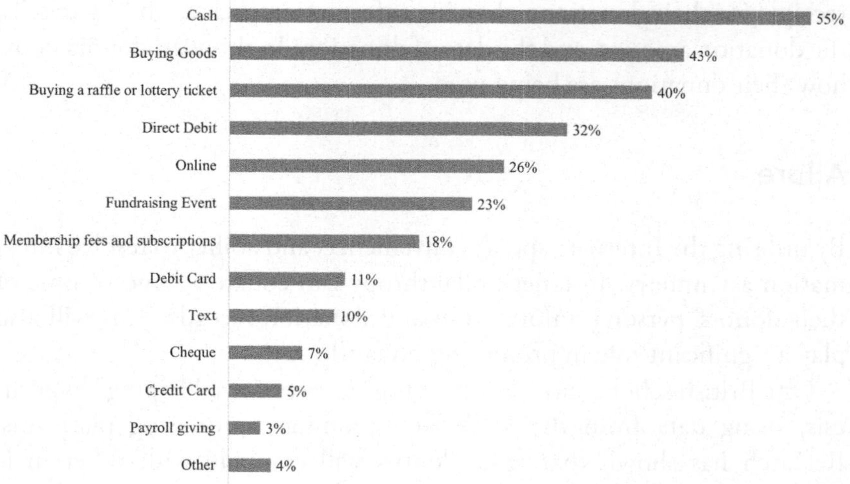

Fig. 7.3 Methods for donating in the UK. (Source: CAF (2018) Giving Report)

fact that most people of this age are too busy with work to have time for in-person charity events. Therefore, online donation, which can be completed in a few minutes without having to actually go anywhere, is the preferred choice. According to another survey, 19% of elderly people (over 65) and 28% of young people (under 24) have made donations online in the past year. (CAF, 2018) Clearly, online donation is spreading among British users of all ages thanks to its convenience and speed. In the future, there will be an even more substantial number of British users donating online.

Transparency

Internet donation platforms allow for all details during a project to be made public for the public to supervise, and donors can learn about the use and whereabouts of their donations in a variety of ways. This helps to lower the level of corruption and improve the social credibility of philanthropic organizations, thus facilitating the development of philanthropy. These platforms can keep records of the personal information of all fundraisers, including their bank information and addresses. Donors receive receipts for their donations, showing information such as charity details, the donation amount, and the date of donation. In this way, donors know how their donations are being used.

Allure

By utilising the Internet's speed, convenience, and ability to resolve information asymmetry, Internet philanthropy can collate a large volume of their donors' personal information and donation records. This will also play a significant role in promoting philanthropy.

One British scholar has confirmed the "Competitive Helping" hypothesis, using data from the UK's largest online fundraising platforms. Research has shown that male donors will compete with other male donors on the size of their donations when facing an attractive female fundraiser. (Raihani & Smith, 2015) Internet fundraising platforms show a fundraiser's personal data (name, photo, reason for fundraising and sponsoring agency) as well as how much others have donated. When this is combined with Competitive Helping and the "Anchoring Effect", when a man makes a contribution on the donation page, he will naturally not make a donation lower than the previous donor. This phenomenon is particularly evident when a male donor faces an attractive female fundraiser. It is clear, therefore, that such platforms indirectly increase the number of participants in fundraising and philanthropic events by taking advantage of the psychology of Competitive Helping.

Problems

Despite the advantages, there are also some potential risks to online fundraising. After the terrorist attack in London in March 2017, many pages popped up on JustGiving raising funds for the victims' families, including the family of Aysha Frade. According to the BBC, the money raised totaled more than GBP 17,000. However, users in the UK found out that someone with the same name as the administrator for the page had been convicted of charity fraud in 2013. JustGiving discovered that the account username had been changed a number of times since it had first opened.

Several other unverified pages were also found on the site raising money for Aysha Frade. Suspecting fraudulent activity, JustGiving decided to take over the page. Additionally, a "Verified by JustGiving" tag was added to the page to assure users that their donations would go to Ms. Frade's family. (CCTV, 2018)

No matter they go about it, laws and regulations seem never to be able to catch up with fraudulent activity. At present, the charity law in the UK is still relatively lax in terms of regulation, and the British public are in the belief that online fundraising is more dependent on self-awareness to prevent scams.

Nevertheless, the combination of the Internet and philanthropy is undeniably promising. As such, the UK, as the earliest country to develop global philanthropy, will no doubt continue to rely more on the Internet to expand its work in this field.

Section 4 Summary

Philanthropy in the UK over the past century could not have flourished without the Christian tradition, British gentleman culture, and elite awareness. We can also see that the development of philanthropy, first led by the rich and the church, then by charities, and then by Internet donation platforms, reflects a culture of benevolence and self-awareness in the UK when it comes to philanthropy. Their strong charitable culture is the foundation for the ever-growing British Internet philanthropy industry.

At the same time, as Internet philanthropy has developed, the British government has also played an important role in terms of supervision and guidance. From the *Old Poor Law* to the *New Poor Law*, then to the *Charities Act 2006*, and the establishment of the Charity Commission, the British government has constantly adapted to new developments in philanthropy, adjusting laws and policies, and supporting the industry's orderly and sound development.

Charity organizations' move to Internet platforms is a significant symbol of how traditional fundraising has been transformed in the digital age. The growth of large charitable fundraising websites such as JustGiving,

Everyclick and BT MyDonate has dramatically facilitated the participation of the British public in philanthropic activities. The combination between the Internet and traditional charity days like Red Nose Day helps to build more interest in charity days. In this way, the culture of philanthropy will only continue to penetrate British society and the world as a whole. Although Internet donation is still experiencing problems due to lax regulation and fraud, we can predict that with the development of digital technology and the improvement of online philanthropy, Internet donation in the UK will step into a more secure and active era.

Ultimately, Internet philanthropy in the UK, influenced by the time-honored philanthropic tradition and the hard work of British society, will continue to play an increasingly critical role in daily life, driving more people to participate in charity.

References

BBC News. (2010, January 25). London boy raises £145k for Haiti quake aid by cycling. *BBC*. http://news.bbc.co.uk/2/hi/uk_news/england/london/8478244.stm

Blackbaud. (2014). 2014 state of the not-for-profit industry survey summary report. *Blackbaud*. https://www.blackbaud.co.uk/files/bbe/SONI/SONI_UKReport2014.pdf

CAF. (2018). CAF UK giving 2018. *Cafonline*. https://www.cafonline.org/docs/default-source/about-us-publications/caf-uk-giving-2018-report.pdf

CCTV(央广网). (2018, June 03). *网络募捐频出问题 看各国如何监管*. *Baijiahao*. https://baijiahao.baidu.com/s?id=1602240950639306940&%20wfr=spider&for=pc

Chen, X. L. (1996). *英国福利制度的由来与发展*. 南京大学出版社.

CM Public Welfare Communication (CM公益传播). (2017, September 18). 国外也有"99公益日"英国人把募捐玩成一种时尚美国人悄悄弄了个公益大IP. Sohu. https://www.sohu.com/a/192689686_712346

CPRI & CCOH. (2013). *慈善与社会体制改革:历史背景和政策导向*. http://www.yifangfoundation.org/wap/sources_view.php?id=71

Gao, H. (2012). 神圣与世俗:《米德尔敦》中的慈善悖论. *杭州师范大学学报(社会科学版), 2012*(2), 114–117. http://xb.hznu.edu.cn/hsdxb/oa/DArticle.aspx?type=view&id=20120217

Give as you Live. (n.d.). Raise free funds for charity with your everyday shopping. *Giveasyoulive*. Retrieved September 30, 2018, from https://www.giveasyoulive.com/

Harris, B. (2004). *The origins of the British welfare state: Society, state and social welfare in England and Wales, 1800–1945*. Palgrave Macmillan.

How does the UK's online charity fundraising work?*(英国的网络慈善募捐是如何运作的)*. (2016, June 01). *Stnn*. http://finance.stnn.cc/gywt/2016/0601/320873.shtml

Huang, H. S. (黄瀚生). (2017, March 25). *英国红鼻子日你的鼻子红了吗*. *Sohu*. http://www.sohu.com/a/130236534_252650

Jordan, W. K. (1960). *The charities of London 1480–1660*. Allen & Unwin Ltd..

JustGiving. (n.d.). Raise more money, change more lives. *Justgiving*. Retrieved September 30, 2018, from https://pages.justgiving.com/charities.html

Lomas, N. (2013, November 13). Charitable donation platform, JustGiving, launches Yimby, a crowdfunding platform for social good. *Techcrunch*. https://techcrunch.com/2013/11/12/yimby/

My Donate. (2016, January 27). 2015 review. *Btplc*. https://www.btplc.com/mydonate/News/2015Review/index.aspx

NPT UK. (n.d.). Charitable giving statistics in the United Kingdom. *Yfanfoundation*. Retrieved September 30, 2018, from http://www.npt-uk.org/philanthropic-resources/uk-charitable-giving-statistics

Qiu, Y. (2014, January 08). *英国慈善机构筹款方式大盘点*. 人民网. http://gongyi.people.com.cn/n/2014/0108/c151132-24055623.html

Raihani, N. J., & Smith, S. (2015). Competitive helping in online giving. *Current Biology, 25*(9), 1183–1186. https://www.cell.com/action/showPdf?pii=S0960-9822%2815%2900211-0.

Salamon, L. M. (2002). *全球公民社会:非营利部门视界* (X. J. Jia & Y. Wei, Trans.). 中国社会科学出版社. (Original work published 1999).

The Charity Commission for England and Wales. (2018, October 18). Recent charity register statistics: Charity Commission. *Gov.uk*. https://www.gov.uk/government/publications/charity-register-statistics/recent-charity-register-statistics-charity-commission

Wang, H. (1998). *文化与公共性*. 上海三联书店.

Wang, M. (2012, October 24). *英国的慈善组织*. *Chinadevelopmentbrief*. http://www.chinadevelopmentbrief.org.cn/news-12230.html

Wang, M., Li, Y., & Huang, H. M. (Eds.). (2009). *英国非营利组织*. 社会科学文献出版社.

Xu, J. X. (2013). *一种历史的视角:英国慈善事业的现代化转型* (Publication No. 10.7666/d.D370151) [Masters dissertations, Qufu Normal University]. Wanfang data.

8

Japan: From Government Supervision to Shared Governance

Section 1 The Development of Japanese Philanthropy

"Philanthropy", as defined in the Japanese dictionary, refers to common and public interest as opposed to private interest, the same as in Western languages. It is widely agreed that "philanthropy" in Japan was something introduced from the West in modern times after the Meiji Reform.

According to Japan's laws on the legal persons of philanthropic groups and philanthropic consortiums in the country, the detailed definition of a philanthropic undertaking is one in academia, art, charity or another field promoting the interests of a broad and unspecified section of the public. From this perspective, "philanthropy" in Japan includes "charity" and all other kinds of "public philanthropy".

Though the word "philanthropy" emerged relatively late in Japanese language and culture, charitable and philanthropic activities started in ancient Japan, just like its Chinese counterpart. This 1500-year history can be roughly divided into pre-Edo Times, the Meiji Reform, and after WWII.

Y. Chen, *Internet Philanthropy in China*,
https://doi.org/10.1007/978-981-16-2566-4_8

Contemporary and Modern Times: Pre-Edo Tradition of Religious Philanthropy and Non-governmental Mutual Aid

When it comes to the historic charitable and philanthropic activities of Japan, mainstream Japanese academia traces them back to the Asuka Period (beginning in 593 AD). At that time, the Regent Prince Shōtoku, who adopted the Chinese idea that the emperor enjoyed unparalleled and unconstrained powers, tried to establish a system of centralization with the emperor as the center in an attempt to push through reforms and solve the social crisis arising from incessant wars among the nobles. One of his major actions was to strongly promote Buddhism among the people in order to impair the power of the nobility. For that purpose, Prince Shōtoku ordered the construction of the first officially administered temple, the Four Devas Temple. Moreover, he initiated the system of the "Four Agents", namely, Agent for the Senior People and the Homeless, Agent for Delivering Medicines, Agent for Curing Diseases, and Agent of the Temple. This is now regarded as the beginning of Japanese charity and philanthropy (see Fig. 8.1). The system of "Four Agents" originated from the Buddhist ideas of "respect for the Buddha, other Buddhists, parents, and the underprivileged", and taught that people should do good for society for the sake of their own virtue, which naturally worked to promote charitable activity. While the "Four Agents" is not in a strict sense a non-governmental organization for philanthropy, it has exerted a great influence on this sector's development in Japan. Following Prince Shōtoku, a batch of eminent Buddhist monks including Dōshō, Gyōki, Chōgen, Eison, Ninshō and Gan'ami, spread the idea of charity by conducting charitable activities like raising funds for constructing bridges, paving roads, relieving disasters and curing the sick. This contributed to the rise of religious charities.

Japan's religious influences, represented by Buddhism, combined with the organizational mode and moral education of traditional Japanese society, an array of local philanthropic organizations concerned with

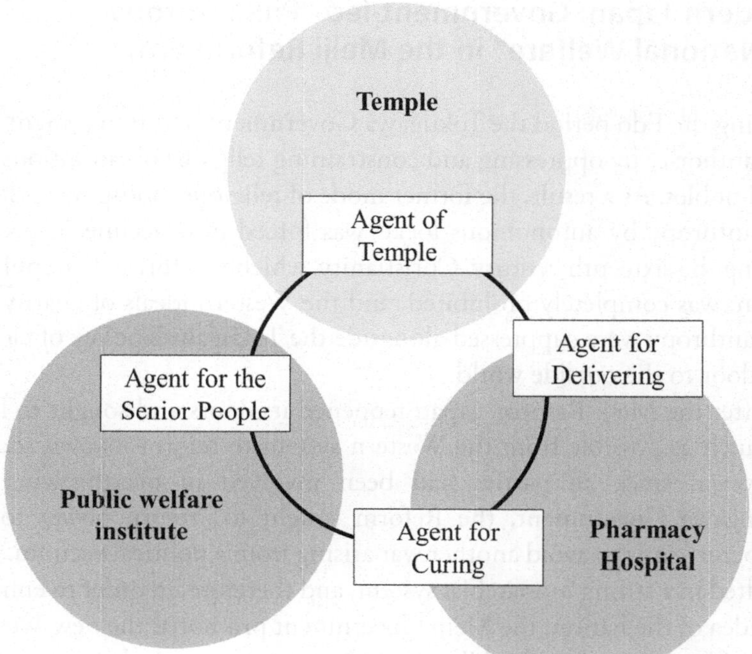

Fig. 8.1 The "Four Agents" System of the Four Devas Temple. (Source: 四天王寺関連サイトリンク)

mutual assistance and mutual benefit were born. The most representative ones were referred to as "Chanting" (講, こう) and "Connecting" (結, ゆい). The former originated from the chanting of Buddhist scriptures and gradually evolved into "an institution of people who share the same beliefs". The latter originally referred to the word "connection", and since the Kamakura Period it has been used to describe small settlements and autonomous units where residents helped each other, including equal exchange of labor, materials and capital. At this point the concept of generalized "philanthropy" had not yet emerged, as the roles of such organizations were constrained within local areas and small communities.

Modern Japan: Government-led "Philanthropy as National Welfare" in the Meiji Reform Era

During the Edo period the Tokugawa Government began to cement central authority by oppressing and constraining religious organizations and local nobles. As a result, the former mode of religious, non-governmental philanthropy by autonomous locals was forced into decline. Especially during the sixteenth century, Christianity, which was formerly popular in Japan, was completely prohibited, and the Western ideals of charity and philanthropy were suppressed alongside the Tokugawa's policy of closing the door to the outside world.

After the Meiji Reform, Japan reopened its doors and sought to learn as much as possible from the Western system to reform its own society. However, since all parties had been involved in overthrowing the Tokugawa Government, the Reform sought to "return power to the Emperor" so as to avoid another war arising from a political vacuum. This resulted in a strong monarchist system, and therefore, in order to enhance the idea of the nation, the Meiji Government promoted the new Western idea of "public interest" (philanthropy) as the new equivalent to national welfare, thereby obscuring the role of "the citizen" and "the citizen's interest".

Under the guidance of these state-administered models and ideologies, the Meiji Government issued the *Civil Code* in 1896, establishing the legal person system for the first time, which divided organizations into those that are profitable and those that are non-profit. However, the requirements placed on non-profit organizations were stricter; they had to be approved by the appropriate governmental department. In other words, the government administration possessed discretionary power over philanthropic organizations, and the public could not conduct philanthropic activities without permission. This mechanism prevented non-governmental philanthropic organizations from expanding to a larger scale, while the majority of philanthropic work was concentrated in the government. This mode of government-led philanthropy lasted nearly a century until WWII.

The Contemporary Age: From Post-WWII Reconstruction to Present, "Joint-governance by the Government and the Public"

WWII left Japan with an unsurmountable amount of work to do, making it impossible for the government to handle the country's reconstruction alone. In 1951, the Japanese government issued the first law focused on charity, the *Social Welfare Act.* The aim of this law was to unite the strength of non-governmental philanthropic organizations and bring them in line with government regulations, without violating the Constitution (Article 89 of Japan's Constitution stipulates that charitable organizations and groups shall not assist the government). The law provided a new method for managing philanthropic activities by establishing a new operational mode, namely the "legal person of social welfare". This enabled non-governmental groups to conduct philanthropic activities by establishing a legal person, or cooperating with another legal person of the same field. This in turn lifted the curtain for non-governmental participation in philanthropic undertakings.

In the mid-1960s, Japanese academics mounted criticism on the country's "state-administered public" (top-down) social system, and advocated instead the legitimacy of a "citizen-administered public" (bottom-up) model. The discussion originated from research on Western "public philosophy" and "modern civil society", and nurtured the growth of Japan's own public philosophy. This school of thought had two main ideas about the public. The first suggested doing away with the dualism between public and private, advocating "public" space to be presided over by the government, "private" space by the individual, and a "shared domain" for both government and individual (see Fig. 8.2) (長坂寿久, 2007). The shared domain belongs to both the government and the individual; it is a space where citizens can freely participate in philanthropic undertakings without interference. This should be a third type of space that cannot be monopolized by the government or the individual. The second idea of Japanese public philosophy involved the denial of "sacrificing self-interest for public interest" and vice versa. It advocated a mode featuring "active individual participation and open public policy" (山脇直司, 2004).

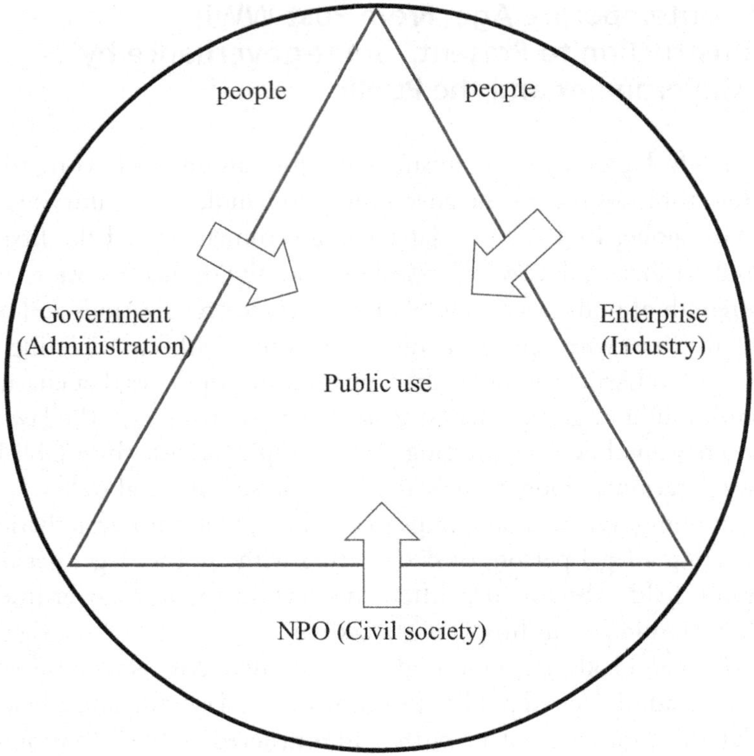

Fig. 8.2 Three Segments of the Tripartite Public. (Source: 长坂寿久.公共哲学と日本の市民社会 (NPO) セクタ")

The rising "public philosophy" in this period took philanthropy to the new stage of non-governmental rejuvenation and joint governance by the government and the public. In the "shared domain," or third sector in Western countries, Nonprofit Organization (NPO) became the government's major target for development. The Hanshin-Awaji Earthquake of 1995 was pivotal in this, because a large number of non-governmental organizations and groups emerged during relief efforts to care for disaster-hit areas. It also accelerated the implementation of the *Law to Promote Specified Non-profit Activities* in 1998 ("NPO Law"), which provide legal groundwork for the establishment of NPOs. In 2006, the strict licensing system for legal persons with philanthropic purposes stipulated in Article 34 of the *Civil Law* was completely removed. In its place, the general legal person system based on a looser standardization (the principle of registering and filing) was enacted, along with a new system of philanthropic legal persons based on determinism. This further relaxed the supervision over NPOs and promoted their rapid development. In 2010, the Japanese government issued the declaration of "New Public Commons", which advocated "a vibrant civil society based on mutual assistance between people, where coordinated voluntary action can take place". A number of other measures were implemented covering donation and tax reform, training for philanthropic workers, and raising social capital, as well as the concept of "joint governance by the government and the public".

The Current Situation: After a Successful Resurgence in Philanthropy, More Time Needed to Expand in Scale and Popularity

The rejuvenation of Japanese non-governmental philanthropy has developed rapidly since the *NPO Law* was enacted in 1998. In one respect, a large number of charitable and philanthropic groups, both old and new, have become legal persons recognized by law, which provides the legal guarantee to carry out non-governmental philanthropic activities. As of July 2018, there were 51,768 recognized philanthropic legal persons in Japan. In addition, the government has accelerated the approval of legal persons, who enjoy preferential tax policies but are subject to strict governmental approval restrictions. The proportion of recognized legal persons to accredited legal persons is increasing, and currently stands at 2.1% with 1085 recognized legal persons (Cabinet Office NPO, n.d.).

With regard to donation amounts, though there have been fluctuations in recent years the overall trend is ascending. Individual donations are particularly high. On the one hand, major disasters have brought great public enthusiasm for donations, especially by individuals. In March 2011, an earthquake off the Pacific coast of Tohoku triggered a leak at the Fukushima nuclear power plant, causing huge losses for Japan. As a result, the amount of individual donations surged, increased by

109% from the previous year. However, in comparison, donation amounts made by legal persons increased by only 18%. This demonstrates the great enthusiasm in Japan for helping others in need and the extent to which philanthropic habits have spread among the Japanese people. The amount of individual donations is nearly the same as those made by legal persons. For example, between 2009 and 2014, the ratio fluctuated between 5:7 and 13:7, but was nearly 1:1 for the most of this period. Overall, the proportion of individual donations exceeded 30%, at one point nearly reaching 69% (2011) (Giving Japan, 2017).

Nevertheless, compared with Europe and America, philanthropy in Japan is still lagging behind somewhat. For example, there are 1 million philanthropic organizations in the US, while the number in Japan is just over 50,000; individual donations in the US accounted for 1.44% of the GDP in 2016, while Japan's figure was only 0.14% (Giving Japan, 2017). As the rejuvenation of Japan's non-governmental philanthropy began only two decades ago, there still remains much room for improvement in the future.

Section 2 The Development of Japan's Internet Philanthropy

Japan's Internet may not enjoy the same worldwide reputation as "Made in Japan" or Japanese anime culture, but with the establishment of Yahoo! Japan in 1996, it has essentially developed alongside the global Internet industry. According to Yahoo! Japan, it was after the 2004 Chūetsu earthquake when the company launched the fundraising website Yahoo! Internet Fund Raising (Yahoo! ネット募金) that Internet philanthropy in Japan began to thrive. From then on, in line with the development of the Internet, Japan's Internet philanthropy has also moved from the desktop onto mobile platforms. At present, not only are the traditional Internet giants conducting philanthropic activities in Japan, but traditional agents of charity and philanthropy have also set up their own websites, and are increasingly adopting online donation methods. Some of the newly-emerging Internet-based philanthropy is having a global impact, as Japan builds its own Internet-based mode for philanthropy and connects itself with the rest of the world.

Portals Plus Philanthropy: Yahoo! JAPAN

Yahoo! JAPAN was Japan's first website, a joint-venture between Yahoo! and Japan Softbank established on April 1, 1996. Representing part of the Web 1.0 era, Yahoo! Japan hasn't collapsed like so many other Internet companies established at the same period, despite the industry's rapid development. Instead, Yahoo! Japan continues to lead the Internet industry in terms of its business scope and market value, through proactive expansion and successful operational methods in the fields of web portal services, advertising, search, auction, wireless value-added services, and online banking.

The breadth of Yahoo! Japan's business is also clearly demonstrated in the layout of its philanthropic work. Yahoo! Japan is involved in Japanese Internet philanthropy via its web portal, e-commerce, payment, and crowd-funding services, all of which play leading roles in the industry. According to the Yahoo! Japan website, the company supports philanthropic undertakings mainly through its platforms and applications in the following five areas: Yahoo! Internet Fund Raising, Yahoo! Foundation, Yahoo! Volunteer, Charity Auction and Links for Good.

1. Yahoo! Internet Fund Raising. Initiated in 2004, the platform is aimed at collecting funds for disaster relief and reconstruction in the disaster-hit areas of the 2004 Chūetsu earthquake. It covers a wide range of activities including disaster relief and reconstruction, children, animals/pets, international cooperation, medical care/welfare, the environment, culture and education. It also provides display and broadcasting of web portal information and an online donation service. Besides regular donations and emergency (disaster) support, it also covers many donation methods such as lotteries and gift return. The major payment methods are through Yahoo! Wallet (credit card), T points, and mobile phones (Softbank), which cover the payment preferences of the majority of online users. In 2016, its online fundraising total exceeded JPY 900 million, making Yahoo! Internet Fund Raising the leader of the entire Japanese industry (Yahoo! Japan, n.d.).
2. Yahoo! Foundation (Yahoo! 基金). Set up in 2006 for the 10th anniversary of Yahoo! Japan, the foundation is constituted from donations

by Yahoo! and users. The major use of the donations is for the safe and sound development of online society, emergency support in the event of disasters, and monetary assistance for NPO activities. In addition, it has established two specialized departments. The first is the IT Funding Department, which provides traditional IT business support to help resolve social problems. The second is the Reconstruction Department, which supports reconstruction projects after the 2011 earthquake off the Pacific coast of Tohoku.

3. Yahoo! Volunteer. Launched on April 1, 2003 for the seventh anniversary of Yahoo! Japan, Yahoo! Volunteer is part of the company's social responsibility commitment. It aims at coordinating volunteer organizations and campaign information by establishing a forum website to help volunteers find suitable activities. The information it contains is taken from three partner websites, which ensure the correctness and authenticity of the information: the first is CANPAN, operated by Japanese Consortium Foundation; the second is Volunteer Platform, the largest volunteer platform in the country with over 39,000 members; and Volunteer Info., which is focused on providing information on voluntary activities and coordinating volunteer resources.
4. Charity Auction (チャリティ“オ”クション). Implemented in 1999 as part of the company's social responsibility projects, the platform supports philanthropic activities through online charity auctions. In November 2011, the auction website established a specialized "reU funding" service for crowd-funding, where the funds paid by the buyer for certain goods are given as donations. In 2015, the total amount of auction proceeds reached approximately JPY 180 million, creating a win-win situation for the buyer, the seller and society as a whole, and a new way of building a cyclical social system.
5. Links for Good. Launched on June 11, 2013 and terminated on September 30, 2016 due to business adjustments, this was a Yahoo! advertisement display network that can be used by NPOs for one year of free promotion. The platform can display their advertisements in a specified part of the Yahoo! web page. With the help of ad targeting technology, these companies are able to effectively catch users' interest by displaying advertisements that are specifically tailored to them.

E-commerce Plus Philanthropy: Rakuten

Rakuten was founded in February 1997. It started as a B2B2C e-commerce site with only 6 employees and 13 merchants. It was not until 1998, when it launched its auctioning service, that it began to explore the C2C market. In 2000, it grew larger by means of an initial public offering (IPO) and subsequent acquisitions, which included securities companies, travel websites and professional baseball teams. It also provides credit card and loyalty rewards services, which add further depth to its commercial transaction abilities. In 2006, Rakuten established the vision of a new business ecosystem based on the Rakuten member system, aiming at diversification and overseas expansion. The company purchased Viber, an Israeli instant messaging company; Slice, an American online-shopping data company; VIKI, a Singaporean video sub-titling community; Kobo, a Canadian electronic reading service; OverDrive, an American digital and media distributor; PriceMinister, a French e-commerce platform; and Ebates, an American cashback shopping website. This has become a model for Japanese Internet companies seeking to expand worldwide. Rakuten provides over 70 kinds of services to its registered 1.2 billion users in 29 countries and regions around the world, and has a total transaction value of JPY 12.9 trillion (2017) (Rakuten, n.d.).

Unlike Yahoo! Japan's method of integrating philanthropy into all of its businesses, Rakuten focuses on its core business sectors—e-commerce and payment, including Rakuten Global Market, Rakuten Payment and Rakuten Bank. In addition, Rakuten has set up two independent philanthropic organizations aimed at the fields they are particularly passionate about, namely "Future Wings of Rakuten", a non-profit philanthropic consortium, and "Rakuten Clutch Special Charity Fund".

E-commerce and Payment Plus Philanthropy

Rakuten Global Market provides channels for philanthropic organizations and causes to improve their publicity and receive donations, with the help of its e-commerce platform and payment tools. In terms of format, philanthropic activities are presented in the form of commercial products, so that customers can donate by buying these products or make their own donations directly. In this way it resembles the online philanthropic shopping model used by Chinese Alibaba. However, it is linked with Japan's unique system of "hometown taxation", which stimulates enthusiasm for donations made by consumers by offering tax exemption or reduction for users. Taobao, Rakuten Global Market's Chinese counterpart, focuses on promoting sales by emphasizing philanthropic donations of the businesses or shop owners.

The system of "hometown taxation" (ふるさと纳税) was set up in 2007, allowing taxpayers to donate to any area they wished to support in order to gain exemptions from individual income tax or residency tax. The system aimed at encouraging people living in cities to donate to rural or remote areas in order to support the area's development. Rakuten Global Market adopted the system in 2015 when it began to help local governments design web pages and establish donation projects for the "hometown taxation" system. Many of the areas give local specialty products back to the donors as gifts, much like other e-commerce on Rakuten. This creates a unique modal of "shopping-donating-tax exempting". Thanks to Internet platforms like Rakuten, more and more customers are getting to know remote areas of Japan in a quick and convenient way. As a result, it is possible for urban residents to donate and pay taxes towards remote areas where they are not even residents (one user can choose five donation targets per year). In this way, users can not only support construction in remote places, but also achieve reductions or exemptions to their own taxes. This single measure produces three benefits, thus greatly increasing its appeal among users.

There are six main steps in Rakuten's "hometown taxation" process (see Fig. 8.3): (1) choosing a municipal government to receive your donation

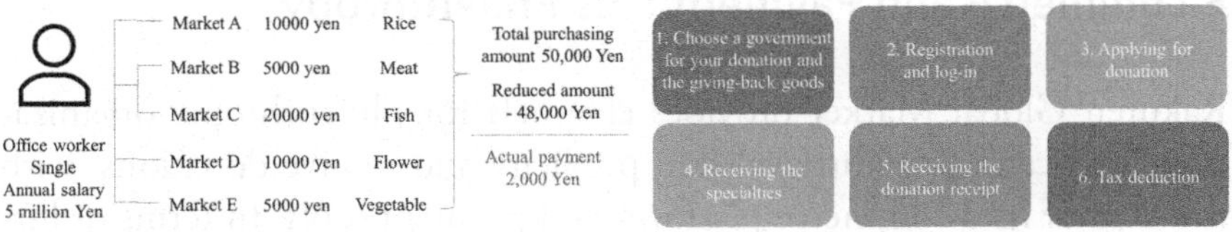

Fig. 8.3 The system of Rakuten "hometown taxation" and its processes

and thank you gifts; (2) registration and log-in (the system can also be used by non-registered members who wish to forgo the points service); (3) applying for donation: viewing the descriptions of the specialty products and clicking "apply for donation"; (4) receiving the specialty products, which may take between one week and several months for delivery as they are not commercial goods for sale; (5) receiving the donation receipt; (6) tax deduction. Both the one-stop special exemption system and the subsequent application and reporting are available. There are three ways of handling donation and payment: the Rakuten card, the Rakuten bank, and Rakuten points that can be directly used for the donated amount, just like T points in Yahoo!. All of them can reduce or exempt taxes.

Establishing Specialized and Independent Philanthropic Organizations

"Future Wings of Rakuten", a non-profit philanthropic consortium, was established on June 1, 2011 through a donation made by Airio Life Insurance Co., Ltd. (now Rakuten Life Insurance Co., Ltd.), it focuses on improving children's welfare. The business scope covers three core aspects. The first is to provide scholarship funding including tuition fees and apartment leasing costs for young people aged 18 who are beginning to live independently. The second is to support technology and education activities to help children increase their competitive edge at school. The third is to provide information, consultations and encouragement to help resolve the psychological problems created by loneliness.

"Rakuten Clutch Special Fund" was launched after the 2011 earthquake off the Pacific coast of Tohoku to answer calls from thousands of users who hoped to provide help. In addition to providing donations for disaster relief and reconstruction, it gradually developed other special projects for philanthropy. The best example is the "Rakuten Forest", aimed at protecting the habitat of the endangered golden eagle. Since then it has developed into a sustainable system for philanthropy combining ecological shopping and tourism, working in conjunction with Rakuten e-commerce and travel services.

Social Media Plus Philanthropy: Line

Line was launched by the Korean company Naver in June 2011 to conduct mobile and instant communication business. It has become one of the most widely used social and messaging apps in the world, with most of its users in Japan, South Korea and other East Asian areas. By combining Japan's characteristic anime with Line's own distinctive and original cartoons and emoji, and making use of the mobile payment function Line Pay, it has gradually developed a unique modal consisting of social messaging, related commercial goods and shops. Line has become a vital component of Japan's Internet industry, especially in the mobile Internet market.

Line's business features are fully integrated with philanthropy in the following four aspects: its official accounts, the emoji shop, mobile payments, and the messaging function.

1. Official accounts and philanthropy. Just like WeChat's official accounts, Line's official accounts allow philanthropic organizations to open their own accounts through which to connect and interact with Line users, helping publicize philanthropic activities online.
2. The emoji shop and philanthropy. Line offers tailored emoji design packages for philanthropic agents. When Line users buy such packages, the payment amount is donated to the philanthropic agents.
3. Mobile payment and philanthropy. If users are interested in any philanthropic activities shown on the platform, they can make donations directly through Line Pay, just like donations made via WeChat.
4. Communication functions and philanthropy. Targeting the frequent natural disasters happening in Japan, Line has launched a series of emergency services and guidance functions aimed at enabling people to rescue themselves and others when disasters happen. This includes: (1) safety notices: in emergency situations, users can use "group communication" as an emergency communication platform, enabling them to report on their current situation using the individual "status information"; (2) current location notices: users can put important information at the top of chat lists using the "notice function", which can help others be aware of their current condition and the evacuation sites. In addition, users can retain important information in the

"annotation" function for review at any time and can share their positions through live mapping; (3) emergency mode: this can be automatically turned on when large-scale disasters happen, allowing users to report the disaster to the Line official account, which then broadcasts it to other users' timelines.

Other Typical Models: Click, Crowd-funding, Action (Offline Activities)

Click-to-donate originated on The Hunger Site in 1999. Users are encouraged to click the "Click to donate" button free of charge on philanthropy websites, which causes a donation from sponsors on behalf of the user (generally, one click is one JPY) (see Fig. 8.4). In September 2000, Sumabo established the first "click-to-donate" website in Japan, devoted to activities like wiping out world hunger, supporting education and medical care in developing countries, and protecting the environment. With over 8 million users, it has contributed over JPY 450 million in donations (Sumabo, n.d.). Since Japanese users prefer this "click-to-donate" method, there is a growing number of such websites in Japan, most of which are related to international philanthropic organizations, each with their own unique features. For example, Brother Earth focuses on environmental protection; Happyrice concentrates on children's hunger with games and question and answer activities, and JWorld emphasizes sponsorship by Internet enterprises.

With loosened supervision on crowd-funding services by the government, the crowd-funding model has developed fast in Japan. Readyfor, an Internet-based crowd-funding platform for philanthropy, was created in March 2011 by students from Tokyo University. It was established as a company in 2014 and has become Japan's largest crowd-funding

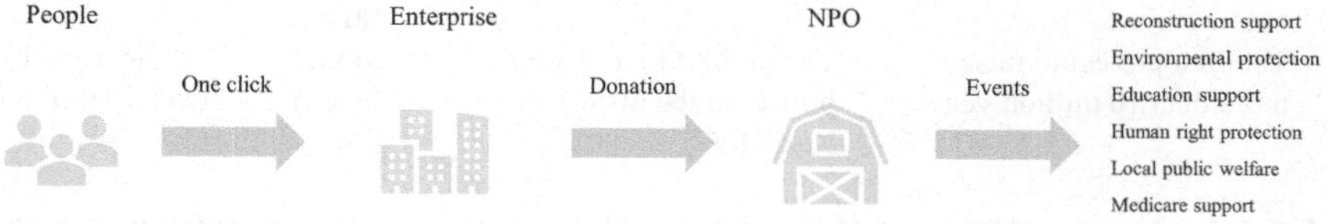

Fig. 8.4 Sumabo's "Click for Donation"

platform. There are two major online projects. One is purchases, in which payers can get back relevant goods or services, similar to commercial crowd-funding. The other is donation, in which the donors only receive symbolic awards like appreciation letters, rather than any physical goods or service. Such platforms fully motivate the new generation of Japanese people to get into the spirit of mutual assistance. As of June 2018, JPY 6.2 billion had been raised through 8300 projects, greatly exceeding many other Internet-based charitable crowd-funding platforms (see Fig. 8.5) (Readyfor, n.d.).

Another characteristic of Japan's philanthropy is bringing donation into everyday scenarios, thus enabling users to donate in their daily lives. The best example here is the catering industry, which is perhaps the heart of the typical Japanese concern with food culture. Take the well-known Table For Two for example. Founded in 2007, Table For Two aimed to

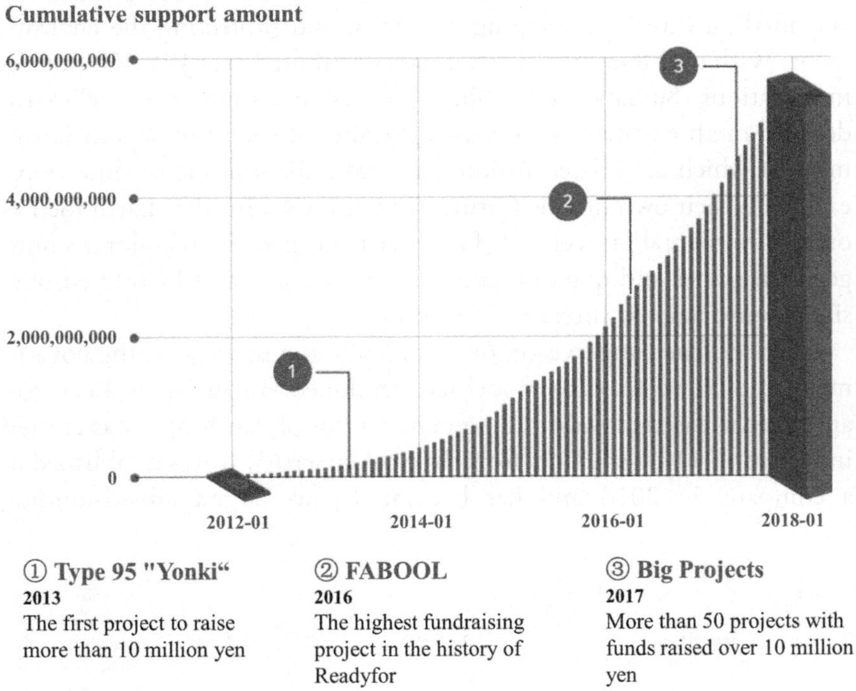

Fig. 8.5 The development of Readyfor and the growth in the total funds raised

resolve the unequal distribution of food between developed and developing countries. This is accomplished as follows: when a donor buys a targeted low-calorie meal or food, JPY 20 from the purchase price is donated through the platform to children in developing countries, providing school meals. In this way, the project creates an opportune combination between healthy diet and charitable donations, which is win-win to both parties and encourages more people to participate. The Internet plays a vital role in making this appetizing combination possible. First, users can conveniently find information about restaurants and food shops that participate in this project through Table For Two, and then make donations during their visit to said restaurants. Second, users can directly donate on the website of Table For Two, or donate while making a purchase from the online store by clicking the links on the website. Third, since Table For Two cooperates with other healthy lifestyle apps like FiNC Walk, users can also make donations by walking or doing other forms of exercise (see Fig. 8.6). Now, Table For Two has gone global. It is in use in many developed countries including the US, and has received worldwide

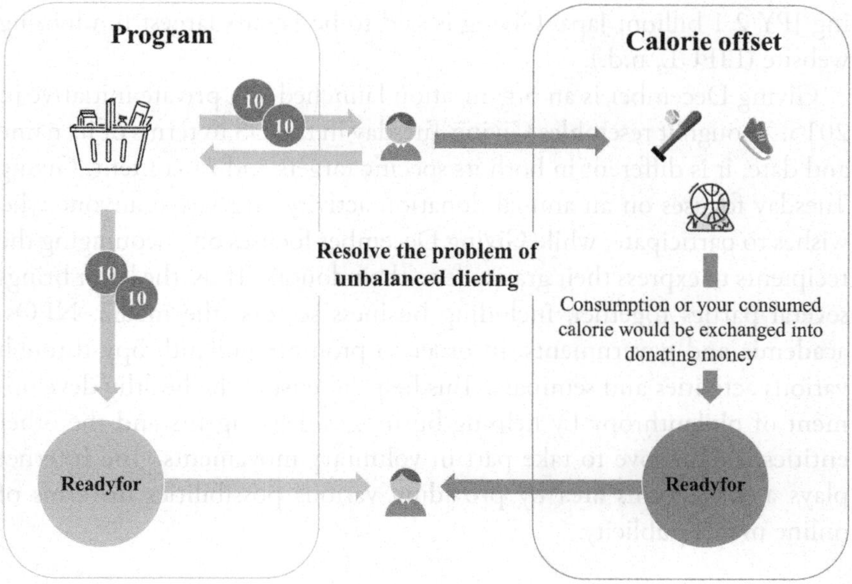

Fig. 8.6 Donation process of Table for Two

recognition. With 641 partner organizations, 7 million people used Table For Two in 2016 (TABLE FOR TWO, n.d.). Table Cross is another similar app focusing on donations made through mobile dieting that is closely integrated with users' mobile Internet activities.

Introduced and Adapted from Overseas: JapanGiving and Giving December

Following the English JustGiving, JustGiving Japan went live in May 2010 and changed its name to JapanGiving in May 2015 after taking on new donors. The name is still in use today.

Following the model of JustGiving, JapanGiving uses its social nature as a platform for promoting philanthropic causes and collecting donations. It is open to all NPOs, which makes it a very helpful way for small and medium-sized agents to reduce their fundraising costs. Meanwhile, users can also receive tax reductions and exemptions from the "hometown taxation" project through this platform, which attracts users just like the Rakuten Global Market does. With 12,000 online projects raising JPY 2.1 billion, JapanGiving is said to be Japan's largest fundraising website (LIFUL, n.d.).

Giving December is an organization launched as a private initiative in 2015. Though it resembles Giving Tuesday in the US in terms of its name and date, it is different in both its specific targets and its content. Giving Tuesday focuses on an annual donation activity targeted at anyone who wishes to participate, while Giving December focuses on encouraging the recipients to express their gratitude to their donors. Thus, the latter brings several parties together, including business sectors, the media, NPOs, academia and governments, in order to promote philanthropy through various activities and seminars. This helps to ensure the healthy development of philanthropy by helping businesses, legal agents and the other entities listed above to take part in voluntary movements. The Internet plays a role in this area by providing various possibilities in terms of online media publicity.

Section 3 Japanese Characteristics and their Effects on Internet Philanthropy

Science and Technology: Internet Philanthropy Is Fairly Widespread But Still Lacks Full Coverage

In terms of coverage, from the perspective of the philanthropic organizations (the "sellers" of philanthropy), as can be seen from the above examples, all kinds of Internet philanthropy exist in Japan. Many philanthropic groups have their own websites, and a growing number of online platforms linking up with philanthropic programs. In this respect, Internet philanthropy in Japan is widespread. Next, from the perspective of the users (the "buyers" of philanthropy), Japan is a world leader in terms of Internet user coverage (92%, the 17th place in the world). In addition, Japan's credit card system like its counterparts in Europe and North America enjoys a high level of development. As a result, many Japanese users have the habit of paying by credit card on philanthropic websites, or making electronic payments (online donation accounted for 25.8% of donations in 2014 (Giving Japan, 2015)). Internet philanthropy has also achieved a degree of pervasiveness on the side of the users (see Fig. 8.7).

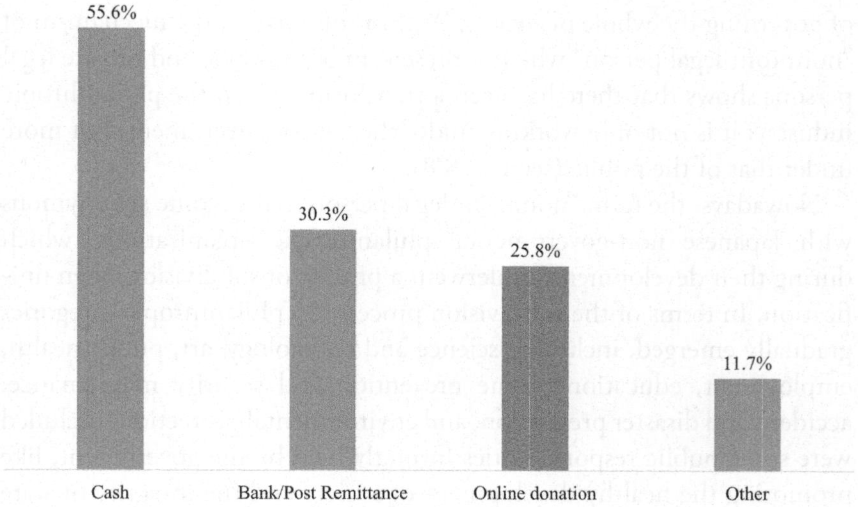

Fig. 8.7 Research on main payment methods for donation

A relatively comprehensive range of Internet philanthropy models exist in Japan. However, the majority of these are desktop-based, with mobile-based applications having yet to enter the mainstream. Even major online donation platforms like Yahoo and Rakuten rely heavily on their desktop websites rather than on their apps. Additionally, as Japan's credit card system matured relatively early on, most online donors choose payment directly by credit card, unlike their Chinese counterparts who rely primarily on third-party payment methods (such as WeChat Payment).

To summarize, since Japan has established multiple convenient payment methods for donations (residents' committee, donation boxes, credit cards, etc.), the Internet has not had a great effect on philanthropy. On the other hand, it plays a greater role in connecting, collecting and optimizing the information in this sector.

Mechanisms: "Joint Governance by the Government and the Public" Provides Space for Free Development

Over the past few decades of development, the Japanese government has formed relatively comprehensive and detailed social management institutions and systems. Japan has adopted the system of legal persons as a way of governing the whole of society. Within this system, the mechanism of "nonprofit legal person" which is present in both public and private legal persons shows that there has been a transformation in the philanthropic industry; it is not only working under the rule of government, but more under that of the public (see Fig. 8.8).

Nowadays, the term "nonprofit legal person" has become synonymous with Japanese non-governmental philanthropic organizations, which during their development, underwent a process of subdivision, then unification. In terms of the subdivision process, 23 philanthropic categories gradually emerged, including science and technology, art, public health, employment, education, crime prevention and security maintenance, accident and disaster prevention, and environmental protection. Included were some public responsibilities formerly held by the government, like promoting the healthy development of society and the integrity of state

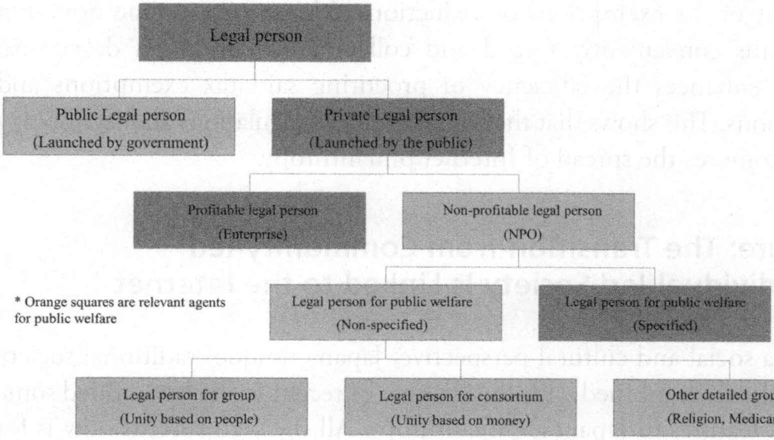

Fig. 8.8 Reference for Japan's system of legal persons and philanthropic organizations

administrations. When under management by different governmental agencies, there was a shift from "governmental management" to "public management". However, due to overly subdivided supervision, the various government departments had different systems and even different legal requirements. Meanwhile, philanthropic organizations were also undergoing intense diversification in their development. Subdivided supervision of philanthropic organizations led to unnecessary conflicts that then affected efficiency. Consequently, the Japanese government has unified supervision of philanthropic organizations under the Cabinet Office, while liberating the NPO registration system. In this way, it has achieved to some degree the goal of streamlining administration and delegating powers to lower-level governments, as well as promoting the development of philanthropic organizations.

However, the Japanese government has not yet established any special legal policies targeted towards Internet philanthropy, which means that as long as people meet the requirements of common laws on philanthropic legal persons, they can conduct online philanthropic activities. This provides Internet philanthropy with ample space for development. Moreover, thanks to the sound development of tax exemption systems for donations, both individual and agency donors are eligible for some amount of tax exemptions or reductions. Meanwhile, online donation platforms conveniently record and collect information on donations, which enhances the efficiency of procuring said tax exemptions and reductions. This shows that the combination of regulations and technology also promotes the spread of Internet philanthropy.

Culture: The Transition from Community-led to Individual-led Society Is Linked to the Internet

From a social and cultural perspective, Japan's unique traditional society and culture, combined with the changes of recent years, have added some special features to Japanese philanthropy. All the sector needs now is for Internet philanthropy to play its role. Due to its geographic location, the prevalence of natural disasters, a relatively monolithic ethnicity composition, the lasting and dominant feudal system, and the influence of Confucianism, Buddhism and Taoism, Japan has developed a unique traditional culture of collectivism. Such uniqueness is manifested in the fact that "smaller communities" have larger influence as opposed to "larger ones". Before the Meiji Reforms, communities in Japan centered on the locality and neighborhood, which nurtured the habit of "mutual assistance among communities". After the Meiji reforms, Japan emerged as a "large community", but time was short before its contemporary influence found itself constrained somewhat following its failure in WWII. As a result, philanthropy has traditionally predominated in the sense of community, for example in the "resident communities". From the "mutual assistance" culture, a traditional Japanese model for charity and philanthropy was born that centred around small communities.

This uniqueness is represented in another way by the lonely "individualism" within Japan's "collectivism," which is commonly known as the country's "Culture of Shame" (Benedict, 2016). The Japanese people care greatly about others' opinions, and their behaviors are ruled and dominated by external social factors. Though this kind of culture also prevails in many other Asian countries like China and South Korea, the culture of "not troubling others" is arguably the most extreme in Japan. For example, a very common phrase in Japanese is "I'm sorry." To some extent, this culture oppresses public activities in Japan, making it difficult for people in need, such as the homeless, and people who are time-busy but money-poor, to actively seek or receive social assistance. Nevertheless, people capable of helping others are refereed as cold if they are afraid of disrespecting those in need. However, alongside the development of mega-cities, the large roaming population is gradually breaking down formerly stable communities. As the young generation care increasingly about their own individual needs, "individualism" in Japan has become ever more apparent. With relationships among neighborhoods, communities and even family members becoming distant, community-dominated philanthropic activity has declined. In 2010, NHK broadcasted a documentary named "*Muen* Society, the Striking Effect of *Muen* Death" (*muen* means "no-relationship"), with an aim to warn people against cutting themselves off from society, their family members, or their hometowns.

This situation highlights the need for Internet philanthropy. First, people in an information society use the Internet, which can easily reunite scattered and highly mobile people. In theory, the Internet society can replace the traditional geographic one. Second, by connecting with the Internet, philanthropy can be combined with the interests of the "online citizens" and extensively arouse goodness in people, who can then spread and implement philanthropy throughout the online environment. Third, thanks to the boundless nature of the Internet, philanthropic activities can play a more prominent role when conducted online. This not only represents the "non-targeted" characteristic of modern philanthropy, but also aptly responds to broader social concerns of the younger Japanese generation. In short, the Internet has the potential to use "philanthropy" to reorganize and bring connection to Japan's quickly deteriorating society.

References

Benedict, R. (2016). *菊与刀* (J. He, Trans.). 浙江文艺出版社. (1946).

Cabinet Office NPO (内阁府 NPO). (n.d.). *特定非営利活動法人の認証·認定数の遷移*. Npo-homepage. Retrieved July 31, 2018, from https://www.npo-homepage.go.jp/about/toukei-info/ninshou-seni

Giving Japan (寄付白書発行研究会), (Eds.). (2015). 寄付白書 2015. 日本ファンドレイジング協会. https://jfra.jp/research

Giving Japan (寄付白書発行研究会), (Eds.). (2017). 寄付白書 2017. 日本ファンドレイジング協会. https://jfra.jp/research

LIFULL. (n.d.). *JapanGiving overview*. Lifull-socialfunding. Retrieved October 15, 2018, from https://lifull-socialfunding.co.jp/

Rakuten. (n.d.). *About Rakuten*. Rakuten. Retrieved October 05, 2018, from https://global.rakuten.com/corp/

Readyfor. (n.d.). *About Readyfor*. Readyfor. Retrieved September 10, 2018, from https://readyfor.jp/proposals/intro

Sumabo. (n.d.). *About Sumabo*. Dff. Retrieved September 10, 2018, from http://www.dff.jp/docs/aboutus

TABLE FOR TWO. (n.d.). *Annual Report 2016*. Tablefor2. Retrieved October 15, 2018, from https://jp.tablefor2.org/files/annualreport/TFT_annual_report_2016.pdf

Yahoo! Japan. (n.d.). *ネット募金結果報告*. Yahoo. Retrieved October 05, 2018, from https://docs-donation.yahoo.co.jp/report/index.html

長坂寿久. (2007). 公共哲学と日本の市民社会 (NPO) セクター--「公・公共・私」三元論と3セクターモデルについて. *国际贸易と投资, 19*(1), 103–138. http://www.iti.or.jp/kikan68/68nagasaka.pdf.

山脇直司. (2004). 公共哲学とは何か. *公共研究, 1*(1), 29–46. https://opac.ll.chiba-u.jp/da/curator/900021003/keynote-yamawakinaoshi.pdf.

Part III

In Retrospection: Internet Philanthropy Reshapes Connections in Atomized Society

When the great way prevails, the world is equally shared by all.
—*The Book of Rites*

The Book of Rites was completed between the pre-Qin Period and the Han Dynasty.

Today, Internet philanthropy is developing rapidly all over the world. From East to West, we have seen the emergence of many innovative models of Internet philanthropy.

At this point, we cannot help but ask: What is internet philanthropy? Why is it so popular around the globe? Was internet philanthropy inevitable or accidental?

To answer these questions, we must explore the basic nature and function of philanthropy.

9

Definition of Philanthropy

What does the word "philanthropy" mean? Under different historic and cultural contexts, we find differing definitions and usages of this term. However, continued improvements have been made to modern philanthropy in the West, which, combined with the trend of globalization, have gradually led to consistency in most countries' understandings and practices of philanthropy. A thorough understanding of the nature and role of philanthropy will help us discern and control the direction of its future development.

Section 1 What Is Philanthropy?

The Chinese word "philanthropy" literally means "public welfare." "Public" designates the recipient of charitable aid as a broad, general population, instead of a particular individual or group. "Welfare" encompasses the provision of the various objective things we need to survive and develop. Together, the phrase "philanthropy" is defined as that which provides the general public with what they need to survive and develop. Put simply, philanthropy can be defined as that which benefits all.

Y. Chen, *Internet Philanthropy in China*,
https://doi.org/10.1007/978-981-16-2566-4_9

To further understand the concept, we can compare two English words that express similar meanings. One is "philanthropy," and the other is "charity." The former derives from the Greek word "philanthrôpía." This word dates back to the Roman Empire during the second century AD, in a description of the super human, written by Greek writer Plutarch. In his description, he used the word "philanthrôpía" to mean "loving that which makes us human." In the seventeenth century, the British philosopher Sir Francis Bacon modernized the term, making it synonymous with "goodness." In the eighteenth century, British writer Samuel Johnson defined "philanthropy" as "love for human beings." This definition is still used today.

The word "charity" comes from the Latin word "caritas," which the Roman Catholic Church used to replace "philanthrôpía" in the Middle Ages (fifth century A.D. to fifteenth century A.D.). Its original meaning, "Christ's love," gave the term a strong religious connotation. In time, the term "charity" gradually evolved to mean "offering support, generosity and dedication to those in need." It is obvious that both mean "love," but the love in "philanthropy" is more extensive and broad than that of "charity."

In the Chinese context, there are also two phrases that correspond to the English terms "philanthropy" and "charity". One is "*gongyi* (公益)," (referred to above) and the other is "*cishan* (慈善)." To be precise, the former means "philanthropy," referring to efforts targeted towards helping society or humanity as a whole, while the latter translates as "charity," or helping those in need. Donating money and supplies to the local inhabitants of a poverty-stricken mountain area falls into the category of charity. However, establishing institutions and initiate poverty relief programs to improve local education, the working environment, and local income; then becomes an act of philanthropy. Charity is like giving a man a fish, and philanthropy is like teaching a man to fish as well as improving the area he is fishing in.

Nowadays, the two concepts are closely related to each other. A charitable event may later become a philanthropic one, or both may be integrated. For example, a fundraising event during a disaster relief campaign is a charitable activity, but the ensuing long-term voluntary teaching programs aimed at post-disaster reconstruction would be more typical of the philanthropic sector. For convenience, we shall consider the two expressions interchangeable (unless otherwise specified) in later discussions.

Section 2 The Development of Modern Philanthropy

Originating in the West, over the past several hundred years modern philanthropy has evolved from its original religious basis, towards a more secular focus. In the religious sense, philanthropy formed a narrow concept of helping the poor and the weak, while the secular idea of philanthropy seeks the broad, structural improvement of society on an institutional level. Western charitable traditions mainly came from teachings in the Christian Bible, meaning that churches were the main organizations to pursue charitable causes in earlier times. Back then, donations were usually sent by donors to churches, which would then distribute the donations to the under-privileged. Consequently, philanthropy at that time was characterized by religious charity, i.e. helping the poor and the weak.

In the sixteenth century, European capitalism started to quickly develop and the emerging bourgeois class promoted religious reform, greatly crippling the resources and power of the Vatican and churches. As charity led by religious institutions could no longer continue, philanthropy started to become more secular and socialized.

There were two typical approaches to secularization. One was "strong government supervision" represented by the British, and the other was the American style of "strong societal volunteering." In the early seventeenth century, the English parliament enacted the *Act for the Relief of the Poor* and the *Statute of Charitable Uses 1601* (often referred as the *Statute of Elizabeth I*) which established the "taxpayer-recipient" system based on mandatory taxation. This system not only showed social awareness, but also demonstrated the important role of supervision and management by the government. Americans brought the ideas and undertakings of British charity to the new world, while also incorporating distinct new elements of their own. Originating from the Puritan belief that "Everyone is equal before God," voluntary assistance among the people was advocated in American society from the very beginning, and positive awareness of public welfare and a sense of responsibility was formed. As a result, various non-governmental charitable organizations have flourished since the 1830s, when the formation of the modern American philanthropic environment began, with a shift from individual to group leadership. Unlike in Britain, there is still no American counterpart to the British charity law at the national level, which reflects the American ideals of regional autonomy and non-governmental self-rule.

Compared with centuries-old modern philanthropy in the West, modern philanthropy in China developed later. Unlike in the western world, religious influence plays little part in the development of modern philanthropy in China, which was more a process of evolution from leadership by government organizations to leadership by civil society organizations. In July, 1981, the China Children and Teenagers' Fund (CCTF) was established. It was China's first modern public fund-raising foundation and charitable organization, which marked the beginning of modern philanthropy in the region (China Children's Fund, n.d.). Since then, a group of foundations have been established. For example, there is the Amity Foundation, the China Women's Development Foundation (CWDF), and the China Youth Development Foundation (CYDF). Thus, charity and philanthropy began to develop quickly in China, further promoting the establishment of various non-governmental charitable organizations and activities. However, the government has played a dominant role in this field for a long time. Established by the central government, foundations are charitable organizations of large scale and influence, and most of them are institutions working under government supervision, leaving little space for the public strength to play a role. It was not until 2004 when the *Regulations on Administration of Foundations* (RAF) were enacted that the Chinese government began to deregulate somewhat and encourage civil powers to take part in philanthropy. Since then, all types of philanthropic organizations have begun to develop rapidly, especially civil society organizations, gradually turning the industry to a non-public sector.

Section 3 Effects of Modern Philanthropy on Society

Today, countries around the world are developing philanthropy to varying degrees. It seems that the more developed a country is, the greater enthusiasm it has towards philanthropy. Why is this? To answer this question, we need to explore the roles of philanthropic civil society organizations in modern society.

We can analyze the roles of civil society organizations from two angles. First, we shall examine whether they aim at pursuing private interest or public benefit. Second, we shall examine whether they seek to achieve such an aim in an enforced or voluntary way. Seeking private interest by enforced means is a feature of the ancient monarchic system; as the old Chinese saying goes, "The rule of the Son of Heaven was over all the land." In this system, the whole country belonged to the emperor, whose interests came first and foremost before that of the nation's. Therefore, there was no real philanthropy at that time. Modern democratic society has broken away from the shackles of monarchism and formed the following three new social structures based on three categories of organization. The first is modern corporate system formed by enterprises that seek private interests on the basis of voluntary choice, or to realize the individual economic rights of citizens by means of free market transactions the second is modern governmental system based on organization seeking public benefit by using enforced measures. In other words, the agents of philanthropy are elected by votes, and are entitled to offer public goods to a statutory extent, thus executing the citizens' political rights. The third is modern third sector system, also known as philanthropy today, which is constituted by organization that seeks public benefit on the basis of voluntary choice, to achieve citizens' individual social rights by directly providing public goods without restrictions (see Fig. 9.1).

If we consider the logic described above, modern civil society organizations are a vital part of contemporary societies. However, what role do they play? There are currently three major definitions of civil society organizations' functions: (i) it "provides public goods," which means

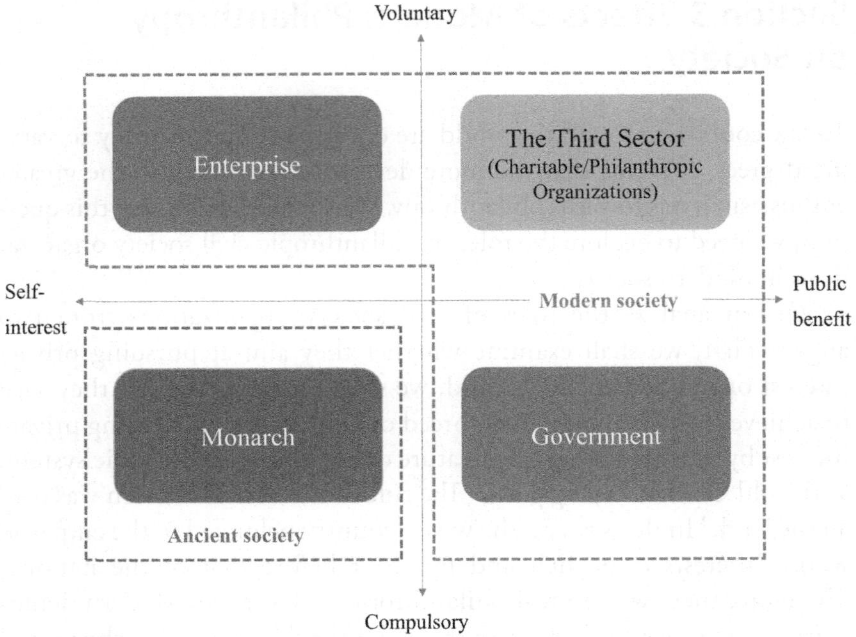

Fig. 9.1 Four basic patterns of organizations

conducting philanthropy in a non-governmental way, i.e. traditional philanthropy among the people; (ii) it "fosters civil society," which constitutes the necessary promotion of social modernization, even civil society itself; and (iii) it "promotes sustainable development," which plays the very modern role of overcoming the dysfunctions of modern governments and markets. In fact, the above three definitions show the interweaving development of civil society organizations. However, present-day organizations can perform several different functions at the same time. We can safely draw the conclusion that philanthropic civil society organizations, as the "third sector" of society, demonstrate a tendency to undertake a diverse range of social functions, thus playing an increasingly necessary role in society's ability to operate successfully.

Reference

China Children's Fund (中国少年儿童基金会). (n.d.). 机构概况. CCTF. Retrieved October 05, 2018, from http://www.cctf.org.cn/about/

10 The Influence of Social Atomization

While modern society has improved the lifestyles of many, there are still flaws to be addressed. Recently, many new social phenomena and problems have emerged on a global scale, among which a trend of "dissociation" can be observed. For example, there is Brexit at the national level, Japan's *Muen Shakai* ("no-relationship" society) at the social level, and China's "empty nest youth" at the community or individual level. This shows that traditional social connections have drifted apart or even been cut off entirely. What is the nature of this trend? What factors have contributed to it? What is its impact on society, specifically with regards to philanthropic programs?

Section 1 Atomized Society

The tendency of social dissociation and disconnection is referred to as "social atomization," a phenomenon which increasingly worries modern sociologists. It suggests a social crisis caused by the disintegration or absence of one's most important mechanism of social connection—the intermediate group. This results in a state of individual loneliness,

Y. Chen, *Internet Philanthropy in China*,
https://doi.org/10.1007/978-981-16-2566-4_10

interpersonal disorganization, moral disintegration, and social alienation, and public isolation (Tian, 2009). The notion is derived from early materialism and was coined by the ancient Greek philosopher Democritus and the Roman philosopher Lucretius, who defined social atomism as "the tendency for society to be made up of a collection of self-interested and largely self-sufficient individuals, operating as separate atoms" (Heywood, 2011). In modern times, research on social atomism has developed further following the industrial revolution and urbanization. The German sociologist Georg Simmel, after observing life in Berlin, proposed in his book *The Metropolis and Mental Life* (1903) that "metropolitan man" is faced with "the swift and uninterrupted change of outer and inner stimuli." As a result, he wrote, "punctuality, culpability, [and] exactness are forced upon life by the complexity and extension of metropolitan existence," and that "one would be completely atomized internally."

The two theories mentioned above actually represent two basic evolutionary paths of social atomization; either resulting from individualism or totalitarianism. In terms of individualism, this kind of atomization arises from the pursuit of individual needs. In extreme cases, overemphasis on equality and freedom of individuals may lead to a focus on concerns about private gains over public benefits. Just as the French political scientist Alexis de Tocqueville described, individualism is "a calm and considered feeling which disposes each citizen to isolate himself from the mass of his fellows and withdraw into the circle of family and friends; with this little society formed to his taste, he gladly leaves the greater society to look after itself," and "individualism at first dries up only the source of public virtue" (Tocqueville, 1989). On the other hand, when social atomization is caused by totalitarianism, it comes from the pursuit of political needs. Overemphasis on a political regime's governance of society, in extreme cases, will force individuals to be completely loyal to the regime and discard all their individual needs, thus becoming an "atom" within the regime. This is explained by the American political theorist Hannah Arendt in her book *The Origins of Totalitarianism* (1951): "Totalitarian movements are mass organizations of atomized, isolated individuals" which "demand for total, unrestricted, unconditional, and unalterable loyalty of the individual member."

Therefore, whether individually or collectively, pursuing the needs of one side while ignoring other will invariably lead to critical levels of social atomization. As a result, neither enterprises, that overly focus on individual needs, nor governments, that start from collective needs, alone can guarantee a sound and stable society in the long term. As a third party, civil society organizations function as a necessary balancing and correcting force. Social atomization happens because of a shortage or weakening of such a force, which can play the role of an intermediary to connect individuals.

Section 2 The Side Effects of Science and Technology

Social atomization results from a variety of factors. Apart from the above-mentioned one-sided risks within modern social systems, the rapid development of modern science and technology also provides tools, creates environments, and even to a certain extent accelerates and amplifies the effects of social atomization.

The history of science and technology is as long as that of human civilization. Since the beginning of the Stone Age when the first tools were crafted, each advance in science and technology has propelled the development of human society. At the same time, science and technology are neutral. For example, the knife can be used as a tool both to cook and to kill. Similarly, science and technology inevitably have certain negative impacts on human society.

For today's society, the information technology revolution is the largest driving factor for progress, yet it has also had an increasingly clear impact on society. The largest difference from technological revolutions of the past lies in its ability to transfer innovation and production from the material world to the digital world. On the one hand, it greatly reduces costs, improves efficiency and enables consumers to get access to informational products rapidly and freely, enriching the market and people's lives. On the other hand, it also transforms traditional social and face-to-face connections into digital, remote interactions separated by screens, thus making direct interpersonal relations more and more fragmented, alienated, or even irrelevant when everything can be done via the internet. People can, for example, watch videos if they are bored, order takeaway when they are hungry, and apply for jobs if they run out of money, but they no longer use physical avenues to accomplish these goals in the real world.

Many things can be achieved easily and independently online, with necessary social activities conducted over virtual platforms. This, coupled with the relatively high costs associated with outdoor society (such as going out, shopping and handling affairs), makes people tend to choose the internet for their own convenience, resulting in individual atomization. From Japan to China, and even in Europe and America, the booming "geek" and "nerd" cultures vividly testifies to such influence and trends. An increasingly greater number of young people have become keen on pursuing private spaces and interests instead of caring about public issues and social responsibilities. The fact that the percentage of youth interested in voting has been declining over the years also reflects this troubling phenomenon.

Section 3 Challenges Facing Traditional Philanthropy

Social atomization exerts a greater impact on charity and philanthropy than on governments and enterprises. Individual income stems from enterprises that pursue private interests, while governments have the legal authority to impose their philanthropic functions upon individuals. Unless completely separated from society, individuals cannot avoid such philanthropy, even in an atomized society. However, atomized individuals can easily avoid third parties that are voluntarily committed to philanthropy. As a result, when social atomization develops, private charity and philanthropy bear the brunt of this social change, leading to the decline of intermediary groups in society and further intensifying social atomization. Without effective intervention, a vicious cycle will emerge and ultimately destroy charity and philanthropy. It is possible that even the stability of modern society as we know it could be irrevocably damaged.

Therefore, while procuring support and collaboration from governments and enterprises, it is of the utmost importunate for civil society organizations to mobilize public and individual voluntary philanthropy as well as to avoid or weaken the force of social atomization. To this end, modern philanthropic organizations should reach out to the public to learn about their concerns, then analyze relevant social groups and environmental factors in order to provide and support plans for improvement. Growing a lasting philanthropic cause from a short-term charitable effort is not an easy task for China's charitable and philanthropic civil society organizations. There are two main reasons why this is so challenging.

First, there are the shortcomings within the charitable and philanthropic sector itself. China's charitable and philanthropic institutions are not as diverse or high in number as they need to be, despite their rapid development. Moreover, given the limited resources and ability of many private groups, a long-term and professional research approach to solving problems in social charity has not yet been fostered. For example, most people chose to work in large enterprises, as opposed to civil society organizations. Since charitable and philanthropic organizations alone cannot solve this problem, support from governments and enterprises is also needed so that human talent and quality resources continue to flow to charity and philanthropy, thus helping it grow.

Second, there is the impact of science and technology. As mentioned above, development in information science and technology has made more and more people connect to each other on the internet, especially among the new generation of young people, which increases the risk of social atomization. Furthermore, traditional philanthropic organizations mainly carry out off-line face-to-face activities, which makes it difficult to reach online users and adapt to their online behavior. As a result, we have been unable to harness the power and influence of the online public to resist the effects of social atomization.

References

Heywood, A. (2011). *Global politics*. Palgrave Macmillan.
Tian, Y. P. (2009). 转型期中国社会原子化动向及其对社会工作的挑战. *社会科学, 2009*(7), 71–75.
Tocqueville, A. D. (1989). *论美国的民主* (G. L. Dong, Trans.). 商务印书馆. (originally published in 1835).

11

Internet Philanthropy Reshapes Social Connections

Given that scientific and technological development has promoted individualism to a certain extent, and that traditional philanthropy is unable to fully play the role of an intermediate group due to limited resources and ability, technology and philanthropy alone cannot effectively solve social atomization. Only by combining the internet and philanthropy can diverse, stable, and lasting connections between intermediate groups be established in a digital society. The purpose of such links is to encourage the public, enterprises, and governments to actively participate in philanthropy and ensure sustainable social development.

Section 1 The Inevitability of Internet Philanthropy

Internet philanthropy is significant and inevitable for both charitable and philanthropic pursuits, as well as for the Internet as an industry.

On the one hand, philanthropy needs the Internet. Of the three bedrock organizations in modern society, private enterprises have taken the lead in embracing the Internet, and have achieved fruitful results in social

Y. Chen, *Internet Philanthropy in China*,
https://doi.org/10.1007/978-981-16-2566-4_11

networking, e-commerce, transport, and countless other fields. Governments are also actively utilizing the Internet to achieve online governance and streamline administrative practices so as to enhance their service to the public. Only by embracing the Internet, integrating with Internet technology, and conducting communications and operations through the Internet can charity and philanthropy attract larger audiences to take part in and support their causes.

On the other hand, the Internet also needs to join hands with philanthropy. As previously mentioned, today's major scientific and innovative technologies such as the Internet are innately neutral. Therefore, while promoting social development, the Internet also brings about both positive and negative side effects. To relieve and offset those side effects, ethics and values need to be fostered with regards to technology and philanthropy, and the Internet is an effective way to do so. Integrating the Internet into charity and philanthropy will create more positive effects for society in a myriad of specific ways.

Section 2 Reshaping Social Connections

The existing risks of atomization in modern society will be amplified via the Internet, which has the power to disassemble many traditional connections in today's digital society. The key avenue of integrating the Internet and philanthropy lies in reshaping social connections. In essence this involves connecting neutral information, introducing positive emotional connections, and fostering stronger social bonds to ensure the healthy development of digital society. There are three main dimensions to the process of reshaping social connections.

First, connecting the public and society. Since modern society is a digital one, more and more public activities are taking place online. Bringing charity and philanthropy online and promoting public philanthropic issues online will be more effective at attracting public attention and involvement. By doing so, more people will be able to connect with one another.

Second, connecting business and philanthropy. Traditional commercial enterprises regard the pursuit of profit as their core aim. As enterprises develop, clashes with social philanthropy are inevitable, on account of issues such as environmental protection. Internet philanthropy creates a more convenient way to connect enterprises with philanthropic causes, and makes it possible for more enterprises to communicate with philanthropic organizations and projects through online platforms and to contribute to philanthropy by launching rapid online donation campaigns.

Third, connecting governments and the public. With the influence of digital society, traditional connections between governments and the public are being weakened. Internet philanthropy can build a bridge between the two. By supporting and participating in philanthropy, governments are able to learn about the public condition in a time-efficient manner. The public can also express problems to governments through Internet philanthropy, thus establishing a new channel for communication and cooperation between both sides.

Section 3 Philanthropy Combined with Technology

Internet technology supports philanthropy by bringing in more scientific and technological foresight. This significantly improves the efficiency, quality, and value of philanthropy the following ways.

Firstly, it improves the efficiency of philanthropy. Traditionally, philanthropic programs are carried out offline through rudimentary digital methods such as television commercials and bank transfers, which are slow in terms of both communication and fundraising. A more efficient method would be a direct link between the philanthropic broadcast and donation, for which the Internet provides an unmatched efficiency of communication. A livestream on a short video platform, or an article on Sina Weibo or a WeChat Subscription Account may go viral within a short period of time. This content is often forwarded to other online platforms, and its influence can be magnified up to hundreds of times over. In addition, online payment tools significantly improve the efficiency of donation, requiring just a few clicks from users' computers or mobile phones. Online philanthropic platforms connect two important functions, communication and fund-raising, and help form a highly efficient closed loop between the philanthropic broadcast and donations.

Secondly, we can improve the quality of philanthropy. The speed at which information spreads online helps philanthropic organizations find a low-cost and highly efficient way to publish information with greater transparency. However, easier ways of publishing information pose the risk of causing an onslaught of public opinion, and therefore it is vital for philanthropic organizations to be prompt and accurate about responding to social concerns on their published information. Currently, social media and other channels are open to public participation and supervision, and upcoming technological advancements such as blockchain will only bring more security and transparency to published information. With the support of these technologies and applications, we can look forward to more carefully supervised and effective philanthropic programs.

Last but not least, we can improve the value of philanthropy. The internet provides a broader platform for philanthropic organizations to carry out their programs more creatively. Creativity plays an important role in philanthropic and charitable activities and helps them better connect with business and social activities such as sports, fashion and cultural performances. Unfortunately, these activities are sometimes expensive and attract less people to take part. However, with internet platforms such as social media apps and websites, creative philanthropic activities can reach hundreds of millions of users in a very short period of time and at a relatively low cost. As a result, these activities will have a broader influence and be able to fully integrate themselves into people's daily lives.

Therefore, the integration between the Internet and philanthropy is the inevitable outcome of social development. Internet philanthropy maximizes the social function of the "third sector" with the use of new technologies, helping society to enjoy sustainable and healthy development under the new technological environment.

Part IV

In the Future: Where Will Internet Philanthropy Lead Us?

~I would address one general admonition to all, that they consider what are the true ends of knowledge…for the benefit and use of life; and that they perfect and govern it in charity.

—Francis Bacon

Preface, *The Great Instauration* (1620)

Since the Wenchuan earthquake in 2008, Internet philanthropy in China has undergone ten years of rapid development with online donations increasing from tens of millions of yuan up to a billion yuan—now becoming a major driver for the advancement of China's philanthropic undertakings.

As we have seen, the country's underdeveloped environment for philanthropy, as well as participants' lack of ability and experience, have stifled the impressive growth of Internet philanthropy. Issues such as misleading information and exaggerated claims, unchecked fundraising and donating, as well as the inefficient implementation and ineffective assessment of philanthropic projects, have had a significant negative impact on the philanthropic sector. Therefore, it is time for the world of Internet philanthropy to reflect on where to go forward in the next decade.

There are three key issues to focus on for the future: the first is technology, which includes the potential which new technologies offer, and how they can be applied in promoting philanthropy; the second is the mechanisms for running charitable activities and how these mechanisms can be achieved online; and the third is culture, philanthropic culture specifically, and how it can be shaped by the Internet.

12

Key Issues and Challenges Facing Philanthropy in China

Section 1 The Application of Science and Technology

Science and technology are major productive forces in society and philanthropy both. It is already clear how the Internet can help charitable undertakings to expand and improve their efficiency. Furthermore, the emergence of new technologies such as big data and blockchain provide yet more opportunities for the future development of philanthropy through technological innovation.

In China's still nascent philanthropic eco-system, a large number civil society organizations, especially smaller and medium-sized ones, face fairly severe "technology gaps" and are struggling somewhat to integrate new technologies into their operations.

The first reason for this is the low penetration rate of digitalization. According to *The Fifth Report* on *Researching Chinese NGOs' Internet Usage and Their Communication Ability* (2016) released by NGO 2.0, even though over 90% of surveyed civil society organizations reported using WeChat and other Internet tools to obtain and promote philanthropy-related information, the digitalization of their internal

Y. Chen, *Internet Philanthropy in China*,
https://doi.org/10.1007/978-981-16-2566-4_12

operations was still relatively low. For example, only about half of organizations surveyed used file-sharing tools such as could storage. Furthermore, less than 40% had ever used any volunteer management tools, and less than 20% had adopted project management and donor management systems. The divergence in digital literacy among organizations will inevitably influence the adoption of emerging technologies.

Second, the lack of technical professionals remains an issue. Like many traditional industries, the philanthropic sector is in need of information and technology professionals. Moreover, the failure to provide financial incentives (e.g., bonuses and stock options, which are more common in the business world) makes it even more difficult to recruit exceptional scientific and technological talent. According to NGO 2.0's report, only a little over 20% of surveyed civil society organizations are staffed with full-time technicians, and nearly 60% use part-time or volunteer technicians, leaving the remaining 20% without any technical support at all. Over three-fifths of those surveyed see the lack of Internet-savvy professionals as a serious obstacle to the expansion of Internet philanthropy.

Therefore, the first challenge for the future development of Internet philanthropy is the shortage of business incentives and technical expertise. New technologies should be integrated into philanthropy in a swift and efficient manner.

Section 2 Building Trust

Loosening restrictions on China's philanthropic sector gave birth to an increasing number of civil society organizations and greatly facilitated their development. The increasing number of people engaged in philanthropy will on one hand diversify China's philanthropic eco-system, while on the other hand, they will also work to complicate said eco-system. To ensure the healthy development of this complicated philanthropic eco-system, it is vital that we establish a rational and efficient mechanism for ensuring mutual trust.

From 2009 to 2018, the number of China's civil society organizations (including social groups, private non-enterprise organizations, and foundations) saw an increase of 225%, from 236,000 to 767,000 (Ministry of Civil Affairs of the People's Republic of China, n.d.). In addition to traditional philanthropic organizations focused on disaster relief, poverty reduction, education, medicine, and environmental protection, a more diverse group of civil society organizations concerned with culture and art, community development, and social innovation were established. An expanded ecology meant a more complex field of interaction.

When philanthropy goes online, the fact that information is easier to access and easier to share means that this complicated eco-system now at risk of any negative information being drastically magnified. For example, the Guo Meimei incident eroded public trust for the RCSC and the Luo Er incident raised questions about the lack of accountability when individuals carry out fundraising on the Internet. These cases show how science and technology may cause damage when used without appropriate regulation.

The second major challenge facing Internet philanthropy is identifying how we can build a mutual trust mechanism in the face of an increasingly complicated industry eco-system, with the added potential risk of negative online reactions. A successful mutual trust mechanism must enable interaction between multiple parties in a way that is sincere, reasonable and accurate. Within this, Internet philanthropy must decipher how to build a system that promotes healthy competition between charitable organizations, so that the philanthropy industry can benefit from active, sustainable development.

Section 3 Cultural Accumulation

Although philanthropy as whole in China had reached new heights since 2008, the success of Internet philanthropy is even more astonishing. However, in terms of per capita statistics, China still lags far behind developed countries in the field of civil philanthropy. In 2016, for example, only 21% of Chinese individuals made donations (China Charity Alliance, 2018), compared to 72% of Americans (Giving USA, 2017).

China's donation average per capita was RMB 97 in 2016,[1] ranking last among the top 10 economies in the world, and that figure was approximately only one-ninetieth of the leading country's total, the United States, which had a per capita donation average 8094 yuan.[2]

These numbers indicate that non-governmental philanthropic activities have yet to flourish in China. One of the root causes is a lack of positive awareness about philanthropy and the habits of participating in charity campaigns. This is due to the absence of a native philanthropic culture within Chinese society. According to the 2017 survey report of the British Charity Aid Foundation (CAF), Chinese citizens' willingness to donate index was a mere 14% in that year, ranking 138 out of 139 major countries in the world. While Western philanthropic culture originated from religion, modern philanthropic activities in China generally do not derive from local religions or beliefs. Moreover, since China's adoption of the modern Western model of philanthropy excluded this religious (Christian) foundation, China's philanthropic culture lacked the foundation of faith. In addition, the Internet boom gave rise to new cultural mindsets. Various developing subcultures are becoming the new trend online, united under the acronym "ACG" (meaning "anime, comics, and games"). These virtual social circles are based on diverse interests, topics, and hobbies, each with their own unique values, communication methods, and beliefs. If traditional sectors, including philanthropy, wish to succeed in the Internet age, they need to adapt and find ways to more effectively interact with these niche groups.

Shaping philanthropic culture is the third challenge for Internet philanthropy in China. Finding its foothold by meeting the cultural demands of the new generation of online users is the most crucial long-term issue that must be addressed for the philanthropic sector to thrive in the future.

[1] Calculation based on the *Annual Report on China's Philanthropy Development 2017* and demographic data from the National Bureau of Statistics of China.

[2] Calculation based on GivingUSA 2017, World Bank's US demographic data, and the Bank of China's data on the China-US exchange rate.

References

China Charity Alliance (中国慈善联合会). (2018). *2017年度中国慈善捐助报告*. Charity alliance. http://www.charityalliance.org.cn/u/cms/www/201809/20232201v09l.pdf

Giving USA. (2017, June 12). *Giving USA 2017*. Givingusa. https://givingusa.org/tag/giving-usa-2017/

Ministry of Civil Affairs of the People's Republic of China (中华人民共和国民政部). (n.d.). 社会服务发展统计公报. MCA. Retrieved October 05, 2018, from http://www.mca.gov.cn/article/sj/

13

Transforming Technological Results into Social Progress

Emerging new technologies are the driving force behind the current progress of human society. In the philanthropic world, embracing technology is necessary to maximize the social and public value of science and reduce the negative impact caused by excessive commercial self-interest. The integration of science and technology with charity and philanthropy is primarily reflected in three areas: efficiency, truthfulness, and transparency.

Section 1 Efficiency

The main role of technological progress is to increase social efficiency. With the trends of continuous networking and the digitization of society, how to further improve operational efficiency through information technology becomes a key issue for the future of the integration of philanthropy and science and technology. From the perspective of economics, we can better understand the trend of efficiency improvement in philanthropy by way of three key factors: the means of production, instrument of production, and producers.

Y. Chen, *Internet Philanthropy in China*,
https://doi.org/10.1007/978-981-16-2566-4_13

Means of Production: Big Data for Philanthropy

Like in other fields, networking and digitization are creating a new type of means of production in philanthropy—big data. In simple terms, big data in philanthropy largely relates to information about communications, donations, and the execution of philanthropic activities. By summarizing and analyzing data, we can gain insight into what is the status quo as well as trends in activities, and then provide suggestions to improve the design, dissemination, and implementation of philanthropic undertakings. In a broader sense, big data in philanthropy also pertains to data associated with participants in philanthropic activities, including the profiles of donors and recipients, operational data of nonprofit organizations, and other useful data in the industry such as information about the environment, education, medical care, and government affairs. The aggregate analysis of this data will provide support for the improvement and optimization of social governance, industry development, institutional operations, and even quality of life for people in society.

Case Study

JustGiving—Personalized Big-Data Fundraising

The rapid development of JustGiving benefited from its integration with social networking sites, its support for mobile donations, its adoption of crowdfunding models, and its experimentation with various creative online systems. JustGiving recognized the significance of the emergence of various philanthropic activities, funding mechanisms, interactive games, and other information that could be tracked to collect data, which helped to further improve the efficiency of crowdfunding through data science. This gave birth to the idea of personalized big-data fundraising. With the help of big-data algorithms, JustGiving implemented optimization in three aspects:

- *Increased the category and number of platform pages.* People's preferences for philanthropic activities have become diversified. For example, not everyone wants to participate in a charity marathon. Some people want to participate on their birthdays by asking their friends to donate money rather than give them gifts. Analysis of big data can provide guidance in the design of new pages.

- *Provided personalized pages and a user guide*. Fundraising is not a daily activity, nor is it easy for most people to do. Many have no idea how to upload pictures, tell a good story, set goals, or contact interested parties. Big data can guide them in terms of what and what not to do, as well as provide support for personalized pages by customizing them for unique purposes.
- *Identified specific reasons that can trigger donors' emotions*. For example, big-data analysis shows that some users continuously reload online fundraising pages to check the progress of an established goal. Only a few want to be the early donors. For these people, as soon as 5% of the goal is achieved, they are less likely to donate. On the other hand, many people won't donate until 95% of the goal is already achieved, so they can be recognized as "donor heroes" by donating the money needed to fully achieve the goal. By identifying donor behavior, it could make for more targeted and effective promotions, which will increase the possibility of achieving the goal.

This case study accurately demonstrates the application of big-data analysis to fundraising in philanthropy. In China, the China Charities Aid Foundation for Children and Ai You Foundation, which are active on Internet philanthropic platforms, are trying to gather data and effectively use it. For example, the Ai You Foundation established its own data center and set up an institute for data application technology. It is important to note that data safety and privacy protection should be carefully considered when conducting philanthropic big-data innovation activities. Ensuring the appropriate degree of data privacy and the proper application of data privacy regulations is necessary for the healthy development of big data in the philanthropic sector.

In the long term, aside from raising the operational efficiency of philanthropic projects, the value of big data in philanthropy can be best realized by using information to increase the efficiency of solving major social issues, including the prevention and treatment of diseases, the development of more sustainable urban planning, and the improvement of environmental governance. These are key areas where big data analysis can make major progresses—enabling change for a better future.

Instrument of Production: AI's Application in Philanthropy

To process massive amounts of data, high-quality algorithms are necessary, and this is true for the philanthropy like other industries. A new generation of AI technology represented by machine learning is now in its mature stage, making it possible to process philanthropy-related data to create innovations. As an instrument of production in the digital world, AI can use its full powers of efficiency and innovation that can be applied to every aspect of charity and philanthropy. In a narrow sense, when speaking of AI's application in philanthropy, most would usually think of its application to the operations of philanthropic organizations and projects. AI, such as intelligent algorithms, can help improve efficiency in operations, for instance, when it comes to automatic analysis and the processing of philanthropic activities' operational data. In a broad sense, AI itself is a global political and social issue that is discussed beyond the scope of its application in the business world. More broadly, the integration of AI and philanthropy serves as an endeavor to explore approaches to technology that can develop positive social values. Solving key social public problems with the help of AI is becoming an important measure that is spurring new developments in science and technology.

Case Study

Microsoft—AI to Solve Social Problems

Microsoft believes that a positive collaboration of AI with society can leave a lasting, positive impact on the world. Teaming up with organizations in the areas of accessibility, healthcare, education, and environmental protection, the world of philanthropy can create an inclusive solution with ultimate goal using AI for positive social values.

- *AI for accessibility*. Based on technologies such as speech recognition and image recognition and following a barrier-free design concept, Microsoft developed applications to assist the disabled in communication and with daily activities. For example, Microsoft partnered with Equadex to develop Helpicto, a pictogram application for children with language disorders like autism to help them communicate using AI by converting speech or text to images. For instance, when using Helpicto to communicate with a child with autism, you can send a speech command like "Do you want to eat an apple?" The application will then generate three images: the child himself, the action of eating, and a picture of an apple, thus helping the child understand the language and give a response.
- *AI in healthcare*. Microsoft uses machine learning to help healthcare providers solve the most challenging medical problems today. For example, Microsoft's Project InnerEye uses machine learning to build innovative tools for automated, quantitative analysis of three-dimensional radiographic images. It does this by carrying out automatic delineation and rapid diagnosis of tumors, thus supporting treatment planning and facilitating precise surgery preparation and navigation.
- *AI in education*. Microsoft uses AI to help students and educational staff address the challenges they face when accessing information and carrying out educational projects. For example, in India, Microsoft is working with local governments, using machine learning to analyze the status of students and identify students with a high potential for dropping out, so as to help schools reduce dropout rates. In the UK, Microsoft launched the Torino Project to help visually impaired children learn physical programming language to provide the opportunity to expand their career possibilities.
- *AI for environmental protection*. Microsoft uses the cloud and AI to help organizations promote sustainable development. It supports ecological protection by creating high resolution and dynamic land cover maps; supports sustainable development of agriculture based on land

environmental monitoring and analysis; and monitors biodiversity by continuously automating the collection of biological data.

Civil society organizations and AI-related technological businesses in China are working together to explore the applications of AI in philanthropy, especially in healthcare and education. For example, Tencent Miying, an AI-driven medical solution developed by Tencent, was integrated into the Lung Love Project to provide identification services and guidance in the early stage of lung cancer diagnosis and treatment.

In the future, the collaboration of AI with philanthropy will continue to develop for a wide range of social issues as AI matures and more applications are found. However, AI is still far from full maturity and its negative impacts are still difficult to mitigate, so it is more reasonable to find ways to use the new technology to promote positive societal values by exploring its application in philanthropy rather than through direct commercialization.

Producers: Professionals Skilled in Information Technology and Philanthropy

For the philanthropic sector, recruiting and developing first-rate professionals is key to keeping up with an increasingly innovative society led by technological development. Similar to most traditional sectors, philanthropy not only needs experienced talent, but it also needs those people who are knowledgeable about new technologies. Only this kind of talent will promote the sector's development. However, compared to for-profit commercial organizations, philanthropic organizations cannot offer the same high salaries to their employees, given their non-profit nature. To some extent, this limits the appeal to top talent, especially those with skills in new technologies. The key to the sustainable and healthy development of philanthropic organizations is attracting and nurturing a stable and professional team.

Case Study

RNIB—Building a Transformative Digital Team

RNIB, an English charity organization with a long history, offers support of all kinds for the blind. The growth of the Internet in recent years facilitated digital transformation in various sectors, particularly for RNIB.

To promote efficient transformation, RNIB built its own digital team. Initially, RNIB used a dozen of part-time "Internet officers." The group gradually evolved into a professional team consisting of full-time experts in digital content and marketing. During the process of development, these experts' knowledge in digitalization was shared with the whole organization through lunch sessions, staff newsletters and intranet articles, speeches and meetings, with positive results.

By encouraging digital literacy, staff members from all departments gradually mastered digital tools (for example, producing their own digital content). Transforming into developers of digital operation standards, the digital team helps the organization and its various departments create guidelines and monitoring methods in order to thoroughly implement digital operations for the whole organization.

Chinese philanthropic organizations have also attached greater importance to attracting tech talent and building a specialized team. For example, the China Foundation for Poverty Alleviation (CFPA) established a department that specialized in the mobile Internet in 2015 to provide full support to the development of online philanthropy projects. Newly established departments like these consist of professionals from both the tech and philanthropic sector. Engaging in hands-on work together has allowed both sectors to be widely integrated.

Of course, when building a tech team, it is necessary to attract professionals. Given the low salaries in the philanthropic sector, "soft skills," including the cultivation of digital awareness among management, cultural inclusiveness and sustained support for talent development in philanthropic organizations, have become key components in recruiting. Sustainable development will only be possible for those organizations that align their values with young people's pursuit of personal fulfillment.

Section 2 Reality

Although IT and digital applications in philanthropy help to improve the efficiency of transmitting information, much of that information is actually lost during the process of digitization. Traditional print media primarily uses text and pictures to communicate with its audience and, hence, can get a charity campaign's message across quickly with effective copywriting and communication. However, it is difficult for a reader to obtain first-hand and more detailed knowledge about specific philanthropic programs through this medium.

Digital-reality technologies (including virtual reality or VR and augmented reality or AR) have helped to solve this problem. By simulating a three-dimensional space in a two-dimensional plane and providing multiple forms of sensory input, digital reality technologies can give users an "immersive" or even "surreal" experience, thus expanding the boundaries of the digital world. This allows audiences to gain an in-depth understanding of a specific philanthropic activity without spending money by going through a website. The significance of this development has led many philanthropic organizations to experiment with these technologies, with encouraging results.

Case Study

Virtual Reality (VR) and Immersive Images Provide a New Form of Storytelling for Philanthropic Organizations

With the development of VR technology, immersive storytelling methods such as 360-degree movies have been quickly adopted. In recent years, many participants in the philanthropic community, including organizations such as the United Nations and philanthropists such as Bill Gates, have offered immersive images and videos based on VR technology, aiming to better promote philanthropic activities. Currently, VR technology is widely applied in philanthropy for 5 major reasons.

- First, to inspire empathy. VR images give audiences a detailed and personal understanding of philanthropic campaigns, and in this way, evoke people's empathy toward those in need. For example, Alzheimer's Research UK designed a VR application called "A Walk Through Dementia" to help people understand the complexity of the disease and experience the challenges in everyday life from the perspective of patients. The National Autistic Society in the United Kingdom launched a similar VR application called "Too Much Information," which gives customers in shopping malls a sense of the feelings of anxiety and sensory overload that autistic children experience when they are in a public space, so that people can better understand what it feels like to have autism.
- Second, to motivate people to make donations. VR's immersive storytelling helps to block out the outside world and forces audience to focus, which is conducive to increasing people's willingness to donation. For example, Amnesty International equipped their staff with VR devices, each worth less than 15 GBP. During fundraising activities, staff members use the device to show people images from Syria, and achieved a 16% increase in regular donations. Another example comes from Charity: Water, an American philanthropic organization, which produced a short VR video called "The Source," which depicted the extent of water pollution in Ethiopia and was screened at a charity dinner at the Metropolitan Museum of Art in New York. The film tells the story of a 13-year-old Ethiopian girl and her family having access to clean water for the first time in their lives. It deeply moved audiences that evening, and they secured commitments from donors that raised more than 2.4 million USD for their initiative.
- Third, to better address recipients' concerns. VR technology provides recipients with diverse experiences, including showing them the services they are going to receive. For example, being sent to a hospice can be a disturbing experience, and that is what Royal Trinity Hospice, the oldest hospice in the UK hoped to tackle this issue with VR technology. It offered patients and their families a virtual hospice care

experience to familiarize them with its facilities, staff and services, so that they could feel reassured.
- Fourth, to help people learn. Like many new IT technologies, VR is becoming an effective teaching tool and has already been adopted by many schools and medical laboratories. Now, it is expanding this educational value to philanthropic organizations that provide information and consulting services. For example, Resuscitation Council (UK) designed an interactive VR application called "Lifesaving VR" to guide rescuers through the steps someone needs to take when someone's heart stops beating to potentially save that person's life.
- Fifth, to express gratitude to supporters. Philanthropic organizations also use VR technology to thank their valuable supporters and encourage legacy gifts. For example, Cancer Research UK built a unique VR garden called "The Life Garden" at the RHS Hampton Court Palace Flower Show to pay tribute to its supporters and celebrate the progress that they made as a result of the funds they received. The garden showcased over 100,000 flowers, one for each person who left a gift in their will to Cancer Research UK.

In China, VR technology has been applied in various philanthropic areas. One example is the Chengdu Research Base of Giant Panda Breeding, which uses VR videos to raise awareness about protecting giant pandas. Similarly, the Xin Kang Le Center for Autistic Children in Shenzhen provides VR social training courses for youth with autism. But VR application in Chinese philanthropy remains small in scale compared to other countries, and its future development still needs further exploration.

Section 3 Trust

As a distributed database technology, blockchain technology offers three principal features. The first is decentralization. Once a transaction is made in the blockchain system, it is immediately transmitted to the entire network, and each node simultaneously records the transaction information received on a ledger. Therefore, the data is open, traceable and tamper-proof for all the nodes in the blockchain. Second, it is anonymous. Since the exchanges between nodes follow a specific algorithm, inter-node communication does not need to be validated (the programming rules of the blockchain will judge whether the activity is valid or not). This means that the parties involved in the transaction do not need to disclose their identity. This helps protect people's privacy and increases the efficiency of transactions. Lastly, it is encrypted. Blockchain technology generally uses asymmetric encryption algorithms, which encrypt a user's identity using a public key and private key. This helps both parties ensure the security of the information and at the same time verify a user's identity.

These features make blockchain ideal for addressing some of the core concerns surrounding philanthropy and financial trustworthiness. Decentralization encourages both the transparency and accessibility of philanthropic information, thus guaranteeing the credibility of philanthropic activities. Anonymity effectively protects the privacy of participants, especially of donors who do not want their names disclosed to the public. Encryption ensures the security of the information, while helping to verify the identity of each participant. The effective solution of these issues is of great significance to philanthropic organizations since these are based on issues of "trust." Therefore, from the day blockchain was born, the philanthropic world was one of the first sectors where it was adopted.

Case Study

Blockchain Enables Transparent and Credible Circulation of Philanthropic Information

Blockchain technology is important for philanthropy primarily because its credit mechanism does not depend on a specific centralized organization, but instead comes from the consensus of all nodes in a network. This ensures the transparency and credibility of information circulated in the network. It is mainly applied to the supervision of three kinds of flows: capital, logistics and human capital.

- Flow of Capital—Real-time supervision of the used funds: Giveth, a donation platform based on Ethereum, has received extensive attention from overseas philanthropic communities. The platform is entirely built on Ethereum's smart contract system, which allows real-time monitoring of how donated money and goods are used and has dramatically changed the way philanthropic information is disclosed. With Ethereum's blockchain technology, donors can keep property rights over their donations after they make a donation and before the money is actually distributed. They can cancel the distribution plan or even withdraw the donated money if they are unsatisfied with how their funds are used. Such a mechanism ensures that donors are updated with the real-time information about money distribution, and they can refuse to authorize the philanthropic organization's use of their money. As a result, organizations are compelled to disclose information to donors in a timely manner. At the same time, blockchain technology gives donors confidence that their information will not be tampered or lost and that they can trust the distribution of donated money.
- Flow of Logistics—Tracking the whole distribution process of donated goods: According to an estimate by Economic Research Service of the U.S. Department of Agriculture, American consumers waste about 60 million tons of food each year. To address this issue, a company called Goodr decided to use blockchain technology to quickly deliver leftover food from companies and restaurants to local charities. When companies and restaurants have leftover food, they can send a message on a blockchain app provided by Goodr, so that the food can be packaged, sent to charities, and then track the shipment. They also receive tips on how to reduce waste from Goodr. On their end, charities can check information about the source of the free food received and its shelf life, so that they can have a better understanding of the donor and the resources that were given.
- Flow of Human Capital—Accurate identification of recipients: Human trafficking, especially child trafficking, is a global issue. To find a solution, the United Nations launched a pilot project, The World Identity Network, which uses blockchain technology to combat child trafficking in Moldova. The first step is creating a digital

profile for the child and linking his/her identity to other family members. Traffickers often fabricate fake IDs, making it difficult to find out the real identity of trafficked children. But blockchain is tamper-proof and traceable, which helps to identify these children more effectively. The second step is establishing a blockchain platform for the integrated identity system to protect the data on blockchain. When a minor wants to go abroad without their parents' permission, the system automatically generates an unalterable record to help spot potential traffickers. Last but not least, blockchain offers automatic communication. Potential or actual victims of trafficking often live in isolation with little support or help. If AI can be used to detect, identify and analyze these behaviors and initiate a communication session with the individual at risk automatically, it may be easier to find traffickers and intervene or even stop them.

Blockchain technology has attracted significant attention from Chinese companies, which focus on the transparent exchange of philanthropic information, much like their foreign counterparts. For example, the Ai You Foundation, the first private foundation registered in China, used it to track capital flow when it launched a public platform for aid and relief in August 2018. It used blockchain to release real-time data on the amount of money donated and how it was allocated. Blockchain has also been used in logistics. When JD Charity worked with the Teach for China program in September 2017, it used blockchain technology to trace the route of donated goods. In addition, the technology has been used to track people. For example, Tencent TrustSQL launched a platform called "Philanthropic Blockchain for Tracing Missing Persons" in October 2017, which connected multiple philanthropic institutions and websites specialized in missing persons to help them share their data and improve the effectiveness of searches.

Since blockchain greatly improves information transparency, it is particularly relevant to philanthropy. As a public industry by nature, philanthropy needs to be under public supervision. In the future, blockchain will continue to exert a profound influence on the way information flows in the entire industry and facilitate the establishment and improvement of a "network of trust."

Section 4 For Social Good

Technology, by its nature, is neutral for human beings. Technological developments may benefit us, but they can also cause harm. From agriculture to industry to information industry, the great leaps in technology have indeed promoted the prosperity of human civilization, yet also brought about new diseases, social contradictions, environmental degradation and other issues. Information technology as represented by the Internet is no exception. Although it greatly enriches and facilitates our lives in several ways, it has also led to new and wide-spread social issues like information overload. As modern technology becomes even more integrated into society, how to make the best use of technology will become an issue that everyone in the society is forced to think about.

Case Study

Tencent—Tech for Social Good

Tencent, a representative of China's Internet enterprise, has long recognized the need to apply technology for the benefit of public welfare. Long before the establishment of Tencent Charity in 2007, Tencent used QQ to disseminate charity information and carry out fundraising activities. After the establishment of Tencent Charity, it actively promoted philanthropy on its main business platforms such as WeChat and WeChat Pay, and took the lead in carrying out innovations in applying new technologies such as artificial intelligence and blockchain to look for missing persons and fund raise.

In January 2018, Tencent launched the Tech for Social Good project to further systematically explore beneficial applications of technology in society. Focusing on the acute and urgent social problems brought about by new technologies, the project aims to build a multi-party platform for dialogue, research and action that involves domestic and international philanthropic communities to seek social consensus, constructive opinions and solutions. The project consists of three core parts: (i) T-Survey, an annual survey of public perceptions of new technologies and Internet product services; (ii) T-Meet, a regular forum for in-depth discussions of social issues brought about by Internet technology and products; and (iii) T-Foundation, which will launch a series of academic and creative support programs.

At the first T-Meet conference, Tony Zhang Zhidong, core founder and former CTO of Tencent gave a keynote speech. From the perspective of a senior IT leader, he elaborated on the "information overload" problem in today's digital world. He believes that technology has greatly empowered people, but also amplified the weaknesses of human nature. What technology and products should do is to take these social issues seriously and attempt to solve them through collaborations with experts from related fields. For example, Tencent developed a growth guard platform for mobile games to prevent teenagers from being addicted to video games. Zhang Zhidong said he hopes that through the experimental Tech for Social Good project, more people in the future will be motivated to participate in the cause of using technologies to solve the problems in digital society.

With technology developing at an increasingly faster pace, its misuse may bring even greater risks. There will likely be serious negatives consequences that result from new technologies, such as artificial intelligence, biotechnology, and genetic engineering, not being effectively regulated. It is for that reason that countries around the world have recently put more effort into encouraging people in society to use technology for good and rolled out initiatives such as Tech for Good and AI for Good. Tech for Good is a cause that focuses on the wellbeing of mankind and can be seen as a standard for other projects to follow in the course of future technological development.

14

Towards More Diversified and Comprehensive Governance Over Philanthropy

Section 1 Mechanisms for Public Participation

As Internet philanthropy took off, the mechanisms for public engagement in philanthropy became more diversified and personalized. In light of this mechanisms for individual participation have experienced a new tendency toward development.

Public participation in Internet philanthropy will create closer connections to online products and services. This will facilitate the establishment of a more sophisticated and comprehensive donation incentive system.

In recent years, many Internet companies created philanthropy-focused accounts online, which recorded users activity and connected them with other services provided by the company. The most popular examples are the Ant Forest and Ant Farm projects, launched by Ant Financial, through which users played games that contributed to philanthropic efforts that benefited society. Through this mechanism, organizations and individuals can establish a positive feedback loop that promotes mutual growth.

Y. Chen, *Internet Philanthropy in China*,
https://doi.org/10.1007/978-981-16-2566-4_14

In addition to Ant Financial, other Internet companies such as Tencent, DiDi, Meituan and Kuaishou are developing similar philanthropy-focused accounts online. These accounts allow companies to connect with users who already use their Internet products and services to promote philanthropic activities, establishing more sustainable and extensive incentive mechanisms. In the future, we may even see an online philanthropy account system working between different companies and products to provide more incentives to users. This system could only exist under the premise that users will be guaranteed full knowledge of their rights and can trust that their private information will be safe. In such a system, philanthropy would be integrated into every aspect of users' online lives, even those who are not always looking to participate in charity events. Looking even further ahead, this system could be integrated with the national credit and reward systems to create a more all-encompassing incentive mechanism for engaging the public. The next stage of development for Internet philanthropy will usher in an improved and advanced donor incentive process.

On the other hand, philanthropic organizations could create a more comprehensive donor service system by simply using emerging digital technologies. In the traditional model of philanthropy, in addition to regular feedback provided by social organizations and project managers, most organizations struggle to provide effective follow-up services for donors. This is due to the lack of any strong connection between donors and organizations, as well as the high costs of transmitting information.

In the era of mobile Internet, philanthropic organizations can use digital technology to provide donors with a series of new services that boost their sense of participation and reward. For example, philanthropic organizations can use smart contracts and other new digital technologies to give donors greater control over how to use their donated funds. In this way, donors can play a more direct role in the distribution and use of the funds, helping donors feel that they are still participating even after they have made their contributions. Likewise, philanthropic organizations can use the Internet to establish closer connections with donors to better understand their real needs, and use digital technologies to provide personalized and customized donor services according to these needs, effectively improving their sense of fulfillment. With the support of digital technologies and tools, we can expect the donor service systems used by organizations to become more diversified and comprehensive.

Section 2 Mechanisms for Information Transparency

Information transparency is undoubtedly of crucial importance to philanthropic organizations. Transparent information in philanthropy helps enhance donors' sense of fulfillment, encourages deeper and more long-term participation in charitable activities, and allows the public to oversee philanthropic organizations and their projects. This kind of public supervision puts checks on the power of those executing the projects, reducing the risk of wasted funds and fabricated reports. Ultimately, it improves the efficiency of implementing philanthropic projects.

The lack of transparency in philanthropic organizations and programs has long been an issue in the sector. Traditionally, philanthropic organizations only disclosed information through financial and executive reports. Many of these reports offered only brief overviews and summaries of projects and paid little attention to specifics or provided limited details about the actual programs being implemented. Essentially, they provided insufficient information, leaving the public in the dark about how these organizations and programs actually operated. Additionally, most people have no access to the complete report, bar a limited few. Therefore, the disclosure of information through traditional means often fails to achieve the desired results.

In the era of Internet philanthropy, mechanisms for information transparency have greatly evolved, contributing to a significant improvement in the overall transparency of philanthropic organizations. Compared to traditional methods, the Internet has a wider audience and information can be shared more efficiently. By disclosing information online, organizations can target more users and exert a greater influence. In recent years, online information disclosure has become a common practice within the philanthropic sector.

Philanthropic organizations capable of creating official websites have published annual reports and audited information regularly for the public to review. New and ever more sophisticated media operations like Sina Weibo and WeChat, along with small and medium-sized civil society organizations, are now able to disclose financial and operational information through third-party platforms, thus achieving information transparency. Internet platforms like Tencent Charity even provide additional tools to help these organizations disclose relevant information about their campaigns to the public, replacing the traditional organization-centered information disclosure model.

Now that the industry has acknowledged the significance of online philanthropy, the philanthropic sector has reached a consensus on improving information transparency by utilizing the Internet. Foundations, civil society organizations, and private non-enterprise entities are all embracing the Internet and actively working on effective means of disclosing information. With the introduction of the *Charity Law*, China's national policy and legislation will no doubt also improve mechanisms for information transparency. With joint efforts from the government and collective public involvement in philanthropy, organizational processes can start to incorporate the relevant provisions of the *Charity Law*, hopefully creating fairer platform regulations and industry standards.

Even though these mechanisms started later in China's philanthropic development, China's is a rapidly evolving system. Influenced by industrial development, technological advancement, the recent development of a philanthropic culture, and innovations in the concept of charity, these information transparency mechanisms are undergoing constant and dynamic refinement. These efforts might even set new standards for the future.

First, private charities must play a crucial part in the exploration of these mechanisms within the philanthropic sector.

Before official rules and regulations were formulated, the philanthropy sector in China did not pay much attention to information transparency. Civil society organizations disclosed information on their own terms, especially since there were no universally accepted mechanisms for publicly declaring such information. As the industry developed, the demand for regulations over the disclosure of information grew. In response, the Chinese government enacted a series of laws and regulations, including the *Regulations on Administration of Foundations* (RAF) and the *Charity Law*, which addressed the demand for proper charitable information disclosure. These laws and regulations became the starting point and basis for the creation of information transparency mechanisms.

However, in practice, the stipulations regarding information transparency in both the RAF and *Charity Law* are broad guidelines. The provisions are neither detailed nor easy to implement. Moreover, they do not differentiate between the different kinds of organizations that exist. The authorities also have not issued corresponding enforcement measures. This leaves significant room for improvement with regards to specifying the standards for disclosing information and modifying the mechanisms for transparency.

This is precisely why private philanthropic entities, on top of their own meaningful work, have also shouldered the responsibility of creating a system for disclosing charitable information. In the past few years, given the increased public attention on information transparency in the philanthropy industry, there has been an increasing demand for the establishment of a widely accepted information disclosure mechanism. Many organizations, most notably the China Foundation Center and Tencent Charity, looked deeply into the matter and made attempts to provide a solution. Many Internet platforms and large-scale philanthropic organizations became essential driving forces for greater transparency within the industry. Because the institutions overseeing this industry rarely take part in building such mechanisms, private charitable entities will continue to play an important role.

Second, the focus of future information transparency should expand to include transparency of the processes as well as the results.

In fact, being transparent about the operations supporting philanthropic activities is a vital part of the industry. It can serve to enhance the authenticity and efficiency of information disclosure efforts, as information on a project's results alone cannot completely eliminate fraud and embezzlement.

With this new wave of Internet philanthropy, some philanthropic organizations have successfully achieved transparency around project results, but the majority of entities have yet to disclose information regarding institutional management and project execution except for a few specialized information-focused institutions. The main reason is that philanthropic organizations are not focused enough on operational transparency. Another factor is that recording or monitoring the implementation of their projects is not easy. For some small and medium-sized organizations, even if they are willing to disclose operational information, the practical difficulties involved with recording their processes makes it hard to achieve operational transparency.

The development of online technology provided the favorable conditions for operational transparency in the philanthropic sector. The first reason for this was because the Internet lowered the cost of disclosing information, allowing more organizations to disclose information on the implementation of their projects. Second, digital tools made it easier for philanthropic organizations to effectively record each step in their process, which paved the way for complete operational transparency. The development of digital technology will also encourage more organizations to better understand the purpose and feasibility of transparency, thereby leading to a consensus throughout the industry on promoting the development of mechanisms for transparency.

Due to the significance of disclosing operational information and the technological development of the Internet, operational transparency will play a more critical role in the next stage of information transparency.

Third, in the future, equal importance should be placed on the transparency of finances and results.

The existing mechanisms for information transparency primarily highlight the overall financial picture of institutions, while failing to disclose the resultant finances of specific projects. In fact, numerous philanthropic organizations are now able to release annual reports just like commercial establishments, which is an effort toward information transparency. Such reports reveal information about the operations of an organization and the implementation of its projects in a more structured manner. Certain organizations even employ third-party audit firms and publish the audit reports both online and offline. Major breakthroughs have been made to improve the financial and managerial transparency of philanthropic organizations. In the near future, as the industry evolves and gains leverage, the financial transparency of organizations will also continue to improve.

However, the progress towards operational transparency remains slow as result of several factors. Traditional methods of information disclosure, such as annual reports and audit reports, focus primarily on organizations' management and finance, while information regarding project results can often be left out. An important factor to consider is that evaluating the wide variety of projects is costly and time-consuming, especially programs relating to issues like childhood education, people with special needs, and ecological conservation. In the pre-Internet era, organizations did not exert much effort evaluating the results of these projects because feedback on their project results was rarely timely or accurate.

Future philanthropic information transparency mechanisms should be able to strengthen operational transparency, lending equal attention to the transparency of both project finances and results.

The digital tools and methods provided by the Internet helped break ground for results transparency. One reason for this is that disclosing information online is more cost effective and efficient overall. Secondly, because most methods are facilitated by massive data sources on the Internet, this will improve the quality of project assessment and reduce the cost of evaluating results. Third, because online technology allows donors to easily follow up on long-term projects, it fosters a deeper understanding of project performance at different stages.

The development of Internet philanthropy reminds organizations of the importance of results transparency. Given the continued development of charitable culture, more donors are now willing to fund the evaluation of project results. Aided by the Internet, there has been an improvement to the different subjective and objective requirements for results transparency. In the future, based on financial transparency, mechanisms for information transparency will give more weight to the transparency of results, encouraging more institutions to publish their evaluations online and in turn make project executions more efficient and transparent.

Last but not least, future transparency mechanisms for philanthropy will make better use of information on the level of transparency achieved by philanthropic organizations and projects. This will consist of providing valuable information for donors' to make informed decisions about donating.

With the development of Internet philanthropy and the specialization of philanthropic organizations, the overall information transparency of the philanthropic sector has significantly increased. In one respect, this is due to the fact that the *Charity Law* clearly defines information disclosure for philanthropic organizations. This can also be attributed to Internet philanthropy platforms such as Tencent Charity actively exploring the best practices in the industry for information disclosure, effectively making the entire Internet philanthropy sector more transparent.

However, the transparency of the information offered by philanthropic organizations seems to have a limited impact on donors. The information disclosed by some organizations only meets the minimum threshold for the industry and may not be directly related to other philanthropic activities. Donors, especially public donors, often do not refer to the detailed information disclosed by organizations when they make donations. This is because they participate in philanthropic activities primarily out of empathy. As a result, some organizations do not attach much importance to information disclosure. They only disclose related information as required by law or the policies set by Internet platforms, unaware of the importance of these practices. Some organizations also think is simply another additional cost, and only take part out of obligation.

In the future, new transparency mechanisms will make more frequent and efficient use of the information disclosed by philanthropic organizations. The mechanisms will also display different transparency levels into each part of public engagement with philanthropic activities. This will give users more accurate and complete information to use as reference. An organization's level of information disclosure may be linked to its rights and interests; that is, organizations performing well in transparency will receive more resources, while those that are underperforming will be penalized. This mechanism for reward and punishment will then give greater impetus to the push for greater transparency.

In fact, the philanthropy industry has already been exploring the connection between organizations' transparency and philanthropic activities. One of the most successful efforts was undertaken two years ago by

Tencent Charity when it launched a new mechanism that linked an organization's information disclosure level to its admission onto the 99 Charity Day program, and the permission to accept user donations. Tencent Charity first introduced this admission criteria for 99 Charity Day in 2017. Accordingly, philanthropic organizations that fail to meet Tencent's transparency standards were prevented from participating in 99 Charity Day. Such a mechanism can compel these organizations to make up for their deficiencies by taking the initiative to disclose information. A special function that went live in March 2018 displays feedback about an organization when a user is about to make a donation. In this way, the donor can achieve a better understanding of the basic information and transparency level of a philanthropic organization before they donate, allowing them to make a more informed decision about donating their money and resources.

Tencent's ventures in philanthropy show a new kind of trend. As the level of information transparency in philanthropy continues to improve, making better use of the information disclosed by organizations is the next big step for transparency mechanisms. In the future, information disclosure by philanthropic organizations will no longer simply be a legal requirement, or a measure reluctantly undertaken to meet the conditions of Internet-based platforms. Furthermore, this ever-evolving process will closely connect information about the transparency level of philanthropic organizations with the full range of philanthropic activities including public donations. In doing so, information transparency will have a more significant role to play in philanthropy, which forecasts a strong pathway of development for transparency mechanisms for years to come.

Section 3 Competition

By definition, public philanthropy is the distribution of social resources. However, social resources are limited and so is public sympathy. The scarcity of these two leads to competition between the different fields, forms, and entities of public philanthropy around the world. This competition can never be completely eliminated since it is part of philanthropy's core nature; the redistribution of resources. Of course, there is also cooperation and mutual assistance among these institutions. But competition is deeply rooted in this industry and cannot and should not be avoided.

At the same time, an industry mechanism to regulate this competition and set some basic ground rules is necessary. While a poorly developed mechanism may lead to unhealthy competition, a well-developed one would promote constructive competition and push institutions to constantly improve their own capabilities. The Internet has not only spurred the development of such a mechanism, but also promoted fairer rules.

The focus of the competition between public philanthropic organizations will shift from a charity's fundraising capabilities to its overall competence. The most significant competition in public philanthropy among different areas and organizations is for donation resources, or in other words, their fundraising capability. At the present stage, this capability has a greater capacity to arouse empathy from the public and donors.

In recent years, public philanthropy in China has seen increased public participation, but compared with the more developed public philanthropic culture in Europe and the United States, there is still room for improvement. Public donations are more driven by empathy than by a desire to solve social problems. Many donors do not necessarily think deeply or rationally when giving donations. Moreover, in the past, the imperfect disclosure of information and a lack of transparency in project execution does not seem to help donors in making decisions. This has led to competition in who can stir the most empathy, resulting in organizations losing focus on more important issues such as how they would effectively use donations, assess follow-up projects, and improve information disclosure.

Under the influence of Internet philanthropy, the processes for competition between public institutions is expected to change significantly. The emergence of the Internet has enabled organizations to disclose information online and improved public understanding of the progress and results of charitable projects. This will further efforts towards transparency that inform donors about the results of project implementation, helping them to make better decisions.

With this mechanism in place, the public will pay greater attention to the level of information disclosed as well as the results of a project's implementation when choosing what programs to support. If one organization lags significantly behind others in both respects, it will struggle to maintain public support and compete with other organizations.

This new process requires public philanthropy organizations to compete in a more comprehensive way. Under this system, any model that relies solely on arousing public sympathy to receive generous support will never become the norm. Organizations need to be competitive in multiple areas such as fund raising, project execution, transparency, and donor services. With this new competitive model, philanthropic organizations will be forced to strengthen their weaknesses and continuously improve their all-round capabilities.

At the same time, innovation and creativity will be the focus of future competition efforts. Before the emergence of Internet philanthropy, the philanthropic sector was quite traditional and conservative, and the public was not an active participant in activities. Competition among public institutions often depended on their resources and fundraising channels. This lessened the importance of creativity and innovation, and organizations were not motivated to make daring enough breakthroughs.

With the global spread of the Internet, innovative models can be replicated quickly, and beneficial ideas can be explored in as much depth as we like. In the online era, the institutions with a more innovative approach are more often the ones to achieve greater success. Public philanthropy products such as Charity Hiker and Ant Forest have achieved tremendous success through pioneering concepts and product design. Projects such as Kids Gallery have gained popularity through their level of creativity. Competition in the public philanthropy sector has undergone a silent but substantial change in the Internet era. In the near future, innovation and creativity will play an increasingly prominent role in the competition of the industry. In the years to come, we will see institutions with outstanding innovative capabilities gaining greater competitive advantages.

In the more distant future, competition among public philanthropy institutions may shift from competition over capital resources to competition for attention. The traditional charity model aims to solve social problems through more indirect distribution methods and the transfer of funds and resources. However, over the past decade, the efficiency of this process was significantly improved by online charity, empowered as it is by technology—most notably in terms of the speed and amount of money that can now be raised. At the same time, online philanthropic projects can be shared through social media, which helps to pool collective knowledge and spread good will.

With the development and large-scale use of emerging technologies such as new energy, big data, quantum computing and artificial intelligence, production efficiency will be dramatically improved, and material resources will flourish accordingly. In other words, money and material resources will be cheaper to achieve, while attention as a resource will become more expensive. Public attention will overtake money as the key to solving social problems, and the core content of public philanthropy activities will gradually shift from the redistribution of money and material resources to the allocation of attention as a resource. Consequently, competition between philanthropic institutions will also change. In the future, institutions with robust, all-round abilities and effective means of accessing the resource of public attention will be more likely to stand out.

Section 4 Philanthropic Organizations and Management Mechanisms

With the rise of the Internet, the thriving philanthropic community may give rise to innovative processes for project organization and management.

The philanthropic community, created by and comprised of engaged participants, is an active philanthropic group with the distinct feature of self-organization. Shared interest in charity brings together individuals within the philanthropic community. Under the traditional model, two donors, even funding the same charity project, would not have been connected in an efficient way. Thanks to the mobile Internet, it can be simple enough to share a contact card or scan a QR code in order to connect different donors. In this way, the cost of connectivity is now significantly reduced, which can help nurture numerous communities that are based on a shared passion for philanthropy.

As the distance between people online decreases, connectivity based on common interests will become an increasingly common practice. As many philanthropic organizations have become centered around community, the wider philanthropic community will be the main force at the core of charitable undertakings, and boundaries will be further blurred between communities and philanthropic organizations. A community may evolve into a philanthropic organization through its commitment to social issues. Equally, by bringing together charitable recipients, supporters, and other organizations, a philanthropic institution can become a community. Philanthropy in the future will focus on mobilizing and connecting people, where communities will play an increasingly critical role in attracting people's attention and organizing philanthropic activities.

With the growth of community-focused philanthropy, all kinds of philanthropic organizations will see their organizational and management patterns further transformed. Thanks to digital technology, new ways of organizing and managing philanthropic events may emerge in the philanthropic sector. For example, participants of charitable activities will be able to quickly assemble themselves to launch a philanthropic project, then disband once the project's follow-up evaluation and feedback are complete. Compared to traditional philanthropy, this form of organizing affords more flexibility. It is a lightweight version of philanthropic organizing that encourages more people to participate in causes they believe in. These new trends in organization will erase the once clear lines separating volunteers and specialized professional staff. Through web-based collaboration, philanthropic campaigns will become accessible to everyone.

Section 5 Co-ordination Between the Third Sector and the Other Two Sectors

Over the years, China has faced various difficulties resulting from the uncoordinated development of its three sectors, particularly the insufficient development of the third sector. At the same time, there have been many problems with both the division of and collaboration among the three sectors. The third sector usually works independently in its mission to solve social problems, limited to its subjective and objective requirements. In many such cases, the third sector does not fully engage with the first or second sectors, compelling them to "reinvent the wheel" with each project, which ultimately wastes resources. Yet the third sector also can play more of a supporting role. It is highly dependent on infrastructure and various resources provided by the other two sectors, but it is very unlikely to provide any help in return. A situation where the first and second sectors set the stage for the third sector to perform its role has existed for quite a long time, and the third sector has failed to play a greater role until now.

With the support of central government policies and the continuous improvement of relevant laws and regulations, the cooperation mechanism between the third sector and the other two is undergoing positive changes with the added power of the Internet. The third sector is engaging more with the other two sectors, while actively taking advantage of its own strengths. It has gone beyond philanthropy and now supports how the other two sectors run. One common example is WeCountry, which is sponsored by Tencent.

WeCountry is a rural philanthropic project initiated by the Tencent Foundation, derived from the foundation's "New Village" project. As early as 2009, the Tencent Foundation noticed that many rural areas lacked Internet access and failed to partake in the benefits of digital technology. They were left even further behind the developed regions of the country as the wave of digital development swept China. In order to help these rural areas, the Tencent Foundation launched the "New Village" project. With the aim of protecting local culture and passing it on to future generations, the project not only helped rural communities in western China to develop, but it also harnessed Tencent's core strengths as an Internet enterprise. Tencent was able to bring together philanthropic forces and promote new models of education, culture, and economic development in the region. Through years of trial and error, the "New Village" project continued to develop and gradually evolved into the WeCountry project.

The most important feature of WeCountry is its connectivity. Tencent tapped into its technological advantages and resources to design a multilevel structure that connected WeCountry nationally. This was achieved by linking the project's operations at various levels, from the provincial level all the way down to city, county, township, and village. At the same time, villages, village committees, Party members, and professionals were encouraged to take part in the project by verifying their real names. This approach successfully built connections between people from rural areas and the outside world, between migrant workers and their hometowns, and between grassroots Party members and the people. Connectivity is no longer an issue for people in the countryside thanks to WeCountry.

WeCountry became an important channel of social connections in rural areas. Many people from the countryside who had no access to the Internet are now able to access it via the WeCountry platform, which has dramatically advanced the development of rural society. WeCountry fulfilled its aim of establishing connectivity, but it also went above and beyond its role in the philanthropic sector by building infrastructure to support the first and second sectors.

Various online and offline Internet workshops were carried out as a result of the infrastructure provided by WeCountry. This improved the ability of grassroots organizers, WeCountry administrators, and the local people to use mobile Internet. With the improvement of Internet literacy, the Party Community of WeCountry became a platform that served Party members, including those at grassroots levels. WeCountry Smart Admin increased the effectiveness of dealing with village affairs and brought about higher levels of information transparency. Moreover, it has provided convenience by allowing people to enjoy public services via the Internet from the comfort of their own homes. The improved connectivity provided by WeCountry helped the Party committees and village committees to significantly increase the level of rural governance.

Furthermore, according to each village's level of Internet development, the WeCountry platform matches corporate resources with the appropriate village and then introduces market-oriented mechanisms and foreign capital to promote rural industries. The platform assists villagers in using market-based approaches, such as e-commerce and established countryside tourism, to close the information gap that has always presented a challenge to poverty alleviation in the past. The improved connectivity driven by WeCountry injected vitality into rural enterprises and promoted the development of the rural economy.

Tencent's WeCountry was initiated, and later known as, a philanthropic project, but it is about more than just philanthropy. With strong support from the government, WeCountry played an important role in many important positive changes, such as cultural inheritance, village governance, and rural economic development. The connectivity platform that WeCountry built further serves as an infrastructure that can help the first and second sectors function better. The three sectors are now making joint efforts to promote comprehensive development in rural areas.

In the future, there will be more examples like WeCountry. Eventually, the third sector will simply perform upon the stage set up by the first and second sectors. Instead, it will assist the other two sectors in building the stage itself with the guidance and support of relevant laws and regulations. The third sector will also support and engage more deeply with the other two sectors, playing an even greater role in modernizing and improving the effectiveness of China's national systems of governance.

15

Culture: Shaping a Philanthropic Culture with Emotionalism, Rationalism and Inclusion

Section 1 Traditional Chinese Philanthropic Culture

The concept of traditional Chinese philanthropy was developed from Buddhist concepts of blessings, Confucian ethics of benevolence and the Taoist idea of "One good turn deserves another." As an orthodox Chinese thought with a history of more than two thousand years, Confucian ethics has the most profound influence on charity and philanthropy. Specifically, that traditional charity and philanthropy is non-socialized, based on patriarchal clans, and controlled by the government.

Taoist Idea of "One Good Turn Deserves Another"

Taoist scholars believe that "Tao" is the rule of everything that exists, which cannot be predicted by ordinary people. They believe that the way of heaven will give rewards or punishments at any time and will reward good while punishing evil. As the traditional Taoist teaching goes, "There is no law in heavenly rewards and punishments, but the way of heaven

Y. Chen, *Internet Philanthropy in China*,
https://doi.org/10.1007/978-981-16-2566-4_15

always stands on the side of the good man". Taoism even connects kindness with longevity to inspire people to help others, saying, "He who desires to live a long life must do good deeds," or "If one does not strive for virtue but practices magic arts, he cannot live a long life." Only virtuous people can live a long life; if people want to prolong their life, they must do good deeds. This kind of utilitarianism-based philanthropy, on one hand, encourages people to do good by using rewards, and on the other, may prevent the public from developing a spontaneous and conscientious awareness of charity and philanthropy, thus inevitably making people seek self-interest while helping others.

Buddhist Ethics of Blessing

This kind of utilitarian charity and philanthropy can be best reflected in Buddhism. The core idea of Buddhist philanthropy is the theory of merits. Buddhism highly praises the theory of karma, saying, "There are three types of karma: Sanchit Karma, which is due to our past actions and what one goes through in the present are the effects of that past; Prarabdha Karma is what we are experiencing currently due to our past and the effects or experiences we are creating at present; and Agami Karma, the future seeds that we are sowing." Karma means that good actions bring good results while bad actions result in the opposite. This embodies the concept of reincarnation or the cycle of rebirth. Influenced by this idea, people think that if they do good when they are alive, they will go to the heaven after death; therefore, they will try their best to help others and place emphasis on relief and charity, contributing to the development of non-governmental philanthropic organizations and social philanthropy.

Confucian Ethics of Benevolence and Benevolent Governing

The core concept of Confucianism lies in benevolence. The basic point of benevolence is love, requiring people to love themselves, their family and their loved ones. Confucianism with characteristics from patriarchal systems leads to the charitable activities of some big families. For example, Fan Zhongyan, a well-known litterateur and statesman in the early Song Dynasty (960–1127), bought about 66.7 hectares of farmland in his hometown and made it common property shared by all his clan members to help them live a better life. This philanthropic culture, focusing on the family's development is quite different from modern philanthropic culture which requires doing good for all of society. Traditional philanthropic culture is also limited by its hometown-centered feature.

Confucius's idea of governing by virtue and Mencius's idea of a benevolent government required governors to love and protect people. Mencius said, "It was by benevolence that Xia, Shang and Zhou emperors ruled ancient China, and by inhumanity that they lost it. It is by the same means that the decaying and flourishing, the preservation and perishing, of a country are determined." He believed that the sovereign should govern the nation with a benevolent heart. When Confucianism became the official philosophy, governors in later dynasties paid more attention to benevolent governing. For example, during the Song (960–1279) and Yuan (1206–1368) dynasties, the government set up various charitable institutions such as Juyangyuan (a nursing home), Anjifang (a physiotherapy institution), Ciyouju (a center that adopted orphans), Ying'erju (a center that adopted orphans), Guanghuicang (a warehouse that stored food for disaster relief), Juzicang (a center that adopted orphans), and Louzeyuan (a place built by the government where unknown bodies were buried). Consequently, socially charitable and philanthropic activities were still under the government's strict control and the social nature of charity was suppressed.

The 2000-year-old culture of charity in China encapsulates the thoughts of Confucianism, Buddhism and Taoism. Confucianism spreads the knowledge of benevolence and morality; Buddhism features the idea of "karma and reincarnation"; while Taoism believes that doing good brings about immortality. However, they engaged people in doing good only from the perspective of personal interest, far from modern culture of philanthropy that prioritizes public interests. With long-standing imperial power in ancient China, the sophisticated, top-down government hierarchy strictly controlled the whole society, holding back the emergence of civil organizations and people's participation in public affairs. That's why the awareness of public interest represented by modern philanthropic culture failed to develop in ancient China.

Section 2 Modern Chinese Philanthropic Culture

Modern Chinese philanthropic culture properly emerged in the 1840s when China was forced to open its door as a result of the Opium War. As western civilizations came to China along with wars and religion, Christianity and its charitable causes gradually spread across China. Following the Hundred Days' Reform of 1898, the National Revolution of the Kuomintang (KMT) and the establishment of the Republic of China, a variety of modern philanthropic organizations were established, such as schools, hospitals and administrative offices. Western philanthropic theories such as "fraternity" and "humanity" were then introduced to China and melded with Chinese philanthropic culture. However, further evolvement of modern Chinese philanthropic culture was interrupted by the outbreak of World War II and the Chinese civil war between the KMT and the Communist Party. In a long period after the founding of the People's Republic of China in 1949, the government implemented a planned economy and controlled most public affairs. There was little room for civil philanthropy to grow, so the public awareness of philanthropic culture couldn't develop. The truly modern philanthropic organizations didn't appear in China until 1978, when China rolled out policies of reform, opened-up to the West and implemented a market economy.

Therefore, true modern philanthropic culture in China has only developed for 40 years and is nowhere near the comprehensive, deep-rooted consensus among the people. Current Chinese philanthropic culture is multi-faceted as diverse theories and cultures constantly collide and merge with each other. For example, it keeps the ancient Chinese theory of doing good for the benefit of oneself and absorbs western notions of fraternity and altruism; it stresses universal responsibility from a national perspective while encouraging mutual assistance among the general public. There are also various viewpoints and discussions in Chinese philanthropic communities and academic circles. Their ideas can be summarized into three major categories: moralism that emphasizes charity for its own sake, marketism that promotes efficiency of philanthropic activities, and populism that advocates inclusive charity.

Moralism emphasizes that the essence of philanthropic value is the core of modern philanthropic culture. Professor Kang Xiaoguang, a proponent of moralism, argues that philanthropy is by definition altruist. However, the interpretations of "altruism" vary fundamentally from Eastern to Western cultures. Altruism in Western culture is rooted in Christian fraternity and it means undifferentiated love for self and others. In Eastern culture, however, altruism is based upon "benevolence" put forward by Confucianism. According to Confucianism, a man of perfect virtue, wishing to be established himself, seeks also to establish others; wishing to be enlarged himself, he seeks also to enlarge others. Confucianism also argues that you should do unto others as you would have them do unto you. Therefore, benevolence in Eastern culture puts individual interest before others. Professor Kang Xiaoguang believes that "benevolence" in Confucianism corresponds with human nature and that we should further explore and carry forward Confucianism to shape China's modern philanthropic culture. "One should pursue immortality of life through three immortal deeds, which are, morality, contribution and speech. That is to say, one's influence can survive the time if one does good to society and mankind as a whole and benefits generations to come" (Bai & Zhang, 2016).

Marketism gives special importance to developing philanthropy with a market driven mentality and methods to solve problems in current philanthropic organizations. This is a newly developed school of thought in China's philanthropy community in recent years. One of its representatives is Xu Yongguang, chairman of Narada Foundation, who points out two deep-rooted problems in contemporary Chinese philanthropy: bureaucracy and moralization. Bureaucracy leads to low efficiency and hinders innovation in civil society. Moralization can turn into moral coercion that makes it hard to transform or optimize philanthropy operations. By contrast, marketization advocates respect for business rules and stresses the importance of efficiency and input-output ratio in developing philanthropy. Xu Yongguang illustrates in his monograph Philanthropy or Business, his core value of marketism. "On the one hand, philanthropic organizations can turn into businesses and deal with social issues with business approaches; and on the other hand, businesses can assume corporate social responsibility and implement their own philanthropic strategy" (*Xu Yongguang*, 2017). According to Xu, this is the ideal development path for China's modern philanthropy.

Populism focuses on the social nature of philanthropy and advocates that philanthropy should play a balancing role in the society. On the one hand, we need to raise the awareness of philanthropy among the general public. On the other hand, we should avoid the trap of alienation caused by moral coercion or pursuit of personal interests. Philanthropy should develop in the way that balances self-interest and altruism. Professor Li Xiaoyun is an ambassador of populism. He raises the idea of down-to-earth philanthropy that especially refers to the inclusiveness of philanthropy. He argues that philanthropy consists of three layers of meaning, which are, civil society, democracy and people's livelihood. According to Professor Li, civil society refers to the general public, democracy means mechanism, and people's livelihood is the goal to strive for. Philanthropy by nature is all about these three aspects. "Rather than a representation of government, philanthropy is about a tacit social contract, where everyone comes together voluntarily to offer whatever they are capable of, be it money or knowledge. When streams of individual strengths converge, democracy will come about in such a strong way that the government cannot afford to neglect. Besides, the goal of philanthropy is to improve people's livelihood. This is not an easy task for any government. When a government is excessively overseen by its people, its power and resource will be limited, thus becoming less able to solve problems. But the opposite wouldn't work either because bureaucracy doesn't help. Therefore, philanthropy in civil society should go hand in hand with government to improve people's livelihood." To this end, China's philanthropic culture must transcend the elite culture of middle class to become mass culture that is rooted in local communities and incorporates all social classes. In other words, China's philanthropic culture should reflect tradition while integrating itself with current mass culture, especially the grassroots culture.

Currently, China's philanthropic culture is still undergoing constant twists and turns. More and more Chinese people are looking back on traditional Chinese culture while actively embracing modern Western culture. We believe China will, through constant practice and reflection, cradle the pearl of philanthropic culture that is widely recognized by its people and absorb the essences of Eastern and Western culture.

Section 3 Three Levels of Chinese Philanthropy

Emotionalism

Influenced by different geographical circumstances and traditional cultures, different from the logic-based rationalism developed in other countries, Chinese people have developed a culture of emotionalism that is mainly shown by expressing emotions through describing concrete objects. Chinese culture originated from the inland river basin which enjoyed good natural conditions and abundant resources for human beings. At the basin, people survived by cooperating with each other. Therefore, an interdependent relationship was developed over time; and, finally, a national culture characterized by mutual dependence and adaptability among people was produced (Li, 2013), which manifested emotionalism and conformity. In China, patriarchal ideas of Confucianism require people to follow the rules of the family and put the interest of the family before personal interest, which hinders the occurrence of rationalism and deepens conformity.

Emotionalism is reflected in all aspects of Chinese society, which, of course, covers charity and philanthropy. In China, people participate in charitable activities because they are touched by a cause. People will provide help of all kinds to the people in disaster-hit areas after natural disasters. A rapidly developing fund-raising platform has become an effective channel to help people in need, and various philanthropic organizations are active in all fields. However, these kinds of philanthropic activities can only touch people in the short term rather than help them to develop the habit of long-term donation.

Due to lax supervision and difficulties in verifying the news on the Internet and other problems, many swindlers appear on online fund-raising platforms and take advantage of people's kindness. For example, one couple from Henan Province, and a father named Luo Er swindled netizens out of donations by making use of their seriously ill daughters. Also, a man from Jiangsu Province exaggerated his mother's illness on a fund-raising platform to get more donations. In recent years, scams of this nature have greatly cooled people's passion for helping others. Take the Guo Meimei incident as an example. Social donation in that year declined by 50% in quarter-on-quarter terms, which made a severe impact on the development of China's philanthropy (*The Chinese*, 2011). The aforementioned incidents have shown us that a new era of participating in philanthropic activities by rationalism and judgement has arrived.

Rationalism

Large-scale Internet companies contributed to the start and development of the rational philanthropic culture. Relying on technical methods, they build mechanisms for rational donations on the donation platforms, gradually leading netizens to develop a rational donation thinking pattern and habit. However, it is impractical to develop a rational philanthropic culture only by relying on Internet companies. Fostering a new kind of culture in people's mind calls for efforts from all sections of society; therefore, the government, philanthropic organizations, new media outlets and the public should work together to push forward with rational philanthropy.

(1) The government improves relative regulations and laws to supervise philanthropic organizations and online fund-raising more strictly.

Since 2005, the *Charity Law* has been revised many times, providing a stricter legal system for charity, especially donation scams. For booming online fund-raising, the government announced the "white list" (i.e. donation platforms recognized by the government) of online fund-raising platforms in 2016, the first batch of which included 13 charitable organizations; in July 2017, the Ministry of Civil Affairs issued two standards: Basic Technical Specifications of Online Fundraising Platform for Charitable Organizations and Basic Management Specifications of Online Fundraising Platform for Charitable Organizations, which clearly require that organizations that launch a fund-raising campaign on fund-raising platforms should be qualified charitable organizations eligible for public fund-raising and fund-raising platforms should not release any fund-raising information of organizations or individuals ineligible for public fund-raising (Kuang et al., 2017). This strict supervision from the government has ensured the openness and transparency of charitable organizations and online fund-raising, which not only earns people's trust but also makes it possible for people to make rational judgement based on the fund-raising information.

(2) The development of philanthropic organizations and the Internet ensure the public's right to select on their own.

The development of philanthropic organizations provides more choices for the public to participate in charitable activities. The donors have the right to make donations to the philanthropic organizations that they are interested in and the right to refuse to make donations to other organizations. The philanthropic organizations cover each field of society, enabling each donor to make donations to the discipline they are interested in. The charitable activities based on interest and love can be frequent and continuous.

The development of the Internet as a means of fundraising has enabled the public to donate in various ways. Except for street fund-raising, charity auctions and other traditional methods, online fund-raising greatly improves the public's participation in charitable activities. At present, some well-known domestic websites and philanthropic organizations have built philanthropy platforms on WeChat and Sina Weibo, and crowdfunding platforms have gradually been standardized. For example, Tencent's innovative annual philanthropic campaign 99 Charity Day came to an end recently. In three days, the company raised more than RMB 830 million through its charity platform with donations from 28 million individuals and RMB 185 million from more than 2000 companies, supporting more than 5498 philanthropic projects (Zhao, 2018). The development of the Internet provides a more convenient way for the public to participate in charitable activities and rich online information enables the public to choose any charitable projects that they are interested in.

(3) The public has adopted the awareness of rights and responsibilities and realized effective altruism in an enthusiastic and professional shape.

As members of modern society, people participate in charitable activities based on their responsibilities rather than utilitarianism or passion. The principle of justice requires that everyone in modern society has the right to be aided by society, which helps to ensure social stability; correspondingly, providing help for people in need becomes the public's obligation. Based on consciousness of the unity of power and responsibility, citizens have begun to participate in charitable activities in fields in which they are personally concerned with consciously and habitually.

When people conduct donations, they need to consider how much they want to donate and who they will donate to. Professional donors will maximize the benefit of their donations, achieving effective altruism. Driven by emotionalism, charity focuses on the goodwill of the donor rather than the result of the donation; however, under the guidance of effective altruism, the purpose of various charitable projects and donations will be evaluated from all aspects of society, and the question of how to maximize the positive benefits brought by everyone to society should be considered.

Under the guidance of effective altruism, the donor will donate money to those who need it most rather than those who have a close relationship with the donor; and, when choosing philanthropic organizations, they will compare the maximum values created by each philanthropic organization from their donations and give their money to the most efficient organization. The professional public, in turn, improves the professionalism of philanthropic organizations. Only professional philanthropic organizations can gain much more trust and support from rational philanthropists.

Achieving effective altruism and maximizing the value of resources requires the public to participate in charitable activities in a more rational and professional way. In the development of rational charity and philanthropy, cooperation among the government, philanthropic organizations and new media outlets provide external guarantees for rational choices from the public. Chinese philanthropy gradually throws off the parochialism of traditional culture and develops into a socialist culture.

Inclusion

Inclusion here means that charity has been thoroughly included in Chinese people's daily life and etched in their mind. The public does not need to think clearly about whether the activity they participated in is charitable or not.

More than two thousand years ago, Confucian scholars mentioned the issue of social inclusion. Mozi said, "It is to regard the state of others as one's own, the houses of others as one's own, the persons of others as one's self." Buddhists also pointed out the concept of "feeling others' suffering as our own", which means that people should regard others' needs and problems as their own. In this case, charity is not out of kindness or to seek the value of existence and there is no right or wrong, failure or success in charitable activities. In other words, participating in charitable activities becomes a habit, or a matter of course.

For society, development of philanthropy signifies the improvement of human civilization and is the result of imbalances of social supply and demand. With the development of technology and the global economy, there is less requirement to stress about the importance of charity. The great success and final level of philanthropy is that one day there will be no need to stress on it because people's basic requirements can be satisfied at that time, they will participate in charitable and philanthropic activities consciously and philanthropy has been thoroughly included into people's daily life and mind as a basic concept.

To accomplish the transition of Chinese philanthropy from emotionalism to rationalism and finally to the inclusion level, Chinese people should continuously improve their philanthropic consciousness. At present, Chinese philanthropy is transitioning from emotionalism to rationalism. Internet philanthropy has accelerated the transition speed and changed netizens' attitude towards philanthropy, transmitting the warmth of practical actions to people's heart (*Chen Yidan*, 2018).

Section 4 Rational Philanthropy on the Internet

Internet culture has such features as taking the users as God, information asymmetry, and fast updates of technology. These features will complement philanthropic culture after Internet culture is brought into the philanthropic field, forming a unique Internet philanthropic culture. With the development of Internet philanthropy, its rational features tend to be more significant.

Users' Rational Participation after Being Treated as "God"

Internet culture emphasizes that users are God, which means to satisfy users' needs and improve user experience as much as possible. Therefore, various online philanthropic platforms such as crowdfunding platforms, WeChat and Sina Weibo's philanthropy have emerged to facilitate users to more conveniently and quickly participate in philanthropic activities, greatly reducing the cost and threshold for users. Most Chinese people can directly participate in philanthropy through the Internet, whether it is donations, even one or ten yuan or philanthropy is supported with actions such as a charity marathon, and ice bucket challenge. The implementation of these activities has both lowered the threshold and diversified the forms of participation in philanthropy, so that more people can join in. The experience of users is also improving, and they are more enthusiastic about philanthropy. This will be beneficial to the improvement of citizens' philanthropic awareness and the development of rational philanthropy habits.

In addition, each "God" has their own "ID" on the Internet. They can use various applications online via their IDs and passwords and make choices on their own. Meanwhile, in the Internet age, users generate plenty of content recording personal consumption and their understanding of life. These "digital citizens" are the first motivators of rational philanthropic culture.

Bridging Information Asymmetry

The Internet provides users with a huge amount of information, which greatly eliminates information asymmetry. In addition to the comments of other donors, the users can refer to the evaluation of specialized charity rating agencies to make rational judgments. In the US, there have been philanthropy research institutes such as GiveWell, which examines the effectiveness of specific philanthropic practices through academic research and data analysis, and the indicators including "the cost for saving one life" and "the economic help brought to the beneficiary by one dollar" are used to evaluate the efficiency of philanthropic organizations and projects. In 2016, they selected the Against Malaria Foundation, which provides donations for the purchase of insecticide-treated bed nets in high-risk areas of malaria as the most efficient (Business Weekly, 2015). The emergence of such rating agencies has greatly improved the efficiency of philanthropy and promoted the Internet philanthropic culture to evolve into rational philanthropy.

The more developed charitable giving is, the more rational its philanthropic culture and habits will be. China's Internet philanthropy has greatly improved the efficiency of philanthropy through Internet technology. At the same time, with further practices in charity and philanthropy in the future and the improvement in legislation by the government regulatory agency, China's Internet philanthropy may also have similar charity research and evaluation institutes as GiveWell. Therefore, China's Internet philanthropic culture will forge ahead into rational philanthropy.

Application of the Blockchain Technology

The rapid development of Internet technology has also become a powerful driver in realizing China's goals for philanthropy. The application of blockchain technology in the philanthropy field is conducive to solving the problem of information asymmetry. The whole philanthropic process can be divided into several nodes. Each node possesses corresponding authentication which means this technology-based process makes the blockchain information difficult to tamper with. Therefore, the system can provide more accurate information to the public to guarantee rational philanthropy.

Large-Scale Internet Companies

In the Internet era, China's favorable sci-tech environment has given rise to several large-scale Internet companies. These enterprises have a large user base and significant advantages in information technology. The network value is high, which has a tremendous impact on shaping rational philanthropy.

Internet companies have powerful control over the platform so that they can provide guidance for the public to participate in philanthropy and raise people's awareness for rational philanthropy. For example, the online "cooler" function developed by Tencent Charity can reveal information about the time, implementation effect, financial disclosure, project progress, etc. of a philanthropic project to the users before donation. After people understand the philanthropic project fully, they can make a well-informed decision.

In this way, it guarantees the donor's right to know and prevents donors from donating money impulsively. Donors who have a good understanding of a philanthropic project will continue to pay attention to the project's progress after making donations, thus ensuring that their donations are used invaluably. They attach importance to the true value created by the project and judge whether it is worthwhile to continue supporting. If they feel their donations are being utilized to the maximum, they will participate more deeply in the project, become long-term donors, and make rational philanthropy part of their life (Zhang, 2018).

At the same time, Internet companies rely on strong platforms to supervise philanthropic organizations and projects to make them more professional and transparent. Internet philanthropy platforms strengthen the review of philanthropic projects, launch a series of transparent projects and continuously upgrade them and supervise non-profit organizations to ensure they cherish their prospects. Also, the platforms require these organizations guarantee "professional disclosure and transparent presentation", fulfill their obligation to disclose information and take the initiative to accept social supervision. Only then is the donor given a satisfactory result. A professional organization that can make rational and effective use of donations will maintain its credibility and gain public support. Internet companies can help philanthropic organizations develop with transparency and follow regulations, while promoting the development of philanthropic culture to rational philanthropy.

References

Bai, X., & Zhang, X. (2016). 康晓光:相比于基督教文明的"博爱", 儒家的"仁爱"更普适. *中国慈善家, 2016*(3), 38–39. https://www.zhangqiaokeyan.com/academic-journal-cn_china-philanthropist_thesis/0201240727802.html.

Business Weekly (商业周刊). (2015, December 28). *科学地做慈善像选股一样较真*. Xueqiu. https://xueqiu.com/3904790550/62581829

Chen Yidan: It's time for rational public welfare (陈一丹:理性公益正当时). (2018, September 11). QQ. Retrieved October 05, 2018, from https://gongyi.qq.com/a/20180911/062952.htm

Kuang, X. X., Qian, Y. B., & Zhao, D. T. (2017, November 02). *人民日报:互联网公益形式出新、监管趋严*. Rmzxb. http://csgy.rmzxb.com.cn/c/2017-11-02/1857971.shtml

Li, H. (2013). 谈中国社会文化中的感性主义. *云南社会主义学院学报, 2013*(2), 327–328.

The Chinese Red Cross admits that personal donations have fallen sharply due to the Guo Meimei incident (中国红十字会承认受郭美美事件影响个人捐款大降). (2011, December 08). Sohu. Retrieved October 05, 2018, from http://business.sohu.com/20111208/n328362672.shtml

Xu Yongguang: Ineffective use of charitable resources is the most unethical (徐永光: 慈善资源的无效使用是最不道德的). (2017, June 16). Sohu. Retrieved October 05, 2018, from http://www.sohu.com/a/149544834_616757

Zhang, Y. X. (2018, September 13). *为何说"理性公益"是大势所趋*. 360doc. http://www.360doc.com/content/18/0913/21/59320440_786460911.shtml

Zhao, M. H. (2018, September 17). *引导公益慈善从感性走向理性*. Baidu. https://baijiahao.baidu.com/s?id=1611809760906231635&wfr=spider&for=pc

Epilogue: Long-Term Pursuit of Rational Philanthropy

On September 5, 2018, when this book was nearly completed, the fourth Tencent 99 Charity Day officially launched. At the launching ceremony, Charles Chen Yidan, the core founder of Tencent and initiator and honorary chairman of the Tencent Foundation, made a speech entitled "Rational Philanthropy Is at the Time". Based on the development of 99 Charity Day over the last four years, Mr. Chen believes that China's Internet philanthropy has reached a new historical turning point. If the success of Internet philanthropy in the past stimulated the public's philanthropic passion, the core task to Tencent's philanthropic undertaking in the next decade is to channel that momentary passion into a lasting "rational philanthropy". Based on a convenient, transparent and open philanthropy platform, Tencent will further improve the industry's infrastructure, connectors and toolkit, to help the Chinese philanthropy industry develop from being spontaneous to being conscious, from being perceptual to being rational, and from being emotional to being professional. When building up a "rational philanthropy" in the era of science and technology, specifically, the following three aspects from Mr. Chen's speech are worth mentioning:

Y. Chen, *Internet Philanthropy in China*,
https://doi.org/10.1007/978-981-16-2566-4

First, we have updated the transparency system and consolidated the foundation of philanthropic ecology.

On the 99 Charity Day of 2018, in order to promote a transparent system for the philanthropy industry, Tencent Charity used technical means to inspire kindness in people and win their trust in philanthropic projects, so that actions can be taken to better solve social problems.

In terms of rules, the 99 Charity Day 2018 invited stakeholders to participate in formulating rules, to promote the healthy development of the Internet philanthropy. It took nearly three months to hold various events including seminars for exchanging ideas, online public collection of opinions and proposals and professional review committee meetings. A total of 231 suggestions were received both online and offline from nearly 80 participants, including scholars, experts, journalists, consultants, lawyers and others inside and outside of the industry. After careful reviews and modifications, these suggestions finally constituted the rules for 99 Charity Day 2018.

Regarding products, Tencent Charity platform has been continuously investigating for the past eleven years, using technology to present different philanthropic projects transparently to the public. This year's financial disclosure has been upgraded again: Tencent Charity introduced Deloitte, a professional third party, to assist philanthropy partners in effectively carrying out "professional disclosure and transparent presentation".

As for projects, the 99 Charity Day 2018 launched a "follow-up plan" to bring transparent changes in the project to the public through video recordings of the philanthropic events that have received attention in the past. Meanwhile, it was designed to arouse public attention to and reflection on social issues by the change from a single project.

Year after year, we draw lessons from the 99 Charity Day and makes them into institutional arrangements, so that the kindness of hundreds of millions of users can be expressed and turned into rational philanthropic deeds which are sustainable and transparent.

Second, we have encouraged nearly everyone to get involved and make life better.

The 99 Charity Day 2018 has created diversified philanthropic participation through a variety of ways. With the joint efforts of enterprises, media and Tencent's products, the influence of 99 Charity Day has been extended from online to offline, from the philanthropy industry to the public, and from the philanthropy platform to local communities.

In 2018, new functions have been introduced, such as "hometown philanthropy", "love-doubling cards", "collection of red flowers", and "interactions with stars through short videos". They are intended to mobilize hundreds of millions of netizens who love giving to take part in philanthropic activities in an easy and interactive way. 99 Charity Day integrates philanthropy into real scenarios and proceeds from the perspectives of food, clothing, housing, and transportation. It combines philanthropy with people's daily life so that philanthropy is not abstract anymore.

Philanthropic organizations are the key forces for the development of philanthropy and the core ties for connecting the public. Strong organizations contribute to more prosperous business. In 2018, the Tencent Foundation will continue to give a total of RMB 299.99 million to match the donations made by the public, and another RMB 100 million to the growth fund to support philanthropic organizations.

Be it through technology, education, or philanthropy, our ultimate vision is to make society a better place. The integration of online and offline contributions will bring together the love of all parties into a revolutionary force, which will turn this dream into reality.

Third, we have made rational philanthropy the main theme and ensured that people in need feel connected to the world.

Over the past four years, 99 Charity Day has experienced rapid growth and promoted the transformation of the philanthropy concept held by a generation of netizens from "fingertips to heart". Philanthropy starts at fingertips and gradually evolves into rationality in the heart, which turns the temporary move into a long-term habit, and sentiment-driven decisions into rational judgment. Therefore, we believe that "rational philanthropy" will become the core of the future philanthropy.

The "cool-off" function of Tencent Charity was a new attempt of "rational philanthropy". The cool-off has been used to encourage users to think twice and check the specific information of a project to make donations rationally.

There was a rule in the Internet industry that an additional step of the interaction chain often inevitably results in user loss. It was even said that the "cool-off" function would be "the first thing that stops you from donating". However, the function has been online for half a year. Although the donation rate on the platform has declined, "promoting the transparency of philanthropy" is a principle that we adhere to.

Good products can help discover kind hearts. Transparency and effectiveness are the expectations of everyone. In the past, you could make a one-off donation out of impulse. Now, in the context of rational donations, you can take one more step to witness a child's growth. You can also make suggestions and sustained donations and better see what you have accomplished through philanthropy.

Take "hometown philanthropy" as an example. No matter how far away our hometowns are, we are still able to care about and contribute to their development and influence people around us to do the same. In other words, it helps everyone grow and be connected to the world.

The 99 Charity Day is in its fourth year. We encourage projects to gain more public support and recognition through well-defined concept, efficient implementation and transparent feedback, during which projects that failed to gain trust from the public will be eliminated.

It is foreseeable that the platform will encounter an adjustment period, which is a necessary process for a virtuous cycle of an ecosystem when a new opportunity emerges. We should be more down to earth, continue to improve the infrastructure of the Internet philanthropy, innovate Internet-based platforms, and promote the development of the industry, with rational philanthropy as a motivator in the future.

To promote rational and sustainable philanthropy, we should not cheer for the digital success, but rather focus on the virtuous cycle and continuity of rational philanthropy.

Supplement: A Chronicle of Events of the Development of Internet Philanthropy (1995–2020)

2020

- December: Most of the well-known Internet technology companies in China had announced the establishment of action plans to use technology to support philanthropy. Take Tencent as an example, the Tencent Foundation launched the first phase of its technology charity platform. It also launched a "Light·Charity Innovation Challenge" with Tencent Cloud and other technical teams.
- November: In order to strengthen the use of Internet technology in the field of charity and support charitable organizations to publish Internet public fundraising information on a larger scale, the *Ministry of Civil Affairs* announced that it will select the third batch of charitable organizations Internet public fundraising information platform, and the total number will not exceed 10.
- October: The first law enforcement inspection report since the promulgation of the *Charity Law* was submitted to the Standing Committee of the 13th National People's Congress for deliberation. The deliberation report suggested to amend the *Charity Law*, add a special chapter on online charity to regulate it systematically, and strengthen platform responsibility.

Y. Chen, *Internet Philanthropy in China*,
https://doi.org/10.1007/978-981-16-2566-4

- September: On September 9th, the sixth 99 Charity Day came to an end. With the theme of "Together We Can", this year's event has raised a total donation of RMB3.044 billion. More than 5780 donors, 500 institutions and 10,000 enterprises participated in the campaign, which broke the record for giving among China's internet charity industry, and has transformed into a festival of national goodwill and philanthropy for society.
- August: Tencent Charity Platform launched the "Flood Relief" topic with 38 projects on July 8, covered Guangxi, Yunnan, Sichuan, Chongqing and other flood-affected areas across China with many charity foundations and organizations. As of August 25, the cumulative number of donations reached nearly 300,000 and the donation amount exceeded 11 million yuan.
- July: The 2020 China Internet Philanthropy Summit was held online, with the theme of "Cross a river in the same boat, grow towards the sunlight". More than 3000 charity organizations, more than 30 well-known domestic and foreign experts, social entrepreneurs, and media professionals attended.
- June: The 17th (2020) China Charity List was officially released. 365 mainland private enterprises donated a total of 9.63312 billion yuan, accounting for 77.65% of the total donation, and each enterprise donated an average of 26.39 million yuan.
- May: The China Population Welfare Foundation (CPWF) and the World Health Organization (WHO) jointly launched a charity fund-raising program in Beijing to fight the COVID-19 pandemic. It will receive donations via some 20 Internet-based Chinese fundraising platforms, including Tencent Foundation, Alibaba Foundation, Alipay Foundation and others.
- April: Alibaba held the "Orange Dot Charity List" awards ceremony, to encourage employees who actively participate in charity activities.
- March: Tencent set up US$100 million global anti-pandemic fund to support fight against COVID-19, more than 25 million pieces of anti-epidemic supplies were donated to more than 30 countries.
- February: Tencent Pledges Another RMB1 Billion to Set Up Anti-Epidemic Fund, which would be deployed in areas such as procurement of medical supplies, provision of technical support, reward for

the people who contribute to the battle, assistance for the infected and their families, R&D of anti-NCP solutions, and improvement of medical facilities.

- January: The China Philanthropy Research Institute of Beijing Normal University and the China Global Philanthropy Institute jointly released the "Top 100 Chinese Donors (2019)" in Beijing.
- January: The 9th Annual Conference of Philanthropy China "Charity Star Story" theme party was held in Beijing.
- January: Tencent Charity Foundation announced a donation of RMB300 million to set up the first phase of a new pneumonia prevention and control fund.
- January: Alibaba announced it set up a special fund of 1 billion yuan for medical supplies.
- January: ByteDance announced it has decided to donate 200 million yuan to the Chinese Red Cross Foundation to set up a special fund for humanitarian assistance for medical personnel.

2019

- December: The 2019 China Annual Conference of Philanthropy was held in Beijing with the theme of "Growing Spirit from Wealth".
- November: Tencent hosted The Xplorer Prize Award Ceremony in Beijing, and 50 young scientists from 9 major fields received awards.
- November: The second "111 Small Good Day" Charity Ceremony with the theme of "Living for Good" was held by Shuidichou in Beijing.
- November: 11 Chinese cities joined the global annual celebration of World Children's Day launched by UNICEF.
- October: The National WeCountry Conference was held in Taoba Village, Datong Township, Qionglai City. WeCountry was a digital assistant for rural vitalization, from one village after another to cover the whole country for the last 10 years.
- October: The Internet Charity Forum was held on the World Internet Conference for the first time.
- September: The 99 Charity Day for 2019 came to a successful end on September 9. The number of charitable organizations and caring

enterprises both exceeded 10,000, which has also set a new high in terms of fundraising, transparency and coverage for the 99 Charity Day of this year: 48 million caring netizens donated RMB1.783 billion through the Tencent Public Benefit Platform, more than 2500 enterprises donated RMB307 million, plus RMB399.99 million provided by Tencent's Public Benefit and Charity Foundation, bringing the total amount of donations raised on this 99 Giving Day to RMB2.49 billion.

- September: The 7th China Charity Project Exchange Exhibition was held in Shenzhen.
- July: The Charity Case Center of the China Global Philanthropy Institute was established and released ten classic charity cases.
- May: The 3rd China Internet Philanthropy Summit was held in Guangzhou, nearly 3000 enthusiastic charity individuals from famous enterprises, charitable organizations, universities, and mainstream media had joined to discuss "rational charity, tech for good".
- April: The Tencent Foundation invested 100 million yuan in funds to jointly release the "WeCare Charity Plan" with WeChat Mini Games and Tencent Games Dreaming Plan to encourage developers to create more charity mini games.
- April: The 16th (2019) China Charity List was released in Beijing, 274 philanthropists and 744 charitable enterprises were on the list.
- April: Sina released the 2018 annual operation report of Sina Weibo Charity.
- April: Tencent Charity released the "Tencent Charity Co-Creation 2.0—UP Plan" to promote the overall capability of the entire philanthropy ecosystem through tools, traffic, training and financial incentives.
- February: The Ministry of Civil Affairs of PRC established the Charity Promotion and Social Work Department.
- January: UNICEF launched a US$3.9 billion appeal to provide emergency assistance to 41 million children affected by conflict or disasters.

2018

- December: The Third Internet Philanthropy Summit was hosted by the Tencent Foundation to investigate the future development of Internet philanthropy.
- September: *The Action Plan on Internet Plus Social Organizations (2018–2020)* was issued by China's Ministry of Civil Affairs, marking a comprehensive and profound advancement of "Internet Plus Social Philanthropy" promoted by the government.
- September: Tencent was awarded the 10th China Charity Award, and the "Internet Plus Philanthropy" model won recognition.
- September: The 99 Charity Day 2018 was celebrated. Public participation reached a record high thanks to the first initiative of "rational philanthropy" during the event, in which more than 2000 businesses participated.
- September: The Green Planet Program was rolled out by Ant Forest, enabling low-carbon practices to become part of daily life.
- August: Shuidichou.cn, in conjunction with the Beijing Red Cross Blood Center, launched China's first online unpaid blood donation program called Blood Donation Season.
- July: Cainiao.com, a logistic company under the Alibaba Group, launched a one-week City Superman Energy-Refueling event for outdoor workers, including couriers, take-out delivery men, sanitation workers and traffic police.
- June: The Digital Patrons of Dunhuang Grottoes, an online charity event, was initiated by Tencent Charity, the China Foundation for Cultural Heritage Conservation, the China Dunhuang Grottoes Conservation Research Foundation, Dunhuang Academy China and Xinhua Charity.
- June: The "Environment Map", an Internet-based public participation platform under the "Take Action for a Beautiful China" initiative, was officially kicked off by the Center for Environmental Education and Communications of the Ministry of Environmental Protection, the Alibaba Foundation, and Amap.

- June: AutoNavi Maps launched the Philanthropy by Your Side function, which allows people to see available philanthropic programs nearby by looking on a map.
- May: The Ministry of Civil Affairs issued the second batch of 9 Internet fundraising information platforms including Meituan, DiDi and Shuidichou.cn.
- May: The E-Charity Alliance was initiated in Beijing by the China Charities Aid Foundation for Children.
- April: The China Young Champions of the Earth award was established by UNEP and Sina Weibo.
- April: The first Behavioral Philanthropy Season was started by Tencent Charity. It is another inclusive online charity program like 99 Charity Day, which links businesses, users and charitable organizations. The theme of the first session was Walking for Philanthropy.
- March: Tencent Charity's 2018 Transparency Mechanism was released, a major upgrade to its 2017 version. It modified the rules for information disclosure mechanisms for different types of organizations, along with a cool-off function to encourage more informed donations.
- February: A charity event called "1M Traffic Donation for a Life Package for Left-behind Children" was initiated by China Unicom and the China Children and Teenagers' Fund.
- January: Alipay announced the official launch of online philanthropy accounts, in which user's philanthropic activities and "assets" donated could be recorded and consulted.

2017

- December: The Alibaba Poverty Alleviation Fund was launched to explore a new model in sync with Internet Plus Poverty Alleviation.
- November: The Union for Land Trust Reserves Conference was held in Beijing. Tencent, Alibaba and other member institutions shared their applications and experiences of Internet philanthropy for nature conservation.
- October: The JD Foundation opened its first ever overseas donation channel.

- September: Jinri Toutiao launched its time-donation philanthropic project called One Minute of Your Love. By accumulating daily reading time on the Jinri Toutiao app, users can convert said time into philanthropic funds that can be redeemed for relief supplies.
- September: In conjunction with CCTV Charity Night, the Alibaba Group kicked off the 95 Alibaba Philanthropy Week, together with the "Three Hours for Charity", where hundreds of millions of funds were raised for those in need.
- September: Meituan and Ele.me, two take-out giants in China, rolled out the Green Mountain Program special fund and Blue Planet Program, respectively. They called for the public attention to ecosystems and more active participation in environmental protection.
- September: The 99 Charity Day 2017 was celebrated, during which new ways of "at your fingertips" philanthropic engagement was first introduced, e.g. "Donation of Philanthropic Coins". Public donations exceeded those by businesses significantly for the first time.
- August: Kids Gallery, a philanthropic program jointly initiated by Ai You Foundation and World of Art Brut Culture (WABC), went viral on WeChat Moments. It became a hit among philanthropic programs, raising more than RMB 15 million within 24 hours.
- July: By combining its advantages in both business and platforms, Tencent launched the "Will You Build the Great Wall?" program to conserve and pass on the Great Wall culture with Internet technologies.
- July: The Breadwinner Program, a philanthropic program aiming to provide health insurance for the breadwinners of poor families, was launched by the China Foundation for Poverty Alleviation, Alibaba and Ant Financial.
- July: Two more recommended industry standards were issued by the Ministry of Civil Affairs: The Basic Technical Specifications of Online Fundraising Platform for Charitable Organizations and the Basic Management Specifications of Online Fundraising Platform for Charitable Organizations.
- July: Ants Farm, an online philanthropic campaign, was launched by Alipay, a platform under Ant Financial services.

- June: The Second Internet Philanthropy Summit launched by the Tencent Foundation was held in Beijing, during which 60 mainstream institutions were invited to discuss the future of Internet philanthropy.
- May: The Philanthropic Blockchain for Tracing Missing Persons was launched on Tencent's TrustSQL, which connects Tencent's internal platforms for the purpose of tracing missing persons.
- May: OFO announced its access to the Version 3.0 of Reunion System, the Missing Children Alert Platform of China's Ministry of Public Security.
- April: The Guangdong Provincial Public Security Department cracked down on Renren Charity's illegal fundraising of RMB 1 billion disguised as philanthropic activities. It marked one of the achievements made by the Department against online pyramid schemes and illegal fundraising practices during the Hurricane 5 operations. More than 60 cases were investigated and closed, with a total of more than RMB 6 billion recovered.
- March: Tencent Charity released the Transparency Mechanism, making it the first online charity platform to introduce structured and systematic standards for information disclosure. The rules for access to the 99 Charity Day were also formulated based on this module.
- March: The Conference of the JD Philanthropic Materials Donation Platform themed on "Donations with Love" was held in Beijing.
- February: The Nuan Dong JD Philanthropic Fundraising Platform was officially launched.
- January: Tomorrow Advancing Life (NYSE: TAL), a leading education and technology enterprise in China, launched www.xiwang.com, a philanthropic education platform, aiming to promote equal education development by means of science and technology.

2016

- December: The Organ Donation Registration function was implemented on the Alipay Medical Service Platform.
- December: Alipay launched its first philanthropic blockchain program.
- November: Xinhua Charity launched its online fund-raising service platform.

- September: The 99 Charity Day 2016 was celebrated. Thanks to optimized rules for donations and matching donations, and to the introduction of company matching, more than 3600 philanthropic programs were funded.
- September: *The Charity Law of the People's Republic of China* has been effective since September 1. It stipulates clear regulations for online fund-raising.
- August: Ant Financial launched the Ant Forest module on its Alipay platform, encouraging its users to participate in philanthropic environmental protection programs through a virtual "carbon account".
- August: The Ministry of Civil Affairs issued the *Announcement of the Ministry of Civil Affairs on Designating the First Batch of Online Fundraising Information Platforms Operated by Charitable Organizations*, in which 13 platforms, including Tencent Charity, Taobao Charity, Ant Financial Charity and Sina Weibo's Micro-Philanthropy platform, won official recognition. China's online charity industry entered a stage of standardized development.
- July: China's first XIN Philanthropy Conference was held in Hangzhou. It aimed to foster grassroots charities, to support global environmental protection, and to provide aid for more than 40 million children and teachers in China's rural areas.
- July: Cainiao.com launched its Charity at a Single Click program, China's first online donation system enabling full process tracking of donations.
- July: Didi Charity launched a "Mileage Donation" program, helping the users to achieve "donation by traveling".
- June: Cainiao.com launched the "Green Action Plan" by teaming up with 32 logistics global partners, with a view to reducing carbon emissions and waste in the express delivery industry.
- June: The first Internet Philanthropy Summit, initiated by the Tencent Foundation, Narada Foundation and Chen Yidan Foundation, was held in Shenzhen. Heads of 39 philanthropic organizations gathered in Shenzhen to conduct in-depth communications focusing on "New Opportunities and Challenges Social Organizations Face in the New Era".

- June: China Media Union for Internet Philanthropy was initiated by Tencent, together with more than 20 mainstream media outlets.
- June: Shuidichou.cn, a social fundraising tool for critical illnesses, was created.
- May: The Reunion System, an online emergency relief platform for missing children was officially launched by the Ministry of Public Security, providing an official channel for publishing information on missing children.
- May: The philanthropic event "Looking for the Missing Children" was launched by Amap.
- May: Baidu kicked off the nation's first Smart Micro-school program in conjunction with the China Youth Development Foundation, aiming to address underdevelopment in schools in remote areas.
- April: Tencent introduced the Guardian Program to combat telecommunications network fraud.
- April: Alibaba joined the China Foundation for Poverty Alleviation, the Amity Foundation and China Charities Aid Foundation for Children in establishing the "Philanthropic Product 2.0" program.
- February: Toutiao rolled out a nationwide philanthropic program for missing persons.

2015

- December: The SEE Foundation, together with Tencent PC Manager, Tencent Mobile Manager, and the Tencent Foundation, launched a "Clean Up Plus" campaign to deal with waste contamination in the Sanjiangyuan ("Source of Three Rivers") area in the south of Qinghai Province.
- December: Alibaba Group and the China Disabled Persons' Federation jointly carried out the "Shape the Future" activity, an Internet employment program for the disabled.
- November: China's first early warning system for missing children was launched on WeChat.
- September: The Tencent Foundation worked with hundreds of philanthropic organizations, well-known enterprises, celebrities and top-class

creative communications organizations to launch the first 99 Charity Day. This day is aimed at mobilizing netizens to participate in philanthropy in a happy and convenient way. This event was created to inspire the public's enthusiasm for philanthropy by using mobile payments, social and meaningful interactions, and by matching all donations made by participants. A total of 2.05 million caring netizens donated RMB 127.9 million on the first 99 Charity Day.

- August: Tencent Charity launched the "Hike for Charity" activity. Tencent would donate in proportion to the steps donated by users, unlocking a wave of behavioral philanthropy.
- August: A fund-raising platform Qingsongchou or "easy fund-raising" for the poor and seriously ill was set up.
- July: JD crowdfunding officially started the "Crowdfunding Plus" plan.
- June: DiDi DaChe, China Merchants Property and the China Social Welfare Foundation's "Free Lunch Fund" launched the philanthropic program called "Family in Charity, All the Way".
- May–August: The 2015 Ancient Great Wall Outdoor Tencent Charity Hike Challenge was held with the theme of "Hiking to Show Your Love for the Great Wall." After the fundraising competition, 1200 people from 300 teams were eligible to participate in the Challenge held in Zhangye City, Gansu Province.
- May: Baidu, Shimao Group and the Shanghai Charity Foundation worked together to re-start the activity of Philanthropy Hour to raise funds for "orphans with a serious illness".

2014

- November: Tencent's "WeCountry", a mobile Internet plan for rural areas, was set in motion.
- October: QQ set up the "QQ Alert: Reunion After Years" program to save trafficked children within the "72 golden hours".
- October: SEE Foundation raised funds for environmental governance through its "Cross Helan Mountains" project.
- September: WeChat started the "The Voice Donor: Reading for the Blind" philanthropic activity.

- August: Tencent's project "Donate Together" (based on WeChat) was introduced, featuring a new model of persuading people to donate.
- August: The Ice Bucket Challenge, which focused on a rare disease called amyotrophic lateral sclerosis (ALS), was popular in China.
- May: QQ Mail and Tencent Charity jointly initiated "A Bright Tomorrow" program, which aimed to improve lighting for students in rural areas by calling on people to delete old emails.
- March–July: Working with 15 renowned universities across the country, Tencent Charity started the "Charity Hiker" activity, calling on college students and alumni to take part in a two-month fund-raising competition as a way to raise money for 100 "Charitable Sportsgrounds".
- January: The Shenzhen One Foundation set up a "Warm Bag Charity Campaign for Children Having Survived Fire Accidents" via the WeChat AA collection.

2013

- October: Sina Weibo officially launched a large-scale Weibo Philanthropy activity and advocated for public philanthropy.
- September: The YouChange China Social Entrepreneur Foundation established its "Dual-teacher" pilot program and explored a remote teaching model.
- September: "One Foundation Monthly Giving" was officially set up on Alipay Wallet.
- June: The app of Xingshan "doing good", an Internet donation platform, was made available.
- April: 30+ hours after an earthquake hit Ya'an city in the western part of Sichuan Province, Baidu established the "Internet Platform for Tracing Missing Persons".
- January: The Tencent Foundation held an event entitled "Press Conference on Tencent's Monthly Giving of 100 Million" to announce the RMB 100 million donation made by Tencent Charity. During the conference, Charles Chen Yidan introduced the concept of "Philanthropy by All", to endow all Tencent products with philanthropic features and to work with the whole industry to build an ecosystem of "Philanthropy by All".

2012

- December: The China Foundation Transparency Index (FTI) was first released and became an important indicator of the foundations' transparency.
- June: Tencent's new project "A Dream for the Countryside" was born, with a planned investment of RMB 50 million for the following five years.
- June: Baidu and 800,000 Baidu Alliance partners inaugurated the "One Hour, One Click" campaign to convey the power of philanthropy.
- May: The Weibo Foundation of Cracking Down on the Abduction of Women and Children was created.
- February: The Sino Weibo's Micro-Philanthropy platform officially went live, providing "one-stop" rescue services.
- January: The Internet Philanthropy Alliance, the first Internet philanthropy organization initiated by industry associations, was set up.

2011

- December: Alibaba Group established a private charity foundation—Alibaba Foundation.
- November: The Shanghai United Foundation initiated a charity hiking event called the "Egg Walkathon".
- June: The Guo Meimei incident caused widespread public concern and heated discussion on Sina Weibo.
- April: The Baidu Charity Open Platform was put in place, promoting digitalization of China's philanthropy programs.
- April: Sohu.com announced the launch of the Sohu Convenient Philanthropy Platform based on Sohu Weibo. It also established the Sohu Convenient Charity Foundation to promote the development of non-public philanthropy.
- February: Baidu officially put forward the "Baidu People Search" open platform, featuring philanthropic interaction.

- February: The response of "taking pictures to save child beggars" blog post led to an effort in "cracking down on the abduction of women and children via Weibo".
- January: The Beijing Baidu Foundation was approved by the Beijing Municipal Bureau of Civil Affairs.

2010

- September: Alibaba opened the Taobao Charity platform to attract more civil society organizations. Taobao donated RMB 10 million to set up the "China Red Cross Society and Taobao Charity Fund" at the China Red Cross Society.
- August: Baidu initiated the Beijing Baidu Foundation.
- August: The Sunflower Club, China's first community for philanthropic interaction, went online officially.
- July: The China Foundation Center, sponsored by 35 well-known foundations, opened with the aim of building an important platform of information disclosure for philanthropy, to provide building services for industrial development capacity, and to ensure industry self-regulatory mechanisms to enhance public trust.
- March: A great number of websites and media channels participated in the "Earth Hour 2010" activity.
- January: The Tencent Netizen Love Foundation was founded.

2009

- December: The Shanghai United Foundation, a public fundraising and grant-making foundation, was set up.
- August: Sohu.com, Amway and the China Environmental Protection Foundation launched the "Green Light Forest" environmental protection campaign at bai.sohu.com, which pursued a low-carbon, green lifestyle.

- July: The Amity Foundation and Tencent Charity worked together to inaugurate "Internet-Driven Growth: Take Action to Support Rural Orphans Online", a monthly donation program.
- June: The Tencent Foundation launched the Tencent New Countryside Initiative, which takes advantages of Tencent's online resources, multiple platforms and influence to provide long-term support for educational and economic development of underdeveloped areas in western China.
- May: "Tencent Monthly Giving" platform was officially launched, and a great number of renowned philanthropic organizations launched monthly giving projects there.
- March: The China Green Foundation launched the Chinese Network Arbor Day.
- March: The Earth Hour global campaign came to China for the first time, helping increase attention to climate change by turning off all non-essential lights for one hour.

2008

- November: Charles Chen Yidan first proposed the concept of Philanthropy 2.0. Philanthropy 2.0 refers to building a new mode of philanthropy by making use of Internet technologies and connectivity, which is "Philanthropy by All".
- October: The Office for Rural Engineering Liaison of the China Association of Poverty Alleviation and Development worked with Sohu.com to hold the "Deliver More Love via the Internet: Computer Donation for Impoverished Areas" campaign.
- June: The Amity Foundation and Tencent Charity jointly launched the Internet-based orphan support program on the Tencent online donation platform.
- May: The website gongyi.yeepay.com went live to promote electronic payment-featured online donations and Internet philanthropy.

- May: During the Wenchuan earthquake, Tenpay and Alipay urgently opened online donation channels, receiving over RMB 60 million by the end of the year.

2007

- December: The China Social Work Association and Sohu.com Inc. jointly launched a philanthropy promotion campaign called "Love under the Blue Sky".
- June: The Tencent Foundation was established, which became the first national non-public foundation registered by a Chinese Internet company at the Ministry of Civil Affairs. Tencent Charity was launched thereafter.
- June: China's first official "blog fund" was established by Sohu.com Inc. Later, the Sohu philanthropic blog group was launched, becoming China's first professional philanthropic platform that operates on the blog.
- May: StormPlayer and FlashGet, collaborating with other famous software companies such as Kingsoft Antivirus, launched the "Let Chinese Films Travel Far" event.
- April: The Sohu blog created the first online philanthropic blog group, drawing attention to the shortage of philanthropic channels.

2006

- December: The Magic Bean Baby Charity project was initiated nationwide by the China Red Cross Society.
- November: The first Internet philanthropy brand "Clean Blue Ribbon" designed to clean up cyberspace was officially launched.
- September: The Sohu philanthropic channel that features special topics was established, becoming the first philanthropic channel incorporated into a commercial website.

2005

- December: With the opening of an online store called "Magic Bean Baby House", the shop owner with late stage cancer attracted attention.
- May: The first Internet Philanthropy Day was organized by the Internet Society of China.
- March: Sohu.com and Global Vanguard co-planned a charitable donation campaign themed "To help Xiangzi". Sohu also invited famous NBA stars to participate in the online donation campaign for "Xiangzi".
- March: Sohu.com launched a donation campaign themed "Concern and love for students in Tibet", where more than 200 computers were donated to the Tibetan Mountaineering School to improve audio-visual teaching conditions and develop Internet education in Tibet.
- January: Sohu.com, together with "Star-Bigstar" and "Entertainment Live" television programs, launched an initiative. Sohu.com, Enlight Media, China Charity Federation, the National Radio and Television Administration, and the China Stars' Badminton Team organized disaster relief activities for tsunami-hit countries in Southeast Asia.

2004

- October: In China, the first government-owned philanthropic website "Chinese Donation" was launched by the Ministry of Civil Affairs.
- August: Sohu Guangdong Station and Southern Metropolis Daily worked together to launch an online essay competition themed "Responsible China".
- July: Zhang Miao'e, a netizen in Kaiping City of Guangdong Province, posted an article titled "Friends from All Over the World, Please Click on This Article" on Tianya's forum, becoming the first recorded case in China of an individual raising money on a large scale through the Internet.
- March: The State Council released the *Regulations on Administration of Foundations* (RAF) which came into effect on June 1, 2004. The RAF clearly differentiates between various foundations and specifies that

only those qualified as public can carry out public fund-raising campaigns.

2003

- May: During the SARS epidemic, Tencent provided each Xiaotangshan medical staff with a dedicated QQ number to share medical information instantly with the medical staff and help them reach their families through QQ videos. It was the first case that combined the function of social media and philanthropy in China.
- May: An anti-SARS initiative called "Offer your kindness in the fight against SARS" was announced by Sohu together with the China Charity Federation and other philanthropic organizations to civil society organizations, community organizations and individual volunteers across China.

2002

- December: Sohu, as the exclusive Internet partner of the "Water Cellars for Mothers" project, joined the China Women's Development Foundation and the China Youth Online to launch the "Pour Out Your Love by Water Donation" philanthropic campaign.
- May: Qianlong.com, a local portal, opened a philanthropic channel releasing philanthropic information, becoming the first comprehensive channel for philanthropy in China owned by an online media outlet.

2001

- June: Amway (China) launched a philanthropic campaign called "Twenty Hours of Life" to unite philanthropic efforts on both sides of the Taiwan Straits to save the life of a girl from Jiangsu named Chen Xia suffering from leukemia.

- January: The new version of the Shanghai Charity Foundation website (scf.88547.com) was formally launched. It introduced year-round Internet-based projects such as helping poor students and low-income families, online donations, and online application for aid.

2000

- April: Sohu and the China Youth Development Foundation launched an activity themed on "Protecting the Yellow River-Green Hope Project Joined by Sohu's Caring Netizens". Following the slogan of "5-yuan donation for a tree and 200-yuan donation for 0.067 hectare of forest", netizens from all social sectors were mobilized through Sohu.com to participate in the activity to donate money for building forests.

1999

- June: *The Law of the People's Republic of China on Donations for Public Welfare* was passed and enacted on September 1, 1999.
- March: The Tianya forum was established and got involved in philanthropy by setting up a section for interaction on philanthropy. Then it also set up sections concerning environmental protection, volunteers, and joint efforts for philanthropy in 2001, 2005 and 2009 respectively.

1998

- November: The "Green Beijing" was established as the first Chinese non-governmental environmental protection organization originating from the Internet.
- October: *The Interim Regulations on Registration Administration of Private Non-enterprise Units* was announced and enforced.

1995

- February–April: A Shandong girl Yang Xiaoxia with a unfamiliar disease and a Tsinghua University student Zhu Ling with thallium poisoning got help through the Internet. These two cases marked the beginning of China's Internet philanthropy.

Index[1]

NUMBERS & SYMBOLS

A

C

[1] Note: Page numbers followed by 'n' refer to notes.

Y. Chen, *Internet Philanthropy in China*,
https://doi.org/10.1007/978-981-16-2566-4

The manufacturer's authorised representative in the EU is Springer Nature Customer Service Centre GmbH, Europaplatz 3, 69115 Heidelberg, Germany. If you have any concerns regarding our products, please contact ProductSafety@springernature.com

Printed and bound by CPI Group (UK) Ltd, Croydon, CR0 4YY

30/09/2026

02225455-0019